INTERNATIONAL PROJECT MANAGEMENT

INTERNATIONAL PROJECT MANAGEMENT

KATHRIN KÖSTER

First published 2009

Apart from any fair dealing for the purposes of research or private study, or criticism or review, as permitted under the Copyright, Designs and Patents Act, 1988, this publication may be reproduced, stored or transmitted in any form, or by any means, only with the prior permission in writing of the publishers, or in the case of reprographic reproduction, in accordance with the terms of licences issued by the Copyright Licensing Agency. Enquiries concerning reproduction outside those terms should be sent to the publishers.

SAGE Publications Ltd
1 Oliver's Yard
55 City Road
London EC1Y 1SP

SAGE Publications Inc.
2455 Teller Road
Thousand Oaks, California 91320

SAGE Publications India Pvt Ltd
B 1/I 1 Mohan Cooperative Industrial Area
Mathura Road, Post Bag 7
New Delhi 110 044

SAGE Publications Asia-Pacific Pte Ltd
33 Pekin Street #02-01
Far East Square
Singapore 048763

Library of Congress Control Number **2009922447**

British Library Cataloguing in Publication data

A catalogue record for this book is available from the British Library

ISBN 978-1-4129-4620-9
ISBN 978-1-4129-4621-6 (pbk)

Typeset by C&M Digitals Pvt Ltd, Chennai, India

To all people in this world who endeavour to discover the wealth of diversity, and who are challenged by complexity!

CONTENTS

LIST OF FIGURES

LIST OF TABLES

LIST OF SNAPSHOTS

LIST OF MINI CASES

LIST OF ABBREVIATIONS

ABB	Asea Brown Bovery
AC	Actual Cost
ACWP	Actual Cost of Work Performed
AMD	Advanced Micro Devices
AoA	Activity on Arrow
APM	Association of Project Management
ASQ	American Society for Quality
BCWP	Budgeted Cost of Work Performed
BCWS	Budgeted Cost of Work Scheduled
BoK	Body of Knowledge
BOOT	Build, Own, Operate, Transfer
BSC	Balanced Score Card
BU	Business Unit
CAD	Canadian Dollar
CCB	Configuration Change Board
CEE	Central and Eastern Europe
CEO	Chief Executive Officer
CFO	Chief Financial Officer
CIS	Commonwealth of Independent States
CMM	Capability Maturity Model
COO	Chief Operations Officer
CPA	Critical Path Analysis
CPFF	Cost Plus Fixed Fee
CPI	Cost Performance Index
CPI	Corruption Perception Index
CPM	Critical Path Method
CPO	Chief Project Officer
CRM	Customer Relationship Management
CSS	Construction Safety Study
CV	Cost Variance
CV	Curriculum Vitae
DCA	Diversity Complexity Assessment
DE	Deutschland (Germany)
EADS	European Aeronautic Defence and Space Company
ECSS	European Cooperation for Space Standards
EDI	Electronic Data Interchange

EFT	Earliest Finish Time
EMS	Engineering and Manufacturing Services
ERP	Enterprise Resource Planning
EPC	Engineering, Procurement, Construction
ESA	European Space Agency
EST	Earliest Start Time
ETHOS	Economic, Technical, Human, Organizational, Social
EU	European Union
EV	Earned Value
EVA	Earned Value Analysis
FAO	Food and Agriculture Organization
FI/CO	Finance and Controlling
FIDIC	International Federation of Consulting Engineers
FFP	Firm Fixed Price
FMEA	Failure Modes and Effects Analysis
FP	Framework Program
FSS	Fire Safety Study
FTF	Face-to-Face
GER	Germany
GIS	Gas Insulated Sensor
GLOBE	Global Leadership and Organizational Behavior Effectiveness
GMP	Guaranteed Maximum Price
GPAI	Global Program for Avian Influenza
GR	Goods Receipt
HAZOP	Hazard and Operability Study
HC	High Context
HPAI	Highly Pathogenic Avian Influenza
HQ	Headquarters
HR	Human Resources
HTS	Harmonized Tariff Schedule of the United States
HV	High Voltage
ICC	International Chamber of Commerce
ICT	Information and Communication Technology
IMF	International Monetary Fund
INCOTERMS	International Commercial Terms
IT	Information Technology
JV	Joint Venture
KPI	Key Performance Indicator
LBA	Luftfahrtbundesamt
LC	Low Context
LFT	Latest Finish Time
LST	Latest Start Time
MIT	Massachusetts Institute of Technology
M&S	Marketing & Sales
MNC	Multinational Corporation

NASA	National Aviation and Space Agency
NC	National Culture
NIH	Not-Invented-Here
NPD	New Product Development
NPO	Non-for-profit Organization
NPR	Non-product related
OC	Organizational Culture
OBS	Organization Breakdown Structure
ODM	Original Design Manufacturer
OECD	Organization for Economic Co-operation and Development
OEM	Original Equipment Manufacturer
OGC	Office of Government Commerce
OIE	World Organization for Animal Health
OLPC	One Laptop per Child
PBO	Project-based Organization
PC	Planned Cost
PDCA	Plan Do Check Act
PD	Power Distance
PDM	Product Data Management
PERT	Program (Project) Evaluation and Review Technique
PESTEL	Political, Economic, Socio-cultural, Technological, Environmental, Legal
PMI	Project Management Institute
PMO	Project Management Office
PPM	Project Portfolio Management
PQA	Parts Quality Assurance
PSO	Project Support Office
QA	Quality Assurance
R&D	Research & Development
ROI	Return on Investment
RZB	Raiffeisen Zentralbank
SA	Substation Automation
SAP	Product name of ERP system
SARS	Severe Acute Respiratory Syndrome
SD	Sales and Distribution
SECI	Socialization, Externalization, Combination, Internalization
SEE	South East Europe
SME	Small and Medium Sized Enterprises
SMI	Supplier Managed Inventory
SOW	Statement of Work
SPI	Schedule Performance Index
SQ	Supplier Quality
SRM	Supplier Relationship Management
STECO	Steering Committee
SV	Schedule Variance

SW	Software
TD	Technical Development
TI	Transparency International
TQM	Total Quality Management
UA	Uncertainty Avoidance
UAE	United Arab Emirates
UN	United Nations
UNCITRAL	United Nations Commission on International Trade Law
US	United States
USA	United States of America
VMI	Vendor Managed Inventory
VoIP	Voice over Internet Protocol
WBS	Work Breakdown Structure
WFOE	Wholly Foreign Owned Enterprise
WHO	World Health Organization

PREFACE

OBJECTIVES

International projects, i.e. projects that reach beyond national boundaries in terms of project purpose or the nationality of stakeholders, are ubiquitous in all organizations around the globe. They are a means of implementing an organization's strategy in order to realize its vision. Hence, competence in the management of international projects is central to the strategic capabilities of today's organizations.

Having said this, it is surprising that most textbooks on project management still focus on standard or traditional projects. The discipline of 'project management' originated in the middle of the last century, and it is still shaped by the industrial age and Taylor's 'scientific management'. In my view, however, the discipline needs to be enriched by other academic fields in order to make it meaningful in the era of a global world economy. Over the last decades, project management has to some extent responded to environmental changes by incorporating areas like context management, communication and other 'soft fields' into its knowledge areas. This is the road I am following further: I attempt to merge project management with other disciplines and fields critical for success on a global scale, such as managing cultural diversity, managing heterogeneous stakeholders, managing intercultural communication, managing international co-operation, and managing the learning process in international projects.

I view international project management as an art. It implies a personal, creative power to deal with the uniqueness, risk, complexity, diversity, dynamics, and limited resources of international projects. It also implies an attitude of curiosity and learning. Special skills are needed to embark on this long journey leading us and the organizations we work in to the successful management of international projects. These skills consist of technical expertise and personal competencies.

Providing a systematic consideration of international requirements and factors, this book is aimed at (advanced) business or engineering students and practitioners. The reader should get an easy-to-read overview of what he or she needs to know and be able to do in order to successfully manage international projects.

CONSTRAINTS

As is true for any project, the project 'writing a textbook in international project management' faces various constraints. I had to sacrifice the detailed discussion of existing academic literature and the multidisciplinary analysis of problems to readability and the provision of numerous examples rendering the complexity of international project management more accessible. Most of the examples given are based on my own experience as well as the experience of project managers from the Americas, Asia-Pacific, and Europe, who contributed to this book in more than 40 interviews.

Readability also results in the prioritization of content. With the emphasis on international particularities of project management, important parts of project management such as value management, requirements management, technology management, value engineering, modelling and testing, configuration management, concurrent engineering, business case management, marketing and sales management, project financing and funding, and critical chain project management are beyond the scope of this book. There are other textbooks available for those areas of project management. I will not explore in detail project quality management, health, safety and environmental management, resource management, budgeting and cost management, change control, procurement, and legal awareness. My explanations regarding those areas will emphasize the points most relevant in an international context.

In spite of those limitations, I think that this book can be of help to advanced students who will soon play a role in international projects. This book may also provide some refreshers for practitioners who are constantly striving on the path towards excellence in international project management.

TEXTBOOK OUTLINE

Chapter 1 elaborates on the characteristics of international projects and international project management as opposed to standard project management. Chapter 2 puts international project management into an overall organizational perspective, providing the context for international project management. Chapter 3 explains the first phase in the project management life cycle, the initiating phase. It elucidates the input for the project proposal, namely scope management, the Work Breakdown Structure, and stakeholder management. It also makes the reader familiar with the concept of culture, especially national culture, and its impact on project management. Chapters 4, 5, and 6 explain the input needed in the project planning phase, such as risk management, planning time, cost, and quality, and structuring the project. In Chapter 7, I proceed to the next phase in the project management life cycle, the implementation phase, providing details on monitoring and controlling tools and techniques. Chapters 8, 9, and 10 are dedicated to the human factor in international project management. Chapter 8 explores the competencies a project manager needs to have to lead and manage international projects. Chapter 9 focuses on communicating and negotiating in international projects with an emphasis on intercultural communication as well as on communication modes and communication governance. In Chapter 10 I outline trust as the basis for successful co-operation in international projects. I also touch on co-operation guidelines and conflict management methods relevant in an international context. Chapter 11 has two aspects: first, I explore learning in and from international projects, again putting international project management in a strategic context as I had done in Chapter 2; second, I close the project life cycle with an outline of the project completion phase.

PEDAGOGICAL FEATURES

To facilitate learning, I have incorporated several features in each chapter of this book:

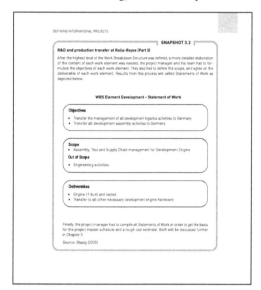

1. **Snapshots**: They provide the reader with real-life examples of how a certain aspect of project management is handled in a particular organization or industry. Snapshots also comprise compilations of the experience of different organizations.

2. **Mini Cases**: Like snapshots, they give real-life examples of the aspects of project management discussed in each chapter. At the end, they have a task or question in order to further the discussion and deepen the reader's understanding.

3. **Chapter End Cases**: At the end of each chapter, there is a longer case with questions and tasks. They help the reader to review the chapter.

4. **Review Tasks**: Three or four review questions at the end of each chapter aim at facilitating a self-assessment. The review questions can also be used to enhance discussions in class. In addition there are one to three exercises to help the reader to think independently about the topics discussed in the chapter and to adopt the subject for his or her own context.

5. **Companion Website**: For most of the chapters, there are additional snapshots and mini cases on the companion website. Depending on the individual needs of students, they can use these to practise their skills further. There is also background information and further resources for some selected topics.

6. **Instructor's Manual and PowerPoint Slides**: Tutors teaching international project management are supported with a compilation of solutions of all Mini Cases and Chapter End Cases. They can also download PowerPoint slides for each chapter.

7. **Glossary**: Technical terms and expressions in the context of international project management are explained in alphabetical order at the end of this book.

ACKNOWLEDGEMENTS

I would like to express my gratitude to all the international project managers who have dedicated their precious time to share their valuable expertise with me and consequently with the readers of this book.

I would like to thank my former student Dora for her great support with the layout and literature search activities. I am indebted to my friend Emily for proof-reading the manuscript.

My creativity is enabled by my best friends – my husband and my parents – who always think outside the box. I am grateful to them for just being different.

INTRODUCTION TO INTERNATIONAL PROJECT MANAGEMENT

1

LEARNING OBJECTIVES

After studying this chapter, you will be able to:

- grasp the concept of a project
- comprehend the main characteristics and components of project management
- identify the major project stakeholders
- understand the concept of a program
- know the historical development and theoretical underpinnings of project management
- assess the constraints of project management methods
- differentiate between a 'standard' project and an international project
- elucidate the characteristics of international projects
- discuss the key success criteria for the management of international projects.

INTRODUCTION

1.1 For three decades globalization has been increasing at an ever faster pace. Huge economies in Asia, China and India have opened up and become very successful competitors to the Western world and the Japanese. Russia, Brazil, and the Gulf region are following suit. Organizations need to become increasingly cost efficient due to fiercer global competition. Global markets were deregulated, allowing for production capabilities to be shifted to low-wage countries. The realignment of global business forces was enabled by advances in technology that have had an enormous impact on how business is done. Most significant were the innovations in telecommunications and computing. Organizations now have the ability to replicate their infrastructure in many different locations. One internationally operating retail chain boasts that it can build up a new outlet on each continent within 60 days (Lientz and Rea, 2003). Organizations can also control remote locations on a real time basis. Thanks to the internet, all entities of an organization scattered around the globe can exchange information easily – at least in theory – due to standardized hardware and software.

Globalization has brought us a more integrated and interdependent world economy. To adapt to this new environment, and to thrive in it, organizations need to undergo major changes. All kind of organizations will initiate a whole range of different international projects in order to implement the necessary adaptations to a changed environment.

Although ubiquitous, international projects are not necessarily leading to organizational success. In 2004, PricewaterhouseCoopers analysed a broad range of companies, large and small, in 30 different countries, which carried out 10,640 projects with an overall value of 7.2 billion US$. They found that only 2.5 per cent of global businesses achieved project success (Stanleigh, 2006). The measure of project success may be debatable, but this is still an alarming number. More needs to be done to make project management more efficient and effective on a global scale. This book aims at providing advanced students and practitioners with hands-on knowledge to enable them to contribute to the future success of international projects.

I will start laying the foundations by explaining the relevant terminology and defining a project, project management, and the main project stakeholders. I will also discuss the relationship between a project and a program. We will also take a look at the historical and theoretical roots of project management to help us assess the global applicability of project management. Based on this foundation, we will dive into the topic of international project management, starting with a differentiation between a 'standard' project and an international project. The emphasis of this chapter is a detailed discussion of the main characteristics of an international project as project management methods need to be attuned to those characteristics. We will also examine the major critical success criteria for international projects. I will wrap up the chapter with an outline of the structure of this book, following a project management knowledge area approach and an open systems approach.

WHAT IS A PROJECT?

1.2 There are a variety of definitions regarding what exactly a project is. For the purpose of this book, I will follow Turner's definition. He sees a project as 'an endeavour in which human, material and financial resources are organized in a novel way, to undertake a unique scope of work, of given specification, within constraints of cost and time, so as to achieve beneficial change defined by quantitative and qualitative objectives' (1993: 8).

In contrast to the routine work in an organization, which could also be called processes or operations management, the objective of a project is usually a new state that is different from normal work. Operations typically are ongoing and repetitive, whereas projects are temporary and unique.

Within the family of projects, however, there are big differences, for instance in size. A project can involve only two people and a relatively small amount of money, like a honeymoon trip to Hawaii. Or it can be a so-called mega-project like one of the biggest cross-national infrastructure projects of the world, the 15.5 kilometres long Oresund coast-to-coast link connecting Denmark (Continental Europe) with Sweden (Scandinavia) which was opened in the year 2000 and built at a cost of roughly 2 billion Euros (Flyvberg et al., 2003).

Projects can also differ in the kind of organization initiating the project, the industry the project belongs to, and the purpose and scope of the project. There can be different stakeholders and customers. Project duration can be long or short. The project can be part of primary activities like Research and Development, Manufacturing, Marketing and Sales, or it can belong to secondary activities of the value chain, such as Information Technology (IT) or Human Resources (HR). You can find a systematic overview of different types of projects on the companion website.

Regardless of the type of project, each project has three main characteristics in common, although these characteristics may be of a different weight for different projects as can be seen in Figure 1.1. Accordingly, projects are limited, unique, and risky. In the following, I comment on each criterion.

LIMITED

A project is intended to have a temporary character, which in reality may take a very long time. According to the research of Cooke-Davies (2002), a project, or at least a well-defined part of a project, should not exceed three years. In general, each project should have a clearly defined beginning and end. A project produces an output which usually is clearly defined, for example a new tangible or intangible asset. This may be abstract, like a higher competence level of managers, or more concrete, like the development of a new drug which has the potential to be a blockbuster. A project typically delivers beneficial change. The value of the outcome of the project should justify the resources invested in that project.

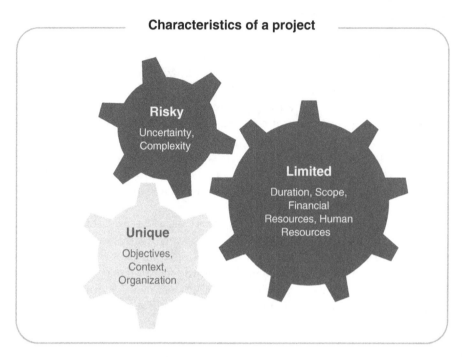

FIGURE 1.1 The main characteristics of a project

UNIQUE

Different projects can have different objectives, can be embedded in a different context, and can usually be launched by different organizations or different entities of an organization. In general, the uniqueness is based on the fact that projects are non-routine endeavours. This is even the case with projects which seem to be repetitive like the establishment of new outlets of a retail chain. They all give customers the same brand feeling; however, the establishment of each outlet will be different and needs to be planned with the legal requirements of the respective country in mind, for instance regarding hygiene regulations and safety standards.

RISKY

Since projects comprise non-routine work, they do involve uncertainty. This means risk which has to be managed. For instance, the requirements of consumers can change quickly. Nowadays, mobile phones without a camera are hard to sell compared to the beginning of this decade. Giving another example, a competitor might launch a similar product earlier at a lower price, as happened with Nintendo's home video game console 'Wii' which was launched in December 2006, much to the chagrin of Sony whose launch of PlayStation 3 had been delayed to spring 2007. To give yet another example, a pharmaceutical company may have discovered dangerous side-effects of a newly developed drug after nine years of research. Hence, it has had to abandon the whole project.

WHAT IS PROJECT MANAGEMENT?

1.3 Section 1.2 defined projects as bringing beneficial change to an organization. In other words, the results of projects should bring value to an organization, rather than destroying value. Consequently, that organization needs to manage the resources used for projects carefully. Project management deals with what it takes to manage projects to create value for organizations. The Association of Project Management (APM) (2006a: 3) defines project management as 'the process by which projects are defined, planned, monitored, controlled and delivered such that the agreed benefits are realised'. This definition indicates that project management takes a staged approach to reduce complexity and ensure efficiency. Several phases connect the beginning of a project with its end. This is also known as a project life cycle or project management life cycle. According to the Project Management Institute (PMI) (2004: 20), 'There is no single best way to define an ideal project life cycle'. Depending on the organization and the nature of the business it is operating in, there may be sub-phases such as the development of prototypes, the approval of such prototypes and the ramp up for mass production in a manufacturing project. Frame (2002) postulates that the project life cycle should by default include after sales service in order to increase customer satisfaction with the outcomes of projects and to smooth the interface between projects and operations management. Typically, the project life cycle consists of four main phases as depicted in Figure 1.2. Let me briefly explain the main tasks of the four phases.

PHASE 1 INITIATING

The initiating phase is also often called the front-end or kick-off phase. The need or the opportunity is confirmed. The project concept is developed after the overall feasibility of the project has been carefully considered and determined. In this phase, the business case for the project is developed. I will discuss the details of this phase in Chapter 3.

PHASE 2 PLANNING

The essence of project planning is to decide what needs to be done in order to deliver the project objectives within the given organizational constraints. As a result of this phase, the so-called project management plan or project master plan is delivered, along with the identification of resources required for the implementation of the project. You can find more details of this phase in Chapters 3, 4, 5, and 6.

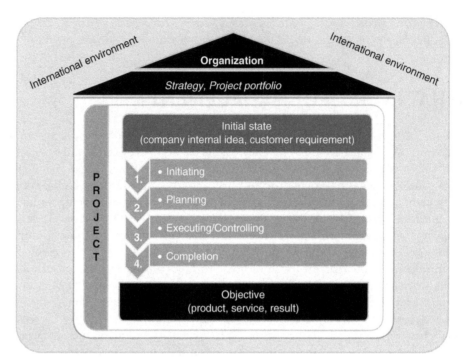

FIGURE 1.2 The project management life cycle

PHASE 3 EXECUTING/CONTROLLING

During the execution or implementation phase, the project plan is implemented, monitored and controlled. In the case of a product, the product design is finalized in this phase and used to build the deliverables of the project. Chapter 7 will provide you with further explanations.

PHASE 4 COMPLETION

The completion, termination or closeout phase consists of the handover of the product or service to the internal or external customer. Moreover, a final review of the whole project is done in order to learn from past mistakes and successes. The project team will be redeployed. Refer to Chapter 11 for more details.

Projects are part of an organization which is endorsed with limited resources only. We speak about organizational constraints. It is the purpose of project management to deliver projects on time, within budget and to scope, with an agreed quality level. This is also called the 'Magic Triangle'. The constraints emerge because on one hand, only limited resources in terms of time, financial and human resources are available. On the other hand, a pre-defined scope has to be delivered with an acceptable quality level.

Project management should ensure that a project is carried out effectively (that the result of the project 'works') and efficiently (that the work is done with minimum effort and cost).

WHO ARE THE MAIN PROJECT STAKEHOLDERS?

1.4

Now we know what project management is. But who are the main players within the context of project management? They are the stakeholders.

Project stakeholders are individuals, groups, or organizations that are either actively involved in a project, or whose interests may be affected positively or negatively as a result of a project completion. Stakeholders may have different interests and perspectives. For the sake of efficiency and to ensure accountability, it is important to identify clearly the responsibilities and authorities of each stakeholder.

Project owner and **project sponsor**: While the project owner provides the resources to deliver the project results, the project sponsor has the responsibility to channel the resources to a project on the owner's behalf. However, there is no standardized definition in the literature. Both terms are frequently used synonymously. According to the Project Management Institute (2004), the project sponsor is the person who provides the financial resources. Kerzner (2006) portrays a project sponsor as a senior executive of the organization who champions and supports the project. The sponsor, for instance, can function as the executive–client contact point or as the final escalation point for project conflicts. Some organizations do not work with one single sponsor, but with a group of sponsors who are structured in a steering committee.

Sometimes, the word 'investor' is used synonymously with project owner or sponsor. But the investor can also be a separate stakeholder, namely the financier, like a bank.

In the case of an inter-organizational project, there can be several project owners in the different organizations involved.

Contractor: The contractor is the group (or individual) using the capital of the owner in order to produce the product/service or result the owner wants to have. In the case of an internal project, the contractors can become the users. Often, the term is used for organizations in a consortium working together to deliver a product or service for another organization, the project owner or customer.

Customer/User: Another role is the customer who takes advantage of the project outcome. The customer also provides the resources for the project (project owner). The users are the individuals benefiting from the project result without directly providing resources for the project.

Project manager: This is the individual responsible for planning, organizing, implementing and controlling the work to ensure that the customer (owner) gets the intended benefits of the project.

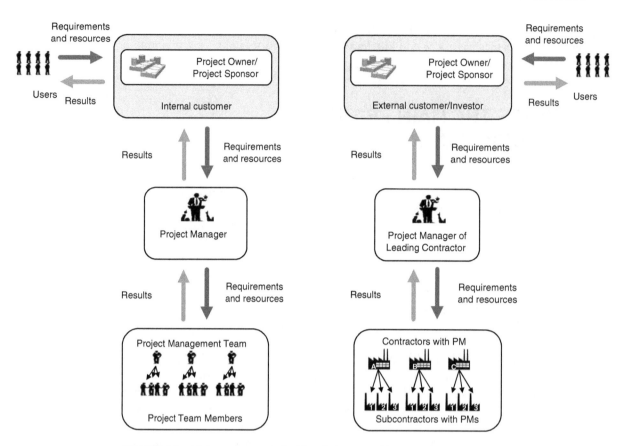

FIGURE 1.3 Main project stakeholders in intra- and inter-organizational projects

Project management team: In a consortium or in complex projects, there are usually sub-project managers, like team leaders with dedicated areas they manage on behalf of the project manager. However, they report to the project manager who is responsible to the customer.

Project team members: The members in the project team who are directly involved in the project and who contribute to its completion.

Figure 1.3 sets out the main stakeholders and their interaction in two kinds of projects: intra-organizational and inter-organizational.

Apart from those main groups of stakeholders, there can be industry lobbies or environmental protection groups who will support or fight the project. In general, the interests of all stakeholders need to be taken into account to ensure successful project management. In the international context, the identification and integration of stakeholder interests are especially complicated, as we will see in Chapter 3.

We have learnt what a project is, what project management is, and who the main actors within a project are. When we take a look at organizations, though, we can't help noticing that they are dealing not with one single project, but with a whole plethora of projects. In order to better co-ordinate projects and not lose control, organizations will create so-called programs.

WHAT IS A PROGRAM?

1.5

A program is a bundle of projects pursuing the same purpose. A program has the same main characteristics as a project (cf. Figure 1.1). However, it usually has a longer duration and requires more resources. Apart from co-ordination benefits, programs allow for the realization of synergy effects between projects. An example of a program is the implementation of a new integrated IT-system in a multinational corporation after the acquisition of a former competitor comprising the following single projects:

- project of stock taking with the purpose of enlisting all relevant information systems in company A and company B
- project of designing the most efficient, new cross-functional processes in the new integrated company
- project of evaluating which existing information systems can support the newly designed processes
- project of benchmarking with other information systems based on criteria like cost, quality, etc.
- project of running a pilot of the new information system in a designated subsidiary
- project of rolling out the new information system worldwide.

'In contrast to project management, program management is the centralized, coordinated management of a group of projects to achieve the program's strategic objectives and benefits' (PMI, 2004: 16). I will further discuss the role and importance of programs related to the implementation of an organization's strategy in Chapter 2.

To complete the basic knowledge about project management, I will outline the history and theoretical underpinnings of project management in the next section, 1.6.

WHERE DOES PROJECT MANAGEMENT COME FROM, AND WHERE DOES IT GO TO?

1.6

Mankinds's accomplishments, like the pyramids in Egypt or the Great Wall of China, can be regarded as early projects. On an international level, Alexander the Great can be viewed as an early project manager who conquered a huge part of the known world.

The relevant management thought underlying project management was already developed in the late nineteenth and early twentieth century by people like the Frenchman Henri Fayol, and the US-Americans Frederick Taylor and Henry Gantt. Fayol was one of the first thinkers to put management on a broader theoretical basis. His philosophy revolves around the optimization of an organization in order to achieve its objectives most efficiently. Taylor, the father of the so-called scientific management, emphasized the optimization of the production process. In contrast to Taylor who focused on repetitive work, Gantt studied the management of navy ship construction that meant work with a beginning and an end. As a result he developed a scheduling tool in the 1910s which carried his name and is still used today – the Gantt chart.

While these early thinkers laid the groundwork, general systems theory emerging in the 1950s has provided project management with its theoretical foundation. General systems theory attempts to analyse and solve issues by assuming a holistic view rather through analysing the single components of an issue. General systems management implies the creation of a management technique that can cut across many organizational disciplines such as Research and Development, Purchasing, Manufacturing, Logistics, Marketing, Sales, Finance, etc., without losing the overview of co-ordinating and managing the whole (Kerzner, 2006). The systems approach and the project management approach both target facilitating change from an initial starting point to a defined final position (Harpum, 2004).

Between 1945 and 1960, the development of project management was pushed by the US-American Department of Defense and NASA, who requested one point of contact for its various arms and weapons projects and space programs. The US government had entered the Cold War and had a strong interest in winning the race to rapidly build weapons of mass destruction. It also had a strong interest in controlling those complex projects with new standards such as project life cycle planning (see Figure 1.2) and time and cost monitoring tools. With the growing dynamics of technological development, private industry, mainly in the USA, started to look for management approaches that were able to deal with a changing environment entailing greater complexity. In the 1960s, the aerospace, defence and construction industries applied project management methodology. During the 1970s and 1980s, more companies, for example in the pharmaceutical or consulting domain, decided to use a formal project management approach to cope with the bigger and more complex tasks resulting from the following trends (Kerzner, 2006):

- technology developments increasing very quickly
- product development becoming more resource intensive
- availability of more information
- increasing time pressures on new product or service development.

In the 1990s and up to today the organizations' environment has become even more complex and more dynamic due to the ongoing globalization process. Organizations in all industries, with different ownership structures, now apply project management to cope with an environment that is increasingly international or global.

At the beginning of this section, I introduced general systems theory. Coming back to this school of thought, I would like to specify that the project management of today needs to be built on open system theory. An organization is regarded as getting input from its environment, transforming it, and then returning it to the environment as output. The key feature of the open system approach which makes it useful as the theoretical basis for project management is that the theory combines the holistic approach of the general systems theory with the context the system is interrelated with. Open system theory ensures that all the relevant factors, inputs or influences on a system, namely the organization, are taken into account (Katz and Kahn, 1969).

If a project is a system, it has to be seen as a sub-system in the light of programs or a whole bundle of programs. These in turn are part of the biggest system in this context, the organization. To view a project as an open and complex system is the basis for effective project management in an international context, as I shall outline in sections 1.9 to 1.11.

The growing popularity and maturity of project management should not let us forget its origins, namely the US military sector. Project management as a kind of applied general systems management was developed by researchers and theorists. Hofstede (1993: 82) argues that '[theorists] grew up in a particular society, in a particular period, and their ideas cannot help but reflect the constraints of their environment'. Project management is engrained in certain values of a certain age. It assumes a normative approach mirroring the values of the Anglo-American world.

The whole approach of project management is based on the assumptions of economic rationality and the analysis of means-end chains, for example: the project management life cycle is based on the assumption that project managers are rational problem solvers working in a sequential way (Muriithi and Crawford, 2003). Project management literature seldom questions the overall validity of those values and the resulting classical project management orthodoxy. If this methodology is transferred to a context with a different set of values, it might at least be partially inappropriate and result in project failure. Milosevic (1999) considers project management as culture-bound. Project members from different cultural backgrounds interpret project management practices differently. He calls this the 'silent project management language'.

It could be argued, though, that values are globally converging towards a Western or even Anglo-American set of values in the wake of a country's economic development towards industrialization. Japan and other East Asian countries demonstrate that there are trends of convergence, but many cultural differences still prevail.

What does this mean for project management in an international context? Cultural differences and their impact on project management tools and techniques need to be taken into account for all international projects. Depending on the (cultural) differences between the parties involved in the project, and depending on the nature of the project, modifications or extensions of the classical project management methods might be needed as I will explore further in this book, concurring with Engwall's (2003: 790) view that 'projects have to be conceptualized as contextually-embedded, open systems'.

WHAT ARE THE MAIN DIFFERENCES BETWEEN A 'STANDARD' AND AN INTERNATIONAL PROJECT?

1.7

Before we turn to the differences between a 'standard' and an international project, let me first clarify how I use the term 'international'. I use the word in a very broad sense, i.e. reaching beyond national boundaries, usually in terms of the project purpose or nationality of stakeholders. International projects can be global, involving the entire world, but this is only a sub-group of international projects. International projects typically are simultaneously multicultural projects relating to diverse cultures, be it national, organizational, or functional cultures. In the following, I will use the terms 'international' and 'multicultural' synonymously. 'Virtual' projects or 'virtual' teams are often a part or sub-group of international projects due to the fact that the stakeholders of international projects are usually geographically dispersed.

International projects are not too different from standard projects when it comes to the nature of the organization, industry, location in the value chain, and duration. There are obvious differences, however, regarding:

- purpose
- scope
- the main stakeholders
- risk intensity.

When I talk about differences, I don't imply cardinal differences. Project management tools and techniques that apply for standard projects also apply for international projects. What I am rather referring to are differences in dimensions and magnitude: the management of international projects simply requires *more* – more disciplines need to be taken into account and more skills are needed, as I will explain in the following paragraphs.

MAIN PURPOSES OF INTERNATIONAL PROJECTS

In the following, I will outline the main purposes of international projects providing selected examples for each purpose.

Search for new geographical presence or new international stakeholders

Non-profit organizations have an interest in gaining new supporters on an international level, thus broadening their fund-raising base. With more international members, acquired by new local offices, non-profit organizations will usually also have a greater influence on different governments or supranational decision-makers which are important in their respective areas. An example is Greenpeace, founded in Canada in 1971. In 1979, it became a centralized international organization. Today, Greenpeace is present in 40 countries across Europe, the Americas, Asia, and the Pacific, with approximately 2.8 million supporters. The organization's strong international presence was accompanied by an increase in its global lobbying power which is necessary to achieve its stated organizational purpose: to change mankind's attitudes and behaviour in order to protect and conserve the environment and to promote peace (Greenpeace, 2006).

Increase of global market share, market power, global political power or global effectiveness

International projects run by governments often have as their purpose to increase the political power of one government on a global level. There are manifold motives: examples are wars led by super powers against smaller countries, for instance to ensure the supply of natural resources. International projects of governmental agencies can also have the purpose of helping other countries to recover from natural catastrophes, like the tsunami in South-East Asia in 2004, by teaming up and joining forces. There are also plenty of projects initiated by the governmental agencies of industrialized countries to improve living conditions in poorer regions of the world. An example is a project financed by the German Ministry for Economic Collaboration to help Egyptian peasants to manage irrigation more efficiently (GTZ, 2006).

Realization of efficiency gains

To reduce manufacturing costs, US car manufacturers have transferred their factories from the USA to Mexico, where the output of assembled cars for the American market has increased steeply in 2006 in contrast to the shrinking output in the home market.

According to a report from the market research firm iSuppli from 2006, 82.6 per cent of PC notebooks sold by multinationals like Hewlett Packard or Dell Corporation are manufactured by Taiwanese companies that in turn have their production sites mainly in the People's Republic of China (The *Inquirer*, 2006).

Access to scarce and unique resources

An increasing number of organizations are trying to develop new products and services with an international workforce. In so-called transnational projects involving members from several corporate units located in different countries, including their headquarters and subsidiaries, companies like the European aeronautics corporation EADS develop new products, for instance satellite equipment.

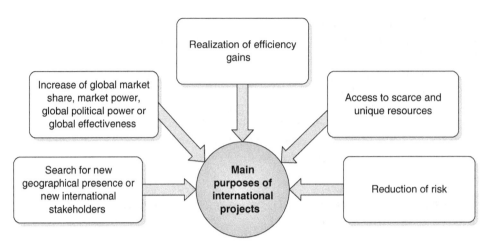

FIGURE 1.4 Main purposes of international projects

Many non-profit organizations short of financial resources will seek volunteers from all over the world in order to recruit talented and committed staff. An example is a small orphanage in Brazil, close to Rio de Janeiro, where a multinational team of volunteers is working together with the local employees to improve the education of the children there.

Reduction of risk

An example of risk reduction by international risk sharing is Boeing's development of their new aircraft the 787, the so-called Dreamliner. Several 'risk-sharing partners' scattered around the globe deliver 75 per cent of all parts and components of the air-craft. The central fuselage sections, for instance, are built in southern Italy. From there, they are flown on special 747 machines to another supplier in the USA located in South Carolina, before the components are assembled by Boeing near Seattle (*The Economist*, 2007a).

Figure 1.4 summarizes the main purposes of an international project.

SCOPE OF INTERNATIONAL PROJECTS

Another substantial difference between standard and international projects lies in the area of scope. By definition, the scope of an international project goes beyond the usual conditions of the home market of any given organization. For instance, there will be several locations involved, which are usually in different countries. In many international projects, several different entities of an organization will be involved, for example headquarters, regional headquarters, and local offices. Due to their strategic importance, many international projects are more visible within an organization. The survival of an organization may depend on the successful management of a single international project, for instance a cross-border merger or acquisition.

Bigger scope usually entails greater complexity, assuming that volume increases complexity in terms of the increase in the number of interfaces, and that organizations and their members have greater difficulty comprehending something 'big' in terms of the parties involved, the countries involved, the budget involved, etc.

STAKEHOLDERS OF INTERNATIONAL PROJECTS

In contrast to standard projects, international projects will typically involve non-domestic stakeholders, especially customers who are very often non-domestic and heterogeneous regarding their nationality. Moreover, there now tend to be more stake-holders outside an organization as collaborative international projects are increasing. A US-based IT consulting company had to work together with 14 subcontractors from Austria, Germany, the Lebanon, Dubai, Greece, and Cyprus to deliver an IT-infrastructure project for a bank in the Gulf region.

RISK INTENSITY OF INTERNATIONAL PROJECTS

International projects usually bear greater risks and uncertainty than other projects. I will discuss the details in Chapter 4. One of the reasons is the complexity of an international environment which is difficult to analyse. Changes are often sudden and unpredictable. Another reason is the complexity of the organizational set-up with a multitude of inter-faces and the large number of stakeholders involved.

Let us close section 1.7 with a Mini Case on Tata Motors covering the main differences between the international and standard projects we have discussed above.

Mini Case 1.1: Tata Motors

According to the New Delhi-based National Council of Applied Economic Research, over 56 million Indians earn over 4,400 US$ annually as of 2006. Against this background, a car priced at half the annual income could be very popular. Hence, Tata Motors, a division of the country's second largest and oldest conglomerate, the Tata Group, wants to launch a US$2,200 car in 2008. In December 2006, the government of West Bengal approved the construction of a new factory near Kolkata. In less than 18 months, the first prototypes of a new low-cost car are scheduled to leave the production line. Tata plans to mass-produce parts and to ship partially or fully knocked-down kits to entrepreneurial-run garages. There, the cars will be assembled, and sold. This 'People's Car', by 2008 known as the 'Nano', will have a rear engine, four or five doors and four wheels. To

Mini Case

lower the weight and cost, more composite materials will go into making the body. The CEO, Mr Tata, wants to achieve his new goal by sourcing technology and materials from 'wherever it makes sense'.

The engine management system will come from the US-automotive supplier, Delphi. Italian design help is coming from the Institute of Development in Automotive Engineering (I.D.E.A) which helped Tata develop its popular Indica sedan. The car project may also be joined by the Italian auto manufacturer, Fiat.

Due to increased raw material prices, the forecast price of the People's Car has risen to approximately 3,000 US$ before taxes in 2008. In addition, in 2008, Tata Motors was forced to transfer its first Nano production plant from West Bengal to Gujarat due to violent peasant protests.

In the last couple of years, Tata Motors acquired Daewoo Commercial Vehicles of South Korea. It also purchased the Spanish automotive manufacturer, Hispano, and announced a joint venture with Marcopolo, a Brazilian bus manufacturer.

Sources: *AutoAsia* (2006); *Financial Express* (2006); Kremer (2006); Tata Motors (2006); *The Economist* (2006); *The Economist* (2008)

Questions and tasks

1 Identify the purpose of the international projects mentioned above.
2 What main stakeholders can you identify in the various projects?
3 Which risks can you identify?

WHAT ARE THE CHARACTERISTICS OF AN INTERNATIONAL PROJECT?

1.8 We have discussed the main differences between 'standard' and international projects. I will now provide you with a systematic overview of the characteristics of an international project that is more multifaceted than a 'standard' project. Figure 1.5 depicts all the characteristics of an international project at a single glance.

Before I comment on individual characteristics, I would like to emphasize that they are interrelated. For instance, uniqueness is amplified by diversity, dynamics, risk propensity and complexity. Complexity and limited resources further contribute to risk, and dynamics and diversity increase complexity.

Let me start with one of the most decisive characteristics, namely complexity, followed by the other characteristics in an anti-clockwise manner.

COMPLEXITY

This means that there is a huge variety of factors the project manager has to deal with. Complexity in this context has mainly organizational and geographical causes. Complexity

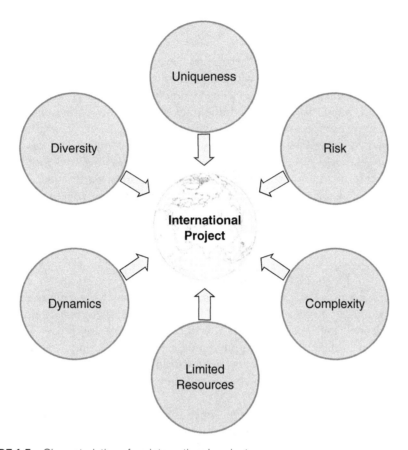

FIGURE 1.5 Characteristics of an international project

from an organizational perspective refers to many intra- and inter-organizational links existing in an international project. Multiple stakeholders with partially conflicting interests, located in different entities of the organization or outside the organization at collaborators' or the client's organizations result in a huge number of interdependent interactions which lead to a very complex project set-up. It is vital for the project manager of an international project to find an adequate structure and system to cope with multi-interdependencies. It is also crucial to get to know the different 'hidden agendas' of the organizations involved and to include these in planning the project. Without the true buy-in of all the parties involved, failure is likely to occur.

Complexity from a geographical point of view resides in stakeholders being scattered around the globe. The organization and the project manager need to establish systems and policies to enable smooth communication and co-operation across different time zones. This is a particular challenge when the Americas and Oceania or East Asian countries are simultaneously involved in a project, as they span time zones with a difference of more than ten hours.

RISK

Due to their complexity, many international projects will see budget and time over-runs, although this is not unusual with standard projects either. The international environment bears further uncertainty, like sudden political instability. Part of the project team might be physically endangered due to guerrilla unrest in the country they are operating in, or members of the team might get hijacked. After a change in political power, the new government might expropriate foreign companies as has happened recently in Venezuela. Western and Japanese oil companies nowadays face huge risks with their international projects like oil and gas exploration, for instance on the Russian island Sakhalin (North-East Asia), because the Russian government wants to regain full control of its natural resources. Different currencies along with local inflation rates, profit repatriation problems, taxation issues, etc. can further add to the risk.

UNIQUENESS

By definition a project is unique. International projects have unique objectives. Daimler acquired Chrysler in 1998 in order to gain a market presence in northern America, grow bigger and benefit from economies of scale and scope. The biggest Chinese PC-manufacturer Lenovo purchased the Personal Computing Division of IBM in 2004 in order to gain access to IBM-technology, to the US-market and to benefit from the well-established IBM-brand they had obtained the right to use for five years.

International projects are also unique when it comes to the organizations involved, like an international network of organizations, international alliances, international joint ventures, etc.

The context international projects are operating in will also be unique. Countries have different economic and political systems, and different societal structures and cultures. They have attained different technological development levels, have different attitudes and laws regarding the environment, and are governed by different regulatory regimes.

DIVERSITY

Bennett and Bennett (2004:150) define diversity as 'cultural differences in values, beliefs, and behaviours learned and shared by groups of interacting people defined by nationality, ethnicity, gender, age, physical status, education, profession, religion, organizational affiliation, and any other grouping that generates identifiable patterns'. In the context of this book, diversity stemming from differences in culture, education, and profession is most crucial. I will use diversity and heterogeneity as synonymous terms throughout this textbook. Different national cultures will have a pervasive influence across all project management phases from definition to completion of the project. Managers and members of international projects must be aware of this fact. Cultural differences must be bridged and managed in an efficient way. Project managers will have to face a situation where their project members might work in entities with different organizational cultures. They may speak different languages. Hence, misunderstandings are the order of the day. Even among native English speakers, the question is: What is 'standard' English? Project stakeholders will have gone through different educational systems which can lead to different skills – some might have accumulated a wealth of knowledge but are not capable of transferring this to new issues and problems, others might have learned different models or are used to different processes and procedures. Diversity is an important characteristic of international problems and a theme throughout this textbook, comparable to complexity.

DYNAMICS

International projects will frequently face numerous and sudden changes. The reasons are fierce competition on global markets, and the fact that there are many parties involved in the project with self-interests which might not be obvious. Besides, this complex environment offers plenty of new opportunities and risks which need to be acted upon swiftly. An example would be the emergence of a new competitor on the global market, like the Korean manufacturer Samsung in the consumer electronics business of the 1990s.

LIMITED RESOURCES

The bigger scope implies a greater amount of resources needed to carry out an international project. More time is required for proper planning, more money is needed due to higher transportation and co-ordination efforts. Moreover, it is a challenge to recruit staff with the language and intercultural skills necessary for in an international project.

Mini Case 1.2 will provide you with the opportunity to analyse an international project in light of the characteristics we have just discussed.

Mini Case 1.2: One laptop per child

In January 2005, Nicholas Negroponte, co-founder and former Director of the MIT Media Lab, founded the One Laptop per Child (OLPC) non-profit association. With the help of other MIT faculty members as well as companies such as 3M, Advanced Micro Devices (AMD), Google, News Corporation, Nortel, Red Hat and others, OLPC aims at designing, manufacturing and distributing laptops at a target price of 100 US$. These laptops shall be sold to governments in developing countries and distributed specifically by schools on the basis of *one laptop per child*. The idea is that the laptops are free to these children. OLPC's objective is to produce a vital educational tool to transform the content and quality of these children's education.

Considering that 60 per cent of the cost of a laptop resides in marketing, sales and distribution which do not occur at OLPC, experts from both academia and industry have come together to provide these ultra-low cost, flexible, power efficient, responsive and durable machines. As of 2007, initial discussions have been held with countries such as

Mini Case

Brazil, Thailand, India, Argentina and Egypt. Each country will receive versions specific to their local language. OLPC has chosen Quanta Computer Inc. of Taiwan as their original design manufacturer (ODM) for the $100 laptop project. Manufacturing was scheduled to begin when 5 to 10 million machines have been ordered and paid for in advance. As of the beginning of 2007, countries like Nigeria and Libya have each committed to 1 million plus units. The preliminary schedule has been met, and in November 2006, the first 875 B1-Test machines left the assembly line. In February 2007, the B2 Test machines were deployed to the chosen launch countries: Brazil, Argentina, Nigeria, Libya and Thailand. To make them useful in their environment, the laptops are equipped with devices to load their batteries manually. Their colour display can be switched to a high resolution mono-chrome display that is easier to read in natural light. However, things turned out to be more difficult than anticipated. As of May 2008, only some 100,000 units had been sold. The cost of the laptop is twice as high as planned.

Sources: dpa (2008);Laptop.org (2007a, 2007b, 2007c); OLPC Wiki (2007); Surowiecki (2007); TED (2006).

Task

Identify the main characteristics making the initiative 'one laptop per child' an international project.

With the main characteristics of an international project in mind, we cannot help recognizing that managing such a multifaceted thing is a daunting task that requires special knowledge and skills. And this is the purpose of the international project 'writing the textbook on international project management': providing you with the relevant knowledge and skills. Let us now take a look at what is necessary in order to lead an international project to success.

WHAT DETERMINES THE SUCCESS OF INTERNATIONAL PROJECT MANAGEMENT?

1.9

First we have to clarify what success means. For the purpose of this book, I will define success as the extent to which the pre-defined project purpose will be attained. We have to be careful, though, not to confuse successful project management with the success of a project. The former might be measured according to the 'Magic Triangle', i.e. in terms of cost, time, and quality. The latter can be subdivided into two questions:

1 What factors contribute to a successful project?
2 What factors lead to consistently successful projects?

Both questions are related to the overall success of the organization. Can an organization develop project management as a competitive advantage? Can it repeatedly use projects as a means to position and reposition itself successfully in the (global) market place? We will deal with the above mentioned questions in Chapters 2 and 11.

In the following, we will focus on what has to be done to achieve the purpose of the project within the given constraints.

We have to distinguish between 'success criteria' and 'success factors'. According to Lim and Mohamed (1999) success criteria are generic assessment standards independent of the type of project whereas success factors are more specific to a concrete project and directly influence project results. Success factors are easily confused with the measurement of success which is done with so-called key performance indicators (cf. Chapter 7).

The literature offers a variety of lists of criteria that are critical for project success (Cooke-Davies, 2004; Pinto and Slevin, 1988). I have selected the most relevant in the context of international projects and will interpret them in light of the particularities of international projects. The order of the points does not imply decreasing importance.

GOAL COMMITMENT OF THE PROJECT TEAM AND INITIAL CLARITY OF GOALS

Due to the great diversity prevailing in international projects, it is extremely challenging to formulate a goal in a way that all project members feel strongly committed to. Another challenge is maintaining the commitment over a longer period of time which is often necessary due to the lengthy duration of international projects.

ESTABLISHMENT OF SMOOTH COMMUNICATIONS AND SUPPORTING INFRASTRUCTURE

It is critical for success to be able to communicate quickly and effectively across temporal, organizational, functional, geographic and cultural boundaries. This requires a common language and intercultural communication skills. All project members need to be able to communicate sufficiently in a common language such as English, Spanish, Mandarin, Arabic, or any other world language. All project members have to be able to use modern communication technology. This might sound like stating the obvious. However, due to different technological development levels of the project sites, ICT and the level of PC literacy might differ hugely between members of the international project.

ADEQUATE PROJECT TEAM CAPABILITIES

In international projects, project members need to have sufficient technical capabilities to perform well, including the communication capabilities outlined above. Moreover, the project members or at least the leaders of the international project need to have more interpersonal competences, namely in the area of intercultural management and languages. Leaders of international projects have to be aware of the nature of cultural differences, and must be trained in efficiently working in and with diversity. Ideally, they can turn differences into greater creativity (cf. Chapter 10).

A CONSIDERATION OF CONTEXT

Project managers have to pay special attention to the diversity and complexity of international projects, partially due to differences in context. The international project has to deal with a variety of heterogeneous stakeholders. It also has to put up with differences in the infrastructure, jurisdiction, and, of course, culture.

THE RIGHT BALANCE BETWEEN COMMON METHODOLOGY AND FLEXIBILITY

Risk propensity and the need for changes in a dynamic environment are high in international projects. Hence, the project manager and his or her team need to allow for flexible and swift responses. At the same time, they have to maintain cohesion among the heterogeneous stakeholders with a common project management methodology such as a project master plan. The project manager needs to be willing and able to take a risk and depart from the original plan, though, in order to cope with a dynamic and complex environment.

A SUPPORTIVE PROJECT CULTURE

A crucial and critical success criterion which is rarely mentioned in classical models is the project culture. Any culture of an international project needs to be ethno-relative. Based on an attitude of open-mindedness, responsiveness and flexibility, no preferences are given to any national (or organizational) culture. No culture should be regarded as superior to another. A supportive project culture allows for fusing customs, habits or behaviours from various cultures if it serves project success. The prerequisite of such an ethno-relative culture is the acknowledgement of differences and their respect. Open-mindedness and respect enable the creation of trust among diverse stakeholders, which in turn is the prerequisite for effective learning in and from projects, as will be explained further in Chapter 11.

Ideally, the project culture supports the achievement of the given tasks and simultaneously functions as a common reference frame in terms of behaviour and communication to all parties involved in the international project. We will discuss project and organizational culture in detail in Chapter 2.

Knowing the criteria for success as summarized in Figure 1.6 is important for efficiently working in and managing international projects.

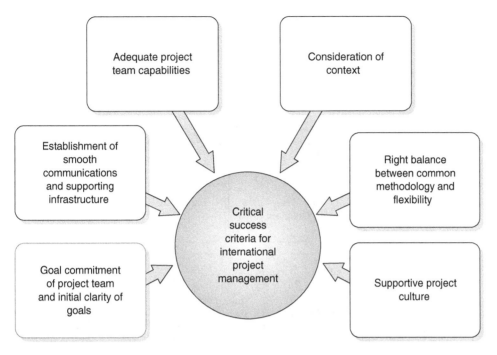

FIGURE 1.6 Key success criteria for international project management

WHAT IS THE STRUCTURE OF THIS TEXTBOOK?

1.10 I will close this chapter by outlining the structure of this book. I have selected two reference frames to explain the main topics, and to indicate the areas which are out of scope. First, this book's structure is described from the perspective of the APM Body of Knowledge in its 5th edition (APM, 2006b). Second, the structure of this book is explained from an open system theory perspective.

APM KNOWLEDGE AREAS PERSPECTIVE

Figure 1.7 illustrates the seven APM knowledge areas with their headings. Below the titles of each knowledge area, you will find the numbers of the chapters of this textbook that chiefly deal with the respective knowledge area.

The APM knowledge areas four and five are only marginally dealt with, whereas knowledge area seven is deeply analysed in this book, with one chapter for each knowledge sub-area. Reflecting the requirements of successful international project management as explained above, I have dedicated special attention to:

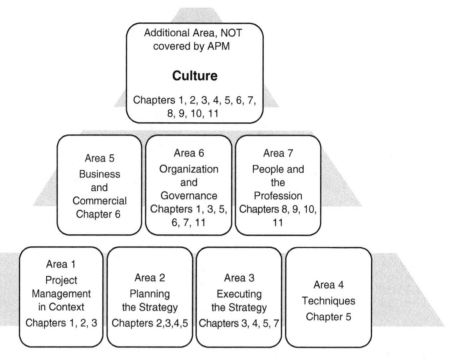

FIGURE 1.7   Coverage of APM knowledge areas in this book

- management methods suitable for a dynamic, complex, fast changing environment
- context management (externalities)
- people management
- culture management.

In the following I relate the content of each knowledge area of the APM Body of Knowledge to the content of the chapters of this book.

1   Project management in context

Comprises project management, program management, portfolio management, project context, project sponsorship, and project office.

This knowledge area is discussed in Chapters 1, 2, and 3 with a special emphasis on project context due to its importance for international projects.

2   Planning the strategy

Comprises project success and benefits management, stakeholder management, value management, project management plan, project risk management, project quality management, health, safety and environmental management.

Project success and benefits management is discussed in Chapter 2. Stakeholder management is discussed in Chapter 3, the project management plan in Chapters 3 and 5, and project risk management in Chapter 4. Project quality management is only touched on in Chapter 5 regarding the particularities of an international project. The other areas are outside the scope of this book.

3 Executing the strategy

Comprises scope management, scheduling, resource management, budgeting and cost management, change control, earned value management, information management and reporting, and issue management.

Scope management is discussed in Chapter 3. Chapter 5 gives an overview of scheduling, resource management, budgeting and cost management. Chapter 7 introduces change control, earned value management, reporting and issue management.

4 Techniques

Comprises requirements management, development, estimating, technology management, value engineering, modelling and testing, and configuration management.

Due to the international focus of the book and the constraints regarding space, the technical areas are only marginally discussed in Chapters 3 and 5. This does not mean that 'techniques' are not important. On the contrary, much more research is needed in this area. I have listed further literature for the interested reader at the end of this chapter.

5 Business and commercial

Comprises business case, marketing and sales, project financing and funding, procurement, legal awareness.

Here again, I have only partially touched on procurement issues and legal awareness issues in Chapter 6, and all other areas are out of scope. For a detailed analysis, further reading is recommended.

6 Organization and governance

Comprises project life cycles, concept, definition, implementation, handover and closeout, project reviews, organization structure, organizational roles, methods and procedures, and the governance of project management.

Project life cycles are discussed in Chapter 1, concept and definition in Chapter 3, implementation in Chapter 7, handover, closeout, and project reviews in Chapter 11, organization structure, organizational roles, methods, and procedures and governance of project management in Chapter 6, and communication governance in Chapter 8.

7 People and the profession

Comprises communication, teamwork, leadership, conflict management, negotiation, human resource management, behavioural characteristics, learning and development, and professionalism and ethics.

The people-related area is the most important when it comes to international project management, especially due to the fact that people cannot be separated from the other areas described above: 'It is not as if there are some factors that involve processes, and others that involve people – people perform every process, and it is the people that ultimately determine the adequacy' (Cooke-Davis, 2002: 189).

I focus on 'People and the Profession' in this book, discussing communication and negotiation in Chapter 9, leadership, behavioural characteristics, and human resource management in Chapter 8, conflict management in Chapter 10, and learning and development in Chapter 11.

Additional knowledge area: culture

People and their actions are heavily influenced by culture. Thus, culture is an important factor impacting on people's behaviour also on projects. However, culture is not mentioned in the APM Body of Knowledge. As culture plays a decisive role in international project management, special attention is given to it throughout the entire book. In each chapter I will point the reader towards the cultural particularities that standard project management methodology may need to incorporate.

Another area which is not explicitly mentioned in the APM Body of Knowledge is 'learning' in the sense of a learning organization. It is argued that the continuous enlargement of the capabilities of an organization creates a strong competitive edge, especially in a globalizing world. Hence, Chapter 11 is dedicated to 'learning in and from international projects', not only touching on individual learning as covered in the APM Body of Knowledge, but also on organizational learning.

Project management standards are useful to provide the student and practitioner with a framework of relevant knowledge in the field of project management. However, you have to be sensitive to not cutting and pasting this standard without further reflection about its applicability in an international context.

OPEN SYSTEM PERSPECTIVE

Let us switch perspectives, turning away from project management standards and looking at international project management from the angle of an open system, the organization. Across sectors and geographical borders, an increasing number of organizations are using project management to implement their strategy. As project management becomes an overarching theme in the management of organizations, it should be more closely tied to the main elements of an organization, rather than viewed as a separate 'thing' existing in parallel to the organization. I think that project management should be integrated into how the organization determines and implements its strategy, how the organization is structured, how the organization ticks, which systems and processes it is based on, how the organization's staff are led, what knowledge the staff have, and what the organization's capabilities are. As projects are managed within the context of an open system, the organization, we have to keep all those organizational

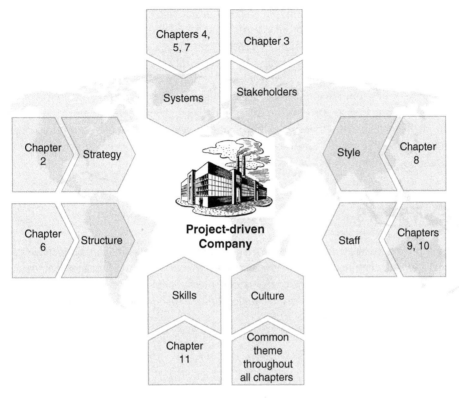

FIGURE 1.8 The content of this book from an open system's perspective

areas attuned to the needs of efficient and effective project management and vice versa. This book aims at providing the reader with a holistic view on project management.

To illustrate this approach, I have adapted (see Figure 1.8) the well-known McKinsey Seven-S-Model comprising 'hard' and 'soft' areas of an organization: Style, Staff, Shared Values (Organizational Culture), Skills, Structure, Strategy and Systems (Bate, 1994). I have extended the Shared Values to Culture in a broader sense, including national and functional cultures, and supplemented the model by another 'S' for 'Stakeholders' to properly reflect the main areas of importance in international project management.

SUMMARY

An international project is typically more complex, dynamic, and riskier than a 'standard' project. It has to address the diversity of its stakeholders mainly in terms of national cultures, organizational cultures, functional cultures, languages, and educational backgrounds. The context of international stakeholders and an international environment with its heterogeneous jurisdictions plays an important role in the management of international projects. Project management emerged from the US military. Hence, it is rooted in Anglo-American values. When applied in other countries and contexts, the methodology might need to be modified. Key criteria for successfully managing international projects are the goal commitment of the project team and an the absolute clarity of goals, the establishment of smooth communications and a general infrastructure, the consideration of context, adequate project team capability and project members' sensitivity to local cultures, the right balance between flexibility and project management methodology as a common reference frame, and the establishment of an ethno-relative project culture reflecting open-mindedness, respect, and trust.

 # KEY TERMS

Project, project management, project management life cycle, stakeholder, project owner, project sponsor, contractor, customer, user, project manager, project management team, program, general systems theory, open system, international project, complexity, risk, uniqueness, diversity, heterogeneity, dynamics, limited resources, success criterion, success factor.

REVIEW TASKS

Questions

1 Where do you see the main differences between a 'standard' and an international project?
2 In your opinion, what can impede the successful management of an international project?
3 How helpful are global standards for international project management?

EXERCISE

Work in groups of five or six people, if possible from different cultures (national, organizational or functional) or with different (educational) backgrounds.

First, you must individually think about your personal experience in the last five years. What would you classify as an international project?

Second, use Figure 1.5 to characterize the project you have in mind and then explain it to your fellow students in the group.

CHAPTER END CASE: FIGHT AGAINST GLOBAL PANDEMICS

EMERGENCE OF HIGHLY PATHOGENIC AVIAN INFLUENZA

In 1997, the avian influenza virus or bird flu first surfaced in Hong Kong. Since then, it has remained largely a disease affecting birds with sporadic infections of humans who have had contact with infected fowl. Hundreds of millions of birds have died or been culled because of the virus since 2003. Until January 2007, 163 people were reported to have been killed by the virus, mostly in Indonesia, Vietnam, Thailand, and China. In 2006, the virus became deadlier: 70 per cent of infected persons died from it.

Between 2003 and 2005, avian influenza was reported in 15 countries, mainly in South-East and Central Asia. By May 2006, the highly pathogenic avian influenza (HPAI), also called H5N1, had spread to 45 countries. In some countries it was only found in wild fowl, in other countries and regions, like India, Africa, the Middle East, and Europe, the virus was identified in domestic and commercial poultry populations. Between 2003 and early 2007, the virus had caused estimated economic losses to the Asian poultry sector of around 10 billion US$. It has destroyed the livelihoods of hundreds of thousands of poor livestock farmers. It jeopardizes commercial poultry production, and is an increasing obstacle to regional and international trade.

RISK OF A PANDEMIC?

The fact that there has been a recent continual increase in the number of known cases of avian influenza transmission has raised concerns over the potential appearance of a human pandemic which could have extremely harmful effects on the health and livelihood of all human beings. However, it is extremely uncertain whether or when a pandemic will emerge. Since the sixteenth century, three pandemics on average have been recorded per century. In the last 100 years, pandemics have occurred in 1918, 1957, and 1968. The most severe was in 1918, the so-called Spanish influenza, with an estimated rate of 50 million deaths within 18 months. A pandemic today would travel faster, given the improvements in transportation. Experts forecast a death toll of between 2 to 50 million for an avian influenza pandemic. This would not only put high requirements on countries' health systems, but would also result in an unprecedented social and economic impact. According to World Bank estimates, the cost of a pandemic could amount to 1.5–2 trillion US$ in a severe pandemic scenario.

GLOBAL PROGRAM FOR AVIAN INFLUENZA

MAIN PLAYERS

In light of the unprecedented potential harm incurred by an avian influenza pandemic, the World Bank, along with other agencies of the UN system (Food and Agriculture Organization (FAO), World Health Organization (WHO), together with the World Organization for Animal Health (OIE), a globally operating intergovernmental organization), started to design a Global Program for Avian Influenza (GPAI) in 2005. Why those organizations? The World Bank has the infrastructure and ability to work across sectors, to raise funds, and to mobilize technical assistance and knowledge-sharing activities at regional and global levels. The World Health Organization specializes in public health on a global level. The Food and Agricultural Organization and the Organization for Animal Health are the experts in agricultural issues and animal health.

The program is scheduled to be implemented over three time-frames: immediate to short (1–3 years), short to medium (4–6 years) and medium to long-term (7–10 years).

It involves numerous players, namely in the areas of health, agriculture, economics, finance, and planning. Apart from the international organizations mentioned above, the world's governments, together with many non-governmental bodies, private entities and international scientific, developmental, humanitarian and security organizations are involved in the program. Some 25 countries received financing under this program by the end of 2006, including Vietnam, Bangladesh, India, Nigeria, Ethiopia, Turkey, and Romania. In the infected countries and the non-infected at-risk countries, governmental agencies committed to controlling trans-boundary animal diseases are part of an integrated, multi-sector response to the threat posed by the deadly disease. In some countries, the military have also to be considered because they play a major role in emergencies.

OBJECTIVES

The long-term objectives of the program are:

- diminishing the global threat of a human pandemic
- stabilizing poultry production
- supporting a robust regional and international trade in poultry and poultry products
- increasing human and food safety
- improving the livelihoods of the rural poor.

What concrete activities can lead to the accomplishment of these objectives? Simply put, it is a careful adherence to basic public health and infection control measures, for instance contact investigation, and infection control at healthcare facilities. Given the uncertainty and the lack of knowledge regarding the spread and persistence of H5N1, the program also supports further research and investigations into avian influenza. Yet, it will not be easy to achieve the goals due to the complex interface between farming systems, the livestock trade, food safety and public health.

The activities described need to be embedded in a strong common vision. It is also important to adapt the global measures to local contexts, tailoring the various activities to local needs. The countries have a great variation in their capacity to deal with the outbreak of a serious disease. The global program consists of many single projects which are dedicated to realizing the above mentioned objectives with measures that are adapted to local conditions.

ISSUES

There are different sources of financial resources: the internal resources of the infected and at-risk countries, funding provided by international organizations, but also funding through a so-called multi-donor trust fund which mainly supports countries that lack financial resources, for example in Africa. By April 2006, the economic heavyweights like China, the EU countries, Japan, Russia, and the USA, but also smaller countries like Saudi Arabia, Singapore, South Korea and Thailand, together with the European Commission, the Asian Development Bank and the World Bank, had provided an overall sum of almost 1.9 billion US$ for the program. Yet, too few financial resources are available for the program as of the end of 2006. Another issue is the lack of support for communications. People need clearer and more comprehensive information regarding the risk and outbreak of the disease.

Recently, more difficulties have emerged as reflected in the following example of Indonesia.

Indonesia is the country worst affected by bird flu. It has recorded 85 cases, of which 64 have been fatal. To protect the world's population from a pandemic, the WHO wants to develop a vaccine against the virus. Consequently, it needs samples of the virus. In February 2007, the director-general of the WHO gave a written guarantee to the Indonesian health minister stating that no avian influenza samples were to be passed on to companies for commercial use. However, Indonesia wants a legally binding agreement before it will share samples with the WHO. The Indonesian government is afraid samples will be used for commercial purposes without its permission. The deputy health minister for research feels that Indonesia has been cheated by the WHO before, as it had allegedly passed on samples to companies. He says that good relationships can be restored quickly, but only if the WHO respects Indonesia.

International avian influenza experts consider the withholding of samples as a great risk to global health because Indonesia is viewed as not having the expertise to determine whether the virus is mutating into a form which could trigger a global pandemic. Other experts understand the tough stance of the Indonesian government as it would have to pay millions of dollars for vaccines to pharmaceutical companies which would have obtained the samples for free. They feel that it is only ethical to share the risks and benefits.

As of May 2008, Indonesia and other countries reluctant to share information about their viruses have started to exchange information using a freely accessible global database. Until then, the WHO had kept crucial information in a private database at a US government laboratory in Los Alamos, USA, with limited access for 15 other laboratories only.

Sources: AP (2008); *Financial Times* (2007); *The Economist* (2007b); The World Bank (2005); The World Bank (2006a); The World Bank (2006b); The World Bank (2006c); The World Bank (2006d); The World Bank (2006e); The World Bank (2006f); The World Bank (2007)

Questions

1 Assuming that the same characteristics apply to a program and project: what are the characteristics of the Global Avian Influenza Program which make it an international program?
2 Who are the main stakeholders in the Global Program on Avian Influenza?
3 What are the key success criteria for this international program?

FURTHER READING

Cleland, David I. and Roland Gareis (eds) (2006) *Global Project Management Handbook. Planning, Organizing, and Controlling International Projects,* 2nd edition. New York: McGraw-Hill. (This reader covers many aspects relevant for managing international projects in great detail. Part 5 provides interesting insights into project management in Austria, China, Australia, Romania, and Japan.)

Murphy, Owen Jay (2005) *International Project Management.* Mason: Thomson. (For those readers who miss a defence industry perspective. The US-American author has a military background.)

Thamain, Hans J. (2005) *Management of Technology. Managing Effectively in Technology-Intensive Organizations.* New Jersey: John Wiley & Sons. (This book gives very detailed insights into project management knowledge areas that are outside the scope of this book.)

Turner, J. Rodney (ed.) (2003) *Contracting for Project Management.* Aldershot: Gower. (This books covers very well the commercial project management knowledge area that is omitted in this book.)

In addition, the following journals publish interesting articles about the topic:

• *International Journal of Project Management* (Journal of the European International Project Management Association)
• *European Management Journal*
• *PM Network*
• *Project Management Journal* (Journal of the Project Management Institute PMI)

THE CONTEXT OF INTERNATIONAL PROJECTS IN TERMS OF ORGANIZATIONAL STRATEGY AND CULTURE

2

LEARNING OBJECTIVES

After studying this chapter, you will be able to:

- explain the concept of strategy and strategic management
- discuss the relationship between strategy and international projects
- describe program management and its relevance for international project management
- understand the concept of project portfolio management
- explain the tasks of a project management office
- discuss project management maturity models
- characterize organizational cultures conducive to effective international project management
- explain the concept 'managing by projects'.

INTRODUCTION

2.1 In Chapter 1, I have stated that international projects have to be seen as open systems embedded in an international context. The context consists of elements outside the organization and inside the organization. In this chapter, the focus is on the institutional context of international projects inside the organization, focusing on corporate strategy and organizational culture.

We know that international projects are steadily gaining importance with organizations worldwide. However, this does not mean that organizations are satisfied with the results of projects. There are many prominent examples of international projects that have failed, such as the merger between German Daimler-Benz and US-American Chrysler in 1998 that ended in the sale of Chrysler to the private equity investor Cerberus in 2007. Whether the Iraq war can be regarded as a successful international project is highly disputed even within the political party of the government responsible for it. The British company Royal Dutch Shell saw a cost leap from 10 to 20 billion US$ in its project of developing liquefied gas facilities on the Siberian island Sakhalin (Stanleigh, 2006). Many more organizations active in the exploitation of raw materials face similar difficulties in their international projects.

The root cause of this dissatisfying situation goes beyond a single project. To understand why projects fail, we have to look at them from a broader organizational perspective. A faulty strategy of the organization is usually a fundamental reason for many projects not obtaining successful results.

Even if a single project is managed efficiently, it still can have inadequate objectives which will not contribute to overall business success as reflected in the organization's strategic intent. To make sure that the initiation of projects is performed in line with the overarching strategy of an organization, projects need to be co-ordinated and managed as one large entity.

This is what we will discuss in this chapter. Based on an introduction into strategic management, we will look at methods to co-ordinate single projects, namely program management and project portfolio management. We will draw on the similarities between these approaches, and work on the differences compared to project management. We will also look at the organization of programs and project portfolios with a special emphasis on the project management office.

To ensure that projects sustainably contribute to organizational success, the organization has to develop skills regarding project, program, and project portfolio management. Based on the discussion of project management maturity models, you will see the link between strategy and skills as I have explained it at the end of Chapter 1 in Figure 1.8. Projects, programs, and project portfolios pursue strategic objectives. They are implemented in the context of the organization which not only has a strategy but also a culture to support its vision. Therefore, at the end of this chapter we will discuss which kind of organizational culture is conducive to the successful management of international projects. We will wrap up this chapter on organizational context with a look at a managerial approach called 'managing by projects'. It focuses on projects as the main organizational form. In other words, such an organization's strategy, culture and structure are solely implemented by projects. With the discussion of project-based organizations, we will close the loop from strategy to projects.

STRATEGY AND STRATEGIC MANAGEMENT

2.2 Over the last 40 years the views on the focus of strategy have evolved. In the 1960s, strategy mainly meant corporate planning with figures based on the past. In the 1970s it changed to the optimization of the overall portfolio of strategic business units within a given organization. In the 1980s, Michael Porter drew attention to the nature of the industry. In other words, the external strategic positioning based on industry and competitors' analysis became an important element of strategy creation. This view was followed in the early 1990s by a shift to the internal resources of an organization. Stress was put on the analysis and development of so-called strategic competences or strategic capabilities (Ghemawat, 2006). Today the focus is more on strategic innovation. Organizations aim at obtaining competitive advantage through superior knowledge management and the development of an effective learning organization (see also Chapter 11).

Whatever the focus of strategy was over the last four decades, Chandler's definition of strategy is still used today: 'Strategy is the determination of the basic long-term goals and objectives of an enterprise, and the adoption of courses of action and the allocation of resources necessary for carrying out these goals' (Moore, 2001: 33). The strategy is usually reflected in an organization's mission or vision (see also the companion website).

The term strategic management is defined by Digman as a '*continuous* process that involves attempts to match or fit the organization with its changing environment in the most advantageous way possible. It clearly includes adapting the organization itself (via internal changes) to fit the external environment' (Moore, 2001: 204). In contrast to strategy itself, strategic management is even more complex and mainly concerned with understanding the strategic position of an organization, strategic choices for the future, continuous change and the fine-tuning of strategy, and strategy implementation.

For the purposes of this book, a model of strategic management which is based on Kaplan and Norton's (1996) four phases of strategic management will be used, as depicted in Figure 2.1. Please note that the terms 'process' and 'cycle' will be used interchangeably in this chapter, as the processes discussed are iterative forming a series of cycles.

Let me briefly explain the strategic management cycle (Kaplan and Norton 1996):

- Phase 1: The senior executives formulate the vision and mission of the organization. They all need to have a clear understanding of the critical performance drivers which can be allocated to four major areas: finance, external customers, internal business processes, and learning and growth (related to the capabilities of employees).
- Phase 2: In the communicating and high-level aligning phase, the upper-level managers need to buy into the vision, and transform it into the goals of their

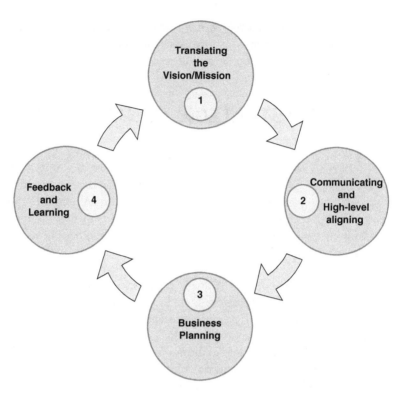

FIGURE 2.1   The strategic management cycle
Source: Based on Kaplan and Norton (1996)

respective organizational entities. The vision along with high-level objectives need to be communicated through the rank and file of the organization using the whole range of communication modes (see also Chapter 9). In parallel, all employees should try to link their individual goals to the objectives of the organizational unit they belong to, and formulate these in a way that makes them measurable.

• Phase 3: In the so-called business planning phase the set of objectives is broken down into concrete activities which could be (international) projects. The same organizational group that formulated and disseminated the vision is now also involved in resource allocation to make sure that the organization's activities will reflect its overall strategy. Measures are decided to monitor the implementation of these activities.

• Phase 4: This phase is dedicated to feedback and learning. It provides the organization with an opportunity to verify its strategies, which might be obsolete after 12 months in a fast changing and unpredictable world. Correlations between different elements of the strategies can be observed and used to improve the formulation of the vision based on the selection of a certain set of strategies. By conducting periodic performance reviews, the senior executives can learn about their strategies and then improve them.

The whole process of strategic management revolves around a tool to monitor and balance different business objectives, the Balanced Score Card (BSC) which will be further discussed in Chapter 7.

THE RELATION BETWEEN STRATEGIC MANAGEMENT AND PROJECTS

2.3

'Projects are ad hoc, resource-consuming activities used to implement organizational strategies, achieve enterprise goals and objectives, and contribute to the realization of the enterprise's mission' (Cleland and Ireland, 2002: 10) How can an organization ensure that projects do indeed contribute to the realization of its vision and mission, and not to its failure?

A crucial prerequisite is the co-ordination between strategy creation and project approval. According to Christensen (2000), many organizations operate their processes to formulate strategies autonomously from their processes in which projects are approved and resources are allocated. In other words, the strategic management cycle needs to incorporate projects as part of the business planning as well as the feedback and learning processes as depicted in Figure 2.2. In the business planning phase, the top management allocates resources to corporate activities, largely projects, or eliminates certain projects which are not in line with the overall strategy of the company, thus synchronizing the process of resource allocation with the strategy formulation process. An organization needs to allow for senior executives to be involved in both processes with each running simultaneously.

Snapshot 2.1 illustrates how international projects are linked with corporate strategy.

SNAPSHOT 2.1

McDonald's

The US-based fast food chain McDonald's has adopted an aggressive growth strategy in Europe. In order to implement this strategy, it will invest up to 800 million US$ in the year 2007 into projects in Europe. The idea is to adapt its products and restaurants in Europe to local habits and customs. Hence, McDonald's has established development teams to create local dishes and to work on a more European restaurant design. These international projects are targeted at increasing the attractiveness and acceptance of the brand with European customers. New soups and coffee specialties have been launched. Chairs in a classical Danish design have been introduced. Other projects like the alliance with a Germany-based organic soft drinks producer have been initiated. All these projects should help the company to achieve its growth targets.

Source: Dengel (2007a); Dengel (2007b)

To facilitate the alignment of the strategic management process with the resource allocation process, projects should be clustered according to pre-defined criteria. These clusters can be called programs (see also Chapter 1) or project portfolios.

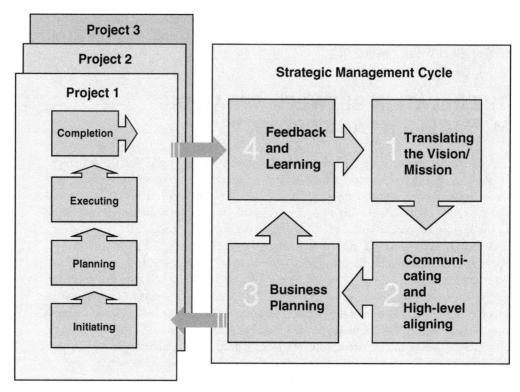

FIGURE 2.2 Extended strategic management cycle
Source: (Adapted from Kaplan and Norton, 1996)

PROGRAM MANAGEMENT

2.4 Let us first clarify how a program is defined. According to Gareis (2006a: 7–3) 'a program is a temporary organization to fulfil a unique business process of large scope. It is of great strategic importance for the company performing the program, and it is limited in time. The projects that are part of the program serve to realize common program objectives'. The program is not limited to projects, though. It can also include non-project actions (Thiry, 2004).

Projects in a program are interdependent. They share the same objectives and scarce resources. They typically have a common infrastructure and share a certain set of risks. The program's objective, though, can be more vague and wider than the rather specific objectives of a single project.

Programs have the following advantages:

- ensuring strategic alignment through the interdependency of objectives
- reducing the complexity of 'large projects', by clearly breaking them down into smaller, easy-to-control projects, which contributes to clearer responsibilities,

minimizes risks, and boosts morale and motivation. It also improves the quality of the results.

Programs are essentially managed in the same way as projects (see also Chapter 1). As is true for complex international projects with a long duration, program objectives might need to be adapted over time. The whole direction and parts of the content of a program might need adjustments because of environmental changes. Thiry (2004) refers to this change requirement as a learning loop. It is also a part of the general strategic management process as depicted in Figure 2.1 in phase four.

THE PROGRAM MANAGEMENT LIFE CYCLE

Both overall strategic management and program management are cyclic processes. The program management life cycle consists of five phases (Thiry, 2004) and strongly resembles the project management life cycle:

1 **Formulation:** The objective of the program is defined. The main purpose of this stage is to identify opportunities and to decide on the most efficient course of action. This phase is equivalent to the initiating phase of the project life cycle.
2 **Organization:** The different projects within a program are selected and prioritized. The project teams and structures are set up. Procedures are installed to enable management of the interdependencies and interrelationships of projects in the program. This phase coincides with the planning phase of the project management life cycle.
3 **Deployment:** It involves the initiation of the different projects (and non-project actions if required). The projects are monitored and controlled in terms of benefit delivery. Necessary changes are made, including the realignment and reprioritization of the projects. This phase is comparable to the implementation and monitoring phase of the project management life cycle.
4 **Appraisal:** This stage is mainly related to an assessment at program level. It looks at critical success criteria and measures the performance of the program with regard to its impact on the organization. This task is subsumed under the third phase of the project management life cycle.
5 **Dissolution:** When the rationale of the program ceases to exist, the program is stopped and all the resources are allocated to other activities. At the end of the program, feedback sessions are carried out. Due to the bigger scope and scale of the program, this phase is longer than a completion phase of a project which would be the equivalent in the project management life cycle.

Figure 2.3 provides you with an overview of the program management cycle.

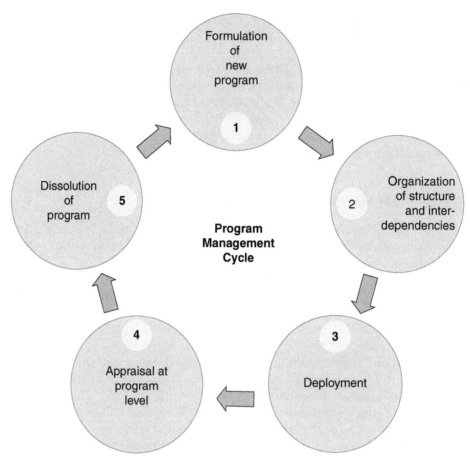

FIGURE 2.3 The program management cycle
Source: Thiry 2004

Mini Case 2.1 illustrates the content of a huge program initiated by the European Union.

Mini Case 2.1: The European Union's 6th Framework Program

Since 1984, the European Union has launched so-called Framework Programs at regular intervals (3–4 years), pursuing two overarching objectives:

1 Strengthening the scientific and technological bases of industry in the European Union
2 Ensuring the international competitiveness of European organizations.

While all programs are tailored towards attaining those objectives, priorities shift over time, reflecting changes in the global environment. At the end of each program cycle the program is evaluated. Based on an assessment of the results, the priorities, budget, and methodology of the programs are then modified. The first Framework Program concentrated on the need to develop alternative energy sources and allocated 50 per cent of its funds to research and development in energy. The subsequent Framework Programs addressed other Europe-level needs, for instance stimulating advances in information technology and communications technology.

For the 6th Framework Program (FP6), the European Commission together with external consultants (technical advisers) selected the projects which would be funded according to their strategic fit and ethical standards.

Strategic fit is given if the project contributes to the strategic objectives of the EU as outlined above and belongs to the following thematic areas:

1   Life sciences, genomics, and biotechnology for health
2   Information society technologies
3   Nano-technologies and nano-sciences, knowledge-based functional materials, new production processes and devices
4   Aeronautics and space
5   Food quality and safety
6   Sustainable development, global change and ecosystems
7   Citizens and governance in a knowledge-based society.

In each of those thematic areas, the 6th Framework Program consists of different international projects. In the nano-technologies, for instance, there is a project called IMPULSE. The objective of IMPULSE is to create a new approach for the design and operation of production systems for the chemical (and related) process industries. Thus, the project contributes to foster knowledge-based manufacturing industry, capable of maintaining substantial production capacity (and highly qualified employment) in Europe.

All the projects in FP6 have to be transnational, which means the projects need to be run by consortia with partners from different EU countries or even from countries outside the EU. In the case of IMPULSE, the main companies co-operating in the project are GlaxoSmithKline from the UK (pharmaceutical), Degussa from Germany (specialty chemicals), and Procter & Gamble from the US (consumer products).

Sources: EU (2002a); EU (2002b); IMPULSE (2005a); IMPULSE (2005b); National Science Foundation (1999)

Task

Identify program management elements in the Framework Programs of the EU.

To manage a program in the way depicted above, the organization needs an adequate structure and dedicated people responsible for program management.

PROGRAM ORGANIZATION

2.5 Looking at the key players in program management, you will notice strong similarities with section 1.4. The biggest difference is an increase in complexity. The following roles and structures are recommended by the British Office of Government Commerce (OGC, 2007).

PROGRAM OWNER AND SPONSOR

The program owner is an individual responsible for ensuring that a program meets its objectives and delivers the projected benefits to the customer (internal or external). This individual should be high ranking. He or she should take personal responsibility for the success of the program and should be acknowledged as the program owner throughout the organization. The program owner is also in charge of periodic program reviews and adaptations if necessary, as well as program controlling, formal program completion and problem solution.

PROGRAM HEADSHIP

The program director provides overall leadership and has the ultimate responsibility for a successful implementation of the program. The program manager is responsible, on behalf of the owner or sponsor, for the successful delivery of the program. In contrast to the program director, the program manager is in charge of the operational day-to-day activities which are necessary for program delivery. This requires the effective co-ordination of the different projects which are part of the program, especially the management of their interdependencies. Typically the program manager works full-time on the program.

In addition, there could also be a business change manager who is responsible for defining the benefits of the program, assessing the progress towards program realization, and achieving improvements.

PROGRAM SUPPORT

Due to the huge spectrum of responsibilities, the individuals at the program management level usually are supported by a so-called Program Support Office (PSO) or Project Management Office (PMO) (section 2.7).

Now that we know how to co-ordinate projects with the program management approach, let us turn to another concept helping the organization to align projects with its overall strategy, namely project portfolio management.

PROJECT PORTFOLIO MANAGEMENT

2.6

In contrast to the projects in a program which all pursue the same objective, projects in a portfolio can not only be related to a common objective, but they can also attain different goals. Project Portfolio Management (PPM) is typically bigger in scope than program management, targeting for an increased competitive edge within the entire organization. Following the principle of transparency, project portfolio management aims at relating all project and program management cycles to strategic goals, rather than to political power plays or emotional attachments.

WHAT IS PROJECT PORTFOLIO MANAGEMENT?

Let us first clarify what is understood by a project portfolio, in this book also simply referred to as a 'portfolio'. It is a collection of projects managed under one umbrella. These projects may be interrelated or not (Thiry, 2004). Project portfolio management is 'the management of the project portfolio so as to maximize the contribution of projects to the overall welfare and success of the enterprise' (Levine, 2005: 22).

The set of all projects and programs an organization runs is called a project portfolio. If an organization has many projects (e.g. 50–60) in its portfolio, it might make sense to create project portfolio networks for projects with certain commonalities, for instance projects which cover the same geographic region, or projects that use the same technology (Gareis, 2006a).

Project portfolios and project networks are clusters. The purpose of those clusters is to ensure an optimal composition of the projects or programs in light of the overall business objectives of the organization. Potentially, conflicts between the objective of a single project or program within the cluster's objective can come to light (Harms et al., 2006).

PROCESSES AND TECHNIQUES OF PROJECT PORTFOLIO MANAGEMENT

Two main management processes within project portfolio management can be distinguished:

1 Selection and prioritization of projects
2 Management of the projects within the portfolio by monitoring target achievement.

Let us first consider the selection and prioritization process. It has to assess which projects or programs are conducive to the organization's overall business objectives. To accomplish this task, the organization has to determine evaluation criteria. Given the complexity of most strategies, the financial success of a project or program, although of paramount importance, does not suffice. Other criteria such as the contribution to innovation or to further internationalization need to be included depending on the foci of the strategy. In addition, the constraints of the organization's resources need to be taken into account.

Usually, there are so-called investment proposals which should facilitate the assessment of the suggested project or program in light of the overall business objectives. It goes without saying that the content of such a proposal needs to be adapted to the respective set of strategies of the organization. A typical investment proposal would comprise the following items:

- field of investment:
  o functional, e.g. R&D, Purchasing, Manufacturing, Marketing, Sales, IT, HR
  o cross-functional, e.g. Supply Chain
  o intra-organization or inter-organizational.

- reasons for the investment
- description of the investment
- goal to be obtained with the investment in terms of:
  - financial objectives, measured for instance in net present value, ROI, amortization period
  - customer-related objectives
  - environment-related objectives
  - innovation-related objectives.
- Business case or cost benefit analysis for investment proposal.

In reference to a portfolio of project and programs, the investment proposals need to be compared with each other. A good structure for such a comparison is an investment portfolio score card which would be based on the Balanced Score Card. As pointed out earlier, the Balanced Score Card can not only be used to compare different projects and programs, but it can also be used to drive the whole strategic management process in the organization. Thus the loop is closed and the link between projects and strategy well established.

Let us now turn to the second main process within project portfolio management, namely, monitoring the projects and programs within the portfolio. This process should provide answers to the following questions:

1 Do the single projects meet their respective objectives? This is related to classical project management as discussed in Chapter 1.
2 Does the execution of the single projects meet the overall portfolio objective? This task implies the regular monitoring of the global environment to cross-check whether the prerequisites for project selection are still valid. If not, the projects may need to be terminated. In Chapter 1, we discussed the fast changing environment that organizations today are operating in. Hence, professional project portfolio management is extremely important for organizations with many international projects.

The tools and techniques suitable to monitor the project portfolios are the same as for project management and will be discussed in Chapter 7.

Figure 2.4 gives an overview of the project portfolio management process.

ROLES AND STRUCTURE OF PROJECT PORTFOLIO MANAGEMENT

As project portfolio management aims at aligning organizational strategy with resource allocation and strategy execution in the form of programs and projects, the managers in charge need to be the executives responsible for strategy and finance. Typically, this would be the Chief Executive Officer (CEO), the Chief Operations Officer (COO), and the Chief Financial Officer (CFO). Some organizations also have a Chief Project Officer (CPO) on board. In an organization where information systems play a strategic role, the Chief Information Officer would be part of the project portfolio management team as well. If the resources are mainly owned and managed by the various functions, their

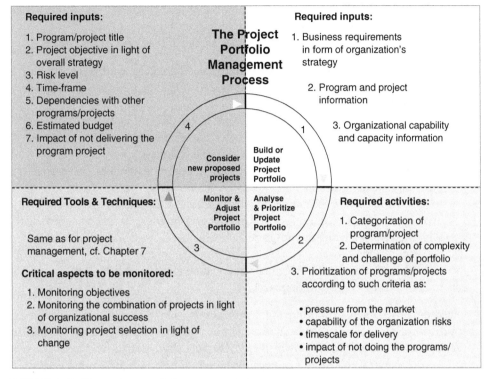

FIGURE 2.4   The project portfolio management process

Source: Adapted from Levine (2005); OGC (2004)

heads need to be included in the team. Marketing must provide market forecasts. The whole process of managing and directing the project portfolio is also called 'governance'. The term 'governance' also applies to the management of single programs. To assure consistency, the governance systems for project portfolio management and single programs should be the same.

As you can see from the paragraph above, no new roles are necessary with the project portfolio management approach. The responsibilities of the executive team remain the same. However, they are carried out within the frame of project portfolio management.

Typically, organizations that practise project portfolio management have a function to support the project portfolio management processes, the aforementioned Project Management Office (PMO). It can also support the programs mentioned under program management.

THE PROJECT MANAGEMENT OFFICE

2.7

The project management office is 'a systematic co-ordination and unified handling of key project-related tasks, as an enterprise-wide resposibility' (Andersen et al., 2006: 32). In other words, a PMO provides the infrastructure and the input to centrally support the work of the project portfolio management team or the program management team.

The main purposes of a project management office are (Englund et al., 2003):

- to develop and deploy predictable, reusable project management methodology and processes (often based on a project model), including tools and techniques as defined in Chapter 1
- to support ongoing projects with advice as internal consultants
- to increase staff professionalism in project management through training and competence development (internal or external training)
- to assure the quality of projects in the form of recommendations based on an evaluation of the decision basis or other documents.
- to support the senior executives in administrating the project portfolio. Typically, the PMO conducts monitoring at certain intervals and provides the senior executives with a go/no-go recommendation. Usually, the PMO lacks decision-making power.
- to help build a project management oriented culture (see section 2.9)
- to retain knowledge (see Chapter 11).

According to Stanleigh (2006) many organizations will fail to see added value in the support infrastructure of a project management office: 75 per cent of 750 global organizations surveyed closed down their PMO only three years after they had set it up. The root cause of this failure can again be seen in the misalignment between project management and the strategies of an organization. Frequently, project management offices are positioned at a hierarchy level which is too low. In order to function successfully, a PMO needs to have sufficient authority as reflected in direct top management support. Mini Case 2.2 will provide you with the opportunity to analyse the effectiveness of the PMOs of two multinational organizations.

Mini Case 2.2: Project management offices at BHP Billiton and LEGO

BHP Billiton, headquartered in Australia, is one of the world's largest diversified resource enterprises. With 41,000 employees working in over 25 countries, BHP Billiton is an industry or near industry leader in major commodity businesses, such as aluminium, energy coal, copper, iron ore, and uranium. Net profits in 2007 amounted to 24.14 billion US$.

As of 2008, BHP has 28 projects in its development pipeline which are either in the planning phase (feasibility) or the execution phase. Those projects represent a total investment of 24.8 billion US$. All are concerned with the exploration and use of natural resources, for instance the development and operation of one of the world's most cost-efficient aluminium smelters in Mozambique. The health and safety of employees and the communities affected by BHP's projects is paramount, especially in light of the increased competition for production licences.

Following a series of poorly managed projects BHP has established a Project Management Office, staffed with 16 people. The PMO is organized as support units distributed across the different subsidiaries. The main tasks of the PMO consist of controlling the project governance process, reviewing projects, conducting training in project management, and providing project management software.

LEGO, headquartered in Denmark (Scandinavia), is the sixth largest toy manufacturer worldwide. Established in 1934, it became famous for its LEGO bricks. In 2007, it had around 4,100 employees worldwide, with manufacturing facilities in Denmark and the Czech Republic (Eastern Europe). In 2007, the net profit was approximately 183 million US$. LEGO needed to initiate projects to react to the following changes:

1 Competition from electronic toys has been increasing dramatically
2 Competition from East Asian manufacturers
3 New product developments needed to be launched on the market much quicker as consumers are becoming more demanding
4 Pressure from the retailers for better service and delivery liability.

LEGO closed its production facilities in Switzerland and South Korea. It transferred parts of the production to its facility in the Czech Republic, and outsourced most of its production to OEMs in low-wage countries. LEGO carried out a project to improve the efficiency of purchases, and to reduce the complexity of its product portfolio. It initiated projects to decrease its new product development cycle from 36 months to 12 months.

In order to achieve these radical changes, the company established a Project Management Office. It is staffed with 20 project managers, and has the following tasks:

* defining and improving business processes across the organization
* providing project managers to projects
* supporting the planning phases of projects
* training new project managers.

Sources: Andersen et al. (2006); BHP (2008); Lego (2008)

Task

Discuss the differences between the project management offices of both organizations and assess the effectiveness of each approach.

To sum up sections 2.3 to 2.7, there are a bundle of measures that an organization should take in order to ensure the alignment of its projects with its overall strategy (examples based on Keller Johnson, 2004):

* **Stock-taking:** First, the organization has to have an overview of the projects it is running. This may sound like stating the obvious. However, big multinationals especially tend to lose control over their project landscape across organizational and geographical boundaries. A California-based business intelligences services firm discovered that it had 400 projects solely in the area of process improvement.
* **Project clustering:** Second, the organization has to structure the projects it has mapped into clusters. The COO here clustered those 400 projects into eight

strategic categories and rated each project in terms of how strongly it contributed to corporate objectives, such as enhancing customer services delivery, boosting revenues, or reducing cost.

- **Prioritization by senior executives**: Then, a process team for each cluster was assigned the task to prioritize projects together with senior management.
- **Establish supportive infrastructure**: This could be a project-portfolio steering committee. Program managers should be responsible for continuous control of the clustered projects. A Project Support Office would also belong to a supportive infrastructure.
- **Communication processes**: To make the project portfolio management cycle and the program management cycles work, fully functioning communication channels across functions and geographical borders need to be established.
- **Software**: Project portfolio management software can facilitate the process.
- **Change management**: This means a continuous screening of the external environment and adaptation of portfolio.

At the beginning of this chapter, I said that organizations needed to build up their strategic capabilities in project management for sustainable success. To measure and control the development of such capabilities, there are so-called project management maturity models that we will discuss in the next section.

PROJECT MANAGEMENT MATURITY MODELS

2.8 An organization gains experience about project management over time. Usually, the organization will start with single projects. It will cluster them into programs which will be summarized in portfolios over time in order to increase professionalism and to better link projects to its set of strategies. This could be called a life cycle as discussed for a single project in Chapter 1. The organization becomes more mature. First, it develops an efficient method of project management. Then, it reaches the stage in which projects perform well as an entirety and are successful in terms of business performance. The final stage is a continuous selection of projects which contribute to a sustainable competitive edge for the organization. The prerequisite for the last stage is a well implemented and smoothly working project portfolio management as outlined in section 2.6.

There are numerous project maturity models, also called capability maturity models or abbreviated to CMM. They are frequently used in the software industry to improve project management efficacy (Cleland and Ireland, 2002). Figure 2.5 outlines the model created by Project Management Solutions, Inc. as a representative of similar models. It is based on five maturity levels.

The existence and activities of a project management office are an indicator of the project management maturity level of an organization.

A project management office goes through the following stages reflecting the increasing maturity of the organization. First, it mainly supports single projects with

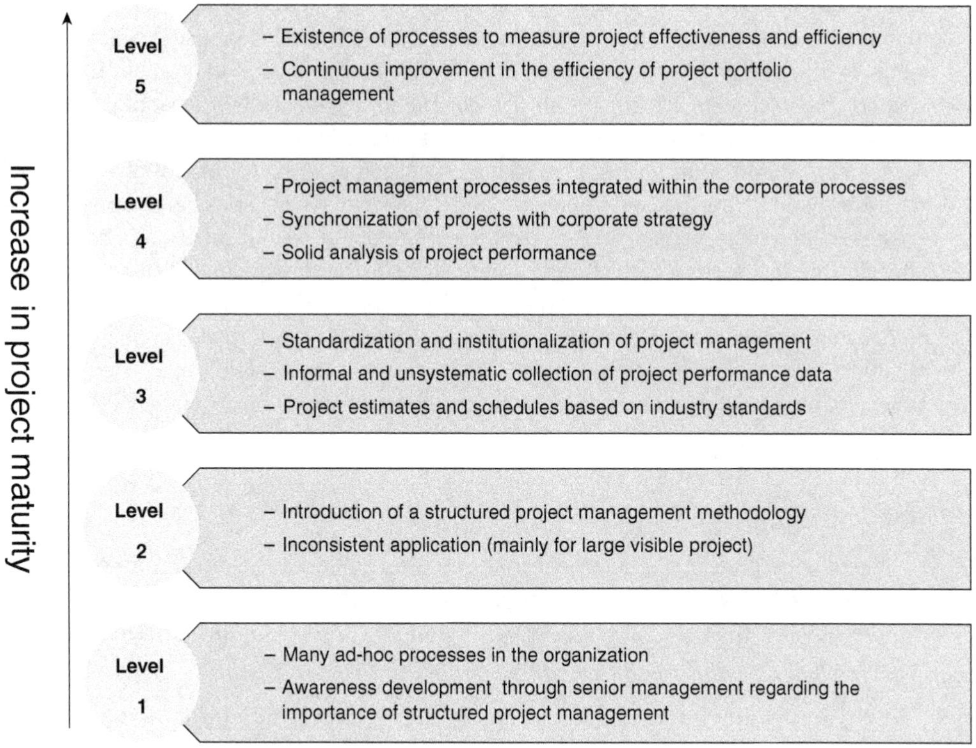

Increase in project maturity →

Level 5
– Existence of processes to measure project effectiveness and efficiency
– Continuous improvement in the efficiency of project portfolio management

Level 4
– Project management processes integrated within the corporate processes
– Synchronization of projects with corporate strategy
– Solid analysis of project performance

Level 3
– Standardization and institutionalization of project management
– Informal and unsystematic collection of project performance data
– Project estimates and schedules based on industry standards

Level 2
– Introduction of a structured project management methodology
– Inconsistent application (mainly for large visible project)

Level 1
– Many ad-hoc processes in the organization
– Awareness development through senior management regarding the importance of structured project management

FIGURE 2.5   Project management maturity levels

Source: Callahan and Brooks (2004)

the development of common tools for project management. This type of PMO is rather an administrative support type with the organization being at level one or two. With rising organizational maturity, it develops into a centre of excellence for project management related issues, reflecting maturity level three. When the project management office intensively supports the executive management with strategy implementation by helping to manage the project portfolio, the organization has reached maturity levels four or five. Mini case 2.3 covers how a CMM is applied in a multinational organization.

Mini Case 2.3: Enhancing project maturity at Ericsson

Founded in 1876, Ericsson is a global telecommunications company, headquartered in Sweden (Scandinavia) with approximately 63,000 employees, and customers in more than 175 countries. Ericsson's strategy is based on technology leadership, for instance in mobile broadband or scalable radio base stations, and simultaneously strengthening its operational efficiency.

Ericsson bases the implementation of its strategy on projects. For more than 15 years it has developed a company-internal project management methodology known as PROPS.

Mini Case

Mini Case

Since 2000, Ericsson has paid special attention to increasing the efficiency of their project management approach across their market units in 25 countries, using a benchmark model to measure project management maturity in all parts of the organization. The model supports the internal benchmark of all Ericsson units internationally against Ericsson-wide standards as well as against external best practice. It is called Project Environment Maturity Assessment PEMA. External benchmarking is realized by the involvement of an external consultancy that runs a global benchmarking network of which Ericsson is a member. A Project Environment Maturity Assessment is carried out at each market unit once a year. Based on the assessment results, recommendations to improve project efficiency are given to increase the maturity of each market unit. The highly visualized results of the assessments are presented to the top management and contribute to a stronger project management focus within the senior executives. The assessment tool fosters project thinking and project management awareness throughout the entire organization.

Source: Bergman (2006); Ericsson (2006)

Task

1 Identify the project management maturity level against the 5-level maturity model introduced above. Give reasons for your categorization.
2 Discuss the special challenges a multinational corporation like Ericsson faces in developing a greater project management maturity.

In sections 2.3 to 2.8 we have learned how an organization can use project management on various aggregation levels to successfully implement its strategy. The path from single projects to project portfolio management is an ongoing development in an organization which can be measured by maturity stages. A high maturity level in project management constitutes a strategic capability, making the organization more competitive in a global environment. Given the high degree of complexity of international projects as depicted in Figure 1.4, more efforts are needed to manage each single project. This is, of course, even more applicable for a whole bundle of international projects. Hence, well-established program management and project portfolio management are vital for an organization handling numerous international projects. It is a prerequisite to sustainably managing international projects towards overall organizational success. Strategy is part of the project context, as is organizational culture. Strategy and organizational culture are interdependent elements of an organization which cannot reach a high maturity level in project management without the underpinning mindset. This leads us to our next topic, organizational culture, or project culture in the context of international project management.

ORGANIZATIONAL CULTURE

2.9

In Chapter 1, I mentioned a project culture rooted in ethno-relativism, based on values such as open-mindedness, respect, and trust as one of the key success criteria for international projects. The same is true for the whole organization applying program management or project portfolio management on an international level. All members of the organization will need to have a special set of values and attitudes which will be explained below. Let us first clarify the term organizational culture.

WHAT IS ORGANIZATIONAL CULTURE?

According to Schein (1992: 12), organizational culture can be defined as 'a pattern of shared basic assumptions [...] that has worked well enough to be considered valid and, therefore, to be taught to new members [of the organization] as the correct way to perceive, think, and feel [...]'. A more simple definition would be the way things are done in a certain organization, like 'the Nokia way'.

WHERE IS ORGANIZATIONAL CULTURE?

According to Schein (1992), we have to distinguish between three levels of organizational culture:

1   **Artefacts:** These are visible organizational structures and processes. In a project environment, these can be project logos, language like acronyms, special terms for milestones, ethical codes for project procurement guidelines, the project structure, the authority level of project managers, etc.
2   **Espoused values:** These are organizational strategies, goals and philosophies which are not necessarily based on the basic assumptions of the workforce. Hence, espoused values often contradict each other or are not suitable to explain the behaviours of employees. In a project environment, project management standards can be an artefact based on espoused values, if the standards are filed somewhere but not implemented. The organization may say it has company-wide standards, but these are not applied. The same could be true for project portfolio management. A management system could exist on paper without being executed.
3   **Basic underlying assumptions:** These are unconscious beliefs that are taken for granted perceptions and feelings. They are the ultimate source of action in the organization. In an international project environment, basic underlying assumptions can differ greatly between geographically dispersed organizational entities as they are influenced by national culture values. Examples of basic underlying assumptions are open-mindedness, parochialism, an autonomous working style, accountability, or valuing diversity.

In other words, organizational culture entails visible and invisible, conscious and unconscious elements. The unconscious, invisible underlying assumptions are the most difficult to manage and change, as you can well imagine. However it is outside scope of this book

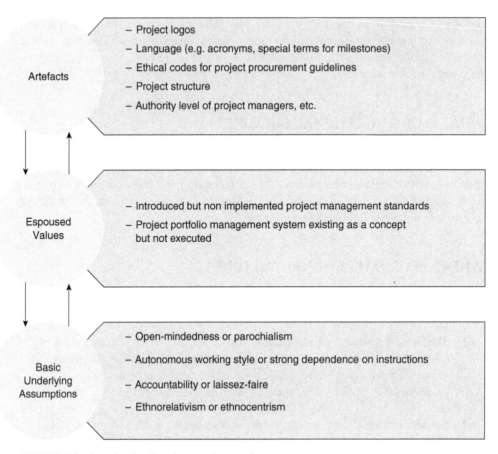

FIGURE 2.6   Levels of culture in a project environment

Source: Culture concept based on Schein (1992), project management examples added by author.
Reprinted with permission of John Wiley & Sons Inc.

to dwell on cultural change strategies and measures that might be necessary in organizations as a prerequisite to establishing an efficient project management approach.

WHAT KIND OF CULTURE DOES SUPPORT EFFICIENT AND EFFECTIVE PROJECT MANAGEMENT?

There are extensive academic debates about whether an organizational culture is manageable or not. In this book, it is assumed that an organizational culture can be influenced by the executives of an organization and can be changed. It is also assumed that organizational culture is an effective tool to support the implementation of strategies, as are the project management processes mentioned above. In addition it can support the efficient use of project management, program management, and portfolio management.

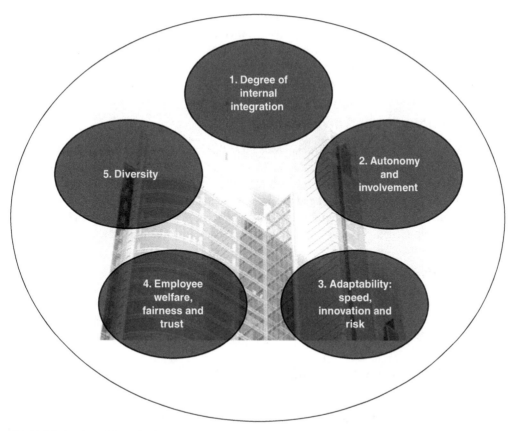

FIGURE 2.7   Five dimensions of organizational culture
Source: Cartwright and McCarthy (2005)

But how can we capture organizational cultures in more detail? There are numerous models on how to classify organizational cultures (Harrison, 1972; Handy, 1991; Cameron and Quinn, 2006). In this book, I will introduce Cartwright and McCarthy's model which is very suitable for the context of international project management, although it has emerged from the context of mergers and acquisitions. Cartwright and McCarthy (2005) distinguish between the following five organizational dimensions as depicted in Figure 2.7.

Let me explain the dimensions in more detail, interpreting them in the light of international projects.

1   Degree of internal integration

This is the extent to which relationships within an organization are co-operative and well co-ordinated. It is the extent to which the sharing of information and ideas is promoted and the achievement of common objectives and goals is supported. A lack or low level of internal integration is conducive to the proliferation of strong sub-cultures and competitive relationships between functional and departmental groups, leading to organizational tensions and conflict. This is especially counter-productive for international projects that span geographically widespread subsidiaries and numerous functions.

2 Autonomy and involvement

This is the extent to which individuals have the authority and freedom to exercise control. The dimension also touches on the degree of authority that organizational members have to make decisions about the way in which they perform their jobs. Project managers together with their management team need to have sufficient autonomy to react flexibly to changing circumstances, which is often the case in international projects. Project managers also need to have sufficient authority to decide on resource allocation and performance rewards.

3 Adaptability: speed, innovation and risk

Adaptability and innovation inevitably involve risk. Like autonomy, a willingness towards risk taking involving decision-making under pressure is conducive to project management performance.

4 Employee welfare, fairness and trust

The employee perceptions of justice or fairness concerning how they are treated with regard to pay, promotions and individual consideration will have important consequences for organizational performance. This is particularly important in international projects where employees from different national cultures, different educational backgrounds, different organizational entities, and different functions will tend to have different views on adequate employee treatment and fairness. As I will discuss in Chapter 10, trust is the prerequisite for efficient co-operation in international projects.

5 Diversity

Ethnocentricity, i.e. the belief that one's own national culture is superior to those of other employees or team members, has been consistently identified as a barrier to the efficient management of international projects. The tendency to view 'what is different is wrong' is counter-productive to building trust, as it strongly shows disrespect regarding diversity and heterogeneity. An international project culture needs to be built on ethno-relativism. What is different has to be considered and evaluated openly. Ideally, organizational members value diversity to the extent that they fuse differences to something new, more creative, and more effective.

To summarize, an organizational culture which has a strong degree of internal integration offers autonomy to organizational members, is highly adaptable and open towards risk, is built on fairness and trust between employees, and manages to cope with diversity is highly conducive to the successful management of international projects. Let me emphasize that there is not one single best or most suitable organizational culture to support efficient project management. It needs to fit into the environment the organization is working in.

The Finnish telecommunication company Nokia is a good example of an organizational culture which has a high degree of internal integration, is strong in autonomy and involvement, and scores high on employee welfare, fairness and trust. This is also reflected in the project portfolio process between the Nokia Research Center and the Business Units of the Nokia Group (Kilpi et al., 2001).

I conclude this section with a special remark on the link between organizational culture and national culture. Hofstede (1997) found in his empirical studies that organizational culture and national culture are closely intertwined. He discovered that the subsidiaries of one multinational corporation in different countries had sub-cultures which showed traits similar to the national culture the subsidiary was located in. It is important to know about this relation when dealing with international projects. Even within one organization, there might be differences in sub-cultures from location to location, which need to be taken into account when transferring management practices, for instance from the headquarters of a multinational organization to its subsidiaries.

In the next section I will introduce a type of organization that is driven solely by projects. This is the most radical form of using projects to implement strategy. The approach is called 'management by projects'.

MANAGEMENT BY PROJECTS

2.10 According to the Project Management Institute (2004), 'management by projects' is a managerial approach adopted by an increasing number of organizations. It extends project management to activities in the area of ongoing operations which are redefined as projects using the same definitions as in Chapter 1. Management by projects incorporates the confluence of the strategy implementation part of strategic management, organization behaviour and project management.

If applied in the extreme, management by projects goes beyond project management, program management, and project portfolio management as discussed in the sections above. In fact, the entire organization is seen as one big project or project portfolio. It is an approach that enables organizations to adapt to a fast changing, global environment. Organizations practising this approach are also called project-based organizations (PBO). Whitley (2006) distinguishes between different types of project-based organizations, depending on the number and similarity of projects they consist of. The extreme is an organization consisting of one large project that dissolves itself after that project's completion. If we consider innovativeness and organizational learning as the competitive edge of organizations (section 2.2), we can wonder at how and when organizational

TABLE 2.1 Differences between project management, program management, PPM, and management by projects

	Project Management	Program Management	Project Portfolio Management	Management by Projects
Main Content of Concept	Managing a single project efficiently within given organizational constraints and context	Clustering projects pursuing the same objectives into a program to support alignment with overall organization's strategy and to increase flexibility	Clustering projects into portfolios to ensure alignment with organization's strategy. PPM supports coordinated resource allocation, increases flexibility of the whole organization and leads to sustainable project success	Managing the whole organization as a bundle of projects based on a supportive organizational culture. At the extreme, the organization consists of one complex project
Scope	Limited to a set of objectives linked to one single project	Business-unit or organization-wide, depending on content of program	An organization-wide management system	A management approach affecting the whole organization, also inter-organizational
Required Project Maturity Level	Level 1–3: Minimum level 1, ideal level 3	Level 3–4	Level 4–5	Level 4–5

learning takes place if the organization only has a limited life cycle, such as a project. Future research will no doubt look into this obvious dilemma.

Let me conclude this chapter here. We have discussed what an organization needs to do in order not only to manage single (international) projects efficiently, but also to have successful projects in a sustainable way. The conclusion is that organizations have to go beyond project management. An organization has to embark on a path towards program management, portfolio management, and might want to develop towards a project-based organization. Of course, this is a simplified normative view which needs to be put in perspective. There is no single best solution that fits all situations. However, I want to highlight the importance of consistency regarding strategy implementation and the benefits of a holistic managerial approach towards project management.

As all expressions and main concepts used in this chapter sound quite similar, Table 2.1 will provide you with an overview of the main differences between project management, program management, portfolio management, and management by projects.

SUMMARY

To be successful in a sustainable way, an organization needs to make sure that its projects are aligned with its strategy. This can be done by clustering projects into programs which will help the organization to use synergies between the projects and make a large number of projects more manageable. Programs are initiated by program owners and have sponsors. Programs are typically part of project portfolios. They help the executives of an organization to select the right projects in light of resource constraints. They are also a tool to adapt swiftly to environmental changes. Project portfolio management, which fulfils the same purpose as program management, is especially important in organizations with numerous, risky, and complex projects. This is the case for many organizations operating on an international level. An organization competing globally needs to build up skills in project, program, and project portfolio management. Project management maturity models measure the degree to which the organization has developed these skills and progressed towards sustainably successful projects. An organizational culture emphasizing achievement, involvement, autonomy, flexibility, openness towards risk and diversity, fairness and trust between its members is most suitable for successfully managing international projects in a sustainable way. Ideally, such an organizational culture concurs with the project culture. The extreme alignment of organizational strategy and projects is given in a project-based organization, where strategy, organizational culture and structure are implemented solely by (international) projects.

 # KEY TERMS

Strategy, strategic management cycle, program management, program, management cycle, program owner, program director, program manager, project portfolio management, governance, project management office, project management maturity model, organizational culture, project culture, management by projects, project-based organization.

REVIEW TASKS

Questions

1 Where do you see challenges for international organizations to introduce program and project portfolio management?
2 What kind of organizational culture is conducive to efficient project management, especially in an international context?
3 In your opinion, does it make sense to strive for a project-based organization?

EXERCISE 1

Go to the website of an organization that is active in the area of commodities, e.g. BP for oil. First have a look at their strategy. Then, search for information about ongoing projects. Try to identify the link between strategy and projects.

EXERCISE 2

Think of an organization you are familiar with. This can be either your current or former employer, or an organization that a family member or friend is working for. Try to analyse this organization's culture using the five dimensions introduced in section 2.9. Would you assess this organization as having a supportive culture for managing international projects successfully?

You will find two more comprehensive cases to test your knowledge on the content of Chapter 2 on the companion website.

CHAPTER END CASE: GOING EAST

The Austrian bank Raiffeisen International is a member of the RZB group. With a market capitalization of 16 billion Euros in 2006, the full service bank RZB is listed among the top 100 banks worldwide.

In 1986, Raiffeisen International was established as a spin off of the RZB group which still holds 70 per cent of its shares. Raiffeisen International should boost the growth of the whole group by taking advantage of strong economic growth in the regions of Central and Eastern Europe (CEE), South-East Europe (SEE), and the Commonwealth of Independent States (CIS). This is a loose confederation of states which was created in 1991 following the dissolution of the Soviet Union. The ten original member states were Armenia, Belarus, Kazakhstan, Kyrgyzstan, Moldova, Russia, Tajikistan, Turkmenistan, Ukraine, and Uzbekistan. Azerbaijan and Georgia joined later. The economies in the region are all so-called transition economies, moving away from a centrally planned economy and opening up their markets for foreign investments and liberalizing their financial markets. The whole region, with approximately 320 million inhabitants, shows strong growth potential.

The move east started in 1986 when Raiffeisen International became a member of an international joint venture establishing the first foreign bank in Eastern Europe, namely in Hungary. This was regarded as a pilot project to find out more about the Eastern European markets. As business opportunities in Hungary were promising, and the project went on smoothly, top management set out the strategic objective to expand swiftly into Central and Eastern as well as South-Eastern Europe in order to become the market leader in these regions as a foreign bank.

The next steps were a joint venture in Poland in 1991 and a joint venture in the Slovak Republic in the same year. Whilst the partners in the Hungarian and the Polish joint ventures were international banks, the partner in the Slovak joint venture was a local bank. In 1993, Raiffeisen International established a wholly foreign-owned enterprise as a 100 per cent subsidiary in the Czech Republic, followed by its own subsidiaries in Bulgaria and Croatia in 1994, Russia in 1995, the Ukraine and Romania in 1996, and Serbia in 2001.

Establishing Raiffeisen International as a new foreign bank in each of the above mentioned countries took 12 months on average, depending mainly on the approval process in the respective economies. The fastest project was the establishment of Raiffeisen International in Serbia. There was a lot of pressure to finalize the foundation of the subsidiary in Serbia due to the planned introduction of the Euro in January 2002. It was expected that many Serbian guest workers in Austria or other Euro-countries would need to convert their savings to Euros. This would be a good opportunity for Raiffeisen International to position itself as the bank of choice for those private customers, who were also mobilizing savings hoarded at home due to a latent mistrust in the (local) banking sector.

In 1999, the organization's strategic focus was redefined, with the second growth pillar shifting from big corporations to 'Small and Medium Sized Enterprises' with annual revenues of more than 5 million Euros, in addition to 'private customers'. This adjustment was due to the fact that the market segment for corporate customers had become increasingly competitive. Hence, margins were shrinking and new growth markets had to be conquered. Speed had become a factor critical to growth in the market. Moreover, the second strategic pillar 'private customers' required a tight net of bank branches across the target markets which would also benefit small and medium sized enterprises.

The new requirements led to a change in the portfolio of international projects. In 2003, the first acquisition of a foreign bank, the Priorbank of Belarus, took place, followed by the purchase of Ukraine's Bank Aval in 2005, Russia's Impexbank, and the Czech Republic's eBanka in 2006.

The Figure on the next page illustrates the timeline of the projects described above.

Today, Raiffeisen International is considered one of the pioneers and leaders in the Eastern European and CIS region. In June 2007, it had approximately 12.7 million customers in the region with nearly 3,000 outlets employing 55,000 staff. It is the foreign bank with the biggest sales network in the region. The company has grown from total assets of 11.5 billion Euros in 2001 to 62.7 billion Euros in the first half of 2007. Consolidated profits jumped from 104 million Euros in 2002 to 594 million Euros in 2006.

Sources: Raiffeisen International (2007a); Raiffeisen International (2007b); Palzer (2007); CIS (2007)

Task

Apply the extended strategic management cycle to Raiffeisen International's Go East initiative. Note: The text does not cover all stages of the cycle.

Dynamic and continuous expansion

• Successful greenfield expansion ...

• ... complemented by targeted and profitable acquisitions.

Raiffeisen International Goes East

FURTHER READING

Dinsmore, Paul C. and Cooke-Davies, Terence J. (2006) *The Right Projects Done Right! From Business Strategy to Successful Project Implementation*. San Francisco, CA: Jossey-Bass. (This book emphasizes the need to align projects with corporate strategy. It is written in a hands-on style and provides numerous ideas on how to align projects with corporate strategy.)

Englund, Randall L., Graham, Robert and Dinsmore, Paul C. (2003) *Creating the Project Office: A Manager's Guide to Leading Organizational Change*. San-Francisco, CA: Jossey-Bass. (This text focuses on improving organizational performance by implementing a project management office system. It gives a lot of details on how to manage change related towards a more project-oriented corporation.)

Phillips, Jack J., Bothell, Timothy W. and Snead, Lynne G. (2002) *The Project Management Scorecard: Measuring the Success of Project Management Solutions*. Amsterdam: Butterworth Heinemann. (The authors provide valuable details on how to effectively use the tool of a Balanced Score Card in relation to project management. It includes explanations on how to build business cases for projects.)

Sahlin-Andersson, Kerstin and Söderholm, Anders (eds) (2002) *Beyond Project Management: New Perspectives on the Temporary – Permanent Dilemma*. Copenhagen: Copenhagen Business School Press. (The authors of this reader all belong to the so-called Scandinavian School of Project Studies. They provide out-of-the-box thinking about project management with a lot of empirical examples.)

DEFINING INTERNATIONAL PROJECTS

3

LEARNING OBJECTIVES

After studying this chapter, you will be able to:

- conceive the main inputs and outputs of the project initiating phase

- comprehend the main components of a project proposal

- explain the process of scope management in an international context

- define and create milestones

- apply a Work Breakdown Structure

- understand the concept of stakeholder management in an international context

- grasp the concept of cultural diversity

- conceive two commonly used national cultural frameworks

- apply the cultural gap tool

- use the diversity-complexity assessment (DCA).

INTRODUCTION

3.1 Now that we have clarified the characteristics of international projects, and discussed the importance of alignment of projects with the overall organizational strategy, I will take you to the starting point of an international project. The focus for the project manager is to set the scene to manage uniqueness, limited resources, dynamics, complexity and diversity (risk will be addressed in Chapter 4). As we have learned in Chapter 1, the project starts with the so-called initiating phase, definition phase or project kick-off. It can be triggered for instance by an idea coming from a manager, or a concrete market demand. First, the project manager tackles the area of uniqueness and limited resources. He or she clarifies the objectives and the scope of the project which we will discuss in the section on scope management. In order to decide whether to proceed with the project at hand or not, the organization needs to have an idea regarding time and cost of the project. To provide this information, the project needs to be made more tangible. This is done by defining so-called milestones. Following the milestone section, we will turn to a more detailed overview of all project activities that is provided by a so-called Work Breakdown Structure (WBS). Milestones and the WBS build the basis of a rough time and cost estimate. This, in turn, is input for the project proposal. In parallel, the project manager has to consider that dynamics as change is omnipresent in an international environment. This is an inherent part of the project proposal.

The project proposal does not only refer to time and cost, but also to the main stakeholders of the international projects. Therefore, we dedicate the next section to stakeholder management. The stakeholder set-up is complex, and stakeholders are characterized by heterogeneity. Hence, the project manager needs to be able to identify the impact that culture (national, organizational, and functional) can have on project management, the topic of section 3.8. As national culture is the most pervasive, it is fundamental to understand the dimensions of national culture (organizational culture is known from Chapter 2). Therefore, I will discuss cultural frameworks in section 3.9, introducing the reader to categories that distinguish cultures from one society from cultures from another society. Based on the cultural frameworks I will familiarize you with the so-called culture gap tool that enables the project manager to systematically assess, first, cultural differences, and second, where these differences show up in international project management. This way, the project manager is well prepared to cope with cultural diversity. In addition, however, diversity consists of factors such as natural and functional languages, time zones, currencies, and jurisdictions. This is what we will discuss in section 3.11 introducing the diversity-complexity assessment which helps the project manager not only to deal adequately with diversity, but also with the complexity of an international project.

In sum, the initiating phase with its main output, the project proposal, is very important for the final success of the international project. The scene is set for the critical success factors I have explained in Chapter 1.

THE START OF A PROJECT

3.2

The project starts with an idea, a customer demand, a bid issued by a government or other opportunities. This is the initiating or definition phase of a project. What could this look like? The business development or the market research department of a Spanish company has discovered that there is huge market potential in Latin America. The details of how this can be achieved and with which kind of projects need to be elaborated. International projects can also be triggered by a change in governmental regulations. For instance, anti-discrimination laws spurred diversity management projects in numerous organizations in North America, Oceania, and Europe.

As outlined in Chapter 1, each international project is unique. Therefore, creativity is essential in the initiating phase. New ideas or technologies have to be found in order to meet the project targets. For international projects with heterogeneous stakeholders, it is very important to allow for diversity when it comes to problem-solving approaches. The process of gathering ideas at the initial stage of the project can be facilitated with tools and techniques such as the tree diagram or the fishbone diagram. You will find more details about those tools on the companion website. Those techniques can be very useful in structuring the wealth of different views and perspectives of the project management team or other stakeholders at this stage. The tools can also serve as a 'common language' in international projects as they are widely used and easy to understand through the high degree of visualization.

It also can be helpful to have facilitators or moderators who are experienced in managing diversity conducting brainstorming workshops. I will get back to the role of facilitators in Chapter 8.

Figure 3.1 provides you with an overview of the main inputs and outputs of the initiating phase. Under controls, it refers to the context the project is embedded in, including organizational constraints. Mechanisms touch on tools and techniques that are appropriate to be applied in this phase in order to achieve the desired output.

PROJECT PROPOSAL

3.3

The project proposal, also referred to as the business case or investment proposal, constitutes the decision-making base for the organization's management to select those projects which are best suited to implement the organization's strategy under given resource constraints. The project proposal would typically comprise information about the project requirements and the resources needed.

The project proposal can be seen not only as a plan providing the basis for go/no-go decisions regarding the project, but also as a basic structure to avoid the cost of chaos in case of unplanned activities.

A formalized approach like the project proposal also gives room to identify potential issues in advance in order to solve them on paper. Most of those potential problems will be related to change. Therefore, a proper change management structure is considered in the proposal, along with the related management of risks.

Initiating Phase: Input, Output, Controls and Mechanisms

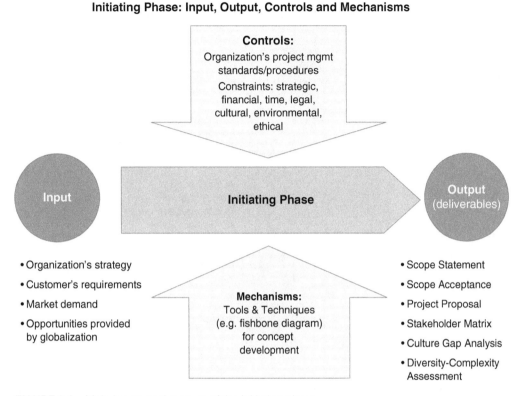

FIGURE 3.1   Main inputs and outputs of the initiating phase

The project proposal should not turn into a straitjacket but should be used as a working paper. In order not to waste too much time on a proposal which could be rejected, it is important to stay at an outline level and not to work out all the details in the project proposal. Yet, the proposal needs to contain a basic estimate of time and cost in order to provide the necessary information for deciding about the future of the project. The basis for the estimates is a structure of the project which leads us to the topic of milestones.

We need three major inputs for the project proposal: first, the scope definition; second, the major milestones; and third, the Work Breakdown Structure. In the following, I will discuss these three inputs.

MANAGING THE SCOPE OF AN INTERNATIONAL PROJECT

3.4

When the concept of an international project takes shape, it is of the utmost importance to clarify from the beginning and as clearly as possible what the project should do, and what it should not do. Throughout the whole project,

Scope Management Process

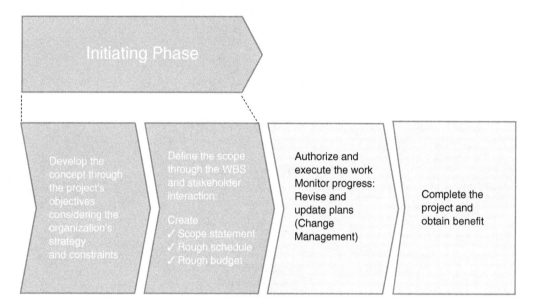

FIGURE 3.2 Scope management process

the project manager needs to check continuously whether the project is still on track in terms of what had been agreed on at the project start. Modifications and changes which had been agreed on also need to be monitored. This process can be described as scope management.

Scope management is important to plan and control the entire project throughout all the project life cycle phases. However, the basis for project success is laid in the initiating phase where the project needs to be clearly defined. Figure 3.2 contains the main steps of project scope management to give you an overview of the entire process. In the following paragraphs, I will explore the scope management tasks that take place in the initiating phase.

SCOPE DEFINITION

The scope management process starts with the definition of the project scope. Especially in the light of the high complexity, risk propensity and diversity of international projects, it is absolutely vital to clearly define the scope in the initiating phase. In order to avoid misunderstandings and to limit manoeuvring room for different interpretations, the scope needs to be formulated in a structured way.

The needs of the internal or external customer have to be defined. It can be a tedious endeavour to extract from each stakeholder what he or she really wants, particularly in international projects with many stakeholders involved. Usually, several rounds have to be made in order to get a clear picture. This is a very important process for the project because the most efficient project management is useless if the objectives of the project do not provide customer satisfaction.

At this stage, it might be helpful to think: What is it that the external client really wants? Typically it is a solution, not only a product. In the case of a large municipality buying trains from a contractor, the city certainly does not want just trains, but also wants to transport people in a certain way.

Customer requirements need to be linked to project objectives, which in turn need to be traceable. To avoid misunderstandings and confusion, we have the SMART rule (Kerzner, 2006: 290–1):

S = specific
M = measurable
A = attainable
R = Realistic or relevant
T = Tangible or time bound

The scope definition is usually documented in a scope statement. This is the document which specifies clearly the content of the project, and what is not covered by the project. For instance, the roll out of the ERP-system SAP to all subsidiaries of a multinational corporation has to exclude the adaptation of the system which might be necessary due to different legal requirements in different countries. This work has to be done beforehand.

The scope statement is typically supplemented by a scope acceptance document. In many organizations, this is a document which is signed off by the project owner and the project manager, and, if necessary, by other major stakeholders. Thus, it creates the mandate for the project manager to go ahead. It also can be used as a reference to measure the progress of the project and finally to assess the project's success or failure. Projects with external customers usually have the scope acceptance as part of the overall project contract to be discussed in Chapters 4 and 6.

SCOPE CREEP AND SCOPE CHANGE MANAGEMENT

The experience of many organizations shows that the purpose of the project gradually changes until it no longer represents the original concept. As the allocation of resources is usually linked to the initial description of the purpose, this so-called scope creep usually leads to project failure in both terms: unsuccessful management of the project, and no successful project because of a misalignment with the organization's strategy. Of course, in the complex and uncertain environments many international projects are embedded in, it is unlikely that all the necessary information regarding a project's requirements is comprehensively available at the start of that project. In many cases, the customer only gradually gets to know his or her real needs, or the international environment changes, which results in modified requirements. Hence, the reality of international projects often requires changes in scope. However, there is a difference between uncontrolled, thus unmanaged changes of scope, and controlled changes. Scope change management therefore is also referred to as scope control. An important part of scope control is stakeholder management, to be discussed in section 3.6, and risk management, which I will discuss in Chapter 4.

Before a scope statement and scope acceptance document can be produced, the project manager needs to elaborate on more details regarding the project. For this purpose, he or she divides the project into the parts that are more manageable.

DEFINING MILESTONES

3.5

This is done by milestones, also called check-points or gates. We understand by milestone a major pre-defined event that represents a measurable accomplishment towards the project's completion. Milestones need to be passed in order to continue with the project. The criteria to pass a milestone have to be formulated in advance. If the criteria are not met at the respective milestone, the project may be terminated. Typically, milestones mark the points in time which are critical for the project according to the following criteria (Longman and Mullins, 2005):

- When are important decisions made?
- When will work packages with an impact on the master schedule be started or terminated?
- When will work packages affecting cost be started or completed?
- When will major deliverables which affect key project objectives be started or completed?
- When will an extremely risky work package be started or completed?
- When will tests that affect project success be carried out?
- When will a sub-project be started or completed?

In some industries like the aeronautics industry there are region-wide developed and applied standards, like the European Cooperation for Space Standards (ECSS) which determines the methodology of project management. This standard even pre-defines which milestones have to be used. The standards aim at facilitating cross-border, intra- and inter-organizational co-operation, thus providing all stakeholders of international projects with a common methodology.

Figure 3.3 illustrates typical project phases and milestones related to new component development in manufacturing. It consists of an 'extended' project management cycle including the 'pre-project phase' called opportunity evaluation, and the entire production of the newly developed component until the organization ceases to produce the component. Opportunity evaluation refers to an opportunity on the market, for instance the tender of a potential customer. If the organization decides on pursuing this opportunity and wins the tender, the project in the narrow sense starts with milestone 1, 'Project authorized'. The following milestones 2–5 refer to the new component development project. As discussed in the list above, these milestones touch on major decisions (milestones 1 and 2) or the major work packages completed (milestones 3, 4 and 5). Typically, the development project ends with serial production. Mass production is usually not considered a project but a routine task (see Chapter 1). The chart still sees production as part of the extended project which ends when the production of the component is terminated (milestone 6), and no more support for the component is needed (milestone 7).

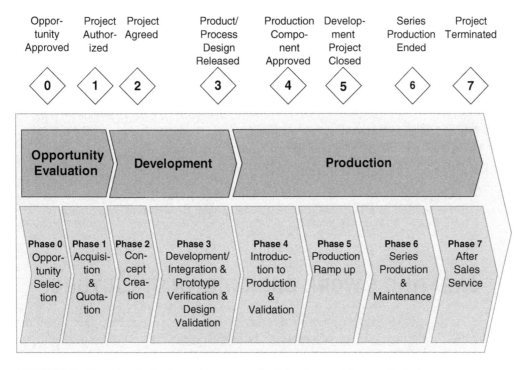

FIGURE 3.3 Sample of milestones for new product development in manufacturing

The case of Rolls-Royce exemplifies with the international project 'Spree', how milestones are planned, and what the criteria for the checkpoints are.

SNAPSHOT 3.1

R&D and production transfer at Rolls-Royce (Part 1)

Rolls-Royce plc operates in four global markets – civil aerospace, defence aerospace, marine and energy. It has offices, manufacturing and service facilities in 50 countries employing about 38,000 people. Its three strategic sites in civil aviation are located in the UK, USA, and Germany. With approximately 2,000 employees, Rolls-Royce Germany offers a complete service from the development of aircraft engines through to production and logistics support.

In 2003, the top management in the UK decided to transfer the development and production of the civil aircraft engine Tay, which powers both regional airliners and business jets, from the UK to Germany. In contrast to transfers from high-wage to low-wage countries, this transfer did not entail job cuts on either side.

As a basis for the project, a Master Plan with the following milestones was developed:

(Cont'd)

1st milestone: last engine produced in the UK
2nd milestone: first prototype built in Germany
3rd milestone: first serial engine built in Germany.

At each of the above described gates, there were review meetings. In those meetings, the status of activities against the milestones was discussed. In case of delay, measures to speed up the process in order to keep the time-frame were decided upon.

Sources: Rolls-Royce (2004a); Rolls-Royce (2004b); Rolls-Royce (2004c); Rolls-Royce (2004d); Blasig (2005).

CREATING A WORK BREAKDOWN STRUCTURE

3.6 The project proposal has the objective of providing basic facts about the time and cost of a project. The definition of milestones alone is insufficient. The project manager needs to structure the project in more detail. He or she has to identify the main project activities. Breaking down large activities into compre- hensible or manageable units is an essential part of project management and a prerequisite for time and cost estimates. This is done by a Work Breakdown Structure

There are different ways of breaking down a project such as:

- product management life cycle phases (such as concept design, feasibility, prototype development, test, mass production)
- components of the product (such as different software layers)
- organizational units (such as Research & Development, or international subsidiaries)
- geographical areas (such as North America, East Asia, South-East Asia, the Middle East)
- cost accounts (such as electrical components procurement, mechanical components procurement, electro-mechanical components procurement, parts quality assurance)
- tasks (such as designing a keyboard).

Breaking down activities according to their logic and sequence is also called chunking or unbundling.

The role of the Work Breakdown Structure is to create a linked, hierarchical series of activities, which are independent units but at the same time part of the whole.

The process is as follows:

1 State the project scope and make sure that all stakeholders have the same understanding.
2 Decompose the project into major elements of work (corresponding to level 1).
3 Decompose each level 1 work element into detailed tasks (level 2, 3, 4, etc.).
4 Identify a deliverable for each task at the lowest level of the WBS.
5 Write a task description for each task.

The Work Breakdown Structure typically looks like a tree diagram (see the companion website). It can also take the form of a checklist.

The project manager needs to properly coordinate the different work elements of the WBS in order not to get out of synch with the overall objective or scope of the project. This is a challenging task when dealing with complex international projects.

Let us look again at Rolls-Royce's project for an illustration of a Work Breakdown Structure.

Mini Case 3.1: R&D and production transfer at Rolls-Royce (Part 2)

The first step in conceptualizing the 'Spree' project was the definition of the milestones. In order to get a rough estimate on project time and cost, a breakdown of the main activities for the transfer of R&D and production of the Tay engine was required. After all, this transfer was more complicated than a standard transfer because different jurisdictions, languages, and national cultures were involved.

On the highest level, project 'Spree' was divided into the following work elements:

1 Systems and Data Migration
2 Build Process and Tooling
3 Pass-Off Testing
4 Logistics and Hardware
5 External Supply Chain
6 Development
7 LBA (German air transport authority) Approval
8 Finance
9 Commercial.

Task

Identify the criteria that the breakdown of level 1 work elements is based on.

Source: Blasig (2005)

Mini Case

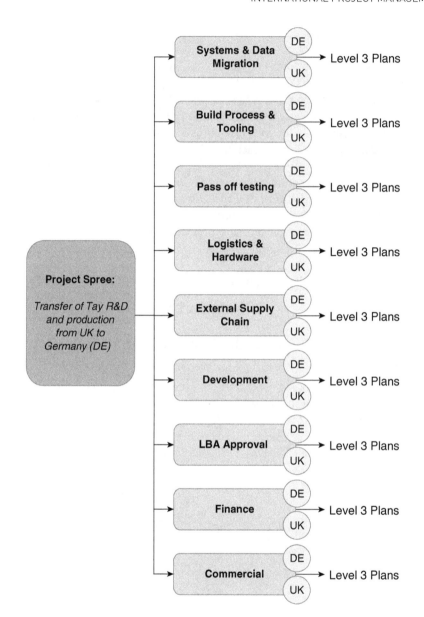

At each level of the Work Breakdown Structure, so-called Statements of Work (SOW) define the objective, scope and deliverable of each set of tasks. The example below shows a statement of work for the work element 6 'development' in the project 'Spree'.

SNAPSHOT 3.2

R&D and production transfer at Rolls-Royce (Part 3)

After the highest level of the Work Breakdown Structure was defined, a more detailed elaboration of the content of each work element was needed: the project manager and his team had to formulize the objectives of each work element. They also had to define the scope, and agree on the deliverable of each work element. Results from this process are called Statements of Work as depicted below:

WBS Element Development – Statement of Work

Objectives

- Transfer the management of all development logistics activities to Germany
- Transfer all development assembly activities to Germany

Scope

- Assembly, Test and Supply Chain management for Development Engine

Out of Scope

- Engineering activities

Deliverables

- Engine 11 built and tested
- Transfer to all other necessary development engine hardware

Finally, the project manager had to compile all Statements of Work in order to get the basis for the project master schedule and a rough cost estimate. Both will be discussed further in Chapter 5.

Source: Blasig (2005)

The lower the work level within the Work Breakdown Structure, the more concrete the activities. Activities are typically integrated into so-called work packages representing jobs of about equal magnitude of effort. A work package should also be of relatively small cost and short duration compared to the total project. How long and how much this would be depend on the industry and nature of the project. Some project management standards suggest that it should not take more than 40 hours to accomplish. Others say that a work package at the lowest level should not represent more than a value of 100,000 US$ in cost and no more than three months in elapsed time (Demeulemeester and Herroelen, 2002).

To summarize, a Work Breakdown Structure serves the following purposes:

1   The work packages of the WBS are the basis for scheduling and budgeting. Thus, the WBS provides vital input for the project proposal.
2   Responsibilities can be assigned to the single identified activities. In this respect, the WBS gives input for project structuring (see Chapter 6).
3   The Work Breakdown Structure provides traceability. It makes the whole project more transparent providing a basis for monitoring and controlling (see Chapter 7).

The Work Breakdown Structure is a vital part of the project proposal. The project proposal, in turn, constitutes the decision-making basis for project approval.

A thoroughly compiled project proposal is a good basis for managing an international project. In order to translate it into a tangible result, however, the project manager has to know who will benefit from the outlined project, and who will oppose it. This leads us on to the process of stakeholder management.

MANAGING THE INTERNATIONAL PROJECT STAKEHOLDERS

3.7 The basis here is the identification of all relevant project stakeholders. International projects usually have numerous, quite heterogeneous stakeholders. This makes good stakeholder management a real challenge for the project manager.

Table 3.1 will provide you with an overview of typical stakeholders in international projects. While the groups of stakeholders are fairly generic, the stakeholders as such need to be specifically identified for each project. A project manager may want to use Table 3.1 as a kind of checklist to facilitate the task of stakeholder identification.

Especially in an international environment, the expectations and needs of the stakeholders may be contradictory. In order to negotiate trade-offs between these sometimes conflicting needs, the project manager together with his or her core team should go through the following steps (Winch, 2004):

TABLE 3.1 Overview of stakeholder groups and stakeholders in international projects

Stakeholder Group	Example of Stakeholders in International Projects
Senior Management	• The organization's board (with different authorities depending on the jurisdiction of the organization's HQ) • Executive management team (often multi-cultural)
Shareholders	• Shareholder groups with a large portion of shares exerting a direct influence on the organization's strategy and project portfolio
Business units with an interest in the project	• Sponsoring business units(s), operating either locally, regionally or globally • Users within and outside the sponsoring business units(s) • Specific function like R&D, Marketing, support functions with links to the sponsoring business unit(s) • Other business units • Subsidiaries of the organization in different countries inside or outside the sponsoring business unit(s)
Employees	• Members of the international project (usually multi-cultural), including the project manager and project management team • Staff of affected business units, usually located in different countries
External Customer	• (Foreign) government, e.g. for infrastructure, defence, or development projects • (Foreign) Corporation • Global NGO
Users	• (Global) consumers of the product or service • Inhabitants of a country or region using a new infrastructure • International community benefiting from environmental protection, or poverty alleviation in the case of NGO projects
Industry	• (International) contractors, usually the case in a consortium • (International) suppliers or service providers • (International) joint venture or alliance partners • Other (international) co-operation partners • (International) competitors
Finance providers	• (International) financial institutions • (International) private equity companies • (Foreign) government(s)

(Cont'd)

TABLE 3.1

Stakeholder Group	Example of Stakeholders in International Projects

Regulators	• Depending on the industry and country, all relevant ministries or authorities, for instance:
	  o Occupational health and safety regulators in different countries
	  o Environmental protection agencies in different countries
	  o Construction and building approval regulators in different countries

Media	• Domestic media • Foreign media (independent coverage or strong influence from local government?)
Communities	• Public in the local area • Public in the region or country • Global public in case of high visibility of the international project

1 Identify the stakeholders or stakeholder groups with an interest in the project.
2 Specify the nature of each stakeholder's interest.
3 Assess each stakeholder's level of influence or power on the project and its related decision-makers.
4 Manage the response to that interest minimizing any potential negative impact on the project.

How can a project manager recognize people with power to influence the project, even in an unfamiliar international context? It helps to include the core team and representatives from different locations involved in the international project in this stakeholder mapping exercise. They will have a better knowledge of the local conditions and the, at times, complex relationships.

The international project manager needs to be able to influence people in a way that turns them from project challengers or sceptics into allies of the project. This requires political skills. All projects are loaded with politics, for instance due to the internal competition for resources (Frame, 2002; Jensen et al. 2006). In an international set-up, the picture is even more complicated. Given the high degree of cultural diversity, a successful manager of international projects needs not only to be an excellent politician, but also a superb cross-cultural communicator (see Chapter 8). Above all, the project manager must be able to establish trust between the major stakeholders, the customer and the contractor (project management team). I will elaborate on concrete measures in Chapter 10.

The result of the stakeholder analysis provides input for project scope definition, which is why it has to take place in the initiating phase. It is also vital for designing the project structure (Chapter 6) and for the communication strategy (Chapter 9), as well as for the conflict management or escalation strategy (Chapter 10).

Let me wrap up this section with a Mini Case that touches on all the topics discussed so far in this chapter. The problems depicted below are also related to what we have discussed in Chapter 2.

Mini Case 3.2: Irritations at the start of a telecommunications project

Headquartered in Switzerland, this telecommunication solution provider operates in nearly 20 countries, among others in Finland. The Finnish subsidiary had well-established relations with an important local customer whose requirements and expectations were well known.

The Finnish customer had a special request: it wanted this contractor to develop a ruggedized communications gateway which would support different interfaces, such as telephony, Gigabit ethernet, fibre, ISDN and specified others. The device had to be ready by the end of January 2008. Any delay would trigger penalty payments.

As the order was quite lucrative, both R&D teams, the Finnish and the Swiss, were eager to develop the product. Both teams started to work on a concept in parallel. The Finnish team favoured a non-platform solution which was fairly cost-competitive. The Swiss team favoured a platform solution which had the advantages of being future-proof, similar to a platform in the automotive industry, and should speed up development of new applications through re-use. In comparison to the Finnish solution, however, it was more costly. Although both organizational units wanted to satisfy their important customer, they were pre-occupied with internal discussions as to what the best approach was. Twelve months were spent on these internal quarrels until the Swiss headquarters decided to develop the product in Switzerland following a platform approach. To kick off the project, a short phone conference was held with the Finnish subsidiary in order to get some input about the customer's requirements. Based on the input from their Finnish colleagues, the Swiss team developed their own design and test specifications.

The internal quarrel deferred the decision on the manufacturing location of the new product. The purchasing function at headquarters claimed they needed three months for evaluating the most cost-competitive manufacturing solution after a freeze on the bill of material. The alternatives were in-house manufacturing in Switzerland, or outsourcing to Finland with a local manufacturer. Due to time and logistical constraints, however, project management did not wait for purchasing and instead decided to pre-assemble parts of the product in Switzerland, and make the final assembly at the outsourcing partner in Finland. Due to the fact that the manufacturing decision was delayed, the milestone of 'product industrialization' including the related resource requirements was simply forgotten. When the project manager checked the Work Breakdown Structure, he did not find the whole set of activities related to manufacturing handover. This meant another delay of three months.

Questions

1 What went wrong in terms of stakeholder management?
2 Compare the task of the initiating phase discussed in this chapter with the activities in the case. What should the organization improve?

MAPPING THE CULTURAL CONTEXT

3.8

As successful stakeholder management is crucial in international projects, it is important to understand the major stakeholders as well as possible, including their social identity. All stakeholders' behaviour is embedded in context. And an important part of context in international projects is local or national culture. If culture is neglected, an incident like that depicted in Snapshot 3.3 easily happen.

SNAPSHOT 3.3

An angry Arab customer

A powerful and resourceful customer from the Gulf region gives an order for aircraft equipment. After a couple of months, he wants a special and complicated technical add-on which is outside the project's request scope. His special request comes at a crucial point of time, shortly before the next milestone. In case of delays, penalties are due. Knowing about the propensity of delay the customer's wish entails, the German project manager of the company replies: 'We cannot do this.' Annoyed by the project manager, the customer calls the CEO of this company threatening to place his follow-on orders with different companies. Another project manager has an idea: What if they offered a slight technical upgrade which was feasible in the given time-frame without any delay and significant cost? It would signal to the customer that the company did value him and aimed to satisfy his wishes. The company could show even more goodwill by offering special discounts for spare parts. This would not cost a lot of money either, especially when compared to the alternative of losing that customer. The project manager adopts this approach, and the customer accepts the proposal.

How can cultural differences explain this problem with stakeholder management? In section 3.8, I will introduce you to different kinds of cultures, focusing in section 3.9 on the concept of national culture which I will explain within cultural frameworks.

NATIONAL CULTURE

There are numerous definitions of national culture, local culture, or just 'culture'. For the purpose of this textbook, I will use a definition by one of the most well-known researchers on cultural differences, Geert Hofstede (1997: 5): Culture 'is the collective programming of the mind which distinguishes the members of one group or category of people from another ... Culture should be distinguished from human nature on one side, and from an individual's personality on the other'.

'Collective programming' refers to deeply rooted values, attitudes, and behaviours, similar to what we have discussed in Chapter 2 concerning organizational culture. Organizational culture, though, tends not to be as deeply ingrained in an individual as national culture. What are values? Values or norms are cultural priorities. Values are also the basis of business etiquette. Examples of values are open-mindedness or respect. What is an attitude? This is a learned tendency to act consistently in the same situation, based on values. And what is behaviour? Behaviour is the action based on attitudes and values. It is easier to change than values and attitudes (Varner and Beamer, 2005).

Let me illustrate those explanations with a concrete example. In a project meeting, a project member does not give an answer to his project manager although he has been assigned a task that is technically not feasible. This is his behaviour. It is based on the attitude that 'Openly disagreeing with superiors is wrong.' Seniority and harmony are underlying values.

Hofstede's definition means that culture is not inherited but learned usually when people are young and easy to educate. As people tend to forget how they have been socialized, culture remains unconscious and needs to be unlearnt at a later age. Until a person gets confronted with different cultures, he or she assumes automatically that his or her values, attitudes and beliefs are normal. This is also called self-reference. It can lead to ethnocentrism, the attitude of people who (unconsciously) operate from the basic assumption that their ways of doing things are best (Adler, 2002).

In international projects, however, such an attitude is counter-productive. A person participating in international projects needs to be conscious of his or her culture, and also needs to be able to view different cultures as *different*, neither better nor worse. It means that the ideal basis for an ethno-relative project culture or organizational culture contains stakeholders who understand their own local culture and can analyse their partners' cultures.

OTHER CULTURAL ASPECTS

National culture is an important influential factor in shaping an individual's behaviour, attitudes and norms. However, it is not the only force. As indicated in Hofstede's definition, human nature – like the necessity for food and sleep, as well as the personality of the individual – has a big impact on someone's behaviour. The same is true for the culture of the organization which we have discussed in Chapter 2.

Another kind of culture is the culture of the profession an individual has. We call this professional culture or functional culture. This refers to a certain methodology, standards, and ethics prevalent in a certain profession, like medical doctors, pilots, accountants, or software-developers, or certain organizational functions, such as Sales and Marketing, Research and Development, or Accounting. A professional culture can to some extent also be observed in certain industries, like banking or IT. Sometimes,

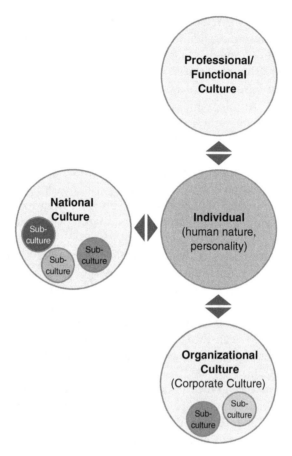

FIGURE 3.4 Different types of culture influencing the individual

functional cultures in organizations are also referred to as sub-cultures and sub-cultures can also refer to a national culture. This is especially true for large countries like Brazil, China, India, and/or so-called immigration countries like the USA, Australia and Canada. Last but not least, organizations can have sub-cultures in their subsidiaries due to the fact that national cultures have an impact on organizational cultures: the organizational cultures of the German airline Lufthansa will differ, depending on whether you are in the headquarters in Frankfurt, Germany, or in a subsidiary in Miami, USA, or in Sao Paolo, Brazil. Like functional cultures, organizational cultural differences between the various subsidiaries usually play a big role in international projects.

Figure 3.4 summarizes the kinds of cultures influencing the individual, in our case the project stakeholder.

We have discussed the importance of cultural sensitization. A project manager needs to understand his or her own culture and the cultures of the project stakeholders. What helps him or her to achieve this? As a first step, the complex construct of 'culture' needs to be simplified in order to understand it better.

CULTURE FRAMEWORKS

3.9

This is what so-called culture frameworks do. They simplify national cultures. They try to describe national cultures by using a certain number of dimensions which characterize a national culture.

STEREOTYPES

Simplification means generalizations. This is what we call 'stereotypes': this is a form of categorization that structures our experience and guides our behaviour towards various groups within a society or between national cultures. A stereotype never describes the behaviour of an individual accurately. Rather it describes the behavioural norm for members of a particular group. Yet, stereotypes are helpful when they are made in the awareness that they are descriptive rather than judgemental, and can be corrected based on further experience (Adler, 2002). One example of stereotypes is held about Germans: they are serious workers, they are extremely structured, and they produce good quality products. However, stereotypes can easily turn into negative prejudices, such as: Germans never laugh, they are cold and arrogant, and their appearance lacks '*eleganza*' – who can take men dressed in short trousers, white tennis socks and sandals seriously?

Although cultural frameworks do stereotype, they can be useful techniques to map international project stakeholders' cultural differences. Let me introduce two of the most commonly used culture frameworks, the first one developed by Hofstede, the second one by another Dutch researcher, Trompenaars.

HOFSTEDE'S CULTURE DIMENSIONS

The national cultures which Hofstede (1997) has covered in his studies were measured with scores in each of the dimensions in which cultures differ from each other. Due to the fact that our culture is changing however, it is not recommended to rely too heavily on these scores. They should instead be used as a rough orientation to prepare the culture gap analysis which I will discuss at the end of this chapter. The following paragraphs basically summarize Hofstede's (1997) explanations with a special emphasis on the implications for project management. Figure 3.5 provides you with an overview of the five dimensions Hofstede has identified.

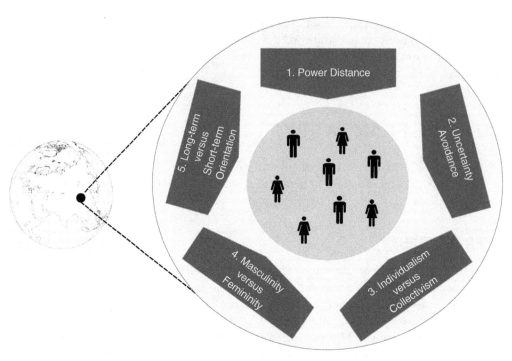

FIGURE 3.5 Hofstede's culture dimensions
Source: Hofstede (1997)

1 The first dimension characterizing a national culture is **Power Distance** (PD).
   It is the degree to which a society accepts that power is distributed
   unequally. When the power distance is relatively high, hierarchical
   differences at the workplace are respected. Managers are expected to take
   decisions in an autocratic way. The ideal boss or project manager is thought
   of as being benevolent, and the employees or project members expect to
   receive clear instructions.

2 The second dimension is **Uncertainty Avoidance (UA)**. It is the degree to
   which a society is willing to accept and deal with uncertainty. Cultures with
   high uncertainty avoidance tend to have a whole array of rules and routines
   they can stick to. They are not tolerant towards unknown risks. Related to
   project management this means, for instance, that clear rules and regulations
   are expected, verbatim or in writing.

3 The third dimension is **Individualism** versus **Collectivism.** This dimension
   refers to the relationship between the individual and the groups to which he
   or she belongs. We can see this as the degree to which individual decision-
   making and action is accepted and encouraged by a society. In individualistic
   cultures, tasks are assigned to individuals in a project team. The project

manager from an individualistic culture aims for variety rather than conformity. Employees in individualistic societies are loyal to their organization as long as it suits their personal interests. Members of collectivist societies prefer to work in groups. They also prefer responsibility to be allocated to a group rather than to an individual.

4   The fourth dimension is called **Masculinity** versus **Femininity**. In more masculine cultures, the social ideal is performance. Sympathy lies with the strong. Conflicts are fought out. Material success and progress are ideal values. Gender roles are clearly differentiated. In feminine societies, the ideal is social welfare. Gender roles are less differentiated. There is sympathy for the weak, and conflicts are resolved through negotiation. This has a direct impact on team work in a project. For instance, is a very competitive attitude within the project team seen as positive or negative?

At a later stage, Hofstede extended his model by including a fifth dimension, called **Long-term orientation** or **Confucian work dynamism.** Societies high on long-term orientation or strong in Confucian work dynamism are concerned with the future and value thrift and persistence. In short-term oriented cultures, organizations focus more on quarterly results (Francesco and Gold, 2005). This has an impact on the selection of projects.

Table 3.2 gives you an overview of the scores that nearly 50 countries or regions have in these five dimensions. A high index on power distance means a high power distance. The same applies to uncertainty avoidance. A low index on individualism means strong individualism. A high index on masculinity means strong masculinity. A high index on long-term orientation stands for a strong long-term orientation. The Arab region comprises Egypt, Iraq, Kuwait, Lebanon, Libya, Saudi Arabia and the United Arab Emirates. East Africa stands for Ethiopia, Kenya, Tanzania, and Zambia. The West African region refers to Ghana, Nigeria, and Sierra Leone.

TROMPENAARS' CULTURE DIMENSIONS

Trompenaars describes national cultural diversity in terms of relationships between people, a relationship to time, and a relationship to the external environment (see Figure 3.6). The first five dimensions deal with an individual's relationship to other people (Trompenaars and Hampden-Turner, 1998; Francesco and Gold, 2005), again explained in light of the relevance for project management:

1   **Universalism** versus **Particularism**: In a universalistic society like that of the US-American, it is the ideal to govern business relationships with contracts and clear rules which are applicable under any circumstances to anyone. In particularistic societies like the Chinese, business relationships are mainly controlled by circumstances and relationships, which can change over time.

TABLE 3.2 Hofsted's country and region index

Country	Power Distance Index	Uncertainty Avoidance Index	Individualism/ Collectivism Index	Masculinity/ Femininity Index	Long- Short-Term Orientation Index
Argentina	49	86	46	56	
Australia	36	51	90	61	31
Austria	11	70	55	79	31*
Belgium	65	94	75	54	38*
Brazil	69	76	38	49	65
Canada	39	48	80	52	23
Chile	63	86	23	28	
Colombia	67	80	13	64	
Costa Rica	35	86	15	21	
Denmark	18	23	74	16	46*
Ecuador	78	67	8	63	
Finland	33	59	63	26	41*
France	68	86	71	43	39*
Germany	35	65	67	66	31
Great Britain	35	35	89	66	25
Greece	60	112	35	57	
Guatemala	95	101	6	37	
Hong Kong	68	29	25	57	96
Indonesia	78	48	14	46	
India	77	40	48	56	61
Iran	58	59	41	43	
Ireland	28	35	70	68	43*
Israel	13	81	54	47	
Italy	50	75	76	70	34*
Jamaica	45	13	39	68	
Japan	54	92	46	95	80
Korea (South)	60	85	18	39	75
Malaysia	104	36	26	50	
Malta*	56	96	59	47	

TABLE 3.2

Country	Power Distance Index	Uncertainty Avoidance Index	Individualism/ Collectivism Index	Masculinity/ Femininity Index	Long/Short- Term Orientation Index
Mexico	81	82	30	69	
Netherlands	38	53	80	14	44
Norway	31	50	69	8	44*
New Zealand	22	49	79	58	30
Pakistan	55	70	14	50	0
Panama	95	86	11	44	
Peru	64	87	16	42	
Philippines	94	44	32	64	19
Portugal	63	104	27	31	30*
South Africa	49	49	65	63	
Salvador	66	94	19	40	
Singapore	74	8	20	48	48
Spain	57	86	51	42	19*
Sweden	31	29	71	5	33
Switzerland	34	58	68	70	40*
Taiwan	58	69	17	45	87
Thailand	64	64	20	34	56
Turkey	66	85	37	45	
Uruguay	61	100	36	38	
United States	40	46	91	62	29
Venezuela	81	76	12	73	
Yugoslavia	76	88	27	21	
Regions:					
Arab Countries	80	68	38	53	
East Africa	64	52	27	41	25
West Africa	77	54	20	46	16

*Based on EMS consumer survey.
Source: Hofstede, 2001. Reprinted with the permission of Prof. Dr G. Hofstede.

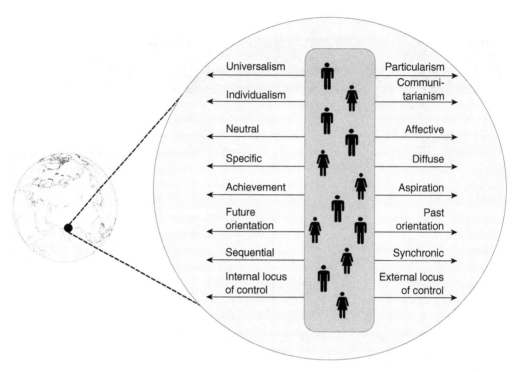

FIGURE 3.6 Trompenaars' culture dimensions
Source: Trompenaars and Hampden-Turner (1998)

2 **Individualism** versus **Communitarianism**: This dimension is comparable to Hofstede's individualism versus collectivism. In a communitarian or group-oriented society like Japan's, it is uncommon that an individual spontaneously contributes his or her ideas without prior consultation with the group. A member of an individualistic society, however, would ambitiously share his or her ideas, for instance in a brainstorming exercise.

3 **Neutral** versus **Affective**: This dimension concerns the range of feelings which are expressed. A person from a neutral culture like Thailand will try to hide his or her true feelings and just smile, even if he or she is very upset. A person from an emotional culture like Egypt would show his true feelings more openly, for instance by raising his voice.

4 **Specific** versus **Diffuse**: A manager from a specific-oriented society like the UK separates the task relationship he or she has with a subordinate from other interactions he or she has with that person. The authority of the manager does not transcend to other areas of life. People from specific cultures tend to break things down into small parts (like a WBS). A manager from a diffuse culture like Russia would expect to be respected as an important person in all kinds of different situations outside work. He or she would think more holistically. A business relationship would be based on a personal relationship.

5 **Achievement** versus **Ascription/Aspiration**: This dimension describes how people in a society gain power and status. An employee in an achievement-oriented society like Australia's relies on the fact that his or her own excellent performance will result in career advancements. People in more powerful positions tend to have special expertise and are skilful. An employee from an ascription-oriented society like Nepal will try to improve his or her relations with important families in that country, for instance through marriage, in order to attain a higher position.

The next dimensions deal with different approaches of cultures towards time (Trompenaars and Hampden-Turner, 1998; Francesco and Gold, 2005):

6 **Past, Present,** or **Future orientation**: Cultures differ in whether they value the past, or are more present- or future-oriented. The system of all business with strategies and planning is future oriented. The same goes for project management. A project needs to be implemented in the future. Societies like that of the Anglo-Saxons or Scandinavians are very much focused on the future and how to make it happen. Other societies, as is the case with many South-East-Asians, tend to attach more importance to the present. Above all necessary planning, they would rather focus on the here and now and enjoy as much as they can which results in an impact on commitment to tasks related to the future.

7 **Sequential** versus **Synchronic**: People from societies which are sequential, like that of the USA, tend to be punctual, follow schedules, and do one thing at a time. Time is viewed as a measurable and controllable thing. The importance of schedules and sticking to them is paramount, as reflected in the approach to project management. People from synchronous societies like Mexico will track various activities in parallel. They view the time set for appointments or schedules as approximate. In general, interpersonal relations are more important than schedules.

The last of Trompenaars' dimensions deals with people's relationship to their external environment.

8 **Internal locus of control** versus **External locus of control**: The inner-directed societies like Canada try to change their external environment by controlling the situation. People from outer-directed societies like Nepal will try to align themselves advantageously with the external environment instead of confronting it head on. Projects are usually based on an attitude of internal locus of control.

As stated at the beginning of section 3.9, the culture frameworks are based on generalizations and therefore are best suited to explaining major differences between national cultures. They do not aim at describing the behaviour of any one individual. You will find more information regarding the constraints of culture models on the companion website.

Let me wrap up this section with Mini Case 3.3, enabling you to combine stakeholder management and culture related knowledge.

Mini Case 3.3: Who wants what in a development project on the Philippines?

The Small and Medium Enterprise Development for Sustainable Employment Program is an international development program that aims to contribute to the efforts of the Philippine government to improve the competitiveness of the country. The program's mission is to facilitate the development and replication of sustainable models for improving the local business climate in the region of the Visayas. This long-term program started in 2003 and is scheduled until 2011.

The trade department of the Philippines is the main partner on the receiving side. Other partners on the Filipino side are the Development Agency, private and public business development service providers and local governments of the region. The donor agency is the German Ministry in charge of development aid, contracting the program implementation to the German development agency that in turn subcontracted two of the four program components to a consulting company specializing in international development projects.

The German development agency has overall responsibility for implementing and administering the whole program. The consulting company has the assignment to implement two program components, namely Business Development Services and Financial Services based on a contractually fixed implementation outline. This contract contains a Work Breakdown Structure, expected outputs, as well as a detailed budget.

To reach agreement on the program objectives and main processes, representatives of the German development agency and the consulting company travel to the Philippines. The meeting with representatives of the Philippines' trade department and development agency starts with a clear agenda. An agreed implementation plan is documented in the meeting's minutes. Hence, the German side is confident that a mutually signed scope agreement is only a matter of days away. However, no observable progress towards a scope statement is made for 12 months, leading to frustrations on both sides. In follow-up meetings, the stance of the German donors gets more aggressive. It takes another six months to receive an explicit answer from the Filipino side: they decline to sign the scope agreement because they do not want any support in the consultation. Rather, they expect to receive mere financial support and themselves act as the implementer of the program. This comes as a shock to the German donors whose situation has changed over time. The budget of the development agency has been cut. Therefore, they expected the consulting company to take over some of their responsibilities. However, the consulting company has their own set of goals determined in the contract, not allowing for any additional task within the specified time-frame. Only after more than two years do the main parties involved in the program agree on what the program is about and who should do what.

Sources: SMEDSEP (2003); SMEDSEP (2006); Ehmann (2007)

Question

What are the causes of the frustration? Base your answer on stakeholder management issues and cultural issues.

THE CULTURAL GAP TOOL

3.10

The culture frameworks help us to understand culturally diverse project stakeholders better. Yet, they are not tailored to the context of project management. Therefore, I have selected the most relevant culture dimensions with regard to project management and summarized them in the so-called cultural gap tool. You will notice that the dimensions conflict versus consensus, task versus relationship and theoretical versus pragmatic are not as such explicitly elaborated in the frameworks introduced above. Those are dimensions derived from business practice. Being bi-polar, the culture gap tool also simplifies cultures and is not suited to describe and analyse the behaviour of a single stakeholder. Used properly, it instead highlights the biggest cultural differences between major stakeholders such as the project manager, the customer, and the project team. It also relates cultural differences to the main areas of project management, sensitizing the project manager to potential differences in the behaviour of stakeholders in a project management context. Knowing about those potential differences, the project manager can plan for them.

In other words, the purpose of the cultural gap tool is to raise the awareness of the project manager regarding the manifestation of cultural differences in his or her project. It also can be used by the project management team and project members to help them in identifying differences and dealing with them.

Figure 3.7 indicates where in international project management the cultural differences manifest themselves. However, it does not go beyond an outline level or provide detailed explanations. Those will follow in the chapters I have listed within the arrows. The list of bi-polar cultural dimensions with their relevance to project management areas is the so-called culture gap analysis or culture gap tool.

Of course, measuring culture exactly is not possible. The gap analysis always contains subjective elements rather than quantifiable, neutrally measurable evaluations.

Therefore, the tool serves as a proxy to become sensitized towards cultural differences. How big is the culture gap between myself as the project manager, for instance, and my customer? This is also called 'cultural distance'.

The gap analysis provides the management team of the international project with valuable input for the stakeholder management process. It highlights any areas of potential issues between participating stakeholders, based on the assumption that big differences or large 'cultural distance', if not managed well, will lead to misunderstandings, conflict, and ultimately to project failure.

DIVERSITY-COMPLEXITY ASSESSMENT

3.11

Stakeholder heterogeneity as reflected in the stakeholder analysis and cultural diversity as reflected in the cultural gap analysis, however, are only two elements in the overall complexity of an

Equality	Managing risk and uncertainty (4) Defining & planning the project (3, 5) Organizing the project (6) Leading and managing the team (8) Communicating (9) Co-operating (10)	Hierarchy
Embracing Risk	Defining the project (3) Managing risk and uncertainty (4) Planning the project (5) Organizing the project (6) Implementing & controlling the project (7)	Avoiding Risk
Individual	Managing risk (4) Organizing the project (6) Implementing & controlling (7) Motivating and leading the team (8) Communicating (9) Co-operating (10) Learning (11)	Group
Universal	Matching strategy with projects (2) Defining the project (3) Planning the project (5) Implementing & controlling the project (7) Learning (11)	Circumstantial
Conflict	Defining the scope (3) Leading and managing the team (8) Communicating (9), Co-operating (10)	Consensus
Task	Managing stakeholders (3) Planning the project (5) Implementing & controlling (7) Leading and managing the team (8) Learning (11)	Relationship
Achievement	Planning the project (5) Organizing the project (6) Implementing & controlling (7) Motivating and leading the team (8)	Standing /Status
Sequential	Defining the project (3) Planning the project (5) Implementing & controlling (7)	Synchronic
Theoretical	Planning the project (5) Executing & controlling the project (7) Learning (11)	Pragmatic

FIGURE 3.7 Culture gap tool

TABLE 3.3 Diversity-Complexity Assessment

Criteria	Low	Medium	High
Diversity			
Number of national cultures			
Number of regional or sub-cultures			
Number of organizational cultures			
Number of organizational subcultures			
Number of functional cultures			
Number of ethnicities			
Number of languages			
Competency level in one common language			
Degree of heterogeneity of educational background			
Heterogeneity of personalities of key stakeholders			
Number of time zones			
Number of currencies			
Number of jurisdictions			
Complexity			
Degree of physical distance/distribution			
Degree of heterogeneity of stakeholder interests			
Number of intra- and inter-organizational interfaces			
Amount of information to be processed			
Degree of novelty (experience in organization existing?)			
Overall assessment of diversity & complexity			

international project. In order to decide whether the project is feasible, and if so, in order to plan well for the complexity, more factors than stakeholders and their cultures have to be considered and assessed. A project manager needs to have all major contributors to diversity and complexity on a kind of radar screen. To support the preparation of the project proposal and further project planning, the project manager can use the diversity-complexity assessment table as depicted in Table 3.3.

The stronger the cultural diversity, and the higher the complexity, the more efforts have to be made in terms of managing the international project. More time is needed for a thorough stakeholder analysis, time and resources must be planned for building and working on stakeholder relations. Communication strategies need to take national cultural differences into account, the risk management plan has to consider the international and multicultural environment, resulting in more time and resources needed to plan for and monitor risk. In general, project planning cannot be based on standard or domestic assumptions. The project manager must be on his or her toes, never taking things for granted.

The diversity-complexity assessment table should be used as a checklist for guiding the project manager through the elements of diversity and complexity prevalent in international projects. The assessment, of course, is subjective. Typically, it depends on the experience of the project manager, the competencies of the entire organization, and the project context. The more information and experience available, the more accurate the assessment can be. The process is similar to risk assessment that I will discuss in the next chapter, Chapter 4.

SUMMARY

What are the main tasks at the beginning of an international project? A concept based on creativity needs to be formulated. The scope of a project needs to be defined according to SMART criteria, usually documented in a scope statement and agreed on by all major stakeholders in a scope acceptance. This is input for the project proposal which functions as a decision-making basis for project authorization. The project proposal with a rough cost and time estimate is based on milestone definitions and a Work Breakdown Structure. The project proposal also includes a stakeholder analysis based on a stakeholder identification and categorization in a stakeholder matrix. In an international project, stakeholder management means managing diversity. Therefore, the project manager has to be sensitized towards cultural differences. Based on cultural frameworks, the project manager can differentiate between national cultures. Planning for diversity in an international project management environment is supported by the use of the cultural gap tool. A diversity-complexity assessment adds complexity to the equation, enabling the project manager to deal efficiently with the requirements of an international project.

 KEY TERMS

Scope statement, scope acceptance, SMART, project proposal, business case, scope creep, milestone, gate, checkpoint, work breakdown structure, chunking, unbundling, statement of work, stakeholder matrix, national culture, value, attitude, behaviour, professional culture, functional culture, self-reference, ethnocentrism, ethno-relativism, stereotype, cultural framework, cultural gap analysis, cultural distance, diversity-complexity assessment.

REVIEW TASKS

Questions

1 What are the most important tasks to be accomplished in the project initiating phase of an international project?
2 What kind of cultures do you have knowledge of, and how would you characterize them?
3 What are the advantages and limitations of culture frameworks?

EXERCISE 1

Think of a project you are familiar with (in a private or business context) and try to formulate the project scope based on the SMART-technique.

EXERCISE 2

Which stereotypes are you familiar with about your neighbouring countries? Please discuss in class.

EXERCISE 3

Look for your national culture on Hofstede's webpage (www.geerthofstede.com). Which national cultures have the biggest gap with your own culture?

EXERCISE 4

Apply the culture gap tool as introduced in Figure 3.7 to Snapshot 3.3 and try to explain the reasons for the behaviour of both parties, the customer from the Gulf region, and the German project manager.

CHAPTER END CASE: THE NEVER ENDING STORY

This case elaborates on an international software development project in Indonesia with the involvement of Australian programmers for the fifth largest financial leasing corporation in Indonesia, BIG (name disguised), worth about 15 million US$ turnover. As a typical Indonesian company, BIG had an organizational culture where a lot of importance was attached to personal relations. These were considered more relevant than processes and procedures of any kind. BIG's information systems were based on software not fully catering to all the needs of the fast growing company. Therefore, the company was looking for a new IT-solution which was finally provided by C-Consulting.

C-Consulting was a spin-off of an IBM subsidiary in Belgium, with offices in Singapore, Indonesia and Australia. Early in 2007, C-Consulting was acquired by an Indonesian consulting company with strong international connections. At its peak in 1998/1999, C-Consulting along with its Singapore-based parent company had a consolidated book accounting turnover of about 6 million US$ and around 25 employees. In the aftermath of the Asian crisis, turnover drastically decreased due to the fact that new investments in information technology were made only reluctantly. C-Consulting was led by two executives, an Australian and a Belgian, the former with an in-depth programming background and the latter with an IBM consulting background. Both executives were well trained in standard project management methodology. They were used to managing projects according to strict milestones and tight schedules with clear procedures to sign off the deliverables on the contractor and customer side. Despite their knowledge, they were not consistent in the implementation of those project management tools and techniques.

In order to obtain suitable customized software for his company, the CEO of BIG called an old friend whom he trusted fully, one of the founders of C-Consulting. Both parties negotiated the following agreement: BIG would pay C-Consulting about 30,000 US$ for the development of web-based leasing software which would integrate all functionalities, from sales to lease insurance and accounting reports. That quoted price came after tough negotiations by BIG and implied a serious cut in price compared to the closest competitor of C-Consulting. Such web-based lease software, developed in Microsoft PSP web-language with the possibility to migrate to a Linux version at a later stage, had the advantage of allowing managers to access the software regardless of their physical location. Although not unique, such software created crucial advantages for BIG. Both parties intended to start a long-term collaboration for the mutual benefit of both companies. They agreed on an indicative price without bothering too much on the detailed specifications. That price was way below the Indonesian competitor's offer, let alone an international software supplier which would have charged roughly ten times as much as C-Consulting. The agreement was based on a kind of partnership with the aim of continuing to supply other leasing companies in Indonesia after the successful implementation of the system at BIG.

When the price was determined, the specifications of the financial lease software were more indicative than precise. Somehow, the high-level specifications were considered sufficient at that stage because of the long-term relationship between the senior managers of both companies. The need for further detailing of the specifications to customize the software to BIG's requirements was not seen since no bad intention by either party was assumed. Such a 'loose' contract implied that the dates were guidelines and that the deliverables were referring to generic modules without any specific features of the modules which needed to be signed off. It was presumed that an attachment with the detailed specifications would follow at a later stage when work was in progress. Of course, the fact that precise specifications did not exist and were never signed off meant that there was no legal reference or basis to refer to.

Nobody, however, made the effort to create and sign off detailed specifications. In the course of modelling the business processes, the client BIG unilaterally decided at least three times to request some changes to the software concerning the information workflow. Those changes seriously affected the information flows and the interdependencies between different modules. In addition, they made a lot of work which had already been done up until that stage redundant. Due to the fact that those changes were not documented, it was as if the requests had never taken place, resulting in a largely modified scope. The project specifications became broader and broader while no real additional substantial fees were granted since the spirit of the contract was that both parties were making an investment. But BIG conceded with a later delivery deadline which was postponed a couple of times.

During the first seven months the work process proceeded more or less according to the initial schedule, or so it seemed, and no real conflicts appeared on the surface. Reports about the work in process were usually delivered orally. Some written progress reports turned out to reflect more the expectations of top management rather than flagging up delays. Over time, those reports became increasingly defensive from both parties since the respective Indonesian project managers on either side did not want to admit to any wrongdoing and did not want to lose face. The lack of open clear reporting against pre-defined milestones was initially compensated for by the two CEOs whose good relationship guaranteed the smoothness of the overall process. The Indonesian project managers for both C-Consulting and BIG were well trained and experienced. However, they were not used to such big change management processes and ignored the requests of the international CEO of C-Consulting to implement some tough formal procedures regarding time performance and progress. The Indonesian project manager of BIG did not rely on formal sign offs, instead using only written statements of specifications without signatures. A formal sign off could have been misinterpreted as distrust which was seen as counter-productive in a business relationship. The project managers of both parties relied on ad hoc management if issues occurred. They did not ask probing questions of their team members, and received only insufficiently detailed feedback about project status.

When the Australian programmers of C-Consulting who were responsible for the quality assurance of the software started to complain about the numerous change requests by the Indonesian client BIG that were accepted by the Indonesian project manager and his Indonesian team, resulting in so-called 'spaghetti programming',[1] it became obvious that the project was facing real time versus deliverables issues. After the CEOs of both companies had found out that the progress reports were mere cover ups rather than a reflection of the reality, the CEO of C-Consulting decided to hire a new project manager to bring the project back on track. The new project manager was a trained civil engineer from a top Indonesian university with an international MBA degree from an Australian university. By the time the new project manager was about to take full control, the project was heavily behind schedule. The change requests had led to delays of 22 months in total. In fact, one could argue that the whole program plan to be finalized within 9 to 12 months (based on limited specifications from C-Consulting's perspective) was dragged up to almost 2.5 years as a result of those changes and add-ons.

At that stage, the Anglo-European executives of C-Consulting tried to install strict procedures and processes in order to rescue the project. The Australian partner of C-Consulting even got involved operationally with the completion of the software, overruling some of the decisions previously made made by the respective Indonesian program managers of BIG and C-Consulting. The Asian project managers interpreted these steps as a sign of distrust and as a way to avoid taking real responsibility for the project. In another effort to rescue the project, one of the lead programmers was laid off, not for incompetence, but because of a lack of commitment. Since his bonus was linked to the successful completion of new projects he did not have any interest in completing the old lingering project, despite an agreed time schedule.

In the meantime, C-Consulting was acquired by a local business consulting company which partially blamed the management of C-Consulting for not having taken appropriate early measures to rectify the project. Ultimately, the project was outsourced to a third party in Indonesia and losses were cut at both ends.

Source: Written by Peter Verhezen (2007)

Task and questions

1 Identify the issues in the project initiating phase.
2 How could the scope creep have been avoided?
3 Where do you see the impact of national cultures in this case?

NOTE

1 Spaghetti programming is a term used by programmers when many ad hoc changes are added without taking into account the possible negative side effects these may have on predetermined well-structured architectural design which accounts for the speed of a software.

FURTHER READING

Gullestrup, Hans (2006) *Cultural Analysis – Towards Cross-cultural Understanding*. Copenhagen: Copenhagen Business School Press/Aalborg Universitetsforlag. (This book provides the reader who is interested in the topic of culture with an in-depth discussion of theoretical and more practical aspects of culture, from the concept of culture, culture dynamics, to ethics and morals in intercultural co-action.)

Schneider, Susan C. and Barsoux, Jean-Louis (2002) *Managing Across Cultures*, 2nd edition. Harlow: Prentice Hall/*Financial Times*. (This book provides the reader with a comprehensive overview of culture and its interrelatedness with managerial aspects like strategy, structure, and human resource management. It also draws on the skills an international manager should have as well as the management of multicultural teams.)

www.geerthofstede.com/ (On this page the reader will find 56 national cultures or regional cultures analysed with Hofstede's model.)

www.thtconsulting.com/welcome/index.htm (Gives an insight into tools and techniques to cluster and analyse national and organizational cultures.)

http://www.crossculture.com/services/cross-culture/ (Short movie on Lewis's cultural model which is very easy to understand and use.)

MANAGING RISK AND UNCERTAINTY IN INTERNATIONAL PROJECTS

4

LEARNING OBJECTIVES

After studying this chapter, you will be able to:

- discuss the nature of risk in an international project
- differentiate between foreseeable risks and emergent risks
- explain the risk management cycle
- apply models to identify risks
- use tools and techniques to prioritize risks
- understand risk response strategies in international project management
- discuss corruption as a special area of risk in international projects
- elucidate how to manage uncertainty in an international project.

INTRODUCTION

4.1

Risk management has become increasingly important following the big corporate scandals in the USA and other countries which triggered harsher laws and regulations (e.g. the US Sarbanes-Oxley Act) to ensure control and transparency. These laws are binding for publicly listed corporations, but also for other organizations in many OECD countries. After the world financial crisis unfolded in 2008, the subject has gained further prominence.

As many international projects involve huge investments and are highly visible in the organization, risks need to be thoroughly managed. This is not only necessary to comply with new laws and regulations, but also indispensable in light of the high complexity of international projects as discussed in Chapter 1. A high degree of complexity leads to high potential risk resulting in financial losses. Risk propensity is amplified by the embeddedness of international projects in a volatile and fast changing environment. According to a study by *Engineering News Record* carried out between 1995 and 2004, 15.1 per cent of the worldwide top 225 global contractors in the construction industry have suffered losses in international construction projects. Only 9.7 per cent of domestic projects, however, incurred losses to those companies. This hints at the higher risks involved in international projects (Han et al., 2007).

Hence, risk management plays a major role in managing international projects. Scope and stakeholder management can be considered as part of risk management in a broader sense. In this chapter, we will focus on risk management in a narrower sense. The first part of this chapter looks at the nature of risk. We will differentiate between risk that can be anticipated and risk which cannot be foreseen. The first category of risks can be managed systematically. Therefore, I will explain the process of risk management, also in light of cultural differences. Divided into different stages, it deals with risk identification, risk assessment, risk planning, and risk control. To some extent, there is an overlap between project planning and risk management because good and thorough general project planning also contributes to risk minimization. We will have a look at the different areas of risks based on a concrete example of the construction industry. Then, we will follow up with various risk identification approaches, before we turn to six major risk response strategies. We will also dwell on corruption as a source of risk which needs special attention in international projects.

In a dynamic, fast changing environment, there is a lot of risk which cannot be systematically managed. Yet, there are ways to deal with general uncertainty, such as an appropriate project culture, a flexible project structure, as well as suitable contract and project governance. These areas indicate again the close connection between risk management and project planning. They also show that risk management affects the entire organization. The section on non-systematic risks links risk management to project portfolio management, and organizational culture. I will wrap up this chapter with an explanation of project flexibility in terms of products, processes and people, and how this relates to uncertainty management.

THE NATURE OF RISK

4.2 The Project Management Institute crisply describes a project risk as 'an uncertain event or condition that, if it occurs, has a positive or a negative effect on at least one project objective, such as time, cost, scope, or quality' (PMI, 2004: 238).

We can differentiate between risks that can be anticipated, and risks that emerge during the course of a project. The two types of risks are also called 'known-unknown' and 'unknown-unknown', sometimes abbreviated as 'unk-unk'. The classical methodology of project management deals with the risks which can be anticipated. Those risks are usually not completely known, but can be identified or modelled. The probability of occurrence and the impact on the project can be calculated (Miller and Hobbs, 2006).

However, due to their characteristics, international projects are often faced with emergent risk. This is linked with uncertainty. High uncertainty means that future events can not be foreseen, nor can they be factored into the overall project planning. In international projects, such events could be the bankruptcy of a (foreign) partner or (foreign) supplier, a radical drop in demand triggered by a distant cause, adversarial attitudes by local authorities after new officials have been appointed, or a coup d'état.

Emergent risk is not only caused by real changes in the project context. They might also stem from the fact that the stakeholders of international projects get a better understanding of their actual needs, or that the original needs of some stakeholders have been misunderstood or misinterpreted (e.g. due to cross-cultural misunderstandings). These turbulences in the environment are called 'drifting environments' by Kreiner (1995).

The success of international projects depends highly on having an effective approach in place to handle both types of risk. Risks that can be anticipated can arise from two principle sources:

1 Risk related to the management of the international project, for example insufficient or non-existent project planning, inappropriate stakeholder management, dysfunctional communication, poor selection of team members. Those risks are also called internal risks because they are caused by the organization itself, either on a broad level, or on a project level.
2 Risks residing in the wider external project environment which are only controllable by (distant) stakeholders or other decision-makers, but which are partially predictable, for instance an increase in inflation in target markets, a high level of corruption, alterations to the tax regime, resistance by (newly emerged) environmental protection groups, or patriotic claims against international projects.

Both sources mentioned above can also be the cause of emergent risks. In addition, emergent risks stem from:

3 Sources that are by nature unpredictable, such as the outbreak of pandemics like avian influenza or SARS, natural disasters, or political revolutions.

Categories 2 and 3 are also referred to as exogenous or external risks that are caused by an organization's environment.

RISK AND CULTURE

4.3 After we have defined what is understood by risk, we have to think of the different meanings and attitudes towards risks in an international context. In Chapter 3 I introduced the culture gap analysis as a tool to highlight where cultural differences can exist in relevant project management areas. The prerequisite to use the tool properly is knowledge of the cultural frameworks, and the application of the cultural frameworks to the main national culture involved in the project. Figure 4.1 provides you with the most prominent differences in attitude towards risk between people from different national cultures. As those differences can turn into project inherent risks and lead to unidentified external risks, the project manager needs to be aware of these cultural differences and include them in his or her project planning. Needless to say, differences in attitude towards risk can also emerge from other factors such as an individual's personality, the organizational culture, or educational background.

Acknowledging the existence of risks, and knowing about potential differences in the attitude towards risks, is a good foundation for properly managing risks – at least those risks that are manageable.

THE RISK MANAGEMENT PROCESS

4.4 Risks that can be anticipated need to be planned for. This is done in the context of risk management, which 'includes the processes concerned with conducting risk management planning, identification, analysis, responses, and monitoring and control on a project' (PMI, 2004: 237). The objective of risk management is to minimize the negative impacts of risks on the project and to benefit from opportunities.

Traditional project risk management deals with the expected consequences of a risk, namely the impact and probability that an event might occur. Contingency plans are created as guidelines for the team members to follow. Flexibility is pre-planned, and only needs to be triggered in case of the occurrence of a risk.

Figure 4.2 gives an overview of the major elements of the risk management process aligned with the project management phases. Like project management itself, risk management is an iterative process. It is important to watch out for risks during the whole duration of the project. It is also important to modify existing risk plans in order to adapt to changes in the environment.

A prerequisite for efficient risk management is to go through the cycle of Figure 4.2 at an early stage of the project. With reference to Chapter 3, this means that risk

Hierarchy		Equality
	Individuals from equality oriented cultures may involve the whole project team to identify and monitor risk. They also may involve all relevant group members in the decision on countermeasures. Project managers from hierarchy-oriented cultures may identify risk on their own and be the only people responsible for taking countermeasures. Group members may be very comfortable with not having any responsibility for this 'dangerous' task.	

Avoiding Risk		Embracing Risk
	Individuals from cultures with high risk avoidance tend to fear unfamiliarity and ambiguous situations. They may try to ignore risk. People from risk embracing cultures may more actively seek risk, and may also turn it into an opportunity.	

Group		Individuals
	People from individualistic cultures might be more inclined to take decisions on their own in risky and urgent situations, whereas persons from group-oriented cultures may want to consult with other group or network members which is time-consuming.	

FIGURE 4.1   Cultural impact on risk management

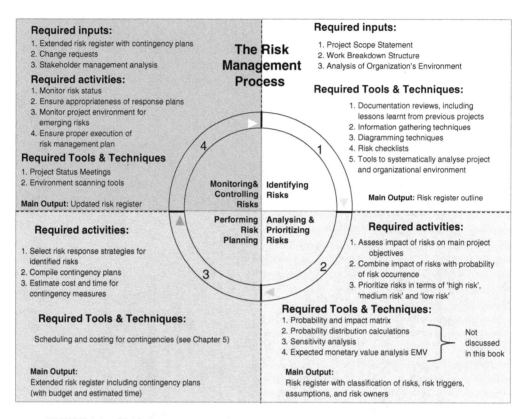

FIGURE 4.2   Risk management cycle

management is already part of the project proposal in the initiating phase, usually in the form of a risk management plan which contains the methodology (tools and data sources used to perform risk management), risk categories, the roles and responsibilities of risk management, and the budget and time needed for contingencies (PMI, 2004).

Especially in international projects, a critical success criterion for effective risk management is communication, which will be discussed further in Chapter 9.

In many multinational organizations, it is mandatory for major international projects to include a list of risks in the bid or project proposal. This is to make sure that sufficient resources are factored into the bid in light of potential risks.

Let me briefly outline the four risk management phases as depicted in Figure 4.2.

1   IDENTIFYING RISKS

This process involves reviewing project documents and checklists (such as the project scope statement), categorizing risks, and finally producing a list of project risks, also called the risk register. Risk categories depend highly on the nature of the project and industry.

2 ANALYSING AND PRIORITIZING RISK

Each risk needs to be analysed in terms of likelihood of occurrence in relation to its impact on the project, the so-called qualitative risk analysis. A ranking of risks according to their effect on the project objectives is part of the process. This is supplemented by a quantitative risk analysis focusing on the numerical evaluation of the likelihood and impact of risks. The whole process is based on assumptions and constraints which need to be reviewed on a regular basis. This is recommended to identify risk triggers, namely events that warn of impending risks. Such a trigger could be elections for a new government, or strikes in a certain country.

3 PERFORMING RISK PLANNING

Based on the prioritized lists produced in the previous phase, the project manager needs to decide on what actions to take to reduce threats while maximizing the opportunities discovered in the risk analysis. Ideally, each identified risk has a risk owner who is responsible for carrying out the risk response or contingency plan.

4 MONITORING AND CONTROLLING RISKS

The main activities at this stage of the risk management process are: first, monitoring the status of risks as listed in the risk register; second, ensuring that risk response plans and contingency plans are appropriate; third, monitoring the project environment in order to detect emerging risks; and fourth, ensuring the proper execution of the risk management plan.

IDENTIFICATION OF RISK

4.5

Now we have an overview of the overall risk management process with its main activities. A special challenge within the process lies in risk assessment, which includes the identification of risks, as well as their analysis and prioritization.

In this section, I will only focus on so-called 'low-tech' tools and techniques for risk assessment. Business practice shows that high-tech solutions are often too costly and time-consuming, and do not necessarily deliver the desired results. Of course, computer-aided risk simulations for new product development and other complex projects are helpful techniques, but outside the scope of this book. The low-tech tools I will discuss in the following paragraphs are sometimes also referred to as 'Problem Structuring Methods'.

RISK BRAINSTORMING OR RISK ASSESSMENT WORKSHOP

As international projects typically deal with a whole variety of risks, it is advisable to include heterogeneous perspectives in the process of risk identification. This could be done by inviting major stakeholders to a workshop on risk assessment, prior to the final decision on whether to proceed with a project or not. If the organization has experience in international projects, it would also be wise to invite the project managers from previous international projects to draw on the lessons they learnt. It is worthwhile to limit the objective of the workshop not only to the risks which can be anticipated, but also to use this opportunity to brainstorm on whether there are gaps in knowledge, i.e., whether it is likely that the international project will have to operate in an environment of uncertainty.

Rolls-Royce's Project 'Spree', which I introduced in Chapter 3, conducted such a risk assessment workshop in the project definition phase. All sub-team leaders were invited to an 'away-day'. The main objective was to go through all the activities within the different statements of work in order to detect risks which would stem mainly from interface problems. The identified (anticipated) risks were summarized in a list and sorted based on their potential impact on the project outcome (Blasig, 2005).

RISK BREAKDOWN STRUCTURE

The identification of risks is specific to the industry. The global construction industry is a good reference here because international construction projects are prone to risk:

- long duration during which currencies can fluctuate, governments can change, laws can be amended, etc.
- typically a local project owner with local attitudes and customs, often in the public sector with a specific organizational culture
- strong dependence on local authorities with issues like postponement of permissions, language problems, corruption
- strong dependence on local (blue collar) workers with their own cultures and languages, religions and local working conditions and laws
- strong dependence on local climate conditions with unpredictable natural catastrophes
- focus on a certain selected host country with a huge sunk cost that cannot be recovered.

For those and other reasons, a deep analysis of the conditions in the host country is of paramount importance. Walewski et al. (2006) have identified 82 risk elements relevant to construction projects as depicted in Figure 4.3. They have covered the risks of the host country under three different perspectives, namely country risks, risk related to the facilities, and risk in production and operations. Han et al. (2007) have identified 64 risk factors for international construction projects, categorized by their effect on profitability under the:

1 Condition of the host country and project owner
2 Bidding process
3 Project characteristics and contractual conditions
4 Characteristics of the organization and participants
5 Contractor's ability.

While the content of the risk breakdown structure is specific to international projects in the construction industry, the approach itself can be used to systematically structure risks that also exist in other industries. Inputs to the risk breakdown structure are the project scope statement and the Work Breakdown Structure as discussed in Chapter 3. Moreover, the risk related documents from previous international projects are valuable sources.

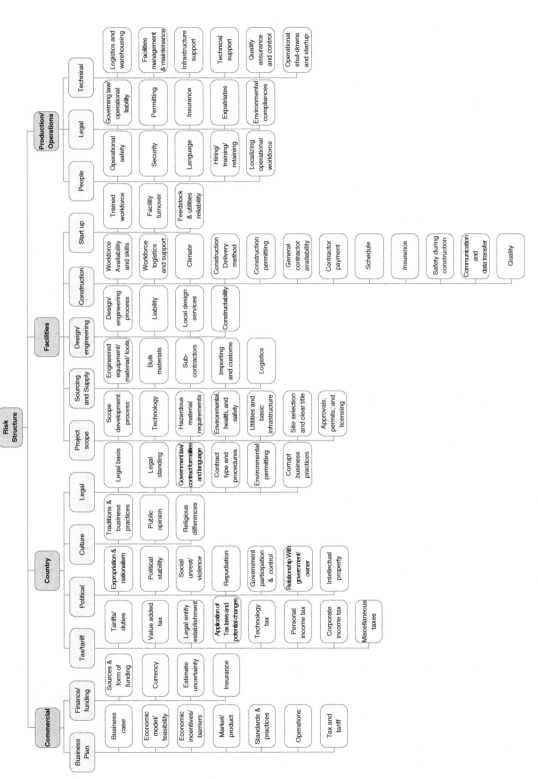

FIGURE 4.3 *Risk breakdown for internal construction projects (Walewski et al., 2006: 6–5)*

Source: Cleland and Gareis (2006): *Global Project Management Handbook: Planning, Organizing and Controlling International Projects*. McGraw-Hill. Material reproduced with the permission of the McGraw-Hill companies.

RISK IDENTIFICATION CHECKLISTS

Checklists are another helpful technique to identify project risks, for instance for off-shoring projects. Before an insurance company transfers services like parts of its claim management process to another organizational unit in a geographically distant country, a thorough risk assessment needs to be carried out. Table 4.1 illustrates how a checklist could support the risk management of the insurance company. Note that this list is only for off-shoring within the same organization. In the case of simultaneous outsourcing, a vendor selection list must be added. The numerical scale can be read as very good (1), good (2), medium (3), bad (4), very bad (5). Where this interpretation does not make sense, it can be modified to 'conducive to project success' or an equivalent. Depending on the project at hand, the listed items can be weighted to customize the checklist further.

This checklist can also be used for country comparisons and later on for a further risk assessment by adding risk scores which will be discussed in the paragraph 'analysing and prioritizing'.

A similar checklist for international construction projects could be created based on the experience summarized in Snapshot 4.1 regarding the most frequently occurring risk in international construction projects carried out by South Korean companies.

SNAPSHOT 4.1

Risks faced by international Korean construction companies

In 2002, the International Contractors Association of Korea identified the following risks that resulted in financial damage to the international construction company:

- an inability or unwillingness to pay on the part of the local government
- misunderstandings regarding contract provisions or specifications
- miscommunication with local authorities
- currency exchange rate risk
- unfair contract clauses
- lower than expected productivity due to unfavourable climate conditions, or problems with labour and materials supply
- conflicts between customers, engineers, contractors, and local subcontractors.

Source: Han et al. (2007)

TOOLS TO IDENTIFY EXOGENOUS RISKS

In order to systematically analyse geographical market or the country the international project will target or be involved with, it is worthwhile to use the PESTEL tool. It covers the political, economic, sociocultural, technological, environmental, and legal aspects of any country selected. For meaningful risk identification, the tool should be applied only to one country respectively.

TABLE 4.1 Risk checklist for off-shoring projects

Country Assessment		1	2	3	4	5
Factors						
Political Factors	Political stability					
	Safety situation					
	Probability of social unrest					
	Extent of corruption					
	Position of labour unions					
	Level of red tape					
Economic Factors	GDP growth trend					
	Availability of qualified labour					
	Salary/wage level					
	Outlook of salary development					
	Inflation rate					
	Volatility of currency					
	Capital supply					
Socio-Cultural Factors	Similarity of cultural norms with organization's home country					
	Work ethics					
	Religious habits & customs					
	Quality of education					
	Language skills					
	Computer literacy					
	Working style of staff in terms of pro-activity					
	Working style of staff in terms of independent problem solution capabilities					
	Extent of achievement orientation					
	Gender roles					
	Demographic development					
Technical/ Technological Factors	Quality of transportation infrastructure					
	Quality of communication infrastructure					
	Quality of utility infrastructure					
Environmental Factors	Environmental regulations					
Legal Factors	Corporate tax					
	Additional federal and municipal taxes					
	VAT					

(Cont'd)

TABLE 4.1

Country Assessment							
Factors		1	2	3	4	5	
	Labour law						
	Health & safety regulations						
	Social insurance laws						
	Protection of intellectual property						
	Reliability of law enforcement						
Process Assessment (on a strategic and operational level) Activities have to precede process transfer		Yes			No		
	Organizational processes categorized as core and non core processes						
	Processes categorized into easy, moderate and difficult to codify						
	Processes flagged for transfer documented						
	Processes documented in a language and style to be easily understood by off-shore employees						
Overall							

The chart depicted in Figure 4.4 provides an example of sub-aspects which could be relevant for the analysis. However, they need to be specified for each international project, as the selection of the important aspects depends on the nature of the project and industry.

The section on national culture in Chapter 3 explored the 'social-cultural' aspect of this tool in more detail.

INDUSTRY SPECIFIC RISK IDENTIFICATION TOOLS

Transportation infrastructure projects, power plant projects, or projects in the pharmaceutical or petrochemical sector all require comprehensive risk analyses in the initiating phase because risk assessment is a prerequisite to obtaining project approval from the regulatory authorities. Instead of a detailed discussion, I will merely mention some of the most well-known risk identification tools and refer you to further reading for more information (Cooper et al., 2005):

- A Hazard and Operability Study (HAZOP) systematically examines the proposed process systems, equipment and procedures with the purpose of identifying potential hazards to people, the environment, the plant or operations.
- A Fire Safety Study (FSS) examines the specific causes and impacts of fires.
- A Construction Safety Study (CSS) aims to identify major hazards in the construction plan.

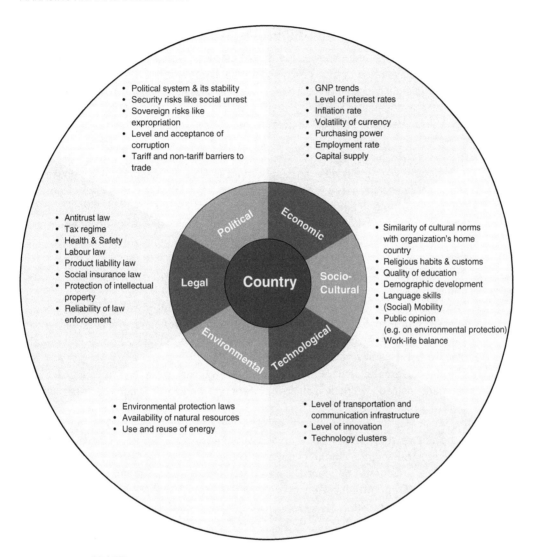

FIGURE 4.4 PESTEL tool

- A Failure Mode and Effects Analysis (FMEA) is standard in manufacturing, identifying step-by-step potential failures in a system or a process. 'Failure modes' refer to the ways in which something might fail, and 'effect analysis' relates to the impact of those failures. The purpose of this technique is to take action in order to eliminate or reduce failures (ASQ, 2007).

Mini Case 4.1 demonstrates the damage that a project can suffer if risks are not identified and are consequently not managed.

Mini Case 4.1: The Panama Canal

A famous early international project in the infrastructure area is the construction of the Panama Canal, initiated by the French diplomat and entrepreneur Ferdinand de Lesseps. In 1879, he established the Panama enterprise with capital raised from the French public. Construction work started in 1880. The canal was forecast to be ready by 1887.

However, the engineers, most of them from France, were confronted with unforeseen problems:

1 The climate was totally different. Eight months of rainy season brought downpours that nobody was prepared for. The rain caused the river close to the proposed canal to flood, resulting in a major threat to shipping and human life. The downpours also caused massive mudslides covering the cut again. Even modern equipment imported from the United States and Europe could not conquer nature. Heavy accidents caused many casualties among the engineers and workers.
2 More casualties were caused by dangerous tropical wildlife like poisonous snakes and spiders.
3 Panama (then belonging to Colombia) was a poor country with a desolate health infrastructure. Tropical diseases like yellow fever, cholera, and smallpox were a constant threat to the workers. Seventy per cent of the employees who caught malaria died from it. This severely affected the schedule.
4 The planned excavation of 74 million cubic metres turned out to be a substantial underestimate. Instead, 120 million cubic metres of rock and earth needed to be removed.

In the end, it took 35 years until the canal was opened for business in 1914. In the meantime the political environment had changed with the foundation of the independent nation of Panama. The scope of the international project had also altered. The new project sponsor, US president Theodore Roosevelt, needed the canal to consolidate his navy from the Pacific and Atlantic. Hence, an originally commercial project had turned into a strategic military project.

Task

Select and apply the risk identification tools introduced in section 4.5 that would have helped to identify the risks mentioned above.

Sources: Cadbury (2003); Kendrick (2003)

I will finish this section on risk identification tools with a remark on risks implied by certain categories of project customers. Government projects, for instance, are riskier than projects with private corporations because there will be much more political influence on such projects. Big infrastructure projects, for instance, tend to be screened after an election or any change of government with the potential consequence of a sudden project cancellation.

Risk register							
Risk No.	Risk description	Cause of risk	Probability of occurrence	Impact on project	Contingency measure	Cost in Yen	Date of entry

FIGURE 4.5 Example of a risk register

RISK ANALYSIS

4.6

The output of the risk identification activities is a so-called risk register. At this stage, it only contains a list of identified risks, including their root causes. This means the first three rows of Figure 4.5 will be filled with data. The risk register may also comprise any uncertain assumptions the project is based on (PMI, 2004). Figure 4.5 provides you with an example of a complete or extended risk register of a Japanese construction multinational which will be completed at the end of the risk planning phase. In the following, we will discuss the activities that will enable us to round off the extended risk register.

Following the identification of a risk including an analysis of its cause, all risks have to be analysed and prioritized in terms of their likelihood of occurrence and impact on the project. Prioritization can be done either in relative or numerical terms. Usually, the risk-rating rules are determined by the organization, based on previous experience and tailored to industry requirements.

A probability and impact matrix is a widespread tool to perform risk prioritization. As is true for risk identification techniques, it is a low-tech tool. More complex tools for quantitative risk analysis are outside the scope of this book (see Further Reading).

TABLE 4.2 Impact Probability Matrix

	Impact				
Probability	Insignificant	Minor	Moderate	Major	Horrible
Almost certain 90%	Medium/ YELLOW	Medium/ YELLOW	High/RED	High/RED	High/RED
Likely 70%	Low/GREEN	Medium/ YELLOW	Medium/ YELLOW	High/RED	High/RED
Possible 50%	Low/GREEN	Low or Medium/ GREEN or YELLOW	Medium/ YELLOW	High/ RED	High/ RED
Unlikely 30%	Low/GREEN	Low/ GREEN	Medium/ YELLOW	Medium/ YELLOW	High/ RED
Rare 10%	Low/GREEN	Low/ GREEN	Low/ GREEN	Medium/ YELLOW	Medium/ YELLOW

Source: Adapted from PMI, 2004; Cooper et al. 2005

The matrix combines the likelihood of risk occurrence with the effect this will have on project objectives. This approach can be used for negative and positive risks.

It provides the project stakeholders with a good overview of the risk propensity of the project. It also visualizes priorities well: the risk with the highest probability of occurrence along with the most severe consequences for project success will have top priority.

To create the matrix, the project manager and his or her team first have to decide which effect a risk will have on major project objectives. Depending on the organization and industry, there are different arrangements for the categorization of impact. Typically, it is either a three-stage or five-stage classification, namely:

- In a three-stage classification the impact on project objectives can be low, medium, or high.
- In a five-stage classification the impact can be insignificant, minor, moderate, major, or horrible.

The next step in creating the matrix is to combine the impact with the probability of occurrence. Table 4.2 uses the five-stage categorization described above to show the severity of potential damage to the project. The categorization of likelihood also differs between organizations and industries. Table 4.2 suggests a five-stage classification with rare, unlikely, possible, likely, and almost certain. A numerical classification is added in percentages.

Those risks which are likely to occur and have a big impact on the project are coded in red. They will require priority action and aggressive response strategies with related cost and time estimates as part of project planning. The customer might be notified about this risk. Action effectiveness needs to be periodically checked.

Risks with a low probability of occurrence and or a low impact on project objectives are coded in green. They might only be periodically monitored and the cost for potential counter-measures factored into the contingency reserve of the project budget.

All other risks, with a medium impact on project results and or medium to low likelihood of occurrence, are coded as yellow risks. Stakeholders need to be aware of the risks, and counter-measures may be recommended with a periodic check on action efficiency.

The colour coding illustrates the priority of the risk very well and supports phase three (performing risk planning) and phase four (monitoring and controlling risk) of the risk management cycle.

The impact-probability matrix results extend the risk register with risk prioritization. This prioritization, in turn, serves as the basis for contingency planning.

PLANNING FOR RISK

4.7

The identification and prioritization of risks only make sense if followed up by actions. What to do about the red, yellow and green risks? This process, the third phase of the risk management cycle, is also called risk planning. Can risks be totally avoided? If not, how can an organization reduce their impact? There are several methods to categorize risk response strategies. I would like to introduce the following five strategies on how to respond to risks: risk avoidance, risk mitigation, risk acceptance, risk transfer, and risk absorption and pooling (see Cooper et al., 2005; Heldman, 2005; Kendrick, 2003). Here I will discuss each strategy in more detail.

RISK AVOIDANCE

A risk can be avoided by adequate planning of an international project. Planning not only refers to project planning, but also to technical product planning. The following scenario provides an example of risk avoidance in new product development. In the case of new product development, for instance, a product architecture which is based on a modular approach reduces the interdependencies between the sub-project teams that are often located at different geographical sites. The product modules enable the various sub-teams to work in parallel without being dependent on the input of other teams. Consequently, the number of interfaces between organizational units is reduced. In other words, modular product architecture decreases complexity, thus reducing risk. For further details, the interested reader is referred to concurrent engineering.

Here is a different example for risk avoidance in the financial area. Big international infrastructure projects or other long-term projects may suffer from delays in installment payments by 90 days or more, either directly caused by the client or indirectly caused by the client's government if it has the power not to allow hard currency transactions. This financial risk can be avoided in different ways. First, crystal-clear milestones at which the instalment payments are due need to be defined. The wording also needs to be as precise as possible, and easy to understand by non-native speakers. Second, the project manager can use letters of credit issued by a bank the organization has good relations with. Against detailed documentation, the bank determines when the requirements for payments are met, and issues the funds to the seller. This also avoids delays due to negotiations and conflict with the customer. However, the bank will charge a fee for this service.

RISK MITIGATION

This approach is about reducing the likelihood of risk occurrence and/or reducing the impact of risk damage. An example here is the development and production of a series of trains for a Scandinavian customer. In order to identify the safety risks and potential non-compliance with local safety regulations as early as possible, the homologation needs to be integrated into the product design process. Test methods have to be determined at an early product design stage and agreed on between the contractor and the customer. The details regarding test methods need to be specified in an appendix of the project's contract. This procedure reduces the risk of undetected local safety demands or customer requirements. Another example for risk mitigation is a currency hedging strategy protecting the project for a certain time-span from strong currency volatility.

SNAPSHOT 4.2

Risk in international infrastructure projects

In the last twenty years, a significant change could be observed regarding the provision of infrastructure services in countries around the world. Governments opened up to private sector involvement, inviting private companies to finance, build and operate in the field of power, transport, water, telecommunications, healthcare, and education. So-called Build-Own-Operate-Transfer (BOOT) projects are financed on a limited-resource basis and operated under a concession from the state or a similar public body such as a private venture. At the end of the concession the project is transferred back to the state or public authority. Such a finance technique spreads the risk for all participating parties; the lenders, user, contractors, operators, and investors.

Yet, investors like banks still have their own risk management strategies, as shown in the following examples from an international bank:

1 Before the loan for an international infrastructure project is granted, it is important to consult with local lawyers, for instance to check property rights. Does the land belong to the people who claim it belongs to them? In some transformation economies, the situation can be unclear due to revoked expropriations.
2 The policy is to have a contract with one single contractor, at a guaranteed maximum price.

3　Standards for risk mitigation are strictest in emerging markets. A building project, for instance, will be only financed if 30–50 per cent of the space of the building is rented out at the point in time of the loan payment.
4　A cost/land conveyor is used to cross-check cost-estimations, and to monitor project milestones. On a need basis, the bank pays personal visits to the construction site to check the progress of the construction work.

Sources: The International Project Finance Association (IPFA) (2007a, 2007b)

RISK ACCEPTANCE

Risk acceptance is a suitable response if the risk is considered manageable and unavoidable. An example here is a Swedish company that had acquired a firm in Northern Spain in order to get access to special knowledge. Most of the local Spanish staff were to be laid off mid-term. The project manager along with his team members were sent to Spain to organize the knowledge transfer. The local employees were so upset about the acquisition and the announced job cuts that they physically threatened the foreign project members. Bodyguards and armed vehicles had to be hired to protect them. This cost needed to be budgeted for.

RISK TRANSFER

This strategy is suitable if the risk can be transferred to another party. As a result of this strategy the risk does not disappear, but the responsibility of managing the risk now rests with someone else. Transfer techniques can be insurance, warranties, or guarantees. However, cost in the form of an insurance premium or another payment is linked to this strategy which is quite appropriate for financial risks (Heldman, 2005). Transfer can also refer to an outsourcing or off-shoring agreement. Especially in the service sector, an increasing number of activities are transferred to third parties, typically non-domestic business partners. Unfortunately, this often invites substantial new risks.

RISK ABSORPTION OR POOLING

It is an appropriate risk response if the risk can be pooled by taking part in a consortium, alliance or joint venture. This strategy is often used in infrastructure projects, and also in new product development projects in industries with extremely high research and development costs.

Mini Case 4.2 will show you the kind of risk responses an international consulting company has adopted in its off-shoring project.

Mini Case: 4.2: Establishing a Shared Service Centre in China

A global consulting company decided to centralize some of its finance and human resource related activities from its Asia-Pacific operations in China. An international project was initiated to move processes like time and expense management, accounts payable, and labour contracting from the South, South-East and East Asian subsidiaries to the People's Republic of China. Overall, 12 different countries were involved in the project.

What kinds of risks were anticipated? What came as a surprise?

1 Language barriers were seen as a risk and planned for: some employees who could speak both Mandarin and Japanese or Mandarin and Korean were hired in order to overcome communication barriers with the Japanese and Korean subsidiaries.

2 Insufficient language qualification of newly hired staff in China: this risk was also anticipated. Readily available templates, for all kinds of email communication, helped local employees with their jobs. Ninety per cent of the information exchange between the Shared Service Centre and its customers was in writing. Hence, templates were very useful.

3 Shared Service Centres only work if all the participating parties follow standardized processes. There was the anticipated risk that staff in the various Asia-Pacific subsidiaries would try to cling to their old habits and processes, avoiding the Shared Service Centre. This risk was counteracted by a very strict and tight software user regime. With the launch of the new SSC, user rights in the subsidiaries were strictly limited to force employees to follow the new, standardized processes.

4 Shortly before the launch of the new Shared Service Centre, a major issue appeared: the selected software system which should support the centre's activities could not handle East Asian language characters. This nearly turned out to be a 'show stopper'. Only at the last minute could software developers find a way round this problem.

Task

Identify which risk response strategies the company applied.

It is important to link the risk response plan to the overall project planning. Time and financial resources for contingencies have to be factored into the schedule and budget in case of risks occurring. This is called contingency reserves or buffers (see Chapter 5).

RISK MONITORING AND CONTROLLING

4.8 First of all, the risk register needs to be constantly cross-checked with the project status and current developments to find out which risks have occurred. Colour-coded risk prioritization facilitates this task. The risk register is a living document which means that it has to be updated. In case of the occurrence of non-anticipated risks, those have to be added to the register.

If risk occurs, the risk owner needs to take action and inform all relevant stakeholders about the risk occurrence. Periodically, the status of action implementation needs to be reviewed.

Risk occurrence will always have an impact on project management in terms of budget, time, quality, and scope. Therefore, the project manager needs to ensure excellent communication regarding the status of the risk.

Part of the monitoring process is the scanning of the project environment to detect risks (planned or new ones). The risk management loop closes here and starts anew with tools like PESTEL or others being used for environmental scanning.

As I have emphasized in Chapter 3, stakeholder management is especially important in international projects. Scope creep is a frequent source of risk. Therefore, both customers and the project scope need to be tightly managed as part of monitoring risks.

Last but not least, monitoring and controlling risks is closely linked to change management. Each change request potentially encompasses new risks. Hence, the risk management system needs to be linked to the project change management system.

After we have obtained an overview of the main tasks of the risk management cycle, I would like to draw your attention to one rather delicate area of risk that many international projects are faced with: corruption.

CORRUPTION AS A SPECIAL RISK IN INTERNATIONAL PROJECTS

4.9

Recent corporate scandals have highlighted the problem of corruption once again. Bribes are often paid to obtain lucrative contracts for international projects. The German conglomerate Siemens, for instance, allegedly paid 4.7 million Euros to government officials in Argentina up until 2003 (*The Economist* 2007d; Jennen, 2008). According to local laws in most industrialized and newly industrialized countries, the payment of bribes is illegal and entails high penalty payments or even imprisonment.

But what is corruption? The not-for-profit organization Transparency International (TI) defines corruption as 'the abuse of entrusted power for private gain' (TI, 2007). The so-called Corruption Perception Index (CPI) can identify those countries where the risk to be faced with corruption practices is highest. The index is published annually by Transparency International. The scores range from ten (no corruption) to zero (extremely corrupt). Transparency International considers a score of 5.0 as the borderline, distinguishing those countries that do or do not have a serious corruption problem (TI, 2007).

In the 2007 CPI index, Finland, Iceland, and New Zealand are perceived to be the world's least corrupt countries, and Haiti is perceived to be the most corrupt.

Table 4.3 provides the corruption perception index scores as of 2007 of the world's 20 biggest economies, in terms of GDP based on IMF figures as of 2006 (IMF, 2006). The ranking follows the size of the economy.

TABLE 4.3 Corruption Perception Index of Transparency International

Country Name	Rank in the CPI 2007	CPI Score (10 least corrupt, 0 most corrupt)
USA	18	7.3
Japan	18	7.3
Germany	14	7.9
People's Republic of China	72	3.6
United Kingdom	16	7.7
France	23	6.9
Italy	55	4.8
Canada	8	8.7
Spain	28	6.5
Brazil	80	3.5
Russia	147	2.1
South Korea	40	5.6
India	85	3.4
Mexico	72	3.6
Australia	9	8.7
Netherlands	7	8.9
Belgium	18	7.3
Turkey	58	4.6
Sweden	1	9.3
Switzerland	5	9.0

Source: Transparency International, 2008

This list indicates that the risk of facing corruption is greatest when undertaking international projects in or with Russia, and quite substantial in China, Brazil, India and Mexico. It depends on the organization planning the international project which risk response strategies it takes. According to the Global Corruption Report (TI, 2007), many Western companies have business codes explicitly forbidding the payment of bribes. Yet, many of those companies still pay bribes by using intermediaries or joint venture partners. The report also says that hardly any Brazilian or Hong Kong-based companies have such codes in place. Certainly, differences in national culture play a role when it comes to the assessment of corruption as a risk.

Mini Case 4.3 demonstrates how the project manager of a Japanese contractor dealt with this risk in Vietnam.

Mini Case 4.3: Bribery payments in Vietnam

As many public officials in Vietnam earn much less than people in the private sector, it is tempting for some individuals to earn some extra money from foreign companies.

In a rural area of Vietnam, a foreign consortium built a pipeline. For the pipeline construction, various parts had to be imported from abroad and also from Japan. The project manager in charge of these imports invested a lot of effort in getting the paperwork complete. As he took care of all paperwork personally and spent a lot of time on it, he was quite confident that all the rules and regulations of the Vietnamese authorities were being adhered to.

The project manager then got a bit nervous – tasks were piling up on his desk, and the customs officer came late to inspect goods at the dock which were urgently needed. After he had browsed through the paperwork, he said that the case was really complicated, and that the inspection could be speeded up by the payment of some additional fees. The project manager refused to do so and said: 'We have time – no problem.' Thanks to the fact that he was Japanese, he could hide his impatience well behind a poker face. The Vietnamese customs officer took nearly a whole day to open every single box painstakingly checking all the accompanying paperwork. However, he could not find any missing documents and eventually released the important components from the dock. The Japanese project manager was relieved. When the next delivery of components for the same project manager arrived, the local customs officer took less time to go through the paperwork and did not mention any additional fees again.

Question

What risks did the Japanese project manager have to consider?

Risk management requires rigour and discipline, not only in the planning phase, but also throughout the whole project. Risks will keep on changing, as well as the likelihood of risk occurrence. Risk management can be aided by a clear separation of the project into phases as outlined in Chapter 1. However, effective risk management is no guarantee for having everything under control. There is always the need to look for the unexpected, especially in international projects. Weick and Sutcliffe (2001) refer to such an attitude as 'mindfulness', which stands for a willingness to watch out for anything unusual and a certain level of sensitivity and capability to identify new dimensions in the context the project members are acting in. It is part of the culture of an organization or project (see Chapter 2).

MANAGING UNCERTAINTY

4.10

It looks like a dilemma: on the one hand, central co-ordination and tight control are the prerequisites for effective risk management; on the other hand, the organization's members should have sufficient autonomy and flexibility to sense the unexpected and cope with it (Williams, 1997). Let us have a look at an ideal project culture to support efficient uncertainty management before we get back to the apparent contradiction mentioned above.

PROJECT CULTURE

De Meyer et al. (2006: 7) suggest a culture of 'learning as you go'. The essence of this approach is that each new activity can provide new input and information, which can be used to modify the project plan in order to better adapt the project to its (changing) environment. This attitude is based on continuous learning and improvement as we shall discuss in more detail in Chapter 11. It requires project team members who are open-minded and skilled to observe an international environment. In light of an effi-cient culture for international projects described in section 2.10, the 'learning as you go' approach builds on information sharing, empowerment, and a strong adaptability towards new situations. The ideal project culture for international projects introduced in section 2.10 concurs with an ideal culture to cope well with uncertainty. Experience from the banking sector shows that a culture that seeks to deal positively with new emergent risks rather than apportion blame helps to identify risks at an early stage. Employees should be encouraged to flag up emerging issues even without having a lot of empirical data to back up their observations (Lucas, 2005).

Flexibility and open-mindedness are decisive elements of a 'risk culture'. To effectively deal with the complex environment and its uncertainties, members of international proj-ects need to have a wide array of competencies, perspectives and backgrounds. Heterogeneous project teams can build on rich and diverse experience and perspectives. Of course, diversity in teams does not automatically result in the effective management of emergent risks. Diverse teams have to be managed actively to avoid the adverse affects of diversity (see Chapters 8 and 10).

How can we reconcile the project culture supporting effective uncertainty manage-ment and the overall effective management of international projects on the one hand with the requirements of risk management on the other hand? For risks that can be anticipated, the risk management cycle with its firm methodology and clear activities needs to be the frame for all project members to act within. At the same time, this sys-tem needs to be open to new internal and external developments identified by autonomously thinking project members.

How can a project be best organized to support the management of uncertainty?

PROJECT STRUCTURE

The project manager needs to ensure that relevant members of the project are linked together in an effective way, enabling them to identify (emergent) risks and deal with them effectively. The prerequisite to choosing the right organizational outline is a detailed stakeholder analysis as outlined in Chapter 3.

Based on the assumption that a project is an open system (see Chapter 1), a structure needs to be built which allows for a continuous interaction with the (wider) context of the international project. This is the prerequisite to detect exogenous risks. With the right mindset as discussed under project culture, the project members will then be able to sense and analyse the emergent risk. Snapshot 4.3 gives a concrete example of a structure enabling constant interaction with the project's environment in the form of the customer.

SNAPSHOT 4.3

Organizing for uncertainty

For more complex projects, a US-based technology company has a structure called the 'Change Control Board'. The establishment of such a structure is laid out in the basic contract for the project (project proposal). Members of the Change Control Board are representatives of the contractor (the technology company) and the client.

This structure allows for a regular interaction between the project representatives and the project context, in this case the customer. It is a forum where emergent risks brought about by the changing ideas of the customer, for instance, can be detected.

All issues affecting specifications, schedule and cost must be raised with the Change Control Board and discussed. Basically, everything which differs from the initial statements of work needs to be approved by the Change Control Board.

The members of the Board are typically senior executives. They usually meet once a month.

In the case of strategically important international projects, the top management of the company additionally pushes for frequent face-to-face meetings between the members of the Change Control Board outside of the official meetings.

Snapshot 4.3 also shows the close interrelatedness of change and risks. As I have pointed out in section 4.8, changes in the project, for instance in the area of specifications, entail a new risk that typically was not planned for and hence needs to be included in the risk management process.

PROJECT CONTRACTS

Apart from an adequate project culture and structure, the right choice of project contract can help with uncertainty management. While Chapter 6 will touch on project contracts in general, here I would like to assume a risk management perspective only. High complexity of international projects often equals high uncertainty. The optimal choice of contract for uncertainty management depends on the locus of uncertainty control – if we can speak here of control at all. Does it lie with the contractor, or with both the contractor and the customer? If both parties need to co-operate to manage uncertainty, for instance with regard to information exchange, a cost-plus contract can be an adequate choice. Another option is an alliance type of contract. Here a gain share pot is created so that all parties involved in the project can share the accomplishments of improved uncertainty management – and other achievements contributing to the client's objectives. High uncertainty and risk usually require contracts which are far-sighted and deal with incompleteness in order to be sufficiently flexible to incorporate emergent risk (Turner, 2003).

Whatever contract form is selected, the contract needs to comprise a clause regarding the duty to inform the customer (whether internal or external) about the occurrence of emergent risks in a given time-frame, for instance within seven days. This reduces the likelihood of emergent risks turning into conflicts between the different stakeholders, as possible alternatives and reactions to the risk can be discussed between the customer and the project manager before the risk has an impact on the time or cost objectives of the project.

However, an adequate contract for managing uncertainty does not replace excellent stakeholder management. This is especially true for national cultures where contracts will play a less important role (see Chapter 3).

FLEXIBILITY IN PROJECT SYSTEMS

In addition to project culture, structure, and contracts that support managing uncertainty, an organization needs to allow for more flexibility in terms of product and process.

A modularization (see section 4.7), of both the product or service and the project processes, supports so-called late-locking, which means that parts of the project will only be decided on at a later stage, usually towards the end of the planning phase.

Milestones have to be able to be modified to reflect information or knowledge that has been acquired during the course of the project. Another area of process flexibility consists of deciding only on basic and essential procedures and policies in order not to suffocate teams with details and regulations. The international project has to be organized and managed in a way that allows for adaptations to local requirements.

TRADE-OFFS BETWEEN RISK AND UNCERTAINTY MANAGEMENT

The project manager needs to strike a balance between the requirements of risk management and the management of uncertainty. The cost and benefits of flexibility need to be traded off. It is often argued that flexibility decreases project efficiency. Indeed, flexibility can endanger deadlines or lead to cost overruns. Yet, as part of a risk culture, flexibility can lead to an increase in project effectiveness (Olsson, 2006). There can be outright contradictions between the right approach to manage risk which can be anticipated, and the right approach to manage emergent risk, for instance in the area of contract management. Anticipated risks can be managed by rigorous contracts. The same contracts, however, can hamper the project in the case of an emergent risk.

In the definition phase of the international project, the project manager has to decide which kind of risk will prevail. Based on this assessment, the manager of an international project needs to make a trade-off regarding those measures which will dominate. Certainly, the need for flexibility in international projects tends to be higher due to their complexity.

SUMMARY

The high complexity of international projects and tighter international laws and regulations regarding risk management and transparency require rigorous risk management. This can collide with the attitude of risk adversity prevailing in numerous national and organizational cultures. Risk can be divided into foreseeable risks and emergent risks. Risks that can be anticipated need to be managed following the four steps of the risk management cycle, namely, the identification of risks, assessment, planning, and controlling of risks. Based on the assessment of probability of risk occurrence as well as the impact on the project's objectives, risk response strategies need to be planned, such as avoidance, mitigation, acceptance, transfer, and absorption and pooling. Corruption is a common source of foreseeable risk in international projects. Uncertainty or emergent risks are best managed by establishing a risk culture, a project structure integrating the external project environment, contracts based on co-operation, and product and system flexibility through modularization and late-locking.

 KEY TERMS

Risk, uncertainty, emergent risk, known-unknown, unkown-unkown, internal risk, external risk, contingency planning, probability, impact, risk management cycle, risk register, qualitative risk analysis, quantitative risk analysis, risk trigger, risk owner, risk response, problem structuring method, risk avoidance, risk mitigation, risk acceptance, risk absorption, contingency reserve, buffer, corruption, risk culture, co-operation contract, modularization, late-locking.

REVIEW TASKS

Questions

1 How would you structure risks?
2 What is the correlation between risks and international project management?
3 What do you think of corruption as a special risk related to international projects? How would you deal with it?

EXERCISE 1

- Reflect about risk. Do you see it as something positive or negative?
- Look for the uncertainty avoidance scores for your national culture on Hofstede's webpage (www.geerthofstede.com).
- Does your personal attitude towards risk concur with the scores given? If not, what might be the reasons for the deviation?

EXERCISE 2

- Work in groups of five or six people.
- Consider the development of an electric car. Most of the world's automobile manufacturers initiate or have initiated projects in this area. You are free to choose the car manufacturer.
- Identify foreseeable risks and write these down as the first step towards a risk register.
- What could uncertainty or emergent risks for this project look like?
- Compare your results with the suggestions of the other groups.

CHAPTER END CASE: COST IN

A multinational headquartered in continental Europe had decided on the following strategy: its IT-services division located at headquarters serving domestic clients needed to become more cost efficient. Hence, management has embarked on a program to transfer the whole bundle of IT-services, including the support for the Enterprise Resource Planning system SAP R/3, to a low-wage country, namely India.

The areas which were part of this transfer were:

1 First level support for SAP R/3 users (employees of external customers): When an SAP user encounters a problem with the system, they can call the helpdesk for support. The helpdesk usually issues a so-called ticket registering the call and describing the issue. As quickly as possible, the user will receive feedback on the solution to the problem.
2 Second level support for SAP R/3: If the problem the user has encountered is more complicated to solve, the ticket is passed on to the second level support people who are responsible for fixing the problem as soon as possible. They inform first level support of their solution, and first level support gives feedback to the customer about the problem resolution.

In an attempt to reduce fixed costs quickly, it was decided to transfer both levels of support from headquarters to the wholly owned subsidiary in India. This was done in a series of international projects which were all part of the overall cost reduction program.

Due to the fact that the customers in continental Europe wanted to continue to talk to the SAP support in their local language, the Indian subsidiary had the task of recruiting employees who had the required language competencies. The project managers of the sub-projects were assured by the Indian subsidiary that feasibility in terms of personnel was given: employees with the right skills, including language skills, were available.

The transfer of the support activities was started. Each manager of a sub-project had the target of moving the activities and tasks within eight months to India. The continental European employees were transferred to a domestic spin-off of the multinational with a 16 per cent lower salary and the prospect of being laid off after the transfer completion. The time estimate for the complete transfer was two to three years.

After a while, customers started to call staff at the new spin-off in Europe, complaining about the support they had received from India:

1 One client got really impatient with the fact that his employees first had to spell their names up to ten times before they were allowed to describe the problem. The Indian counterparts frequently could not understand them. This, however, was a mutual problem, as the customers also had difficulties understanding the Indian helpdesk people.
2 Another corporate customer said that his employees were receiving tickets which could not be understood at all. Translated back to English it was something like:

  'Acknowledging running figures on the screen'

3 The next company complained about a lack of support from India. They had the impression that they were not taken seriously by the Indian helpdesk. In a very friendly manner, the helpdesk people said: 'Yes, Madam, yes, Sir. … This is very unfortunate. Does the system work now? … No, I hope you are ok. Yes, we certainly will take care of it …'

Many times, however, they never got any feedback as to whether the problem had been resolved or not. There were also strong doubts regarding the technical capability of the Indian helpdesk. Some problems were not resolved at all, or resolved very late. The process usually needed to be followed up by the customer which was a nuisance.

4 Yet another client pointed out that the helpdesk came back a couple of times to ask for screenshots. This was perceived as a waste of time and not the usual procedure. Moreover, the request for screenshots frequently only came after one or two days, leaving the users with a dysfunctional system in the meantime.

The employees at the spin-off in Western Europe who were not yet laid off were unhappy, as they sometimes had to work 14 hours a day to fix the problems their 12 Indian colleagues could not get to grips with. In addition, they received all the customer complaints.

After the first year, management was alarmed due to the fact that some corporate clients had changed their supplier for IT-support. The program manager figured out that more training for the Indian staff was needed. Therefore, training programs for the Indian staff were arranged, mainly in Continental Europe. For two months, the Indian employees were trained in application management, and the different modules of SAP. However, the effect of the trainings was not as positive as expected. A consultant found out only by coincidence that many of the Indian trainees did not sufficiently understand the English spoken by the Western European trainers with their thick local accents. In order not to cause any embarrassment, no feedback on this matter was provided by the Indian subsidiary. In only one sub-project, this resulted in an additional training cost of roughly 81,600 Euros. Of course, this was a comparably small amount compared to the loss of a whole range of customers. Still, it was an unbudgeted, additional cost.

The program manager had to realize that more non-budgeted costs needed to be accounted for:

- Due to the fact that the fluctuation in the Indian support teams was at about 20 per cent per annum, training measures needed to be carried out on a continuous basis.
- The salary of the Indian support staff had to be increased by an average of 18 per cent annually in order to attract any people at all and to retain staff for at least one or two years.
- Training in the local language of the European headquarters had to be carried out, as hardly any personnel could be found who possessed adequate language skills.
- More staff from headquarters needed to be sent to the Indian subsidiary in order to facilitate the knowledge transfer, but also in order to bolster up capacities in India. Due to the economic boom, it turned out to be increasingly difficult to hire the necessary number of people there.

Another headache was security. It happened that some temporary staff was 'smuggled' into the Indian subsidiary in order to help out without undergoing the proper procedures. They were also granted access to the intranet and other electronic data of the company. The problem was uncovered by a customer in Europe who had insisted that only internal staff would support his company. The whole incident revealed security gaps for the multinational as a whole. In addition, passwords were shared and passed on within the Indian subsidiary, resulting in a loss of transparency and control regarding who was responsible for which changes in the SAP system. This posed a threat to quality.

Having laid off most of the staff at home, the multinational had difficulties taking back responsibilities and tasks from the Indian subsidiary. There were no short-term fixes to the above mentioned problems either. The whole program looked to be doomed.

What had they done wrong? After all, other multinationals, mainly US- or UK-based, have transferred parts of their business successfully to India.

Question and task

1 What risks can you identify?
2 Create a risk register of this project in the third stage of the risk management process (a risk register with a classification of risks, risk triggers, assumptions, risk owners, and contingency plans). Note: For some categories, there is no information available or only limited information.

FURTHER READING

Chapman, Chris and Ward, Stephen (2002) *Managing Project Risk and Uncertainty: A Constructively Simple Approach to Decision Making*. Chichester: John Wiley & Sons. (Project and risk management are put into a broader perspective, including to some extent strategic and operational management. Emphasis is laid on marketing, financial, contracting, and safety management, aspects which have not been explored in detail in this chapter.)

Cooper, D.F. Grey, S. Raymond, G. and Walker, P. (2005) *Project Risk Management Guidelines: Managing Risk in Large Projects and Complex Procurements*. Chichester: John Wiley & Sons. (For quantitative risk analysis refer to Part III.)

Hillson, David (2004) *Effective Opportunity Management for Projects: Exploiting Positive Risk*. New York/Basel: Marcel Dekker. (Especially Part II which provides a good introduction into managing risk as an opportunity which is not explored in detail in this book.)

PLANNING INTERNATIONAL PROJECTS IN TERMS OF TIME, COST AND QUALITY

5

LEARNING OBJECTIVES

After studying this chapter, you will be able to:

- discuss the planning cycle for an international project

- understand the cultural impact on planning

- conceive methods to estimate time duration and sequencing activities

- turn a Work Breakdown Structure into an Activity on the Arrow Network Diagram

- create a Gantt chart, and a resource loaded Gantt chart

- describe the main relevant cost components and their specifics in international projects

- create a cumulative budget spreadsheet

- elucidate the particularities of planning for quality in international projects.

INTRODUCTION

5.1 As the famous Greek philosopher Aristotle put it: 'Well begun is half done.' Although he did not have a project in mind, this saying is very true for a project which needs to be thought through and structured, before it can be implemented. In fact, many projects face difficulties because of poor planning at the beginning. After the organization has decided on the realization of a project in the initiating phase, it has to work on more details to prepare for project implementation. This happens in the second phase of the project management life cycle, the so-called planning phase. It is this phase that we will discuss in this chapter. Rough estimates and the Work Breakdown Structure elaborated on during the initiating phase will be worked out in more detail in the planning phase. At the end of the planning phase we have the project management plan or Master Plan, which is a deliverable, along with the identification of resources required for the implementation of the project.

Planning reduces uncertainty and brings structure to chaos. However, in the fast changing environment which many international projects face, planning is difficult and needs to be revised constantly in light of multiple changes. Yet, a starting point which is based on estimates that come close to reality is important. In this chapter, I will introduce selected basic tools and techniques to plan time, cost, and quality. I will explain the interdependence between scheduling and resource planning as well as scheduling and budgeting. However, I cannot provide a comprehensive overview of planning tools and techniques in general due to space constraints. As the focus of this book rests on the particularities of international projects, I will explain the cultural impact on the attitude towards planning, on the concept of time and the understanding of quality. Apart from cultural differences, I will discuss other particularities of international projects relevant in the planning phase such as differences in the qualification levels of project staff, heterogeneity in labour laws and salaries, and variations in holiday entitlements. We will learn about specific elements of cost components in international projects. Finally, I will wrap up this chapter with a discussion of different understandings of quality depending on the stakeholders involved, different quality standards in different countries, and the importance of self-explanatory specification sheets.

THE PLANNING PROCESS

5.2 The degree of detail necessary for planning a project depends on its nature, complexity, and stakeholder expectations. As pointed out above, planning is not a one time event. Estimating time and cost is a repetitive task due to changes in the environment and unknown input.

You may remember the characteristics of a project, one of them being 'uniqueness'. With regard to planning this means dealing with unknown information. The greater the uncertainty, or 'unknown-unknowns' as introduced in Chapter 4, planners need to factor sufficient contingencies or buffers into the estimates. They should always be sceptical about being too optimistic on technical assumptions. Experience shows that nearly all projects will have technical glitches. Contingency reserves, however, may not exceed the time and resource constraints linked to the overall project goal.

The scheduling, staffing, and budgeting process as well as the quality planning process need to fulfil efficiency requirements within the magical triangle as introduced in Chapter 1: projects need to be delivered on time, within budget and to scope with a certain quality level. The challenge for planning is to:

- minimize the project duration
- minimize the resource availability cost
- maximize quality.

Depending on the nature of the project, priorities as to what effort is more important might differ. Although each project is unique and requires its own estimates, the planning process is usually facilitated by company procedures, templates and checklists rendering the estimates of different parts of the organization more consistent and realistic, at least in organizations with a higher maturity level regarding project management (see Chapter 2).

Figure 5.1 provides you with an overview of the planning process which I will discuss in more detail in the following sections of this chapter. Please note that I will not explain all the tools and techniques mentioned in the chart. I would like to refer the interested reader to the further reading at the end of this chapter.

In the last couple of years, tremendous progress has been made to support the whole range of planning activities with integrated Information Management tools. As most of them are industry specific, they will not be introduced in this book in detail (see further reading). The technical progress, however, should not hide the fact that systems need to be fed with data. The project team has to be prepared to collect data actively and accurately, and to share and update it. Moreover, not all relevant data are easily accessible and quantifiable, especially in international projects. Information resides with multiple stakeholders who need to be identified and managed properly (see Chapter 3). Information Systems do save time. They enable project managers to simulate complicated products requiring integrated system engineering. However, they do not replace the other skills necessary for international projects which will usually focus more on the soft side of project management. The human actors in a project management context remain of critical importance.

CULTURAL IMPACT ON PLANNING

5.3

In modern project management, planning plays a vital role. The reader should keep in mind, though, that different national cultures or sub-cultures may have a different attitude towards the impact human plans can have. Typically, national cultures with an external orientation towards nature and a past or present orientation (see Chapter 3) tend to see plans as limited in their effectiveness because of higher forces like destiny or God(s) that have outlined the course of life in advance. Hence, detailed planning may be regarded as a waste of time or even managerial hubris. In Thailand, there is an often-shared joke among project members: 'If you take the word planning, it contains the words "plan" and "ning". "Plan" means "plan", ok, but "ning" in Thai means: "Stand still, don't move." So that is very funny for the Thai, because if Western people talk about planning, for us it sounds like "make a plan and stand still"' (Rathje, 2004: 127).

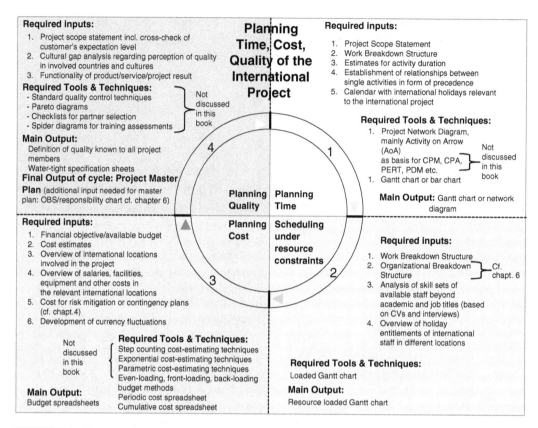

FIGURE 5.1 The planning process for an international project

This joke exemplifies the doubts Thai people tend to have regarding detailed planning which is often perceived as insufficiently flexible.

Apart from religion and philosophy, planning is influenced by the physical environment, the systems within which planning takes place. Plans only make sense in an environment which is predictable and transparent. Hence, plans traditionally bear more importance in societies with a well-structured public infrastructure and an infrequent occurrence of natural disasters. This would be the case in the USA (although the number of natural disasters seems to have increased in the last few decades), some East Asian countries or in some European countries. The frequent occurrence of unforeseeable events, like strikes or a force majeure of any kind, renders plans useless. People need to rely on improvisation instead. A reluctance to spend much time on planning on the one hand, and great resourcefulness in coming up with ad hoc solutions on the other, can be observed in India, but also in countries like Italy. Figure 5.2 provides you with a systematic overview of these cultural dimensions and how they can affect the attitude of an individual regarding planning.

I have to state, however, that these are general impacts that culture may have on planning. Figure 5.1 only reminds the project manager that the inclination towards detailed planning among project stakeholders might differ. These differences, in turn, need to be included in the overall planning which is essential in international projects due to their complexity and diversity.

| Equality | Project managers who are rather hierarchy-oriented will tend to create a plan on their own. More equality-oriented PMs will tend to involve their team. | Hierarchy |

| Embracing Risk | Project managers and members who are afraid of risk tend to put more effort into planning details than risk embracing project managers and teams. | Avoiding Risk |

| Universal | Project managers and other stakeholders with a universal background tend to create a Master Plan which is to be applied at all sites and to situations. Circumstantial people tend to stick to high-level planning with flexibility. | Circumstantial |

| Task | Project managers and other stakeholders who are task-oriented tend to create Work Breakdown Structures and To-Do lists. Relationship-oriented individuals tend to spend much more time on networking with main stakeholders than on creating a plan. | Relationship |

| Achievement | Project managers who are more achievement-oriented tend to 'follow the textbook' in order to obtain the given targets. Project managers and members with a stronger status orientation might have a separate agenda partially contradictory to the project goal. | Standing/Status |

| Sequential | Project managers and members with a sequential approach tend to follow the planning process, with the creation of estimates of time, cost, and links to resource availability. People from synchronic cultures may put less effort into sequencing. | Synchronic |

| Theoretical | Project managers and members who are more oriented towards theory tend to attach more importance and put more effort into planning. People from pragmatic cultures may tend to focus on learning by doing and spend less time on the creation of plans. | Pragmatic |

FIGURE 5.2 Cultural dimensions and their impact on planning

SCHEDULING

5.4 Let us now move towards the first area of planning that touches on the activities which will find out how much time the project will take. For this purpose, the project manager and his or her team need to go through each activity identified in the Work Breakdown Structure, to estimate how long the activity will take, and to think through the logical order of those activities in order to come up with a plan at the end. This requires a certain attitude towards time as we will learn below.

THE CONCEPT OF TIME

In general, the discipline of project management sees time as a measurable, scarce resource. As briefly explained in Chapter 3, not all cultures share this approach towards time. Although it has become widely used and adopted since the introduction of industrialization, not only in established industrialized countries but also in newly industrialized countries and emerging markets, there are societies which do not or only partially share those views. Time can also be regarded as something flowing, indefinite, and unimportant.

Although modern project management methodology as outlined in this book is spreading internationally, there are still differences in the application of the approach: for instance, schedules might be regarded as not binding which will result in project delays.

TIME PLANNING TOOLS AND TECHNIQUES

Yet, there are no alternatives to thorough planning. Hence, the project manager and his or her team will need to be familiar with adequate techniques.

The purpose of scheduling is to aid project implementation in order to optimize efficiency. This can be reached through the minimization of the overall project duration. Time planning involves an estimation of the durations of activities as well as the sequencing of project activities. In order to plan activities in a time-efficient way, they need to be executed in a logical order. This also means that interdependencies between various activities need to be highlighted. Under resource constraints, activities also need be prioritized.

Having said this, the first important step in scheduling is to look at all activities that are part of the project (cf. WBS) and estimate their durations.

ESTIMATING ACTIVITY DURATIONS

The project manager and the team need to put forward realistic time estimates for every activity in an international project. The activity duration is typically expressed in units such as working days, hours or weeks. Nowadays, computer-aided models using fuzzy logic can support the project manager and his or her team with estimation efforts.

Estimating activity durations depends on the availability of resources. Usually, tradeoffs need to be made (Demeulemeester and Herroelen, 2002):

1 **Time versus resource trade-off**: An activity estimated with an effort of 48 person-hours can take eight hours using six workers, 12 hours using four workers, 24 hours using two workers, etc.
2 **Resource versus resource trade-off**: An activity can be performed within four hours by two experienced workers, or by one experienced worker together with two trainees.
3 **Time versus cost trade-off**: A mail package may need three days to be delivered by normal mail for five Euros, or one day when delivered by express mail for 20 Euros.

It is the decision of the project manager whether to prioritize time, quality, or other resources depending on the project's scope and stakeholders' expectations.

THE NETWORK DIAGRAM

After we have estimated the activity durations, we need to put them into a logical order. Which one has to precede another one? Are the activities dependent on each other, or can they be done in parallel? The task is to put all the activities in relation to each other in the form of a network. To begin with, this is done without considering the availability of resources.

In this book, I will only focus on one of the most widely used techniques, the Activity on Arrow (AoA) tool, also known as Activity-on-Arc. Its name stems from the fact that each activity is represented by an arrow, and each milestone or event by an activity box or node. The event at the end of the activity arrow represents the start of the activity, and the event at the head of the arrow represents the completion of that activity. The inter-dependencies between activities are marked by arrows.

An example of a simple network diagram with the name of the activities or events and their duration in days is shown in Figure 5.3. It was created for a project on the process integration of different organizational entities after a cross-border merger.

In order to ensure transparency, the name of each activity should equal the activity name in the Work Breakdown Structure.

As you can see in Figure 5.3, the arrows connect the different activities with each other. Among the basic types of relationships between activities, the following three are relevant in a network diagram (Demeulemeester and Herroelen, 2002):

1 **End-to-Start**: Activity A (for instance, the decision on new, optimized processes) has to finish before activity B (for instance, the specification of a new information system) gets permission to start. This is the typical relationship in a network diagram.
2 **Start-to-Start**: Once activity A (for instance, designing new procurement processes) has started, activity B (for instance, general process training) can also start. Both activities are then running in parallel for most of the time.
3 **End-to-End**: The same is true for end-to-end, where activity A (for instance, the definition of new processes) must finish before activity B (for instance, feeding the newly created intranet with the new processes) can finish.

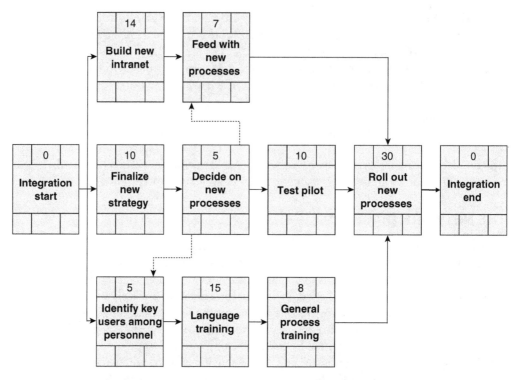

FIGURE 5.3 Example of a simple network diagram

Figure 5.4 illustrates the three relevant types of activity interconnection in network diagrams.

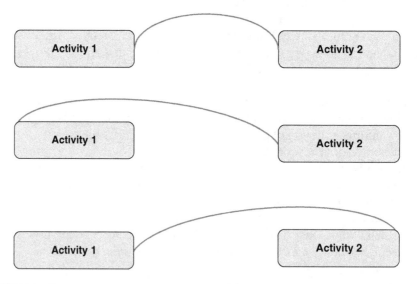

FIGURE 5.4 Three main types of activity relationship

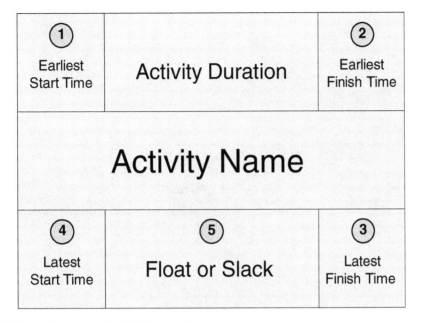

FIGURE 5.5 Structure of activity box

The network diagram must not contain cycles. It may also have only one initial starting node and one ending node. In order to fulfil these requirements for visualization, it might be necessary to introduce so called 'dummy-activities' which do not consume resources or time. A dummy activity also can be used to clarify the precedence between several parallel activity strings. In Figure 5.3 we have two dummy activities between the activity 'Decide on new processes' and 'Feed intranet with new processes' as well as between 'Decide on new processes' and 'Identify key personnel'. Those two dummy activities indicate that the activity 'Decide on new processes' needs to be finished before the other two activities can start (precedence relationship). We have to consider those relationships in the duration calculation that I will now explain.

In Figure 5.3 you see some empty fields in the activity boxes or nodes. During the process of creating the diagram, they will be filled with the following information as depicted in Figure 5.5:

1 Earliest Start Time of the activity (EST)
2 Earliest Finish Time of the activity (EFT)
3 Latest Finish Time of the activity (LFT)
4 Latest Start Time of the activity (LST)
5 Float or slack, which is basically the buffer time you can use for other activities.

How is this information obtained? The project manager and his or her team will first go through the diagram from left to right, i.e. from start to end. The purpose of the exercise is to come up with the earliest time when the project can be finished.

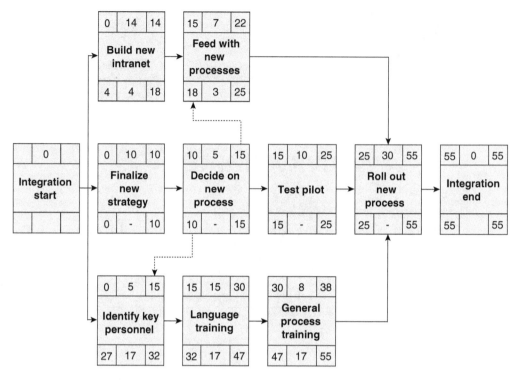

FIGURE 5.6 Complete activity on arrow network

For each activity, the earliest start time (EST) and the earliest finish time (EFT) will be decided. The EST for the first activity is zero. The EFT for an activity is always calculated by adding the duration to its EST. The EST for all remaining activities is the same as the EFT of its immediate predecessor. If there are several predecessors, the EST is taken from the path having the highest EFT. The EFT of the last activity is the expected duration of the project.

At this point the project manager has to identify both the critical activities and the float of non-critical activities. For this purpose, the project manager and team members have to go backwards through the network diagram establishing the latest finish time (LFT) and the latest start time (LST). The LFT of the last activity is the same as the expected project duration. The LST is always calculated by subtracting its duration from its LFT. In case one activity has several immediate successors, the LFT is taken from the path having the numerically lowest LST.

Figure 5.6 illustrates the entire calculation process. Its basis is Figure 5.3 with a calculated EST, EFT, LFT, LST and float where applicable.

The activities leading to the earliest finish time without any float or slack which have the longest duration in sum build the so-called critical path. In a network diagram this can also be indicated by bold arrows. In other words, the critical path reflects the expected duration of the project. For the manager of the international project, it is of utmost importance to make sure that the activities on the critical path are conducted on time to ensure the on-time delivery of the overall project. The activities which are not on the critical path are less time-critical.

Network diagrams can offer a good illustration of all activities with the right sequence and indication of inter-dependencies. They can also support a detailed calculation of activity duration with the earliest and latest event times. A network diagram can be used to calculate the earliest possible completion date for the project. Moreover, it offers a good basis for project control as it can indicate the most critical tasks (see Chapter 7).

Over various decades, many techniques to illustrate those networks of activities in a project have been developed, among them the Critical Path Method (CPM) and the Program or Project Evaluation and Review Technique (PERT). The network diagrams are especially suitable for complex and long-term projects with many inter-dependencies and many stakeholders, which is often the case in international infrastructure or for new product development projects in a multinational corporation.

GANTT CHARTS

Another scheduling technique is the so-called Gantt chart introduced in Chapter 1. As this form of illustration is easier to create and interpret than network diagrams, it has very widespread use for all kind of international projects. So how does it work?

Activities are arranged from top to bottom. The time scale is horizontal. The activities are depicted by a series of horizontal lines or bars with one for each activity. The length of each of these bars is proportional to the time needed to complete the activity that it represents. Critical activities can be highlighted (e.g. bold bars) thus indicating the overall project duration. This allows us to see the critical path described above.

Gantt charts can be extended to show additional information as float which could be reflected in dotted float envelopes. Arrows can be added to indicate inter-dependencies between certain activities. However, the more complex the project gets, the more confusing the Gantt chart becomes with all the necessary additional information included. In this case, a network diagram may be recommended.

In Snapshot 5.1, you can see a typical example of a Gantt chart related to the 'Spree' Project by Rolls-Royce which we have discussed in previous chapters.

SNAPSHOT 5.1

R&D and production transfer at Rolls-Royce (Part 4)

Project 'Spree' was targeted to be completed within 12 months. The team met the schedule. In order to transfer the R&D and production of one type of aircraft engine between two different subsidiaries of one, MNC, the following efforts were necessary:

- 7,000 parts were created in the SAP-system of the German subsidiary
- 400 modifications of the parts lists were uploaded in the ERP system and cross-checked
- contracts with 120 suppliers were modified

(Cont'd)

- 8,000 drawings were scanned, revised and uploaded into the system
- Eight huge files of assembly manuals were translated from English into German.

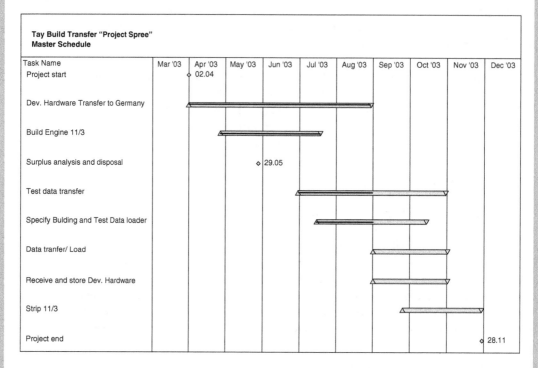

FIGURE SNAPSHOT 5.1 Gantt chart

Source: Adapted from Blasig (2005)

Project management software packages can easily convert network diagrams into Gantt charts and vice versa. This software usually also provides the functionality of summarizing activities to a high level for the Work Breakdown Structure. Thus, the technique can also be used as a reporting tool for different stakeholders, as well as a controlling tool for project members and managers (see Chapter 7). Snapshot 5.2 depicts a very high level Gantt chart referring to the schedule for the integration of an acquisition.

SNAPSHOT 5.2

Planning the integration of an acquired bank

In October 2005, the Austrian bank Raiffeisen International (cf. Chapter 2) acquired the Ukrainian Bank Aval. As of March 2007, the new Raiffeisen Bank Aval is the second biggest bank in the Ukraine with total assets of 4.3 billion Euros, 1,312 branches and 4.1 million customers.

The integration of Bank Aval into the operations of Raiffeisen International was planned based on the following high-level Gantt-chart:

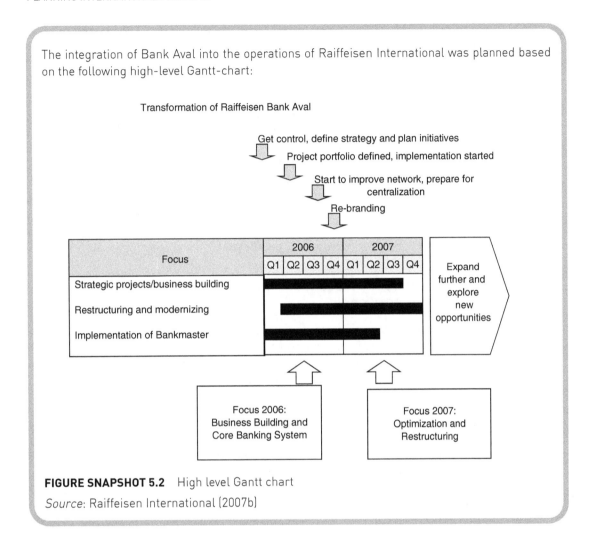

FIGURE SNAPSHOT 5.2   High level Gantt chart

Source: Raiffeisen International (2007b)

With the Activity on Arrow network diagram and the Gantt chart, we have discussed the two most widely used scheduling methods in project planning. Let us now turn to the specifics that need to be considered when scheduling international projects.

FACTORS INFLUENCING THE SCHEDULING OF AN INTERNATIONAL PROJECT

Extra time for co-ordination, communication and training

The more complex a project becomes, the more time needs to be planned in for communication and co-ordination. For instance, the project should start with a meeting between the sponsor and the international project manager where the scope needs to be discussed very thoroughly in order to clarify the expectations and demands of the customer. Such a meeting is also necessary for standard projects.

However, this usually takes less time. As we are talking days, not hours, this will have an impact on planning. Moreover, scope meetings with customers need to be repeated in order to constantly cross-check expectations.

In many relationship-oriented cultures, like Brazil, Russia, India, or China, co-ordination and information about the project may involve many more stakeholders than in task-oriented cultures. Those people might not be directly responsible or involved in the project, but can still be highly influential on the project result. Therefore, local team-leaders should be included in the scheduling process, or at least in the rough milestone planning to ensure a realistic approach and a benefit from local expertise.

When newly hired employees or employees with different educational backgrounds are part of the project, time needs to be planned to train them. Time also needs to be planned for the trainers who cannot work on the same project at the same time. Experience shows that more people need to be trained in international projects because more knowledge is required from the project members and users.

Additional time for local adaptations (of processes, products, or services)

Local sites involved in the international project may have different legal requirements that will need to be taken into account. Products or services sold internationally have to meet local customers' tastes and comply with local regulations. Adaptations to local conditions and demands need time.

Extra time for team building activities

Davison and Ward (1999) state that if it takes you one month to establish a national team, it takes three months to set up an international team. Two hundred per cent more time than in standard projects is also needed to prepare for important meetings, like milestone reviews. The reason for this much longer preparation duration lies in the complexity and diversity of the international project and the international team.

Consideration of additional public holidays and vacation time

Moreover, the planners need to pay attention to different public and religious holidays. It is advisable to include all relevant holidays of the participating stakeholders in the schedule. The culture gap analysis and the stakeholder matrix discussed in Chapter 3 can help with this exercise. On the companion website, the reader will find a useful link to all international public holidays.

Consideration of different calendars and auspicious days

Most Western countries will base their schedules and timing on the gregorian calendar. A project manager however should also be aware of the importance of the lunar

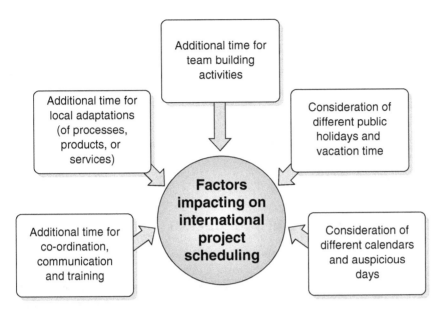

FIGURE 5.7 Factors impacting on international project scheduling

calendar in many cultures, for instance to determine the Islamic month of fasting, Ramadan, or the festival of the New Year in Chinese societies.

In addition, many cultures such as Indian or Chinese regional culture can display a high degree of superstition that will extend to certain days that are considered to be inauspicious. According to Ramaprasad and Prakash (2003), in construction projects Indian workers from certain rural areas will not start important work on a Tuesday. Both Indians and Chinese will consult astrologists to determine lucky days for important events. Project managers in those countries should be aware of the heavy influence of astrology. In China, they should avoid planning important milestones like the start of a project on dates with a 'four' in them, because 'four' is regarded an inauspicious number due to the homonym with death.

Figure 5.7 summarizes the factors that need to be considered when scheduling an international project.

Mini Case 5.1: Delay in software roll out

An Enterprise Resource Planning System project was initiated and planned in the US headquarters. The new ERP system was to be rolled out in international subsidiaries, for instance in the company's factories in France. Much to the annoyance of the project manager, an overall delay of 12 months occurred with the French roll out due to the following problems:

Mini Case

1   Local factories in France had additional requirements for the ERP system. Some of these factories also produced for the defence sector. Hence, strict specifications and security rules applied to those sites.

2   The requirements among the local factories in France differed because the sites manufactured a variety of products. Some factories stored chemicals which needed to be treated away from other materials. Expiry dates needed to be entered into the system. Special disposal rules also had to be followed.

Question

What could the project manager have done to avoid the delay?

TECHNICAL SUPPORT FOR SCHEDULING

Most companies will use Microsoft Project (MS Project) for scheduling projects. For complex international projects in the construction industry, military, software development, etc., more powerful and specific software tools are necessary. Construction projects, for instance, consist of 4,000 to 10,000 planning items which cannot be managed any more by using standard and cheaper software like MS Project. For complex projects, software like PRIMAVERA is frequently used. Besides scheduling and planning, this entails functionalities that can help enterprises to analyse the possible outcomes of ongoing projects, and simulate upcoming risks. PRIMAVERA is used by market leaders in the industry, for instance by General Electric and Siemens.

Beyond a straightforward functionality, globally widespread software has the advantage of serving as a common language between the project owner and contractor or between subcontractors in the case of international consortia.

Let us now broaden the planning task to go beyond mere time planning and to include resources in the planning process.

ADDING RESOURCES TO SCHEDULING

5.5
So far, we have not considered resource allocation as part of the scheduling process. We have only looked at the duration and logical relationship between the activities, and not at the people who have to carry out these activities.

QUANTITATIVE ASPECTS

The project manager needs to make sure that sufficient people are available to carry out the tasks depicted in the WBS. If resources are overcommitted, it is the responsibility of the project manager (Knutson, 2001) to:

Task Name	12	14	16	18	20	22	24	26	28	30	32	34	36	38	40	42	44	46	48	50	52
Project start		◇ 02.04																			
Dev. Hardware Transfer to Germany	△													▽ TL[10%]							
Build Engine 11/3				△					▽ TL[40%]												
Surplus analysis and disposal						◇ 29.05															
Test data transfer								△								▽ TL[50%]					
Specify Bulding and Test Data loader										△					▽ TL[50%]						
Data transfer/ Load													△			▽ TL[10%]					
Receive and store Dev. Hardware													△			▽ TL[10%]					
Strip 11/3														△				▽ TL[10%]			

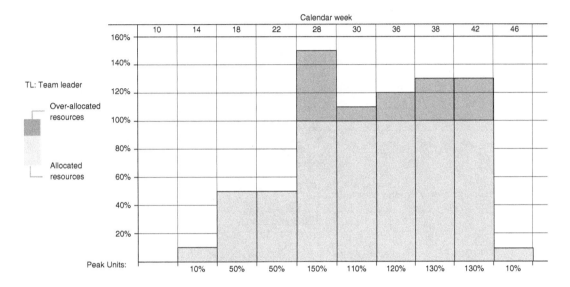

FIGURE 5.8   Resource loaded Gantt chart

- re-schedule tasks
- re-prioritize tasks
- negotiate for additional time or resources
- reduce the scope of the project.

On the basis of previously created schedules, planning the staffing of a project will involve the following main activities:

1 Determining whether the team members are 100 per cent dedicated to the project, and if not, how many per cent each team member can dedicate to given tasks. To be as realistic as possible, this step should include a self-assessment by each project member. However, the results of such self-assessment need to be interpreted with cultural differences in mind. Figure 5.11 shows how a resource can be added to the various activities planned in the Gantt chart, based on parts of the Spree-Project schedule

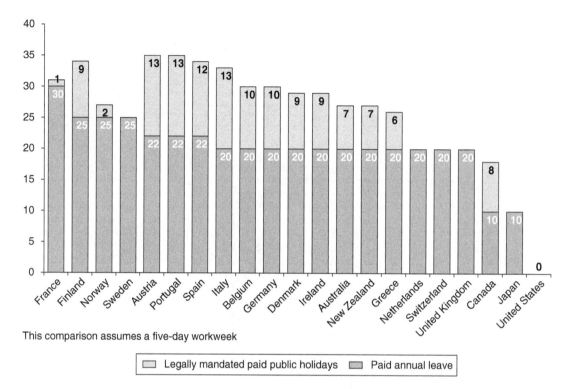

This comparison assumes a five-day workweek

☐ Legally mandated paid public holidays ▨ Paid annual leave

FIGURE 5.9 Paid annual leave and paid public holidays in OECD nations in working days
Source: Ray and Schmitt (2007)

(snapshot 5.1). An assessment for the imaginary team leader is made for each time window. This is the period of time during which no new tasks will start or end.

2 In case of over-commitment by any project member, for example, it is noted that the team leader is over-committed in some time windows, so the project manager needs to perform so-called resource levelling. The options, such as extending the duration of the task if the task has some float, or adding on resources, are listed above.

Looking at the numbers, however, should not defer the project manager from taking into account those individuals who are behind the numbers. In other words, the project manager has also to consider the availability and quality of people. Availability is influenced by labour laws in the respective countries the international project is involved in. The project manager has to keep in mind that different countries will have different labour laws, especially regarding vacations as you can see in Figure 5.9. In Brazil, the United Arab Emirates and Norway, each employee is entitled to six weeks' holidays, whereas it is only eight days in Mexico. Of course, these numbers reflect the minimum legal requirements and not necessarily the actual number of days that organizations will voluntarily grant their employees. In addition to paid holiday entitlements, the minimum number of legal public holidays needs to be taken into account.

Beyond human resources, general resources like materials and equipment could cause potential issues for scheduling the international project. Typically, materials or equipment will need to be exported to international sites. This requires export codes like HTS (USA) or TARIC (EU) and export licences. It can take time to get the necessary codes and licences. The project manager also needs to think about export bans for certain countries which could cause major delays or even put the project on hold.

QUALITATIVE ASPECTS

Availability of qualified staff

The project manager needs to pay special attention to this aspect. The staff or at least key persons in the international project will have to be able to speak the common project language. You cannot take this for granted in every country. Moreover, the content of academic qualifications will differ from country to country. An engineering graduate from an Indian university might have obtained different knowledge from an engineering graduate in Canada. Hence, comparability is not necessarily a given. The project manager or planner needs to make an effort to determine which qualifications he or she needs. He or she then has to select project members carefully according to those qualifications. I will discuss more details of this aspect related to quality management in section 5.7.

Limited mobility and flexibility of employees

Even if qualified staff are available, the project manager has to consider whether these are located in the right places. Is this engineer willing to move to a foreign subsidiary because she is needed there? Not necessarily. Here is one example from Europe. Due to the increasing integration of tax regulations in Europe, certain practices have changed over time. Employees who are transferred temporarily to non-headquarters subsidiaries outside the domestic market, but are still in Europe, have to be given the status of a local subsidiary employee. The employee will then be subject to the local tax laws and to the general local jurisdiction. This move can thus entail a high degree of uncertainty for the person involved. If the contract with her domestic company is replaced by a contract with the foreign subsidiary – what will happen after the duration of the project? A non-European project manager especially needs to keep in mind that employees in countries or regions with strong labour laws, like Scandinavia, France, the Benelux, Germany, and Italy, cannot be ordered to relocate with the same ease as others elsewhere.

Task allocation to minimize interfaces

Many international projects are very complex. Hence, planning should also aim at reducing this complexity, rendering the project more manageable. If possible, a project manager should allocate the different sets of tasks in a way that people at the same geographical location can work together. Experience shows that a reduction of interfaces across different sites, i.e. fewer virtual teams, can lead to faster results. This is closely linked to the organization of the project that we will discuss in Chapter 6.

Time planning, including the consideration of resource availability, is a very important task in international project management. This is also reflected in the cost occurring in case of flawed time planning. In many industries, high penalties may be due when delays happen. In the automotive industry, for instance, a delay in a production start by one week will usually cost the supplier who caused it approximately 200,000–300,000 US$. This is unplanned cost not included in the cost estimates which I will explore in more detail in the following section.

PLANNING COST IN THE PROJECT BUDGET

5.6 Any international project is determined by the limited amount of money that it has at its disposal. Some projects will have more financial resources available than others, like disaster relief projects in Sri Lanka after the tsunami in 2004. Typically, however, financial resources will be scarce, and cost will need to be minimized.

Cost planning works in a similar way to scheduling. Cost needs to be estimated and controlled in a budget. The estimates can be based on historical data like bills of materials of similar products, or quotations and prices. The budget is the financial plan to allocate resources to project activities. In other words, the project budget is the project plan based on the Work Breakdown Structure, expressed in financial terms (Portny et al., 2008).

TYPES OF COSTS

There are direct and indirect costs. Direct costs are solely linked to the project that the budget is planned for. Indirect costs can be divided into overhead costs that cannot be clearly allocated to one single project and administrative costs. These are expenditures that are essential for the survival of the organization as a whole. Out of the plethora of cost components, I will explain the most important ones for international projects.

1 **Labour** The labour cost can be measured by annual gross salaries as depicted in Figure 5.10, or by man-hours. The latter can also be referred to as work-content and measure the total effort which is required to perform the work, independent of the duration and the number of people doing the task. In international projects, it is advisable to convert effort into monetary terms because costs can differ widely across the sites involved. Salary levels and the cost for social benefits will vary from country to country. The project manager also has to pay attention to additional costs related to relocation of project

Labour budget for expatriate project members 2006

	Person 1	Person 2	Person 3
Local wage	$42.168,00	$39.229,00	$32.115,00
Expatriate allowance	$64.291,00	$19.625,00	$23.088,00
Subtotal salaries (CAD)	$106.459,00	$58.854,00	$55.203,00

	Person 1	Person 2	Person 3
Look and see trips	$3.000,00	$3.000,00	$3.000,00
Relocation	$23.000,00	$12.000,00	$12.000,00
Moving allowance	$3.108,00	$2.516,00	$2.516,00
Accommodations (temporary & long term) & transportation	$2.500,00	$1.500,00	$1.500,00
Real estate fees	$5.000,00	$0,00	$0,00
Driver's licence	$120,00	$60,00	$60,00
Work permit	$300,00	$150,00	$150,00
Home flights	$7.120,00	$2.000,00	$2.000,00
Home flights additional – emergency	$7.120,00	$2.000,00	$2.000,00
Health and long term care insurance (re-entry)	$1.776,00	$1.776,00	$1.776,00
Life insurance premiums paid by local subsidiary	$1.896,00	$636,00	$636,00
Employment insurance	$1.022,00	$1.022,00	$1.022,00
Canada pension plan	$1.911,00	$1.911,00	$1.911,00
Premium 10 % (contingency for other costs/exchange rate fluctuations)	$11.182,00	$4.035,00	$4.524,00
Subtotal expenses (CAD)	$69.055,00	$32.606,00	$33.095,00
Total cost (CAD)	**$175.514,00**	**$91.460,00**	**$88.298,00**

FIGURE 5.10 Budget for expatriate Labour related to a manufacturing project

members. Figure 5.10 gives an overview of the additional costs to be calculated for project members who had to be sent to Canada for a manufacturing project. Differences in wage and allowances stem from differences in the local standards of the three project members listed in the budget. The labour budget also comprises a buffer labelled as contingency (Chapter 4). When converting effort into cost, the project manager also needs to consider the different entitlements for paid leave and public holidays.

2 **Materials**   These may be materials contained in the final product or consumables used on project tasks. In engineering, procurement and construction projects, major materials will include vessels (towers, reactors, drums), heat exchangers, boilers, pumps, and storage tanks. Examples for bulk materials are concrete, underground piping and sewers, fencing and railroads (Turner, 1993).

   In many international projects, certain materials may have to be imported. Hence, the project manager needs to check potentially longer lead times for transportation and customs clearance (time planning), import regulations and taxes.

3 **Plant and equipment**   These are items which are not consumed and can be reused for other projects. Therefore, only part of the price needs to be factored into the budget. In engineering projects, the cost for welding machines or earth-moving machinery is included (Turner, 1993).

4 **Travel and transportation**   Typically, travel and transportation costs are much higher in international projects than in domestic projects. Policies such as flying economy-class can only reduce travel costs not avoid it. The same is true for modern telecommunication equipment for video-conferencing. If purchased for the project, costs need to be included under the item plant and equipment. Costs that tend to be overlooked are hotel surcharges for internet connections, business centres and meeting rooms (Murphy, 2005).

5 **Subcontract**   This item includes external resources such as consultants or contractors. The manager of an international project needs to be aware of differences in availability and salary across the regions. IT consultants, for instance, are difficult to find in continental Europe and Latin America due to scarcity, at least as of 2007. In metropolises, the cost is quite high due to strong demand. The salary gap between industrialized countries and emerging markets is getting smaller. An international project might need support from cross-culturally trained facilitators or coaches to resolve conflicts or to support the team generally with its processes. Although this is an expense at first glance, usually the opportunity costs will be much higher if no facilitator is used and the international project reaches a stalemate.

6 **Training**   I have mentioned before that extensive training might be needed in international projects. This includes language training, intercultural training, technical training, training on learning how to transfer knowledge, and communication and leadership training.

7 **Legal support**   Due to internationally different regulations regarding customs, taxes, health and safety, environment, labour laws, and various others, the project manager may need legal support, either via internal or external experts.

8 **Investment cost** (interest rates, etc.)   In the case of larger projects, for instance construction projects, the cost for invested money in the form of interest needs to be included in the budget.

9 **Rent** (for project-related offices, buildings)   Some international projects
will have a very large scope. Therefore, additional space for project
members, like programmers or developers, might be needed. In urban areas
the rent for office space can be extremely high.

10 **Overheads and administration**   This includes general administration costs,
for instance for the project's use of shared services in the areas of pay-roll
administration, IT, procurement and others.

11 **Fees and taxation**   Fees will include items such as insurance, finance or
licence agreements. Taxation can be regarded as a special type of fee.

12 **Inflation**   To include inflation makes sense when different cost components
are expected to have different inflation rates. Currently, this is especially
true for raw materials like steel or oil and gas.

It also makes sense when the product or service resulting from the
project will be sold in countries with extremely high inflation rates. In
general, the project manager has to be aware of the different inflation rates
in the countries involved in the project.

13 **Contingency**   In addition to the quantifiable cost items listed above, a so-
called estimating allowance or contingency will be added to the overall
budget. This allowance should cover oversights or unknowns, with the latter
linked to risk management as discussed under contingency reserves or buffers
in Chapter 4. Figure 5.10 also includes a contingency amount.

As this book focuses on the particularities of international projects, I will not go into
detail regarding cost estimating methods. Methods of assessing project viability like ROI
or NPV are also beyond the scope of this book. In the following, I will only discuss how
the various types of costs I have explained above can be compiled into a budget.

Resource loaded Gantt charts build in the basic input for the budget because these
help to determine the labour budget. The cost for each resource only needs to be multiplied by the allocation to the project.

In general, the budget should be based on the project schedule which in turn will be
based on the Work Breakdown Structure. This helps to avoid major omissions which
could result in cost overruns at the implementation phase.

Usually, the budget is entered onto a spreadsheet. It may be helpful to begin with to
create a so-called periodic cost spreadsheet that lists the cost per relevant planning
period, for instance for one week or one month, depending on the nature of the project.
Usually, the costs in the planning periods are added up and planned in a so-called cumulated spreadsheet that is shown in Figure 5.11, using the example of a project transferring production from Europe to China. This project is scheduled to take ten months. To
keep it simple, I have summarized the detailed cost components into three categories:
labour, travel, and others. Labour consists of the salaries of the project manager (40 per cent
of the production head), the salaries of two foremen (20 per cent of their resource), and
the Chinese employees'. In a business reality, costs are split per cost centre between the
European and Chinese sites which is not reflected on the spreadsheet below. As the local

Chinese workers and foremen have to be trained, European staff will need to travel to China and vice versa. This cost is summarized under travel/expenses. The last row, Others, comprises costs such as consulting costs for local product approval (health and safety), supplier development cost, cost for prototype testing, logistics, etc.

You will see an additional column for actual figures (A) next to the planned figures. A cost spreadsheet is typically used in the implementation phase for controlling purposes which we will discuss in Chapter 7.

PARTICULARITIES OF INTERNATIONAL PROJECTS REGARDING COST ESTIMATES

In international projects, the project manager has to pay special attention to currency conversion rates which can fluctuate widely over the time-span of a project. For the estimates in the budget for an exchange rate for a certain date should be used, based on the organization's policy (in line with the financial department). An extra line should be added to the budget spreadsheet in order to follow up any development in the currencies involved.

SPECIFICS OF INTERNATIONAL PROJECTS IMPACTING ON COST *AND* TIME PLANNING

Travel expenses

As explained in Chapter 3, it is highly important for the success of the international project that the project goals are clear to everyone. However, a thorough understanding of the tasks and assignments is usually best achieved by the intense personal involvement of the project stakeholders. In an international project with geographically dispersed stakeholders, this means a lot of travel activities in order to enable face-to-face meetings, typically at the beginning of the project. The related cost and time need to be budgeted for.

It is important to consider that in many cultures, personal meetings are mandatory to motivate people and push things ahead. Hence, even if phone or video conferences would theoretically do the job and be more cost efficient, this usually works better in task-oriented cultures. Thus, more travelling might be needed than first anticipated.

Selection of sites involved

Selecting sites to be involved in the international project can have a big impact on the time and cost. For instance, an underdeveloped infrastructure might disturb communication which in turn can lead to delays. Another example is local laws requiring health and safety relevant project-related documents to be translated into the local language(s). This effort takes time and costs money. I would recommend using the logic provided in Figure 4.4 in Chapter 4, focusing on the political, economic, sociocultural,

Simplified Cumulative Cost Spreadsheet: Production Transfer from Europe to China

Total Budget € 1 million

P = Plan
A = Actual

Cost Categories		Period to date in months									
		1	2	3	4	5	6	7	8	9	10
Labour	P	20,000	45,000	75,000	115,000	200,000	260,000	330,000	410,000	480,000	550,000
	A										
Travel/ expenses	P	16,000	32,000	64,000	96,000	130,000	170,000	200,000	240,000	300,000	380,000
	A										
Others (consulting, supplier dev., prototypes, logistics, etc.)	P	0	3,000	7,000	14,000	20,000	28,000	35,000	43,000	61,000	70,000
	A										
Total		36,000	80,000	146,000	225,000	350,000	458,000	565,000	693,000	841,000	1,000,000

FIGURE 5.11 Sample of a cumulative cost spreadsheet

technological, environmental, and legal aspects of the country and region that each site is located in. This point elucidates the interrelatedness between planning and risk management. Now that we have discussed the time and cost areas, let us proceed to quality, another pole of the 'magic triangle' introduced in Chapter 1.

PLANNING FOR QUALITY IN INTERNATIONAL PROJECTS

WHAT IS QUALITY?

5.7 The contemporary approach to quality focuses on prevention. An emphasis is laid on avoiding defects, while reducing costs and meeting the customers' requirements at the same time. To translate this into the management of international projects, it would mean 'faster, better, and cheaper' as Ireland (2006: 15–1) coins it.

Quality is not restricted to products or services. It also extends to processes and people.

In this book, I will not discuss generic quality management approaches such as business process re-engineering or Total Quality Management. Nor will I discuss systems to measure and control quality like Six Sigma. I will also not go into detail about ISO-certifications specific to the management of some international projects, as in the construction industry with the 'certificate for project management including design, construction and maintenance of building and civil engineering project for overseas'. There are plenty of textbooks about those areas which are beyond the scope of this book. I will rather explore some of the selected characteristics of managing quality in international projects a bit further.

QUALITY MANAGEMENT IN THE FORM OF PROJECT PLANNING

It is important to have a consistent approach to quality within the international project. This is difficult due to the diversity an international project is characterized by. Differences in national cultures, organizational cultures including sub-cultures, functional cultures, languages, and educational background will all have an impact on quality management. It starts with the word 'quality' which was defined in the paragraph above. Would it be the same definition and association in Japanese or Arabic? Quality expectations might be lower in some countries where scarcity is the order of the day, and consumers are happy to get their hands on a TV set at all, whereas in other economies where competition between manufacturers is high, and products are readily available, quality expectations might not only include a defect-free product at a competitive price, but also additional service or maintenance offerings. Differences do not only exist between less developed and industrialized economies, but also among industrialized countries. There are far fewer service requirements in Germany, for instance, where consumers are usually satisfied with low prices and a good quality product. In Japan, by contrast, friendly and swift service and maintenance have to be part of the product.

So what is the conclusion for planning quality in an international project?

1   *Never take things for granted*

This is especially true for the scope definition with the (non-domestic) customer. Additional features or services might be required, for instance manuals in different languages or consulting services to support local staff after the product or service has been transferred to the customer. Particular attention needs to be paid also to specifications:

- Are the specifications clear? Usually, it is helpful to illustrate as much as possible, even going beyond the drawings that are part of the specifications in any case. Also, be careful with illustrations. In Japan, a cross means 'no' or 'no good', whereas in Western countries, it frequently illustrates the existence of a given functionality.
- Are the specifications comprehensive, or do they require internal company knowledge, for instance to understand the abbreviations used, or to understand certain policies or procedures?
- Is the applied measurement system commonplace in the countries participating in the project? If both a metric system and the Anglo-American system are used, a comparison table is recommended. To avoid rounding up errors, the detailed value should be provided in both measurement systems.
- Specifications also need to be cross-checked as related to their suitability for a certain market. Are the features needed in the market the product is being sold to?

The differences in quality expectations can be cross-checked as part of the cultural gap analysis and the assessment of the diversity and complexity of the project. The expectation levels of the customer regarding quality need to be defined as part of the stakeholder management process. Both areas were discussed in Chapter 3 of this book.

2   *Training needs*

Time and a budget need to be available to train project members in the adopted quality approach. We know that qualification levels differ from country to country, sometimes even within countries. However, all project team members have to work towards a common goal and they must to be enabled to do so. Hence, special training might be necessary. If additional training in some technical areas like welding is required, not too much time will need to be planned in. The situation however will look differently in the development of new products. If engineers first have to learn how to use their acquired knowledge creatively, training is a more radical education and might take quite a long time as it will touch on the basic values of the employee.

Differences in capabilities are often ignored. According to Rauwerdink (2005), research in software-related projects has shown that the productivity of employees can differ by a factor of 10 between the best and worst performing employees. This is not necessarily related to a difference in intelligence or commitment. Usually, the educational background and the working style of employees from very distant cultures will vary considerably. Moreover, newly hired employees will need to be familiarized with the corporate culture and internal company knowledge. The Chapter End Case of Chapter 4 shows what happens when this point is neglected.

3   Selection of co-operation partners

A project will only be successful with the full contribution of all participants. Hence, the project manager needs to check upfront whether the potential business partners such as suppliers, subcontractors, outsourcing partners or others have the capacities and capabilities to fulfil the project requirements. Checklists can help with the selection of business partners, focusing especially on quality issues, which will not only address technical quality, but also commercial quality such as the soundness of the business. Many international projects suffer from the sudden bankruptcy of one of their business partners. This can potentially cause project failure.

You will have noticed at this stage that managing quality is very similar to what we discussed in Chapter 4 concerning managing risks. Let us keep in mind that good and thorough planning is a prerequisite of risk management. Planning for quality is part of this, though not exclusively.

Mini Case 5.2 provides you with an opportunity to re-cap on the main activities and issues related to planning an international project.

Mini Case 5.2: Building malls in Russia

A Scandinavian retail company has adopted a diversification strategy: it invests in big malls in Russia. These malls usually consist of a furniture store, a huge supermarket, a do-it-yourself-store, an ice rink, a multiplex cinema and other smaller stores.

Who are the main stakeholders of these international projects? It is the investor, namely the Scandinavian retailer. The investor also selects locations they consider suitable for such a mall. The selected site is then developed by a Scandinavian-based company which takes care of the basic design. A project management company based in Germany is responsible for the co-ordination of tasks between the different stakeholders, namely the investor, and the suppliers. It defines the interfaces between the different parties involved in the project. Another stakeholder is the Russian building authorities, especially the departments that approve the construction plans. The construction itself is carried out by a corporation based in Turkey and some local Russian companies.

The investor has clarified in the contract with all suppliers that the project language needs to be English. When contacts between the different stakeholders were first established, it soon became obvious that there was a language barrier.

The Russian authorities only spoke Russian. The Turkish construction company had staff who could speak Turkish and Russian. The project manager of the German project management company was fluent in German and Russian, with basic English only. The Scandinavian parties were all very fluent in English, but could not understand any Russian. In breach of the contract, English was not commonly spoken by all the stakeholders. Consequently, additional resources had to be factored into the overall calculation to plan for translators who could translate documents backwards and forwards, and could give help with interpreting at meetings.

Another requirement of the contract was a bi-weekly meeting between the suppliers involved. As one of those projects was located in the middle of Siberia, this turned out to be a requirement which was hardly realizable. The Swedish and German teams would have needed to travel for two full days for meetings in the Siberian city. Therefore, a compromise with the investor was negotiated, agreeing on a monthly meeting in Moscow with photo documentation of the progress instead of an on-site meeting.

Question

What are the lessons learnt from the case above when it comes to international project planning?

SUMMARY

The prerequisites for project implementation are detailed estimates about the duration of all activities, how these interact with each other, whether sufficient human and general resources are available, and what the whole set of activities will cost. Network diagrams such as the Activity-on-Arrow technique and Gantt charts can help to schedule and sequence these activities. In an international context, special attention needs to be paid to planning additional time for co-ordination, communication, training, the adaptations of processes and products to local requirements, and team-building activities. Moreover, differences in public holidays, vacation times, calendars, and auspicious days need to be taken into account. Spreadsheets can contain the budget with different cost components like labour, materials, travel and transportation, and training. These are more complex to estimate for an international project, where special attention needs to be paid to currency conversion changes. Travel costs are usually higher than expected in an international project. The selection of the sites involved in the project will have a big impact on time and cost. Quality also needs to be planned for, by checking on the qualification level of staff, the appropriateness of specifications in the local context, and the thoroughness of contractor selection. Although planning is essential in international projects, different national cultures and religions attach different importance to it. Diversity also exists related to the concept of time which may be seen as something flowing and infinite, colliding with project management scheduling techniques.

 # KEY TERMS

Project master plan, time estimate, activity duration, sequencing, network diagrams, Activity-on-Arrow, dummy activity, float, slack, Earliest Start Time, Earliest Finish Time, Latest Start Time, Latest Finish Time, critical path, Gantt chart, resource loaded Gantt chart, cumulated budget, indirect cost, direct cost, specification sheet.

REVIEW TASKS

Questions

1 In your opinion, how much planning is needed in international projects?
2 What does the planning cycle for international projects look like?
3 What are the specifics in planning the time, costs, and quality of an international project?

EXERCISE 1

- Think of a delay you have been involved in. This could be related to your job or studies.
- Analyse the reasons for that delay.
- What could you have done to avoid it?

EXERCISE 2 (WORKS BEST WITH MULTICULTURAL TEAMS)

- Work in groups of five or six people.
- Reflect individually on what you spontaneously associate with quality.
- Discuss in your group about your associations. Do these differ? If so, what could be the reasons for these differences?

CHAPTER END CASE: GAMING IN SPAIN

A leading multinational corporation in the gaming industry planned to expand its operations to southern Europe, namely to Spain. Two project managers were assigned to achieve this goal: one project manager to establish a wholly owned subsidiary in the new market, another project manager to identify suitable locations for the new gaming outlets.

ESTABLISHING THE SUBSIDIARY IN SPAIN – THE 'PHYSICAL HARDWARE'

The first milestone of the project was the establishment of a local company as a wholly owned subsidiary of the gaming multinational including all administrative issues linked to this process, such as obtaining a licence to run a gaming company from the Spanish government. This was supposed to take approximately two months. Including the search for a reliable bilingual lawyer, this process finally took four months. On the financial side, a bank account needed to be opened, an independent external accountant had to be contracted, and an audit firm had to be found. All these activities were planned to be finalized within two months. However, problems with the selected audit company occurred: in the first meeting with the audit company, the project manager noticed that in contrast to the written quotation, the selected audit company did not have multilingual employees. Therefore, another audit company had to be found and contracted. This activity took three months. As far as the infrastructure was concerned, suitable facilities for the newly established subsidiary needed to be identified and a rental contract signed. Office supplies and furniture had to be purchased, and IT and telecommunication systems set up. Accommodation for the project managers had to be provided. The infrastructure related activities were planned to take roughly two months. A delay of one month was due to the plumber and the phone company. After five visits, the plumber had still not succeeded in installing the toilets in a way they could be used. To this day, the employees have to fight with a malfunctioning flushing system. The greatest challenge for the project manager, however, was the division of work at the phone company. To get three RADSL lines, he needed to fill in four forms for four different departments of the phone company. After frequent calls, begging, and pleading, the technicians in charge eventually came, one after the other, to fix the lines. Unfortunately, they came at intervals of three to four weeks, which resulted in a lead-time of three months until the phone connection was up and running.

In addition, insurance requirements needed to be identified and a contract with an insurance company signed. The project manager responsible for the subsidiary foundation had planned two weeks for this process. With intensive support by the project manager the insurance company was able to finish this process in five weeks, although their normal process typically took nine to ten weeks.

ESTABLISHING THE SUBSIDIARY IN SPAIN – RECRUITING STAFF

The second major step was related to recruiting and training personnel, both in the new subsidiary and in the outlets which were to be opened afterwards across the whole country. Both responsible project managers estimated roughly two months for recruiting, selecting, and training new employees for the subsidiary. They experienced the first difficulties when they tried to find an appropriate Human Resources search company. Amazingly, the differences in price and quality were huge on the Spanish market, much greater than back home. Another hitch came with the first interviews they conducted. They did so in Spanish and English. Much to their surprise, they discovered that 80 per cent of the applicants had somewhat exaggerated their capabilities in their written CV. For instance, some of them could not switch to English in the interview, or lacked other skills that the two project managers could test during the interview. Consequently, the two had to run many more interviews than originally expected and planned for, resulting in another delay of one month.

EXPANSION – ESTABLISHING OUTLETS IN THE SPANISH MARKET

The third milestone was the establishment of outlets in metropolitan areas of the new market. Each shop opening was considered a sub-goal or sub-milestone. In order to reach it, a bundle of measures needed to be conducted.

SUITABLE LOCATIONS

The first set of actions was linked to the identification of suitable locations: definition of criteria for a good location in the local market, selection of real estate agents and property developers, selection of potential locations, closing of tenancy contracts, and acquisition of municipal gaming permits based on police regulations.

NEW OUTLETS

The second set of actions was related to the design and equipment of the new outlets: defining shop standards, designing the location of the machines and furniture, planning the interior decoration, issuing the tender for the construction or refurbishment of the building, application for a construction permit with the local community, granting of a building permit, contract award to general contractor, implementation of a construction plan, final acceptance by project manager, planning of outdoor advertising, approval of outdoor advertising by local authorities, installing of outdoor advertising, furnishing the outlet, contracts with utility companies.

On average, achieving these activities was planned to take eight months. In the end, it took the project manager 14 months due to a low degree of reliability and a high level of red tape encountered at all levels – from local municipalities to central governmental authorities. To give one example: he could not believe it when he made an appointment with the planning office at 09:00 a.m. and the officer eventually showed up at 11.30, commenting that he had just some coffee. Another shock for the project manager was the fact that an important planning officer went on holiday for three weeks. When he asked for his holiday replacement, he was told that there was none. So the project manager had to wait three weeks until the person in charge returned from his vacation.

The construction companies also posed a challenge to the project manager. When he heard from them 'No hay problema!' (no problem), he knew they were running into difficulties. Headquarters pushed him to announce the opening dates for outlets well in advance. However, the deadlines were not taken at all seriously by the construction companies. Even though he followed up personally, and supervised the work, it still took much longer than agreed. Dates were seen as non-binding. They would do their best to meet the deadlines, but if not, it couldn't be helped. Headquarters did not understand at all what was happening, and why the planned opening dates could not be firmly adhered to. Needless to say each delay in opening an outlet meant a cost in the sense of lost profit.

Another budget issue was caused by the semi-legal practices of some construction firms. All materials used needed to be checked on site because the invoices tended to list more expensive materials. The project manager spent a lot of time controlling all the details of the invoices, and still the costs exceeded the budget.

GAMING MACHINES

In parallel to the second set of activities, a third series of actions was to be carried out related to the gaming machines: the composition of a suitable mix of machines, ordering the machines, importing the machines to Spain, processing payment, getting the calibration and local approval of gaming machines, adapting the configuration of the machines to local demand. For instance, roulette was known to be quite popular with Spanish gamblers. All those activities were forecasted to be finalized within six weeks. Due to long procedures for customs' clearance and other bureaucratic issues, the tasks were only completed after eight weeks.

SERVICE AND MAINTENANCE

Last but not least, the project manager had to take care of a fourth bundle of activities: service and maintenance partners needed to be selected and contracted. A security concept needed to be outlined and implemented, a very important issue in the gaming industry as a lot of cash is involved. In parallel, marketing activities needed to be ramped up. At home, it would take the project manager about four weeks to complete those tasks. However, he did not account for problems with the information flow between headquarters and the subsidiary in Spain on one hand and between the new outlet and headquarters on the other, which led to another delay of four weeks.

Despite their language skills, and although they each worked until they fell over, the project managers were still very much behind schedule and over budget. What a pain …

Task and question

1 Create two Gantt charts: one for the original planning, and one for the actual project. (Note: Not all scheduling details are in the text – just refer to the available data.)
2 What are the particularities in this case in terms of planning time, cost, and quality, due to the fact that this is an international project?

FURTHER READING

Benator, Barry and Thumann, Albert (2003) *Project Management and Leadership Skills for Engineering and Construction Projects*. Lilburn: The Fairmont Press Inc. (Chapters 3, 4, 5, and 6 offer a good overview on scheduling fundamentals, financial management and cost estimating. Moreover, the authors touch on the role of computer tools in the planning process. Concrete examples and checklists for construction and high-tech projects are provided.)

Goldratt, Eliyahu M. (1997) *Critical Chain*. Great Barrington: The North River Press (Goes beyond classical scheduling and Goldratt criticizes scheduling techniques. In his opinion, human behaviour is not sufficiently taken into account.)

Huemann, Martina (2004) 'Improving quality in projects and programs'. In Morris, Peter W.G. and Pinto, Jeffrey K. (eds) *The Wiley Guide to Managing Projects*. Hoboken, NJ: John Wiley & Sons, pp. 903–936. (Provides a comprehensive yet concise overview of improvement methods focusing on quality as a process, including quality audit and certification systems such as ISO.)

Portny, Stanley, Mantel, Samuel J., Meredith, Jack R., Shafer, Scott M. and Margaret M. Sutton (2008) *Project Management: Planning, Scheduling, and Controlling Projects*. Hoboken, NJ: John Wiley & Sons. (This book is pedagogically well thought through and structured. Apart from a good overview of relevant planning tools it contains additional features to use the tools and practise the techniques.)

ORGANIZING INTERNATIONAL PROJECTS

6

LEARNING OBJECTIVES

After studying this chapter, you will be able to:

- grasp the relevance of organizational structures for project management

- compare different organizational structures: functional, 'projec-tized', matrix, and virtual

- conceive the cultural particularities of organizational structures and responsibility charts

- discuss internal co-ordination mechanisms in international projects

- elucidate external project co-ordination in international projects

- comprehend communication structures in international projects

- explain the Organization Breakdown Structure

- create a responsibility matrix

- understand best practices for organizing international projects.

INTRODUCTION

6.1 International projects tend to be highly complex. One way of managing complexity is by simplification through detailed structure and design. The relationship between the different participating organizations and the interface between the respective functions and departments strongly affect the efficiency of managing the international project. There are a variety of organizational forms which can be selected for structuring a project, namely functional, 'projectized', matrix, and virtual structures that all have advantages and disadvantages which I will explain in this chapter. The discussion will include culture and how it impacts on our views of organizational structures. The organizational structure has to be seen in line with other inputs in the planning phase, namely the planning of time, cost, and quality. Seen from a project management life cycle perspective, this chapter provides the last input that is needed in the planning phase in order to create the project master plan.

The selected project structure provides the frame for a further co-ordination of internal and external stakeholders of the international project. I will introduce the project office, steering committees, project champions, and so-called war rooms as mechanisms to support the internal co-ordination of the project. External relations between the project and its stakeholders are mainly governed by contracts. Hence, I will provide in this chapter an overview of the main types of contracts such as fixed price contracts, cost reimbursement contracts, and incentive contracts, touching on certain particularities of international contract forms. Contracts as formal co-ordination mechanisms are one side of the coin. The other side consists of informal co-ordination mechanisms such as institutionalized high-level meetings, for instance between the project manager and the customer, and continuity in personal relations. The right project structure and adequate co-ordination mechanisms aim at reducing complexity. The same is true for communication structures, internally and externally, which should be low in terms of the number of interfaces. Project structure and co-ordination mechanisms are filled and used by people. I will close this chapter by explaining the tools to link structure with project members. The basis is laid down by the Work Breakdown Structure introduced in Chapter 3. It comprises all the work packages that need to be accomplished to realize the project goal. Each work package has to be implemented by the project members. Both tools, an Organization Breakdown Structure (OBS) and a responsibility chart, match tasks with project members. The responsibility chart lists all the work packages with all the related activities and links these to project members in the form of a matrix.

FORMS OF PROJECT STRUCTURES

6.2 International projects will involve numerous heterogeneous stakeholders. The project structure defines how these stakeholders interact with each other. The definition of the organizational structure of the project is intertwined with the definition of the project scope (see Chapter 3). Based on the organizational form of the project, the project manager and team can determine how much the project will cost, and how long it will take. In other words, the organizational structure is an important input for managing the time, cost, and quality as discussed in Chapter 5.

In detail, the project's organization structure defines who reports to whom, and which processes, policies and systems will be applied. There is no perfect or optimal organizational structure. Each structure has its advantages and disadvantages. The objective is to select an organizational form which is most suitable to the special circumstances of the international project.

In general, an organization's structure determines the placement of power, responsibility and authority in the organization. Authority is defined as the power granted to individuals to enable them to take the final decisions. Responsibility refers to the obligation incurred by individuals in their roles in the formal organization to effectively perform assignments (Kerzner, 2006).

An organizational structure is characterized by the following four dimensions (Galbraith, 2002):

1 Specialization: type and number of job specialties.
2 Shape: number of people constituting a unit and number of hierarchy levels in an organization.
3 Distribution of power: centralization versus decentralization.
4 Departmentalization: building structural units around the themes, functions, products, work flow processes, market segments (customers), and geography.

As mentioned before, there is no single structure which ideally combines those areas. In this section, I will discuss the most frequently used organizational forms to organize a project: functional, product (or projectized), and matrix. In many international projects, there is a trend to virtual organizational structures which I will also briefly outline. You will find a systematic overview of the pros and cons of each project structure in the form of tables on the companion website.

THE FUNCTIONAL STRUCTURE

The functional structure, also called the traditional or classical structure, is the most frequently used organizational form in an organization. People are grouped by discipline and their level of authority in a top-down hierarchy. The focal point and commitment instead lie with the function rather than with the internal or external customer. Figure 6.1 illustrates how a project can be organized within a functional structure. The people within the dotted line are project members. The project co-ordination is carried out by the functional managers. Please note that the figure does not show the full structure of the organization but only the project relevant parts.

When management in a functionally structured organization decides to implement a project, the different segments of the project are usually delegated to the respective functional units. In this set-up, the project manager tends to have little

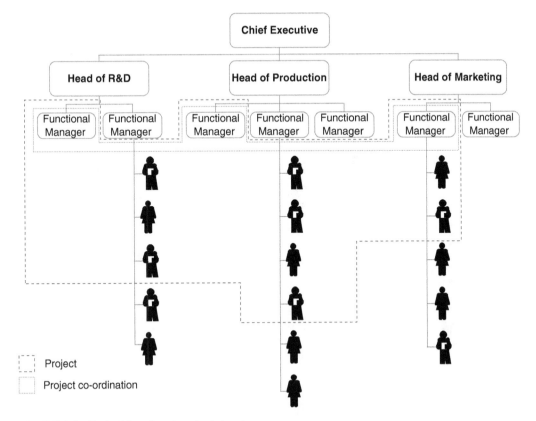

FIGURE 6.1 Typical functional project structure

authority and can barely influence resource availability (PMI, 2004). Moreover, a functional structure tends to be quite bureaucratic and slow. Therefore, it is not suitable for the fast changing environment in which the majority of international projects are operating. Functional structures are better suited for projects which are dominated by a certain function, for instance a new marketing campaign (even with international reach).

THE 'PROJECTIZED' ORGANIZATION

Let us have a look at another form of structuring project, the so-called 'projectized' organization, also called the 'stand-alone' organization. This refers to a structure revolving around a product, program, or project (PMI, 2004). A dedicated project team operates as an independent unit separated from the rest of the organization. Employees working on a certain product or project are typically collocated and are recruited from within and outside the organization. Project managers will usually

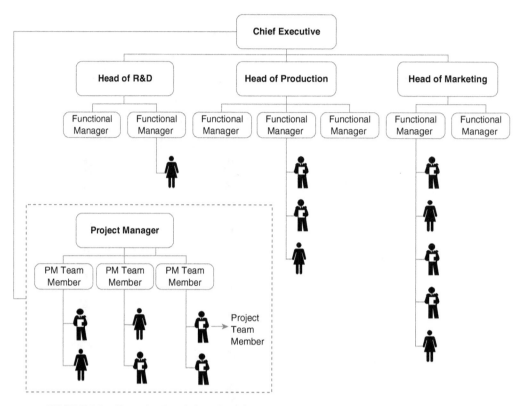

FIGURE 6.2   Organizational chart for a 'projectized' organization

have full autonomy. It depends on the organization how it manages its interface with the 'stand-alone' project. Figure 6.2 illustrates the independence, and autonomy of the stand-alone project organization in which the project manager's authority tends to be high. Typically, project managers' jobs are full time. The same is true for project management administration staff (PMI, 2004).

Depending on the industry, organizations can only consist of such stand-alone projects, as for instance in the software or construction industry. This is what we discussed in Chapter 2 in section 2.10 with regard to project based organizations.

THE MATRIX STRUCTURE

Another way of organizing projects is by using a mixture of a functional structure and a product or project structure which is called a matrix structure. This is a hybrid form. Beyond a project context, a matrix structure on an overall organizational level can also be a hybrid of other structuring themes. For instance, it can be a combination between a regional structure and a functional structure.

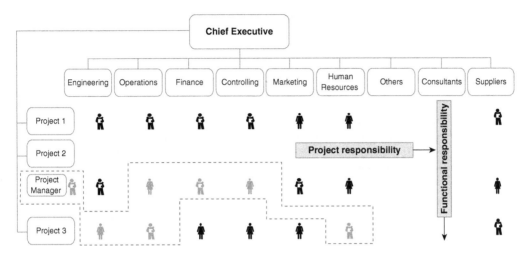

FIGURE 6.3 A project matrix organization

In a project matrix structure, vertically organized functions still exist. However, they are supplemented by horizontally organized projects which cross all functions. The purpose of the matrix structure is to provide greater cross-functional integration, visibility and management control to projects within a big and complex organization while maintaining specialist expertise and synergies in the form of functions. It also aims at increasing flexibility by having individuals working on multiple projects, fulfilling their functional tasks in parallel. In theory, the project manager is responsible for integrating functional input and controlling project completion. Functional managers will usually own the resources in their units and manage the functional contribution to the project. Many Western multinational corporations have adopted matrix structures (see the Chapter End Case).

Due to their high complexity, many international projects are organized in the form of a matrix. This does not mean, however, that the project structure as such guarantees successful project management. In practice, dual reporting can lead to tensions between the functions and projects. The proliferation of reporting and communication channels can result in confusion and information log jams. Overlapping responsibilities between functional managers and project managers can produce turf battles. Team members within a matrix structure may tend to feel themselves pulled into two different directions which are difficult to reconcile (Bartlett and Ghoshal, 1990).

The scale of those difficulties depends on various factors. The most important one is the organizational culture (see Chapter 2). A matrix organization which still maintains a strong awareness of inter-functional boundaries or 'silo-thinking' is said to have a 'weak' matrix structure, also called a lightweight or functional matrix. For project managers, this means that functional managers are usually less co-operative and will tend to have a stronger power base in the organization. A 'strong' matrix (also called a heavyweight or project matrix), on the other hand, is typically based on an organizational culture which reflects a strong customer focus and process thinking. Project managers in strong matrix structures will tend to have more authority and will face less conflict with functional heads.

As the organizational culture is intertwined with the structure and systems, there are more factors contributing to either a weak or a strong matrix (Larson, 2004):

- Reporting relationship: a project manager who reports to the Chief Technology Officer certainly has more clout than the manager of an electrical engineering section reporting to the head of a foreign subsidiary.
- Location of project activities: typically, a project manager has more impact on project staff when people work in his office and not in the office of the functional manager – and vice versa.
- Reward systems: if only the functional manager is responsible for performance appraisals, he or she carries more weight with the project staff than the project manager, and vice versa.

If there is a balance of power between the functional and project management side of the matrix, it is called a balanced matrix. This, however, is rare in real terms.

In general, the main problem with a matrix structure resides in goal conflicts, either between projects and/or between projects and functions. An organization implementing a matrix structure needs to be sufficiently mature from a cultural point of view. Training for employees and managers acting in a matrix structure needs to be provided, focusing especially on the skills that are requisite to deal with conflict. In other words, the main challenge with the matrix structure lies in its proper implementation. Mini Case 6.1 provides you with the opportunity to practise your knowledge of project structures.

Mini Case 6.1: EADS Astrium's project structure

EADS Astrium is a subsidiary of the European Aeronautics Defence and Space Company (EADS). Headquartered in France, it has subsidiaries in the UK, Spain, the Netherlands, and Germany. With 12,000 employees in 2008, EADS Astrium is active across all sectors of the space business – from launch capabilities, orbital systems and manned space activities, to satellite systems, payloads and equipment for civil and military applications. It also offers a portfolio of space-based services.

EADS Astrium operates in an industry which is driven by highly complex international projects: product development is often linked to novelty with long development cycles, high interdisciplinary and intercultural complexity, and strong cost and schedule pressures due to fixed cost contracts.

Big projects usually involve 50 to 130 international co-operation partners, most of them deeply integrated in the new product development process.

EADS Astrium's projects are organized on the basis of a matrix. This is due to the high demand on expert knowledge on the one hand, and the strong focus on customer satisfaction and goal achievement on the other. Most of the project team members are only assigned to a project and stay in the line organization. Only a few members of the staff, like the project leaders and some specialists, are completely transferred to the project as a full resource. The projects will usually have greater weight in the organization compared to the functions because they generate the revenue of the company.

Sources: Benz (2005); EADS Astrium (2008)

Questions

1 How would you classify the kind of matrix that EADS Astrium uses for organizing its projects?
2 Why would using a functional structure not make sense?

VIRTUAL STRUCTURES

The virtual organization was born out of the necessity of an ever faster changing organizational environment coupled with fiercer global competition. By overcoming the physical limitations of distance, time, and organizational boundaries, virtual structures can allow an organization to draw talent quickly from different functions, locations, and organizations, be it different subsidiaries or external partners. The purpose is to apply leverage to intellectual capital and employ it as quickly as possible (Duarte and Snyder, 2006). Moreover, such virtual structures are cost effective. They vastly improve cycle times by moving information instantaneously, improving co-ordination and accelerating work processes. As it is likely that the locations of the members of virtual teams will span the globe, team members in different locations can take turns in conducting activities by using a hands-off arrangement. We call such an approach 'follow-the-sun'. The Japanese team member starts with a task, then hands it over to his European colleague, who in turn passes it on to his American counterpart.

Summarized, virtual structures are characterized by the fact that:

- members work across distance, time, and organizational boundaries
- team work in a virtual structure is based on the use of electronic collaboration technology.

Virtual structures are not confined to the management of projects. Virtual structures can also be applied to management teams within a global corporation, or task forces which can solve emergencies within an organization. In practice, virtual structures will tend to be combined with project matrix structures. They could be said to be even more complex than matrix structures due to the following facts (Kumar et al., 2005):

- Team members need to co-operate across different time zones thus hampering synchronous communication. Therefore, team members need to be skilled in non-synchronous communication modes (see Chapter 9).
- Team members will typically work across national boundaries which means they will have to deal with cultural diversity, language diversity, etc.
- Team members will typically belong to different organizational, governance, social, environmental and economic contexts. Hence, they need to bridge those differences in their collaboration.

In light of these challenges, an organization needs to pay special attention to the implementation of a virtual structure.

Project managers and team members in virtual structures need to have reliable real-time communication and collaboration technology. Moreover, suitable training and development measures for team members, standard organizational processes, an appropriate organizational culture and leadership need to be in place. Work packages must also be adapted to an asynchronous working style. In other words, activities have to be carried out with the minimum of inter-dependencies in a sequential way in order not to lose time. This task is easier to achieve with a low degree of uncertainty.

Let us now wrap up this section on different forms of project organizations with a brief checklist supporting the choice of project structure.

SELECTING THE RIGHT PROJECT STRUCTURE

There is growing empirical evidence that project success is directly linked to the amount of autonomy and authority project managers have. A 'projectized' structure or a strong matrix structure would best meet those requirements. However, projects are contextual. Therefore, each project may need its special structure. The following seven factors can influence the choice of project structure (Kerzner, 2006; Larson, 2004):

1 Size and duration of project
2 Strategic importance
3 Novelty and need for innovation
4 Need for integration (number of departments involved)
5 Environmental complexity (number of external interfaces)
6 Budget and time constraints or resource availability
7 Project location.

International projects tend to be big in scope with a long duration, relatively high strategic importance, a strong need for integration (at least regarding overall co-ordination), a high environmental complexity, and dispersed project teams located around the globe. These characteristics point to a strong matrix organization combined with a virtual structure.

This statement, however, has been made here without considering cultural differences. Let us now take a look at the relation between project structures and national culture.

CULTURAL IMPACT ON PROJECT ORGANIZATION

6.3

In Chapter 2, I explained that organizational structure and culture support the achievement of an organization's vision. Broken down into a project context, organizational structures serve the purpose of accomplishing

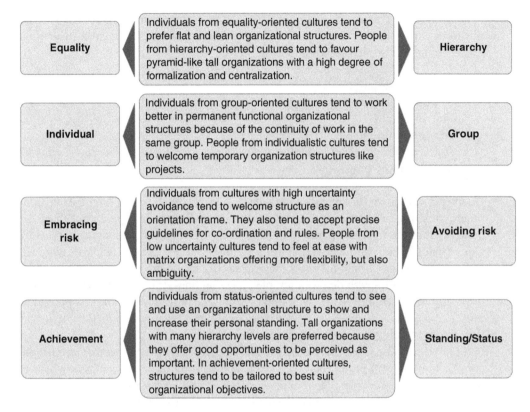

FIGURE 6.4   Cultural impact on organizing projects

project goals. Moreover, they provide organizational members with a frame for orientation, with hierarchies and reporting lines. Hence, organizational structures satisfy needs of belonging and esteem. These can differ between individuals and national cultures. Figure 6.4 summarizes the main cultural dimensions that can have an impact on organizing and structuring. The cultural gap tool for organizing aims at sensitizing project managers and members to cultural differences in this field in order to enable project managers to consider these differences when organizing an international project in the most efficient way.

THE CULTURAL EMBEDDEDNESS OF MATRIX STRUCTURES

Several studies (Guillén, 1994; Pant et al., 1996) suggest that differences in national cultural values can cause variations in organizational structure. Chapter 1 has argued that project management as such is contingent on certain national cultural values, mainly those of the Anglophone world. This implies that organizational structures used for project management are also embedded in and impacted on by cultural values.

As the matrix structure leads to numerous issues in international projects, I will use this form of project structure to explain the interrelation above. The matrix structure is rooted in the following basic assumptions:

- low power distance
- low uncertainty avoidance
- individualism
- strong task orientation
- strong achievement orientation
- sequential way of working.

Chapter 3 has shown that many national cultures in the Arab world, on the Asian continent, in Africa, in Latin America, and Southern and Eastern Europe do not share the basic assumptions mentioned above. In these rather relationship-oriented cultures, loyalties cannot be split and will usually lie with the physically present manager who will typically be the functional manager. High power distance in these cultures may contribute to difficulties with dual or multiple reporting lines. It may be considered insubordination by an employee of a high power distance culture if he or she is supposed to report certain tasks or issues to people who are different from the functional manager they would typically see as their legitimate supervisor.

A (2004) study by Chen and Partington revealed that Chinese project managers in the construction industry prefer their own stable and existing team to a temporary project organization. They are not prepared to share power and leadership with line managers either. Hence, Chinese project managers seem to see their project as a company within a company, with all specialists being part of 'their' sub-organization. The temporary character of a project seems to be disliked in terms of the change of personnel.

What are the consequences for organizing international projects?

1   If a matrix is applied to the whole project across international sites, additional training measures might be needed in order to establish the right environment for a matrix organization. This training, however, takes time to be effective, and involves company resources. From this point of view, the suitability of a matrix structure needs to be reassessed.
2   The matrix might need some fine-tuning to be adapted to local requirements and expectations. For instance, a strong general matrix could be established as a weak matrix in certain subsidiaries with a great cultural distance from the Anglophone world.
3   The project manager might leave the decision on project structure to the local sub-leaders who can choose the most adequate approach. This runs the risk of a lack of co-ordination and control which need to be established by strong communication governance and other means instead.

Having dealt with different project structures and the link between organizing and culture, I will now turn to the other mechanisms used to structure and co-ordinate an international

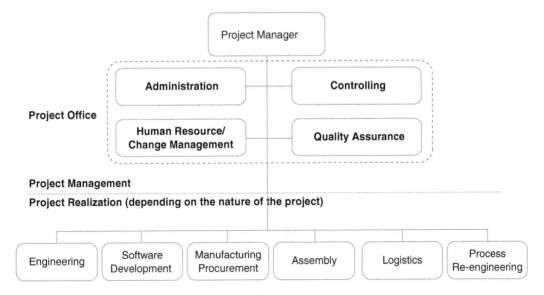

FIGURE 6.5 Typical project structure with a project office

project externally and internally. Section 6.4 following will look at the internal co-ordination mechanisms.

INTERNAL PROJECT CO-ORDINATION

6.4 In section 6.2 we discussed the greater organizational frame, namely the project structure. Within this frame, there are different means of mechanisms on a more detailed level that support the project structure. I will now introduce the mechanisms that are most suitable for international projects.

THE PROJECT OFFICE

The project office needs to be differentiated from the project management office (PMO) discussed in Chapter 2. The project management office provides input and the infra-structure for efficient multiple project management in an organization. The project office, in contrast, is a central unit supporting a single project. It usually consists of administrative support, and covers controlling, quality assurance and legal functions. In bigger projects, there might be additional support for human resource management and change as exemplified in Figure 6.5. Figure 6.5 refers to a comprehensive project with sub-projects across the value chain of Research and Development and Manufacturing.

While the project office will support the project manager from an administrative and functional perspective, international projects will usually also need strong support from top management. This can occur in various forms as I shall now explain.

SUPPORT BY SENIOR EXECUTIVES

Project champion

As many international projects will have a big impact on an entire organization, it is recommended they increase their profile by assigning one of the senior executives of the organization to that project as a kind of project champion or project mentor. This increases the visibility of the project. It also convinces other stakeholders to support it, for instance when the time comes for the release of human resources.

Steering committee

Another method is the steering committee. It will usually be staffed with senior executives of the organization who have a special interest in the project and the power to release resources. With multiple stakeholders, international projects will normally require strong steering committees in order to ease the potential tensions between functions and projects, between different international subsidiaries, between international partners, etc. It is also recommended for big international projects to include the customer in the steering committee. Such a structure ensures an adequate information flow and change management (see Snapshot 4.3). A strong and competent steering committee also allows for more flexibility at the operational level of the international project. If all stakeholders understand and accept the common goals of the international project, regularly reinforced by the steering committee, less effort has to be put into detailed control of the project implementation at every single site where the project is implemented. This allows for flexibility in managerial practices giving sufficient leverage to sub-projects to cope with the requirements of diversity.

CENTRAL WAR ROOM

Another way of internally co-ordinating the international project is the use of a so-called central war room which is particularly beneficial for projects with a virtual or semi-virtual structure. This would be a fixed location, a room where all the project team members from different locations can meet, exchange and store their information. The geographical location of the war room should be decided at the beginning of the project as this decision bears cost consequences.

DUAL LEADERSHIP

Last but not least, I would like to refer to leadership in its co-ordinating function. In projects spanning national boundaries it can make sense to establish dual leadership in project teams. For instance, each work package of Rolls Royce's 'Spree Project' was headed by two sub-project leaders: one person from the British side, one from the German. The purpose was to ensure the acceptance of both sides and to secure information flows. Of course, the efficiency of this co-ordination mechanism depended on the personal relations between both individuals.

Let me now turn to some typical problems that the internal organization of international projects may be confronted with.

FREQUENT ISSUES WITH THE INTERNAL ORGANIZATION OF INTERNATIONAL PROJECTS

Size of the team

Teams in international projects tend to be heterogeneous. Various perspectives have to be unified into one decision and one way forward. The more people there are in a team, the more difficult such a process can get. The project manager needs to strike a balance between the knowledge and diversity needed, and the manageability of the team. Of course, the absolute size of the project team is highly dependent on the nature of the project.

In general, though, it is probably best to have no more than ten members in a team. Even in complex international projects, the team size can be kept small by using the following measures (Hoegl, 2005):

1 Have several sub-projects with respectively small teams.
2 Create a core team and an extended team (e.g. specialists from the line organization appointed on a need basis).
3 Define the team's external contributions and outsource them.
4 Keep team members only for specific project phases or sub-phases.

Overcoming language and cultural barriers, with structure

Communication barriers need to be taken into consideration when designing the internal structure of the international project. Do the various parties share a common language? I am not referring to the natural language only, but also to the functional language they need to understand. It facilitates co-ordination if responsibilities are allocated to people in various sub-teams who share a similar educational background and who have experience in the same functions. This means pairing logistics and logistics people with each other and letting them interact directly, without any intermediary or supervisor. Experience shows that such a set-up works best if the respective individuals know each other personally or at least can share some personal information on the phone, and maybe a photo. The project manager should ensure that the communicating parties are on comparable hierarchical positions across the organization to facilitate open information exchange. This is particularly important for cultures with a high power distance.

Let us now address the mechanisms best suited to co-ordinate international projects with external stakeholders.

EXTERNAL PROJECT CO-ORDINATION

6.5

The most important external stakeholder is typically the customer. With the customer and other external stakeholders such as contractors or partners, co-ordination is usually formalized in the form of a contract.

CONTRACTS IN GENERAL

A detailed discussion of project contracts goes beyond the scope of this book (see further reading). As a result, I will only briefly outline the basic contract forms, emphasizing that the importance and weight of a contract will differ between national cultures and jurisdictions.

The following explanations of the three major contract types are based on Gardiner (2005).

1 Firm Fixed Price (FFP)

It is said to be the most common form of contract, also called 'fixed price' or 'lump sum'. The customer buys a certain product or service from the contractor for a fixed price. The risk that the contractor calculates this fixed price in a way he or she can make a profit lies with the contractor. The Firm Fixed Price is appropriate when customer requirements are easy to define. This is inappropriate in a highly uncertain environment, including a strong dependence on customer's internal information or knowledge. The contract form encourages efficiency increases on the side of the contractor. Due to the fixed price, lower costs will directly result in a profit increase.

If the project takes longer, for instance more than one year, the contract can be made more flexible with the inclusion of price adjustment clauses which will cater for fluctuations in certain commodity prices such as oil.

2 Cost reimbursement contracts

In cost reimbursement contracts, the contractor is reimbursed the cost incurred with the product or service delivery. Most commonly, this form of contract is modified to a so-called cost plus fixed fee contract (CPFF). On top of the cost reimbursement, the contractor is paid an additional fixed fee. For both variants, the contractor is only entitled to be compensated for those costs which can be fully documented and which are usually approved by the customer. In the CPFF type, fees are fixed unless re-negotiated due to a change in project scope. Cost reimbursement contracts bear fewer risks for the contractor but also allow for stronger customer involvement and control. These are typically used in an environment with great performance uncertainty on the side of the contractor, or if the customer insists on strong control. As administrative costs for this form of contract are rather high, for instance due to documentation needs, it is typically used for high-value projects. This often applies to international projects.

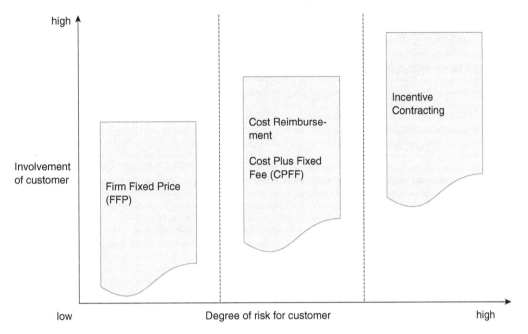

FIGURE 6.6 Common types of contract

3 *Incentive contracting*

The last of the three major forms of contract aims at sharing the savings of the contractor between the customer and contractor. The purpose is to encourage performance improvements in different areas, depending on the nature of the project, such as cost, schedule, quality, or safety. Incentive contracting can result in a win-win situation between the contractor and the customer, promoting performance and supporting a relation of partnership between both parties. Contractors are very motivated to outperform, hoping also to be awarded new projects if the customer is satisfied by their performance. Usually, incentive sharing is based on a pre-defined ratio.

Figure 6.6 summarizes the most common forms of contract, indicating their risk potential and the intensity of customer relations.

INTERNATIONAL CONTRACTS AND INTERNATIONAL CONTRACT LAW

Whatever contract form is chosen, we have to remember that contracts bear different importance and weight across national borders (more details can be found on the companion website). In order to simplify the situation for international project managers, associations of mainly project driven industries have endeavoured to introduce contract templates that are now accepted within respective industries across the globe. Let me introduce just one international contract standard (more details can be found on the companion website).

International Contract Standard UNCITRAL

The United Nations Commission on International Trade Law (UNCITRAL) was established in 1966. Its purpose is to further harmonize and unify the laws of international trade. In 1996, the Model Law on Procurement of Goods, Construction and Services was finalized. It deals with competitive procedures to select suppliers and contractors. In general, the organization provides international project managers and organizations with international projects with conventions, model laws and rules which are acceptable worldwide (UNCITRAL, 2004; 2008).

Regardless of the form contract of chosen, it may be helpful not only to use globally accepted templates, but also to refer to the International Commercial Terms (INCOTERMS) maintained by the International Chamber of Commerce as an international codification of terms used in international contracts. INCOTERMS are adhered to by most countries and are available in all the major world languages. Referring to them clearly defines which party incurs which cost, making misunderstandings less common and speeding up contract negotiations (ICC, 2008).

For the sake of maintaining good relationships to external stakeholders, arbitration is usually favoured over law suits. According to Murphy (2005), contract arbitration in a neutral country like Switzerland or in a country with a positive track record of legal fairness is recommended.

Common reference frames play an important role in the formulation of contracts as co-ordination mechanisms with external stakeholders. In addition, the project manager should pay attention to clarifying seemingly unimportant details in contract annexes in order to anticipate any potential sources of conflict. Snapshot 6.1 provides typical examples taken from international projects.

SNAPSHOT 6.1

Important details for international project contracts

1 Especially in infrastructure projects with many contractors and subcontractors, there is always quarrelling about invoices. Who gets how much money? How are the amounts split fairly? To avoid this, clear rules should be established in a contract annex before the work starts. The implicit should be made explicit. Qualifications, specifications, etc., should be made explicit and detailed, for instance in a contract between the project partners.

2 In the case of a project which has its own organization ('projectized' structure), or in the case of intra-organizational projects, it is important to determine at an early stage where the work will physically be done, and where the team will be located. In other words: which cost centre bears the rent, and who pays for the travel expenses?

The mentioning of misunderstandings and potential conflicts leads us to another mechanism related to the management of external stakeholder co-ordination, namely claim management.

CLAIM MANAGEMENT

This concerns the structured handling of obligations arising from the contracts closed between the contractor and customer. International projects, especially huge ones like infrastructure projects, require active claim management in order to mitigate risk and control cost. You can see the strong controlling component of this mechanism. Therefore, I will discuss the details in Chapter 7. Claim management also has an organizational aspect, though: a dedicated manager or unit (for instance as part of the project office) might be needed to track and implement claims.

EXTERNAL GOVERNANCE STRUCTURE

Suitable contracts are the basis for smooth external stakeholder co-ordination. In addition, there need to be mechanisms in place that continuously allow for an exchange of information and opinion between the contractor and external stakeholder, mainly the customer. Experience shows that monthly high-level meetings between the customer and the project management team of the contractor are helpful, even if there are no concrete issues to be discussed. The role of such meetings lies more in securing a regular information exchange. Before a topic starts to become an issue, things can be discussed in an informal set-up and frequently potential issues can be de-escalated before they turn into serious problems. This is especially important with customers who do not belong to the same national culture, as the likelihood of the occurrence of misunderstandings, for instance due to language problems, is much higher than with a domestic customer.

Information exchange and co-ordination is enhanced by staff continuity, even if the duration of the international project is several years. As it takes so much time to establish trusting relationships, especially across borders, it would be highly inefficient to alter key personnel every six months just because they may want to be involved in other projects or tasks. This stability requirement needs to be considered when internally and externally hiring staff for the international project.

ORGANIZING COMMUNICATION FROM A STRUCTURAL POINT OF VIEW

6.6 Structuring aims to reduce complexity. This is also true for the communication structure governing external and internal project relations.

The interfaces need to be minimized, either by creating work packages that only one organizational unit is responsible for, or by limiting the number of communication

Maximum number of communication relations (in theory):

$$C = \frac{N \times (N-1)}{2}$$

(C = communication relations, N = number of employees)

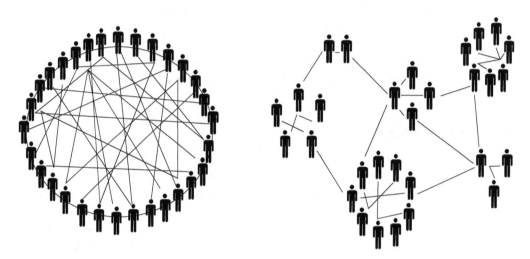

FIGURE 6.7 Building communication nodes

relations. If all the project members in a project with 300 staff communicate with each other, this would result in 44,850 communication relations. To prevent this potential communication chaos, the project has to be divided into sub-projects with sub-groups. Each of these sub-groups is called a communication node. Only one person in the node is allowed to communicate with another node which reduces the number of communication relations tremendously. Apart from slashing the amount of time needed for communication, a communication node structure helps to avoid misunderstandings and lessens the change of obsolete or outdated information flowing uncontrolled through the project.

Mini Case 6.2 provides you with an example of external project governance and communication structure in an international project in the rolling stock business.

Mini Case 6.2: How to communicate with the Scandinavian customer

A Scandinavian customer had placed an order regarding dozens of trains with a multinational corporation. Apart from 120 employees on the contractor's different sites, 48 major suppliers were involved. This meant a lot of information needed to be passed between the different stakeholders. The project language was English. To avoid misunderstandings, misinterpretations

Mini Case

and dysfunctional information flows, it was decided that the entire official communication between the customer and the contractor had to be conducted via the project managers on both sides. Over the four years' project duration, 1,300 letters were sent from the contractor to the customer, and 600 documents from the customer to the contractor. In addition, there were informal information exchanges between the various persons in charge on the operative levels between the customer and the contractor.

In order to continuously maintain an efficient information flow as well as a de-escalation forum, the leading teams of both sides regularly met on a monthly basis.

On the customer side were the: Project manager, Technical Manager, Deputy Project Manager, Safety & Security Manager, and Commercial Manager.

On the contractor side were the: Overall Project Manager, Commercial Project Manager, Technical Manager, Safety & Security Manager, Production Manager.

These persons met once a month to update each other. They went through the open issues list making sure that they were both on the same side talking about the same things. Those face-to-face meetings were mandatory, even if there were no pressing problems.

Task

Identify how the customer was integrated in the project. Assess the underlying co-ordination and communication mechanisms.

I will discuss the details regarding communication guidelines and principles in Chapter 9.

RESPONSIBILITY IN ORGANIZATIONAL STRUCTURES

6.7 After having selected a suitable organizational project structure, determined the mechanisms for internal and external project co-ordination, and decided on the communication interfaces, the structure needs to be 'filled' with people. Who will do what?

The 'what' is reflected in detail in the Work Breakdown Structure introduced in Chapter 3. The 'who' is part of the so-called Organization Breakdown Structure (OBS) which shows all the people who are carrying out the project. In other words, the Organization Breakdown Structure gives a comprehensive overview of the human resource requirements of a project. Simultaneously, it indicates from which parts of the organization people will come. It also shows whether the resources are internal, or whether external resources are required.

Together with the Work Breakdown Structure and the risk management plan, the Organization Breakdown Structure is an important element of the project master plan. And the project master plan, in turn, is the major output of the planning phase (see the companion website for details on an OBS).

PROJECT RESPONSIBILITY CHART		Functions/Roles												
Project: Production Transfer to China		Logistics GR	Procurement SQ	Procurement PQA	R & D Technology	R & D Material	Production QA	Production Assembly	Marketing	Sales	Legal Affairs	Sub-Project Mgr A	Sub-Project Mgr B	Project Manager
Sub-Project	**Description of work packages**													
Logistics	Goods Receipt	R						I				A		
	Warehouse Layout	R						S						A
	Commissioning	R									C	A		
	Interim Storage	R						C				A		
	Dangerous Goods	R			C	C								A
	Commodity Codes	R												A
	Packaging	R										A		
	Returned Goods	R										A		
	Documentation – export	R									S	A		
	Specification and validation of packaging	R										A		
Manufacturing	Change Mgmt Assembly Drawings							R					A	
	Assembly Facility Layout	I						R						A
	Assembly Function Tests						C	R					A	
	Generation of working plans							R					A	
	Material ordering process			S				R						A

FIGURE 6.8 Sample of a responsibility chart

A common format of merging a Work Breakdown Structure with an Organization Breakdown Structure is the so-called responsibility chart or responsibility matrix. It lists all the activities which need to be done, and links them to roles and/or concrete people in the form of a matrix. This systematical overview of who assumes which responsibility facilitates co-operation, especially in large complex projects. Based on the responsibility chart, the resource availability at each location or party involved in the international project needs to be checked. The responsibility chart also serves as a communication tool within the project to ensure all the project members are aware and informed about their concrete tasks.

The matrix usually lists the tasks or activities on the vertical axis, and the people who are supposed to carry out the tasks on a horizontal axis. It can be used at any level of the Work Breakdown Structure, for instance in a rather detailed one as depicted in Figure 6.8. You can

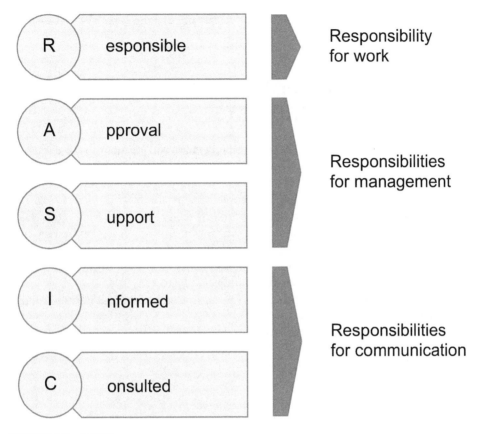

FIGURE 6.9 RASIC

see that the responsibility chart in Figure 6.8 is related to the project discussed in the previous chapter, namely the transfer of production of a medical device from Europe to China. For the sake of simplicity it covers only selected sub-projects and responsibilities at a high level.

The basis of a responsibility chart is a clarification of the types of responsibilities and the roles which go along with them. Experience has shown that the nature of involvement of different people is best described in the responsibility matrix in the form of letters in order to make the chart as self-explanatory as possible. A commonly used system is RASIC as described in Figure 6.9.

Roles and responsibilities need to be clearly communicated, not only internally, but also to external stakeholders. Otherwise, misunderstandings can easily occur like those depicted in the following example. In international infrastructure projects, the customer will sometimes send a delegate to supervise what the contractor is doing. This delegate is not supposed to assume project-related tasks, instead he or she should just supervise the contractor in order to ensure that the customer does not overpay or that specifications are closely adhered to. The same structure exists between a contractor and their subcontractors. Misunderstandings and mistrust can arise if the project stakeholders do no not clearly understand who it is that assumes which role and what this entails.

SPECIFICS OF RESPONSIBILITY IN INTERNATIONAL PROJECTS

6.8

Typically, the project responsibility chart will stir up a lot of discussion in the organization: functional managers will not want to release people who they would need otherwise; and project managers of different (international) projects will compete for people who are specialists in their fields. This is the case for all projects. As international projects tend to have heterogeneous stakeholders, the internal and external negotiations for human resources can be very time consuming. In addition, more politics are typically involved in international projects, with stakeholders pulling the strings behind the scenes as a result of motives that are not necessarily related to the international project at hand.

Another issue in international projects is the cultural embeddedness of responsibility charts, similar to matrix structures.

A responsibility matrix is mainly based on the following basic assumptions:

- individualism
- strong task orientation
- strong achievement orientation
- sequential way of working.

Again, this means for national cultures in the Arab world, on the Asian continent, in Africa, in Latin America, and Southern and Eastern Europe, a limited efficiency of this tool which may need modification.

One of the purposes of a responsibility chart is to clarify roles and assign responsibilities for each activity, usually to one individual. This individual typically is selected because he or she is thought of being the most capable of doing the job (achievement orientation). The individual is seen as the smallest unit of an organization which is the best to motivate and control. This process might not be applicable in a collectivist culture with strong status orientation. It might be perceived as paralysing by an individual from such a culture when he or she sees his or her name next to a certain task or activity. Used to working in a group he or she might not feel capable of doing a job on his or her own. This can cause a feeling of frustration or de-motivation resulting in non-achievement of the task. A person from a collectivist culture might feel safer and more motivated to work in a small group, under the natural leadership of the most senior member in the group who has the most experience. In collectivist cultures like Latin America, a feeling of solidarity is also very important. Even though individuals will have their specific tasks, it is considered sheer common sense to help this person in case of an emergency, regardless of priorities or other tasks. Many collectivist cultures would regard it as highly unfair to leave a colleague on their own with a problem. Even if they cannot do anything for him or her professionally, they will help in order to keep colleagues motivated through feeling with them. Empathy is a prevailing value rather than competition. Rationally seen this is a waste of energy, and slows down the other individuals and their task accomplishment process.

What does this mean for responsibility charts? It should allow for sufficient flexibility to assign tasks to small groups of two to four people. The project manager should leave it to the group as to how the work is split internally within the group and should only interfere in the case of non-performance.

Let us finish this chapter with a checklist which comprises good practices when it comes to the organization of international projects. You may find it helpful when you organize your own projects.

SNAPSHOT 6.2

Checklist for organizing international projects

- ☑ Try to visualize the structure as much as possible.
- ☑ Integrate key stakeholders in the organization's activities.
- ☑ Create organization charts.
- ☑ Explain and clarify what is meant by roles and responsibilities.
- ☑ Be flexible regarding individual or group responsibility.
- ☑ Make a list containing all the project members, their photos, contact details and their respective responsibilities and/or expertise.
- ☑ Ensure that all the project team members know about the organizational structure.
- ☑ Provide access to all organization related documents to all project team members for reference.

SUMMARY

Organizing an international project is another important part of the definition and planning phases. First, a suitable project structure has to be selected among the most frequent structures, namely functional, 'projectized', matrix, and virtual. Then, the project manager has to decide which mechanism he or she will implement in order to co-ordinate the internal and external stakeholders. For internal co-ordination of the project, the project office, steering committees, project champions, war rooms, and dual leadership can be used. For external co-ordination, the right contract form (fixed price, cost reimbursement, incentives) as well as the appropriate governance structure have to be decided on. In general, interfaces need to be minimized and governed by communication nodes. As a last step, the project manager has to plan for who will do the work outlined in the WBS. For this purpose, he or she creates an Organization

Breakdown Structure or typically a responsibility matrix in which roles have to be clearly defined following the RASIC codification. Both, matrix structures and responsibility charts are rooted in Anglo-American cultural dimensions such as individualism, achievement, task orientation, and low power distance. Therefore, these tools have to be adapted to local requirements.

 # KEY TERMS

Organizational structure, responsibility, authority, functional structure, 'projectized' structure, stand-alone structure, matrix structure, weak matrix, balanced matrix, strong matrix, project office, steering committee, project champion, war room, dual leadership, firm fixed price, cost reimbursement plus fee, incentive contracts, INCOTERMS, Organization Breakdown Structure (OBS), responsibility chart, responsibility matrix, RASIC.

REVIEW TASKS

Questions

1 What methods to structure a project do exist and which potential issues are to be expected with an international implementation of these structures?
2 What is important for the efficient internal and external co-ordination of an international project?
3 In your opinion, what are the critical success criteria for organizing an international project?

EXERCISE (FOR STUDENTS WITH BUSINESS EXPERIENCE)

Check with the class as to who has experience with matrix structures.
Class members who have experience with a matrix structure should:

1 Present the situation where they had a matrix structure to the class.
2 Reflect on what went well and where they perceived problems.

This presentation is best done using a flipchart.

After three or four presentations, the whole class should discuss the reasons for the perceived problems and suggest countermeasures.

CHAPTER END CASE: GOOD STRUCTURE PAYS OFF

PROJECT BACKGROUND

The ABB Group (Asea Brown Boveri) is a multinational company headquartered in Zurich, Switzerland. Since 2005, it has focused on its core competences and has been organized in five business units, namely Power Products, Power Systems, Automation Products, Process Automation, and Robotics. In 2007, ABB operated in 100 countries and employed more than 110,000 people.

The corporation was formed by the merger of ASEA AB (Sweden) and BBC Boveri (Switzerland) in 1988 and grew inorganically through numerous acquisitions worldwide in the 1990s. During this decade the corporation was organized de-centrally, developing new products in 550 facilities scattered around the globe. However, globalization urged the company to speed up the designing, developing, engineering and maintaining processes. New product development saw increasing complexity, with a cross-functional integration into an overall system with interface compatibility as a major challenge.

In response to the new market and product requirements, a new project was launched with the objective of creating a common product platform for substation automation systems for power transmission. This platform should ensure a quick and easy integration of the single sub-products from different ABB sites into one system configuration determined by global customers. The ultimate purpose was to reduce engineering time and complexity. The platform which was to be created as a result of the international project contained the following hard- and software products:

- control and protection terminal units for medium and high voltage (HV)
- intelligent gas insulated sensors (GIS)

- substation automation monitoring systems
- engineering tools and others.

In addition, new functions needed to be integrated into the platform such as functions for the medium voltage feeder and motor protection, new functions in HV protection, and more. Part of the project plan was the delivery of the new platform as a pilot system to an Australian customer who needed the system in order to connect two power grids. Hence, on time delivery was crucial for project success.

   Due to the fact that specialists for the different platform elements were located around the globe in different ABB subsidiaries, the project needed to work with global development teams. The subsidiaries which had the necessary core competences were located in Finland, Germany, Italy, Sweden, Switzerland, and the USA. Hence, this project crossing geographical, organizational and cultural boundaries needed to be organized in a way that would meet the demand created by the global distribution of the team members. At peak times, 150–200 employees were involved in this international project.

ORGANIZATIONAL STRUCTURE OF SUBSTATION AUTOMATION 2.0

The overall project was called Substation Automation 2.0 (SA 2.0) and comprised several product development projects which in turn were broken down into sub-projects. SA 2.0 was sectioned into three organizational levels: overall project management, project co-ordination at business units and sub-projects. Six main roles with responsibilities and authority were defined:

1   Program manager: This individual hero overall responsibility for the success of the project and its integration with other projects the company was implementing (see also Chapter 2)
2   Release manager: This individual headed the project organization as the responsible project manager with support from three groups responsible for the system specification, the validation of developed products, and delivery to the end customer.
3   Steering Committee (STECO): The steering committee of this project consisted of some senior managers at the top of different business units. Their main task lay in conflict resolution in the case of conflicting interests between the international local subsidiaries and the project.
4   Configuration Change Board (CCB): The board met on demand which was more often than the steering committee could have met. It consisted of a group of selected line, project and product managers familiar with the technology and market. Their task was to take quick operational decisions in terms of development priorities and functionality for single products. The CCB had full authority to take any kind of technical decisions. This ensured the timely implementation of the project and prevented delays.
5   Project co-ordinator: They needed to coordinate different sub-projects across national boundaries. Their main tasks were to update diagrams indicating the dependence on inputs from the different locations, to co-ordinate and resolve issues between the sub-projects, to co-ordinate reports for the milestone meetings, to initialize decisions where necessary, to report on the status of the sub-project, and to decide which sub-project managers should participate in the high-level status meeting (release meeting).
6   Sub-project managers: A sub-project was created with the purpose of enabling it to work as independently as possible. Typically, a sub-project was therefore limited to one geographical location and was focusing

on a single product. Sub-project managers were responsible for the project plan of their sub-project, for defining the functionality of the product developed in their team, for updating the time and milestone plan, for the project follow-up and reporting, as well as for requesting deliverables from other sub-projects.

These were the main roles and how they referred to each other in terms of an organizational structure.

GOVERNANCE STRUCTURE OF SUBSTATION AUTOMATION 2.0

In an international project with many parties geographically dispersed, it is of the utmost importance to think of a suitable governance structure in order to ensure the necessary information exchange between the parties involved in the project. Hence, the following platforms were established.

RELEASE MEETINGS

The release meetings were a forum where all sub-project representatives and other key persons met on a regular basis to inform each other about actual problems with the development of the new product. With new product development, it is natural that unforeseen problems will occur. Discussing those in the release meeting fostered an awareness of the joint responsibility for the overall outcome of the project, and prevented a 'blame-game' culture which pointed at other teams to look for the reasons for project failure. The release meeting also provided the release manager with an opportunity to reiterate the common project goal, to identify dependencies among sub-projects, to co-ordinate interfaces among the different sub-projects, and to assure a common understanding of the status in relation to the overall goal.

MONTHLY STEERING COMMITTEE (STECO) MEETINGS

The steering committee had the task of aligning the interests of different stakeholders, mainly the goal of the project manager and sub-project manager, with the special interest of the management of the different local subsidiaries involved, e.g. the Italians, Americans, or Swedes. The steering committee needed to make sure that all stakeholders, inside and outside this international project, understood the strategic importance of the project for the overall success of ABB. Hence, the top management members of the steering committee ensured project support by local entities. Project status was reported to the steering committee on a monthly basis, comprising critical issues where a decision was needed and the status regarding punctual delivery measured against milestones.

CONFIGURATION CHANGE BOARD (CCB)

Substation Automation 2.0 was a project without a formal contract regarding co-operation between the different national sites of ABB. This is typical for geographically dispersed new product development projects. As a result, it is very important to keep all the major parties involved in the decision-making process in order to maintain the flow of crucial information, to have the necessary expertise available, and to keep commitment and motivation flowing. New product developments come with a lot of uncertainty. Thus, frequent changes in the light of emerging technical problems are the order of the day. The configuration change board had to make sure that change decisions were taken quickly and consistently.

In addition to these formal forums, there were so-called information meetings carried out at irregular intervals on the different local sites involved. Their main purpose was to inform all members of the sub-projects on one site about the project status, and to conduct more informal measures to keep everybody motivated.

Sources: Eriksson et al. (2002); ABB (2008a); ABB (2008b)

Tasks

1 Create an organizational chart for the project SA 2.0.
2 Create a responsibility matrix for the roles mentioned in the case.
3 In your opinion, which are the critical factors contributing to the successful organization of this international project?

FURTHER READING

Conclaves, Marcus (2005) *Managing Virtual Projects.* San Francisco: McGraw-Hill. (Chapters 4 and 5 are especially relevant in the context of organizing international projects.)

Francesco, Anne Marie and Barry, Allen Gold (2005) *International Organizational Behavior,* 2nd edition. (Chapter 12 in particular provides the reader with a good overview of the relations between national culture and organizational structure, going beyond project management.)

Marsh, Peter (2003a) 'Contracts and payment structures'. In Turner, Rodney, J. (ed.: *Contracting For Project Management.* Aldershot: Gower, pp. 19–31. (An overview of various contracts in terms of structure, prices, and terms of payments is provided.)

IMPLEMENTING AND CONTROLLING INTERNATIONAL PROJECTS

7

LEARNING OBJECTIVES

After studying this chapter, you will be able to:

- elucidate the main activities in the implementation phase
- conceive the link between the control cycle and the PDCA cycle
- understand the impact of culture on monitoring and controlling
- explain different methods of monitoring data collection and types of reports
- apply easy-to-use tools to control international projects
- discuss Earned Value Analysis
- use the Balanced Score Card for controlling international projects
- manage operational change in international projects
- understand and use claim management.

INTRODUCTION

7.1 This chapter leads us to the third phase of project management, the implementation or execution phase. Typically, this is the longest of the four project phases. In an international infrastructure project such as the construction of a big dam, for instance, the implementation phase, i.e. the construction work, may last six years in contrast to the initiating and planning phase which would altogether take roughly three years. The quality of the output of the planning phase has a major impact on the implementation phase. If the course is set well, realizing the project and controlling whether everything goes as planned should be a smooth process. However major problems will occur in the implementation phase if planning turns out to be superficial or downright wrong. In the case of flawed time estimates, for instance, an overall project delay of 25 per cent may result in lost profits of 33 per cent (Jungkunz, 2006). To rectify problems and ensure project success, the project manager has to check the status of project implementation at regular intervals. I will start this chapter by explaining these activities in the framework of the Plan-Do-Check-Act (PDCA) concept. Based on the knowledge of the main tasks of the implementation phase, we will explore how and where national culture has an impact on the activities of this phase.

I will delve deeper into the field of monitoring and controlling, as these are the key activities in the implementation phase. The term 'monitoring' is used in a broad sense, i.e. tracking progress against set targets, whereas 'controlling' is used in a narrower sense, namely, to verify by evidence. I will introduce guidelines and approaches for data collection, data analysis, and report creation, placing emphasis on the importance of speed and information customization in an international project.

After the elaboration of the monitoring system, I will introduce controlling tools and techniques relevant in international projects, namely the traffic light concept, milestone checks, the Earned Value Analysis and the Balanced Score Card.

As international projects are typically embedded in a fast moving environment, the project master plan discussed in Chapter 5 cannot usually be strictly adhered to. In this chapter, we will discuss approaches on how to cope with change that is unavoidable during project implementation. This is closely related to active claim management as a tool to control the obligations and rights towards external parties that will emerge during project execution and that are often triggered by change.

Control has two sides, one being the more direct and fact-oriented side of controlling resources with tools and techniques. This is the side we will focus on in this chapter. The other side is more indirect and person-oriented, such as stakeholder management, leadership, motivation, negotiation, and conflict management. As stated in Chapter 1, the interpersonal side plays a very important role in international projects. Therefore, these aspects of control will be discussed in detail in Chapters 8, 9, and 10.

MAIN TASKS AND OUTPUT OF THE IMPLEMENTATION PHASE

7.2 The implementation phase requires all the inputs we have discussed in Chapters 4, 5, and 6 to be integrated within the project master plan. Following the so-called plan-do-check-act cycle taken from Total Quality Management, the project manager and his or her team will start to carry out the activities outlined in the project master plan. Each project member will pursue the tasks that were assigned to him or her, as documented in the responsibility matrix.

Implementing these planned activities can lead to undesired results. It is the task of the project manager to continuously monitor the process of task accomplishment by collecting, recording, and analysing data. The purpose of all monitoring activities is to detect any deviations from the original plans and discover the undesired results.

These can be caused either by the dynamic environment of international projects which may result in additional risks or any unexpected and unforeseeable emergencies, or by inaccurate planning that is rooted in the complexity of the international project.

Analysing the reason for the problems occurring in the 'do' phase will bring the project manager to the 'check' phase. Based on the analysis results, he or she needs to continuously improve the quality of the planning and align the plan to an ever-changing environment. This is the 'act' phase. Counter-measures could consist of adding additional resources (people, money, or time), reducing the scope, compromising quality, increasing risk, or providing incentives to employees or contractors.

The plan-do-check-act cycle shows us that the added value of the implementation phase not only consists of turning a plan into reality, but also of making its implementation as efficient and effective as possible in a changing context.

Figure 7.1 provides you with an overview of all the relevant activities in the implementation phase. As this is not a one-off endeavour but an ongoing effort, we call the process characterizing the implementation phase the monitoring cycle.

While the monitoring cycle provides us with an overview of all major activities in the implementation phase, we have to know more about controlling, which is one of the major tasks of this phase.

THE CONTROL CYCLE

In Figure 7.1, controlling takes place in the third phase of the cycle, in the 'check' phase. The basic control process in an international project does not differ greatly from the general controlling activities in the line organization. 'It is based on the definition and

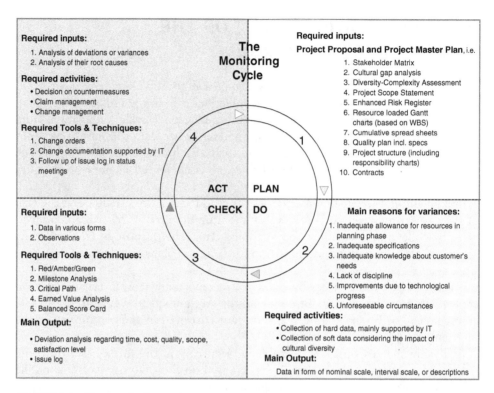

FIGURE 7.1 The monitoring cycle

establishment of key measures, then the comparison of those measurements to some desired values or standards to formulate algebraic formulas usually called metrics' (Brandon, 2004: 831). If the differences between what is measured and what is desired exceed a certain threshold, corrective actions will need to be taken. Depending on the extent of the variances, the ultimate ratio might be to stop the project all together. Such a radical decision might also be taken if the organization's strategy is greatly modified, resulting in a strategic misfit between the project in hand and the new organizational strategy (see Chapter 2).

One can measure process outputs or the process itself. In general, project results consist of scope, quality, time and financial resources, as depicted in Chapter 1. This is the basis for project control. One can measure:

- **Scope:** Have stated needs (requirements, deliverables) and unstated needs (major stakeholder's expectations) been met?
- **Quality:** Has the level of built-in quality (less noticeable aspects) and inspected quality (visible) been met?
- **Resources:** Has the scope been achieved within the given time and cost?

Figure 7.2 depicts the main activities linked with controlling.

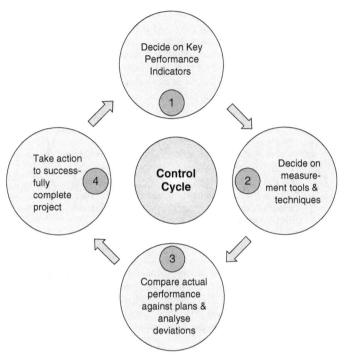

FIGURE 7.2 The control cycle
Source: Brandon (2004)

CULTURAL IMPACT ON MONITORING AND CONTROLLING

7.3 As is true for all areas of project management, monitoring and controlling is also influenced by cultural diversity. Figure 7.3 provides the reader with a systematic overview of cultural dimensions and how these tend to affect the behaviour of individuals in the implementation phase. As stated before, this cultural gap analysis should support the self-assessment of the project manager and/or team members to reflect on behavioural differences within the team. It should also raise awareness regarding the selection of suitable monitoring and controlling approaches in the given international project.

Let me just highlight here one major difference between task-oriented and relationship-oriented cultures that frequently leads to problems in the implementation phase. In many relationship-oriented cultures such as Brazil, Russia, India or China, personal presence is mandatory. For instance, it is very difficult to expedite deliveries via the phone from a remote place. If nobody shows up personally to put pressure on the local team or to support it, the issue is not regarded as important. People tend to feel neglected and do not put as much effort into the project as they could.

Embracing Risk	The higher the inclination to avoid risk, the more likely it is that important decisions due to a changing environment get delayed due to the fact that more details are needed for decision-making. If decisions are avoided, plans cannot be modified, and monitoring becomes meaningless.	**Avoiding Risk**
Individual	Data collection and reporting: persons from individualistic cultures tend to feel more comfortable responding to non-anonymous interviews or questionnaires for data collection. They also tend to feel more comfortable with measurement of their personal performance compared to team members from collectivistic cultures.	**Group**
Universal	Individuals from rather circumstantial cultures might feel that it does not make sense to monitor and revise 'old' plans. They might feel that it is sufficient to adapt to changes when they come, without documenting deviations from the original plan.	**Circumstantial**
Task	Individuals from relationship-oriented cultures could have difficulties in reporting issues or anything bad in order not to ruin the relationship with the person they are reporting to. They also may need more direct physical follow-up in terms of encouragement rather than virtual status meetings.	**Relationship**
Achievement	Project managers from achievement-oriented cultures may tend to invest some time in monitoring on a regular basis in order to counteract quickly. More status-oriented project managers might spend their time on presumably more rewarding activities like politics or building networks.	**Standing/Status**
Sequential	Prioritization of tasks under time constraints might be difficult for individuals from synchronic cultures.	**Synchronic**
Theoretical	Individuals from more pragmatic-orientated cultures may prefer quick action and countermeasures over a thorough analysis of the cause of deviations from the plan.	**Pragmatic**

FIGURE 7.3   Cultural impact on monitoring and controlling

Mini Case 7.1 illustrates how difficult monitoring and controlling in an international project can be.

Mini Case 7.1: Production transfer from Denmark to India

The Danish company LK, now belonging to Schneider Electronics, decided on transferring their labour intensive switch production to its Indian Joint Venture operation. During the planning phase, the company invested a lot in training all project team members on both sides, in Denmark and in India, in the following areas:

1. Language: as the Indian project members had a high proficiency in English, their Danish colleagues needed to be brought up to a similar level by intensive language training.
2. Basic rules of project management: all project members were familiarized with the company's internal methods regarding scheduling and budgeting. The meaning of responsibilities and deadlines was also explained to ensure a common understanding of critical terms and approaches.
3. Reporting: all company internal reporting templates were translated into English and explained to all project members as the new standard for reporting and monitoring.

The Danish project manager created the project master plan including all activities. She travelled to the Indian site to present and discuss her plan with the Indian part of the team. As everything seemed to be agreed on, she returned to Denmark and was happy that all was going so smoothly. Two months later, she went on another trip to India to check the project progress against her plan. Of course, she expected all the activities for the first period to be completed as she hadn't been told otherwise. She was quite irritated to see that nothing at all had happened in those two months.

Source: Adapted from Vonsild and Jensen (2006)

Tasks

1. Identify the reasons for the problem the project manager has.
2. What would you have done to avoid this delay of two months?

As we have now obtained an overview of the implementation phase and knowledge about potential differences in the behaviour of project members, we will delve into the more technical parts of monitoring and controlling, starting with tools and techniques in the area of monitoring.

TOOLS AND TECHNIQUES FOR MONITORING INTERNATIONAL PROJECTS

7.4 Project monitoring consists of the collection, documentation, and reporting of project information that is important to the project manager and other relevant project stakeholders.

	Completion	**Satisfaction**
Internal	1. Resources: time, cost 2. Productivity of Human Resources (due to cultural diversity) 3. Quality 4. Scope 5. Delays in input from other projects 6. Support level from HQ/ top management 7. Efficiency and consistency of business processes across locations	1. Executive management 2. Steering Committee 3. Line managers 4. Heads of subsidiaries 5. Project team members 6. Users within the organization
External	1. Economic situation of the countries the project operates in 2. Government regulations and approvals (changes, delays) 3. Natural disasters or untypical weather changes 4. Technological problems like power outages *For more details see Chapter 4*	1. Customer 2. Suppliers 3. Subcontractors 4. Consultants 5. (International) users outside of the organization

FIGURE 7.4 Monitor matrix for international projects

Source: Adopted from Lim and Mohammed (1999)

Before a project manager can set up a monitoring system, he or she has to decide on relevant performance indicators as depicted in phase one of the control cycle. We call these Key Performance Indicators (KPI). The project manager also needs to decide on how to measure the key performance indicators. Experience shows that it is not only hard facts, easily quantifiable data like time, cost, or quality, which need to be measured. If we think back to Chapter 1 and the critical success criteria listed up there, we can see that there are also a lot of 'soft things' which will need to be tracked because a lot can go wrong there, for instance:

- the goal commitment of the project team and the initial clarity of goals
- the establishment of clear communication
- adequate project team capabilities, including communication and conflict resolution capabilities
- a project culture of respect and trust.

The project manager needs to turn all the success criteria (hard and soft) into success factors. For all of those factors – data collection, feedback, and reporting – systems need to be established.

After the project manager has decided on what data are important to track, he or she has to decide on how to get these data. Systems and processes for data collection will have to be established.

The difficulty in establishing adequate monitoring systems for international projects is their complexity. The project manager needs to monitor more areas than in 'standard' projects. Context plays a big role. The project manager must keep an eye not only on what is going on within the project, but also on what happens around the project. This might have an impact on the final project success. He or she also needs to differentiate between areas contributing to the completion of the project, and areas contributing to the satisfaction of project stakeholders, a differentiation introduced by Lim and Mohamed (1999). Both categories are important for managing the international project successfully. In light of the critical success criteria and the most frequent reasons for failure, we can create a radar matrix of those areas which need to be monitored, as shown in Figure 7.4. The project manager can use this as a template and only add priorities to the various areas depending on the nature of the project.

After the project manager has mapped the monitoring areas, he or she needs to decide on the data collection methods.

HOW TO COLLECT DATA?

The monitoring system can include elements like telephone logs, tracking documents, records of significant changes, or documentation processes for formal and informal communications. Data which might not be available in (information) systems can be collected via interviews and questionnaires. The reader might recall qualitative and quantitative data collection methods from his or her academic research courses. Let me just mention that in international projects, language and cultural differences need to be considered when carrying out interviews or designing questionnaires (Harzing et al., under review). In organizations with a Project Management Office, it is the task of the PMO to provide the project manager with an adequate methodology for data collection.

There are several generic formats which could be used to obtain data. I will outline selected formats in the following list (Frame, 2002; Portny et al., 2008):

1   **Frequency count or nominal scale data:** This is a simple count of the occurrences of events which is usually done over a certain period of time like a month. It could be complaints per month (broken down by various stakeholders), conflicts in teams, interaction of certain parties in one month, or delays in finishing a certain process.

2   **Raw numbers or interval scale data:** These are actual numbers such as Dollars/ Euros/Yen spent, hours required, material consumed, fractions of efforts achieved. It is important that the basis, time period, and collection process to get the raw material are always the same in order not to create any biases. The raw data then need to be compared to the plan and the variances calculated.

3 **Verbal characterizations**: Less tangible variables such as the commitment towards goal achievement or team motivation can be measured in the form of verbal characterizations. However, the project manager needs to make sure that there is no room for an interpretation of those statements, which is a challenge in the complex and diverse context of an international project.

We have to keep in mind that data as such are not necessarily objective. Heterogeneity and a high number of stakeholders will add to subjectivity, mistakes, and errors. Therefore, the manager of an international project needs to pay a lot of attention to data collection guidelines. He or she also must keep in mind that measured data might not be correct. The project manager along with other groups in the organization has to scrutinize continuously whether the data collected are valid at all. Do they cover the areas which should be measured? For instance, does the absenteeism of an employee measure the commitment of this employee? Again, the judgement is context sensitive. In spite of all these caveats, data collection is a prerequisite for controlling an international project.

As a starting point, the project manager can refer to the responsibility matrix along with the WBS for an orientation as to who will collect which data.

HOW TO ANALYSE DATA?

Data collection as such is a very important task of the project manager and his or her management team. However, it bears no value if the data are not analysed. For instance, are five incidents of conflict in a team per month good or bad? And where do these conflicts stem from?

The analysis can consist of simple aggregation of the data, for example to average the values. It could also be something more complex like applying a statistical distribution function to the data to ascertain a particular trend. For raw data on cost, schedules and human resources, there are many software packages analysing and forecasting performance (see Snapshot 7.4).

However, no system support is available to analyse the 'soft data'. Are five conflicts in a team per month normal? Or is this already a major problem and a signal to engage an external mediator to get the team back on track? Especially in international projects where success depends heavily on soft issues, the project manager needs first to have an awareness of the importance of these factors. Second, he or she needs to be able to collect relevant data. Third, the project manager has to have the capability to interpret the data in the right way thus turning these into information. Due to the huge variety of soft data, it does not make much sense to explore every single analysis method. Let me remind you of some tools and documents which can help the project manager to analyse the root causes of 'soft issues', such as the stakeholder matrix, the scope statement, the cultural gap analysis tool, and the diversity-complexity matrix. The use of these tools and techniques can help the project manager in finding out the reasons for misunderstandings, conflicts, or delays.

HOW TO REPORT THE MONITORING RESULTS?

After project data have been collected and analysed, the resulting information needs to be communicated to the relevant stakeholders, usually the customer and senior management, but also the project management team or all project members. This can be done in different formats (Portny et al., 2008):

1 **Routine reports**: These are reports issued on a regular schedule, for instance once a week.
2 **Special analysis reports**: These aim at disseminating the results of a special study in a project concerning a particular challenge beyond the borders of the project. An example could be the first time the organization uses an innovative technology. I will get back to this format in Chapter 11.
3 **Exception reports**: They are intended for special decisions related to unexpected situations which usually need to be taken by senior management. International projects will typically have a lot of exception reports.

The following snapshot illustrates the good practice of an exception report format which targets obtaining quick decisions from senior management or the client. As international projects are dynamic, changes are common and the time to adapt plans to the new conditions is scarce. This requires quick decisions. If the decision is beyond the project manager's authority, the project manager can push for a quick decision using the 'decision preparation checklist' depicted in Snapshot 7.1. You can download the form from the companion website.

SNAPSHOT 7.1

How to get quick decisions from the project owner

Project owners of international projects are usually high ranking executives, either internal or external. They do not want to be bothered by lengthy discussions about potential issues and their root causes. Instead, they want to be faced with possible solutions and their costs. This is the opportunity for the project manager to influence the course of action according to his or her ideas.

☑ What is the problem?
☑ What is the cost incurred by the problem?
☑ What is the status regarding the solution of that problem?
☑ How urgent is the decision?
☑ Are the costs covered by the budget?
☑ Recommended course of action/countermeasure.
☑ Suggested decision.

Confronted with this information, the customer will typically discuss the formulation of the suggested decision, without questioning the decision as such. It is especially important to draw on the consequences if no quick decision is taken.

CUSTOMIZING REPORTS

Reports need to be targeted at the needs of their receivers. Not all stakeholders involved in the project have to get a report with the same level of detail, or with the same frequency. The external customer might be most interested in reports about delays because his business may depend on the timely introduction of new software. The internal owner might be more interested in both time and cost and some project members might want to know about the schedule of the task they depend on.

Customization, however, does not only refer to the frequency of distribution, level of detail or selection of relevant content. It also touches on areas like the method of communication. Is a written report always best, or should it be an oral report face-to-face? Should it comprise only key facts and be concise, or should it have some appendices and provide a lot of background information? Should it be in English or in the native language of the customer? Snapshot 7.2 describes some major differences regarding the expectations held towards a management report of a US-American, East Asian and European Steering Committee.

SNAPSHOT 7.2

Customization of reports

A seasoned international project manager recalls: 'I have experienced that reports to steering committees are culture-bound. Steering committees consisting of US-Americans usually expect crisp and quick status reports. They quickly lose their patience if issues are reported which are not directly relevant for them. They want a brief and relevant summary of the issues and solutions they can decide on. East Asian Steering Committee members need more details and would like to have more background information: Why have issues occurred? What are the possible consequences? They typically would like to have more details than they really need, also for later reference. Western European Steering Committee members are usually in the middle: They want to know a bit of context, but only the relevant issues brought forward in a timely manner.'

The astute reader will have noticed that Snapshot 7.2 contains stereotyping. It reflects the personal experience of one individual rather than a generic 'truth'. Yet, it might be helpful as a rough rule of thumb.

REPORTING GUIDELINES

At the beginning of the implementation phase, the project manager should issue clear reporting guidelines to the project members. An example could look like this (Longman and Mullins, 2005):

- Get approval for any overtime of more than five hours or unbudgeted expenses of more than 500 Euros.

- Report the completion of tasks in percentages on a daily basis to your sub-project leader, including any issues if relevant.
- Report task completions to your sub-project leader on the day of completion, confirming Actual versus Plan for time and cost.
- Use e-mail for routine reporting.
- Use the phone or voice mail for any urgent issues.

Reporting guidelines may differ between the sites involved in the project. However, there should be some basic guidelines which are for the overall project standard. The project manager can use the responsibility matrix created in the planning phase to confirm who to communicate with which monitoring guidelines.

The whole set of monitoring tasks is quite time consuming. It can easily capture 20 to 35 per cent of a project manager's day (Zagarow, 2003).

Let me mention at the end of this section that collecting data and reporting information are particular forms of communication. I will deal with more details on communication guidelines in Chapter 9.

TOOLS AND TECHNIQUES FOR CONTROLLING INTERNATIONAL PROJECTS

7.5 While monitoring carries the association of keeping track of or checking a situation for a special purpose, controlling carries an element of influence and the exertion of power to rectify undesired situations. In this section, I will explain selected tools and techniques such as the traffic light system or the milestone analysis to control the progress of projects. These tools are appropriate when controlling international projects which are not too complex. I will continue with more complicated tools, namely the Earned Value Analysis (EVA), expert systems, and the Balanced Score Card.

TRAFFIC LIGHT APPROACH

This tool with its simple colour coding is very suitable for international projects because it is fairly straightforward and self-explanatory.

Green: Activities or milestones running on schedule
Yellow/amber: Activities or milestones which run a high risk of being delayed or bearing a cost overrun
Red: Activities running behind schedule or milestones not achieved on time, or any other showstopper.

Most international projects will use this approach to control project progress. However, it is a visualization method rather than a generic control tool. Colour coding only makes sense when compared to a plan or other underlying criteria according to

Criteria for project status
light setting

Total project traffic
light status

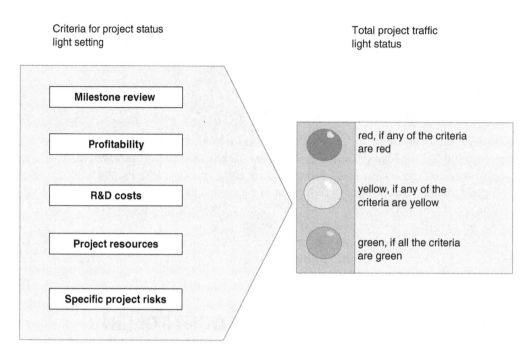

Milestone review

Profitability

R&D costs

Project resources

Specific project risks

red, if any of the criteria
are red

yellow, if any of the
criteria are yellow

green, if all the criteria
are green

FIGURE 7.5 Traffic light tool

which the colour coding is applied. Figure 7.5 gives examples of such criteria that each relate to the project proposal and project master plan.

Hence, the traffic light tool is typically combined with other controlling tools, such as the milestone analysis explained in the next section.

MILESTONE ANALYSIS

This approach uses milestones as defined in Chapter 3 to control the international project. Review meetings are conducted around the pre-defined milestones of the project. To make this approach meaningful, it is important to have clear criteria to pass a milestone, previously defined in the planning phase. Controlling consists of comparing the pre-defined criteria with what has been achieved, along with the costs and schedule.

The review meetings scheduled around a milestone are suitable for discussing the consequences of delays, cost overruns, quality problems or other issues with the project team or senior management. The approach is easy to use and easy to learn. It provides all the main stakeholders with a quick overview and facilitates an ongoing assessment of the project. However, it requires project phases with well-defined deliverables or interim results.

Experience in international projects shows that it is good to hold milestone review meetings at sites outside of the office, for instance in a hotel or any other place which is somehow impressive. The advantage is that people will always remember the place easily. Thus, it is also easier for them to remember the decisions taken at those meetings. Places outside the office are also more suitable to combine a milestone review meeting with a team building meeting to brainstorm about issues which have emerged during the implementation phase or for other purposes. The downside, of course, is additional cost.

EARNED VALUE ANALYSIS

A more comprehensive and complicated controlling tool is the Earned Value Analysis (EVA). The purpose of this tool is to show the relationships between variances in cost, schedule and project performance. Compared to more traditional control mechanisms such as cost versus budget, EVA is more suitable for controlling long-lasting, complex international projects, for instance in engineering and construction, because it integrates different parameters, namely cost and time, based on a pre-defined level of scope and quality. Earned value (EV) is the value expressed in a currency of the work accomplished at a certain point in time based upon the planned or budgeted value for that work. Another term for EV is Budgeted Cost of Work Performed (BCWP) (Brandon, 2004).

A prerequisite to apply the earned value analysis is the availability of the following information which we have discussed in Chapter 5:

- budgeted cost
- planned schedule
- actual cost
- start and completion of different tasks
- milestone checks.

If we feed the Work Breakdown Structure along with the estimated time and cost into any given scheduling program, the program will give us total budgeted cost at any given point in time of the overall project. These figures are named Planned Costs (PC) or Budgeted Cost of Work Scheduled (BCWS). Figure 7.6 shows such a cost curve in relation to time based on the Europe–China production transfer project discussed in Chapter 5.

As the project progresses throughout its execution, actual costs are incurred. These can be directly compared with the curve of the budgeted costs, thus illustrating neatly the deviations as depicted in Figure 7.7.

So far, this has been the usual procedure with an actual versus planned cost comparison. What EVA provides on top, is the integration of the work performed at any given point of time. Therefore, the (aforementioned) parameters are needed, integrating the schedule, costs, and work accomplished (Brendon, 2004):

1 Planned Cost PC (Budgeted Cost of Work Scheduled)
2 Actual Cost AC (Actual Cost of Work Performed)
3 Earned Value EV (Budgeted Cost of Work Performed).

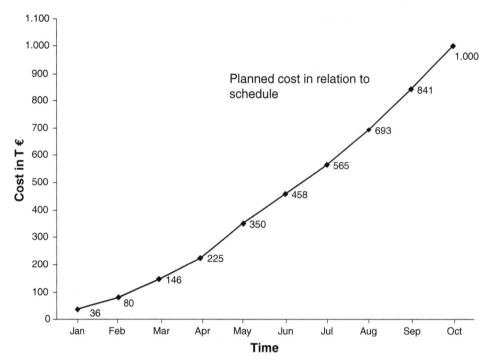

FIGURE 7.6   Planned cost in correlation with time

With these parameters, we can control cost and time deviations by using pre-defined formulas:

- Using a first formula, cost deviations can be determined in monetary terms:
  Cost variance = Earned Value − Actual Cost (= BCWP − ACWP)
- With the following formula, cost deviations can be determined in per cent:
  Cost variance = (EV-AC) × 100%/EV
- The following formula helps to control schedule deviations by determining the Schedule Variance (SV) in monetary terms:
  SV = Earned Value − Planned Costs (= BCWP − BCWS)
- To determine the Schedule Variance (SV_m) in months the following formula has to be used:
  SV_m = (EV − PC)/(Planned costs for the actual month)
  For reporting purposes, charts as depicted above can be used.

Other values that can be determined using EVA are project performance indices which can help in assessing how well the project is performing.

- With respect to budget we can determine the so-called Cost Performance Index (CPI) as follows:
  CPI = Earned Value/Actual Cost (= BCWP/ACWP)

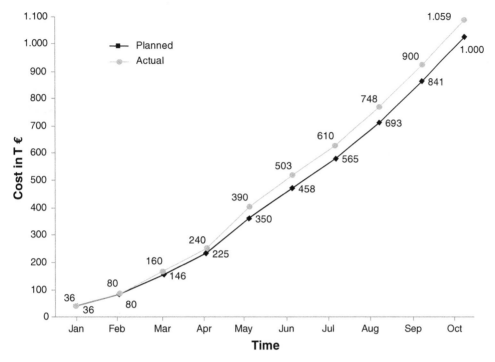

FIGURE 7.7 Actual costs versus budgeted cost in correlation with time

A CPI of 1.0 or more means that the project is at or below budget.

- With respect to time we can determine the so-called Schedule Performance Index (SPI) as follows:
  SPI = Earned Value/Planned Cost (= BCWP/BCWS)
  If SPI is 1.0 or more, the project is at or ahead of schedule.

Figure 7.8 illustrates the cost variance (CV) in monetary terms, the schedule variance (SV) in monetary terms, and the schedule variance (SV_m) in months based on the data presented in Figures 7.6 and 7.7.

Figure 7.8 assumes that we are at the end of June. In accordance with Figures 7.6 and 7.7 we can see that overall PC is 458,000 and that the planned costs for the actual month (June) are 108,000 (see Figure 5.9). However, we now receive a report showing that AC is 503,000. Furthermore, from our scheduling tool we can determine the earned value (BCWP) as 404,000. Applying the formulas given above, we now receive:

CV = 404,000 − 503,000 = − 99,000
SV = 404,000 − 458,000 = − 54,000
SVm = (404,000 − 458,000)/108,000 = − 0.5

This means that the project is 0.5 month and 54,000 € behind schedule and the actual cost is 99,000 € above the earned value (BCWP).

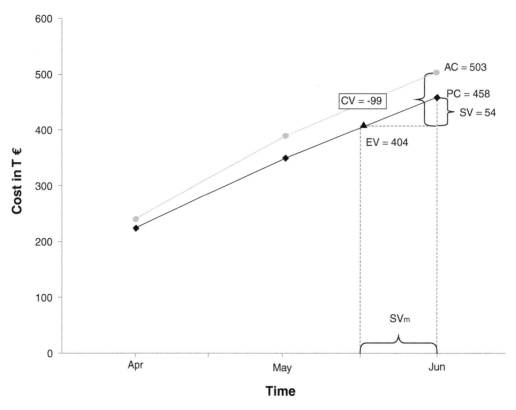

FIGURE 7.8 Illustration of earned value

Although EVA is a suitable controlling tool, the caveat comes with data availability. This is especially true for the completion of activities or work performance, which in turn is input to the earned value. To make the data available, it should be provided on a report template. The data themselves might be determined using known estimation tools. Of course, calculations are only as good as the underlying estimates, and the organization needs to trade off how much time it can afford to spend on very detailed estimates. People also need to be trained in this control tool on an international basis to make sure that it is understood and applied in the same way across the organization.

AUTOMATION OF PROJECT CONTROL BY USING EXPERT SYSTEMS

Integrative information management systems were developed to tackle problems with data availability, complexity, and dynamics. Their output looks very precise. However, the input of these systems will frequently still rely on traditional data collection methods as described in section 7.4. Each industry has made progress with automated controlling systems. So-called expert systems can fulfil such tasks as tracking adherence to specifications. Mini Case 7.2 provides you with an example of an automated controlling system used for international aircraft development projects.

Mini Case 7.2: Product Data Management (PDM) controlling at EADS

EADS is a global leader in aerospace, defence and related services. The group includes the aircraft manufacturer Airbus. As of 2008, it employs about 116,000 people at more than 70 production sites, above all in France, Germany, Great Britain and Spain as well as in the US and Australia. In 2007, the company had revenues of € 39.1 billion.

The development of new aircraft with teams dispersed around the globe is a tremendous challenge. Due to the long project duration, it is extremely important to detect any deviations from plan as early as possible. EADS solves the problem of the unreliability of monitoring data by linking its Product Data Management (PDM) system for aircraft with project controlling. The PDM system contains information about product/component development status. This input is difficult to access via traditional methods. Through a synchronization of the semantics of the PDM system, the company can integrate work performance data, schedule, and cost data. In addition, the automated controlling system tracks changes in terms of additional requirements or specifications. The expert system visualizes the project status in so-called work performance diagrams. These comprise information on groups (structure) working on the project along with the planned milestones of their work. Vertical bars show the changes regarding work packages over time. Another line depicts the work performance in terms of developed components.

Source: Jungkunz (2006); EADS (2008)

Question

Which advantages does the PDM-based controlling system have over the EVA method discussed above?

THE BALANCED SCORE CARD

To cater for the complexity of international projects, performance needs to be measured and controlled from different perspectives in a systematic way. A suitable tool is the Balanced Score Card which I introduced in Chapter 2. Ideally, this controlling approach should be applied to each single (international) project, each program, and the organization as a whole. For the financial side of the Balanced Score Card, the project manager can use tools like EVA.

In addition, the project manager needs to turn his or her attention towards more intangible performance areas like customer satisfaction, internal business processes, and learning and growth. The last area refers to the investment in human capital through training, motivational techniques, or the development of an organizational culture that will be further discussed in Chapter 11.

As a controlling tool, the Balanced Score Card not only looks at past activities, but at the same time also uses the feedback gathered from the different areas to improve the performance of the international project. Table 7.1 provides you with an overview of the metrics that could be used in the respective fields of the Balanced Score Card.

TABLE 7.1   The Balanced Score Card and Project Management Metrics

Perspective	Activities	Examples of Metrics Measurement methods
Learning and Growth	Effective planning and execution of project communication	Quality and use of communication matrix Meeting minutes for each important meeting
	(Facilitated) Team Building Workshops	Number of problems of conflicts Project members survey regarding motivation and job satisfaction
	Carrying out assessment centres and development programs for international project managers with internal certification	Training funding Number of certified international project managers
	Establishing a mentor program	Mentor reviews
	Establishing communities of practice among international project managers	Survey of effectiveness of community of practice among users
Customer	Customer expectation analysis	Track record of changes of customers requests
	Regular customer involvement	Minutes of meetings with customers with issue log
	Clear contract	Zero claims
Internal Business Process	Detailed planning phase	Detailed Gantt-Chart or network plan Precise milestone definitions
	Sizing	Estimation accuracy in per cent
	'Built-in Quality'	Zero defects, no claims, high customer/user satisfaction checked with questionnaires
	Testing and inspection	Compliance with standards
	Scope Control	Transparent and comprehensive tracking of change orders
	Stakeholder management	Quality of stakeholder map, frequency and quality of stakeholder communication
	Issue management	Accuracy and control of issue log
Financial	Use of Resources Contracting/Procurement	EVA Procurement Standards

Sources: Adapted from Kaplan and Norton (1996); Brandon (2004)

The Balanced Score Card requires processes to gather feedback, for instance through surveys, interviews, focus groups or other methods (Phillips et al., 2002). Especially in international projects, it is important to control all fields of the project as they are interdependent. If problems in the 'soft areas' are disregarded, they will turn into financial problems eventually.

ANALYSIS OF CONTROLLING RESULTS

7.6

Now that you have been familiarized with controlling tools, I will guide you through some common issues causing deviations from the original plans. You may find this list helpful as a kind of checklist for your own activities in international projects.

If variances between the actual schedule and the planned schedule are discovered, possible reasons could be:

- People are spending less time on the activity than was estimated. Why? It is important to keep in mind that the project is not an isolated island in the organization. This means the employees assigned to an international project probably still have tasks and commitments stemming from previous projects and their line duties. Moreover, employees are human beings and cannot work at 100 per cent on a given task from 8.00–12.00 for one project, and from 13.00–18.00 on another. Interruptions from customers, colleagues and suppliers need to be factored in. There might be unexpected additional efforts related to a previous project due to a production line standstill. A lot of time is also needed for meetings which are not necessarily related to the project an individual is planned to be part of. According to Rauwerdink (2005), 40 to 70 per cent of the time of a single team member could be used for the activities mentioned above.
- The activity is taking more work effort than estimated.
- People are expanding the scope of the activity. In international projects, the reason for this could be a misunderstanding of the task at hand. It could also be different the standards or expectations that locals have towards the task as compared to the project manager who has estimated the durations.
- Work which was not identified in the WBS is needed to perform the activity.
- The capability level of the people working on the activity is lower than expected.
- People are not correctly recording their schedule performance.

For cost variances or cost overruns, a similar list of possible causes can be created:

- Goods or services that were not included in the plan were needed. This could be due to the fact that technological solutions were more complicated than anticipated.
- Exchange rates have changed greatly in an unexpected way as was the case in 2008 with the US-dollar against the Euro.

- Penalty payments were due and exceeded the contingencies in the budget.
- Risk registers were incomplete, and/or newly emerging risks exceeded the contingencies.
- Inflation in one or more countries has risen sharply.
- Much more travelling was needed than expected.

You will have noticed that the most possible reasons for delays and cost overruns are directly related to time-planning factors and cost-estimate factors as discussed in Chapter 5. The more accurate the planning, the less risk there is for variances in the implementation phase.

Cost or time overruns also may simply be related to internal or external changes.

MANAGING CHANGE

7.7

Experience shows that plans will always have to be adapted to a changing environment. We have to keep in mind, though, that this is operational change. The overall objective of the international project should remain stable, unless the project is cancelled due to a major change of strategy which renders the project obsolete. While the project objective functions as a common denominator of all project members, project implementation may need to be adapted to a fast changing environment.

PROCEDURES TO MANAGE PLANNED AND UNPLANNED CHANGE

Managing the various variations occurring in an international project is a challenge. It needs to be systematically done in order to keep control over the project. Changes can be planned or unplanned as discussed in Chapter 4. In any case, these are referred to as 'issues'. Depending on the quality of our risk register, we will have planned for change when it eventually occurs, or otherwise it is not covered in the risk register and the project manager or senior management has to improvise. For both planned and unplanned change, it is important to detect any variations from the plan. The process looks as follows:

1 Identification of issue through context scanning. The monitoring matrix depicted in Figure 7.4 is a helpful tool to perform this task.
2 Entering the issue into a special form called an issue log. The issue log should contain the date when the issue was discovered, the tracking number of the issue, the description of the issue, the impact of the issue in terms of project completion, the suggested solution to the issue (the proposed change), the responsible person to implement the change, and the date of completion of change implementation. Helpful input at that stage can be provided by the risk register discussed in Chapter 4.
3 Depending on the impact of the issue on project completion, resources are allocated to solving the issue based on a suggested solution.
4 Following up the progress of implementing the change to solve the issue until completion.

Issue Log						
No.	Date	Description	Impact (in terms of project completion)	Suggested solution	Responsible person	Date of completion

FIGURE 7.9 Sample of issue log

Figure 7.9 provides you with a sample of a typical issue log as it is used in many international projects.

Regardless of the causes of the variations, the project manager must keep control of the overall picture. Authority to change the project master plan therefore should be centralized and restricted to the project manager and a few deputies or sub-team leaders. To keep a clear overview, all changes need to be documented with tracking numbers. The impact of the changes on the pre-defined project scope (in relation to cost, time and quality) needs to be assessed continuously and reported to the organization's senior management.

CENTRAL VERSION CONTROL

International projects tend to have numerous interfaces. They also tend to involve staff who are dispersed around the globe and working virtually together. In this context, tight change control is absolutely mandatory. Change requests or changes in progress need to be administered by a central database in order to avoid delays caused by the fact that teams are working from an invalid master plan. In an international software project, this only became obvious afte several weeks, when different coding packages needed to be integrated, that some sub-teams had not considered the changes in the product specification thus resulting in weeks of project delay.

Transparency and accessibility of change data are paramount. However, this does not guarantee efficient change management. In addition, the project manager needs to establish ground rules that will discipline teams to make use of the centralized data. Easy-to-understand scenarios of what will happen if they ignore change management guidelines will help to create the necessary awareness regarding this issue. The link between change management and the final success of the project needs to be elaborated in a simple way and must be understood by all project team members across the globe.

I will now touch upon a special case of change management, namely claim management.

MANAGING CLAIMS

7.8

Figure 7.1 shows that contracts are input to the implementation phase. During project progress, the project manager has to control whether all the contracts are honoured. Usually, contracts contain clauses to deal with the unusual as I have explained in Chapters 4 and 6. Yet, many variations will occur during project progress, for instance due to design changes or changes in the customer's requirements. Variations may result in a claim for additional payment. Some of these claims may be accepted, others might not.

Stakeholder management clearly helps peaceful agreements on claims. The last resort is a legal dispute which should be avoided in an international context, as this can take a very long time and incur immense costs. Regardless of how claims are dealt with, a lot of money is at stake. In the aeronautics business, claim management currently contributes to a 10 per cent increase in project revenue (Benz, 2005). As a result, the project manager needs to pay special attention to managing claims when they occur, which is typically the case in the implementation phase.

I will not discuss claim management in detail here because contracts depend on the legal context which can be quite different for single international projects due to different jurisdictions. I will instead outline the general process of managing claims which needs to be modified depending on the legal context (Marsh, 2003b):

1   Claims need to be identified (reasons and costs). For instance, they can be caused by delayed supplies. They can also be rooted in modified specifications resulting in additional design or process costs. In addition, more capacity in administration may be needed to cope with those changes resulting in decreased profits.

2   As a second step, the claim needs to be passed on to the customer. However, this has to be done in a sensitive way. Depending on the jurisdiction, the supplier may need to provide hard evidence about the cost induced by the customer. In general, it may be easier to convince the customer about accepting a claim by creating an awareness of the related cost that the variation ordered by the customer has caused. Hence, numerical evidence regarding additional cost is always helpful. This requires a fully-functioning monitoring and control system.

Let me close this chapter with Mini Case 7.3, which illustrates what happens if claims are not monitored and controlled – even if it is 'only' due to a misunderstanding.

Mini Case 7.3: Cultural misunderstanding in claim management

A European consortium selling customized investment goods to China assessed claims as a potential source of conflict. Hence, the consortium agreed internally on a 'zero-claim-policy' in order to maintain harmony with the Chinese customer. The purpose was to secure follow-up orders. The consortium did not communicate this policy to their Chinese customer as they thought it would be a basic assumption by the Chinese.

However, the Chinese customer was mainly interested in getting access to innovative technology and not in purchasing more investment goods. In order to pursue his interest, the Chinese customer issued claims against the consortium after the product had been delivered and handed over to the Chinese side. The consortium was accused of having withheld technology from the Chinese. According to the Chinese interpretation of the contract, the technology in question should have been transferred to China.

The consortium was shocked at this approach because they had assumed reciprocation on the 'zero-claim-policy'. When they were confronted with claims from the customer's side, they realized that they had made a mistake. They did not have any leverage against the customer by lodging their own claims because they had unilaterally abstained from forwarding their (numerous) claims during the course of the project.

A study (Chen and Partington, 2004) comparing Chinese and UK project managers in the construction industry has revealed different attitudes to claims and contract penalties. For the Chinese, negotiation was the only way to resolve a conflict between the customer and the contractor. Claims were considered as something extreme resulting in a loss of 'face'. The UK managers had a more impersonal attitude. While they preferred negotiations, they saw claims and contractual penalties as normal management practice.

Probably, the Western consortium had in mind what the study above revealed. But what went wrong?

Question

How do you explain the contradiction between the study and the behaviour of the Chinese customer?

Mini Case

SUMMARY

International projects operate with great complexity in a fast changing environment. As a result, the project manager needs to constantly monitor deviations from the original project master plan. He or she needs to collect reliable and valid hard and soft data, analyse these, report these in an adequate format and push for quick decisions. Cultural differences in attitudes towards reporting, communication, and measurement need to be considered to monitor the project effectively. There are different tools to control the progress of the project, such as the Traffic Light Approach, the Milestone Analysis, the Earned Value Analysis, IT-based automated expert systems, and the Balanced Score Card. Based on the results of continuous control activities, the project manager needs to take corrective actions. These are embedded in effective change management. Issues need to be solved and emerging claims must be handled in order to ensure project completion and customer satisfaction.

KEY TERMS

PDCA cycle, monitoring cycle, control cycle, nominal scale data, interval scale data, data reliability, data validity, Traffic Light Approach, Milestone Analysis, Earned Value Analysis, Earned Value, Budgeted Cost of Work Performed, Actual Cost of Work Performed, Budgeted Cost of Work Scheduled, Cost Variance, Schedule Variance, Cost Performance Index, Schedule Performance Index, Balanced Score Card, change management, claim management.

REVIEW TASKS

Questions

1   Where do you see the link between the planning phase and the implementation phase?
2   Which cultural differences do you have to cope with in the implementation phase?
3   Why is it so challenging to monitor and control international projects?

EXERCISE

- Work in groups of three or four people.
- Go back to the Chapter End Case of Chapter 1 regarding avian influenza (www-links to retrieve further information provided in the references).
- Create a list of data that need to be monitored in order to check project progress. Put your results on a flipchart.
- Search for issues that have occurred in the year 2009 and put these in an issue log. Then put the issue log on a flipchart.
- Present your results to the other groups and discuss in class the challenges of monitoring and controlling such a complex project.

CHAPTER END CASE: CONNECTING THE WORLD IN HONG KONG

In 2004, a multinational consumer electronics manufacturer re-adjusted its strategy from outsourcing manufacturing to Engineering and Manufacturing Services and Original Design Manufacturers to regain full control by manufacturing a significant percentage of the products in their own factories.

In order to reduce the risk and make production more flexible, the company decided on establishing a central hub for so-called Supplier Managed Inventory (SMI) or Vendor Managed Inventory (VMI). This is a business model in which the buyer of a product provides electronic information to component suppliers. The component suppliers take full responsibility for maintaining an agreed inventory of the parts, in this case at the manufacturer's central hub. A third party logistics provider is involved to make sure that the buyer has the required level of inventory by adjusting the demand and supply gaps. Based on Electronic Data Interchange formats, EDI software and statistical methodologies, the suppliers and the manufacturer can obtain a better understanding about each other's situation, enabling more accurate forecasts and the maintenance of correct inventory in the supply chain.

As the main factories were in Asia, the location of the first hub for most of the product components should be in Asia. Due to an excellent infrastructure, the absence of major natural catastrophes, tax and duty advantages, and ease of doing business, Hong Kong was chosen as the hub location.

The main stakeholders of the project were:

- the consumer electronics manufacturer
- 115 suppliers located in Europe (e.g. Hungary), Asia (e.g. China, Vietnam, the Philippines, Japan), and the Americas (e.g. Mexico and Brazil) that were supposed to deliver their components to the Hong Kong hub
- thirty internal and external factories for sub-assemblies and finished goods which had to procure components from the SMI hub
- the logistics partner.

This complex international project had a very long planning phase which started in 2004. The concept needed to be worked out, and the right logistics partner found. Lead times needed to be calculated with different local customs regulations in mind. For instance, the operations in Brazil and India caused uncertainties due to frequent strikes and customs clearance issues. An extra week for those deliveries needed to be factored in. India posed an additional challenge because in some states electronic invoicing was not allowed. In addition, a poor infrastructure and power outages had to be considered.

The implementation phase started in 2006. The project was divided into four smaller sub-projects:

1   Processes: responsible for the re-design of supply chain processes
2   IT: responsible for information technology support
3   Legal: responsible for a consideration and adherence to global rules and regulations as well as contract management
4   Business control sourcing: responsible for a global integration of suppliers and EMS/ODMs with the new hub.

In total the project had roughly 200 members, with 175 of them being external contractors and only 10 permanent employees assigned to the project's core team. The project had a steering committee with the Head of Sourcing and Supply, the Vice President of Supply Chain Operations, the Director of High Volume Sourcing, and the Director of Sourcing Business Management. The project sponsor was the Senior Vice President of Operations. The organizational chart in the Figure on the next page illustrates the structure of the project.

All necessary communication needed to go through the consumer electronics manufacturer. The suppliers were not supposed to get in touch directly with the logistics company.

The implementation phase started with a pilot that was carried out manually, i.e. without information system support. Some pre-selected component suppliers located in France, the USA, and Germany took part in the pilot to validate the process. They were selected based on their experience with the RosettaNet system. This is an organization working on common standards between companies to electronically process transactions and move information within extended corporate supply chains. RosettaNet member companies represent 1.2 trillion US$ in annual revenue and in moving billions of US$ within their trading networks using RosettaNet Partner Interface Processes (RosettaNet, 2008).

In the middle of the first part of the implementation phase, the sub-project leader for processes noticed that the team had to spend time on a task they hadn't been aware of: the alignment of processes between the suppliers and their own processes. The bigger the suppliers, and the lower the transaction volume they had with the manufacturer, the more challenging the negotiations were regarding process synchronization. No quick fix was available for this issue apart from an additional resource that was allocated to the sub-team to accelerate negotiations.

The sub-project 'business control sourcing' was contacted by an upset US supplier regarding the following problem: the hub staff in Hong Kong registered parts according to Hong Kong local time. For instance, they will register a goods receipt at 10.00 a.m. on July 1st. However, the local time of the US-American supplier will be 1 p.m. on June 30th which represents a different quarter of the year. This caused inconsistencies in the quarterly book closing. In a brainstorming meeting, the sub-project team came up with the solution to send the information to the South-East Asian operations of the US-American supplier located in the same time zone as Hong Kong. It took the team two weeks to work out this countermeasure and establish it.

All sub-teams encountered communication problems they had not expected. First, it was very difficult to understand project members from Singapore and Hong Kong, due to their local accents and high talking speed. Second, the meaning of the words turned out to be different between various stakeholders. Industry standard terms like 'Inventory Balance' can have different meanings. Is this total inventory? Do you include inventory committed to production, inventory with quality issues, inventory in incoming inspection, etc.? Another

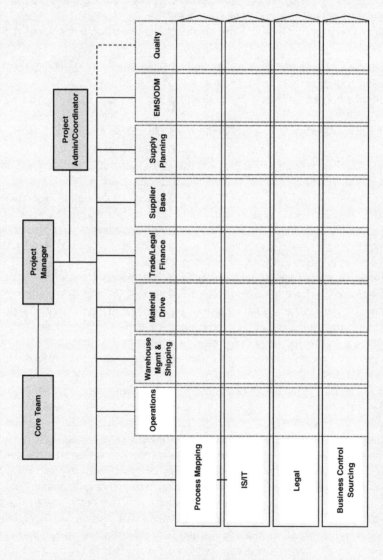

Organization chart of consumer electronics manufacturer's global hub project

example is the term 'delivery date'. Is this the date when the logistics provider picks up the goods? Or is it the date when the goods arrive in the hub? Or is it the date when the supplier places the goods at the pick up location? The project manager established a task force to clarify all critical terms with all major parties involved. This additional effort took three months and prevented team members from pursuing other tasks in the meantime.

The legal sub-project team had to negotiate Trading Partner Agreements with each of the 115 suppliers and 30 factories comprising the technicalities and details regarding process and data flows via the B2B communications. The contract was a written and legally binding agreement about the responsibilities and liabilities of each party. These started with the selected suppliers that had RosettaNet experience. Early on in the process it became obvious that the negotiations would take much more time than had been anticipated. This was due to the necessary process alignment which had not been taken into consideration. Another issue was the interdependencies between all agreements. When the project manager received the report about the prolonged negotiations he escalated this to the steering committee, highlighting an expected project delay of at least three months due to a lack of additional resources. Although unhappy, the steering committee accepted the delay because of resource constraints. To minimize delays, the sub-project leader and his team made it a priority to learn from the first Trading Partner Agreement negotiations. Together, they created a checklist which reduced the negotiation period from six to two months. In addition, an interdependency diagram was created in order not to lose the overview of what had been negotiated with the impacts on further negotiations.

The project manager was taken by surprise by a near showstopper for the whole project, namely internal politics at the participating global suppliers. When the negotiations with the first suppliers started, they quickly reached a stalemate due to internal fights on the suppliers' side. The reason was conflicting interests in different subsidiaries. This was especially true for suppliers without global account management. A common conflict was the allocation of sales revenues within the international supplier. Has the European or the Asian operation sold the components to the manufacturer? Before the introduction of the Hong Kong hub, the factory they did business with, for instance, was in Hungary. Now, they needed to sell the components to an international sales unit of the manufacturer in Hong Kong. The European operation of one supplier 'lost' 100 million Euros sales volume to the Asian operation, which led to unpleasant arguments.

In one of the first weekly status reports, the project manager was informed about this issue. Immediately, he put the traffic light on red. As this issue was outside of his control, he escalated this to the steering committee. He urged members of the steering committee to meet with high level managers at the component suppliers in order to overcome their internal deadlock and save the project.

After six months of manual testing, the automated information system was introduced in phases which took about twelve months. During that time, more issues emerged.

The business control sourcing team leader together with the IT team leader reported another problem they had encountered with training the internal users of the new system. Legal requirements and regulations could not be met because of a lack of knowledge inside the consumer electronics manufacturer. The employees had no understanding of applicable tariff rates and statistical categories for merchandise trading, such as HTS-numbers or export control classification numbers. According to international standards, the net weight of components needed to be indicated on the invoice. Again, the manufacturer did not have this information.

The project manager received a project report with a red light. He negotiated with line managers to get additional resources for a task force that obtained the missing information. In parallel, he suggested to the steering committee that internal procedures and systems needed to be changed. He got approval, for instance, to modify the request for quotations. Simultaneously, training in export and import regulations of the main trading zones was provided to the internal users of the SMI system. This led to yet another delay and increased costs.

The go live of the SMI hub with all the parties involved finally took place six months after the scheduled date. Additional training and other counter-measures had also led to a cost overrun.

However, the project manager was still successful due to the creativity of his team: in one of their status meetings, they had the idea of adding a simple additional feature to the existing software which protected the commercial information belonging to the component suppliers against unauthorized access by OCMs/ODMs or even direct competitors, which is a frequent issue with UMI management. As the component suppliers benefited from this software change, they were prepared to reciprocate by granting additional commercial benefits to the consumer electronics manufacturer. Thus, the manufacturer could amortize the investment in the SMI hub with the related software within six months.

Questions and tasks

1 Apply the monitoring matrix illustrated in Figure 7.4. What areas would you have prioritized if you had been the project manager?
2 Identify the issues emerging during the implementation phase and put them in an issue log as exemplified in Figure 7.9.
3 Where do you see the links between project planning and project implementation?

FURTHER READING

Phillips. Jack J., Bothell, Timothy W. and Snead, G. Lynne (2002) *The Project Management Scorecard: Measuring the Success of Project Management Solutions*. Amsterdam: Butterworth Heinemann. (Provides a very detailed and hands-on overview on how to break down a Balanced Scorecard in a project.)

LEADING INTERNATIONAL PROJECTS

8

LEARNING OBJECTIVES

After studying this chapter you will be able to:

- analyse how a national culture impacts on leadership, decision-making, feedback, and motivation in international projects

- conceive leadership theory dimensions

- deal with challenges in leading virtual teams

- describe important areas in the knowledge and skills of an international project manager

- analyse the crucial characteristics, attitudes, and behaviours of an international project manager

- understand the main tasks of an international project manager

- elucidate the different steps in managing international project teams at the project start.

INTRODUCTION

8.1 Leading international projects entails the challenge of spanning cultural, organizational, geographical, and time boundaries. Hence, the manager of an international project has to perform tasks beyond the application of standard project management techniques within the magic triangle. While it is crucial to have these 'hard skills', they become a threshold in the context of international projects. The international project manager has to lead heterogeneous stakeholders in a sensitive and creative way to ensure the accomplishment of challenging objectives. This is related to the 'soft side' of international project management, namely people management. Certainly, it is crucial for the success of all types of projects, but it is especially complex and challenging in international projects. The following three chapters are dedicated to the soft side of project management. In this chapter, I will start our excursion into people management with a discussion of leadership. In Chapter 9, I will explore communication, and in Chapter 10 I will focus on effective collaboration in an international context.

At the beginning of this chapter, I will outline the impact of cultural diversity on leadership tasks. The manager of an international project needs to keep in mind that team members from collectivistic, risk avoidance and high power distance cultures will have to be led differently to team members from individualistic, high risk and low power distance cultures. We will follow this up with the link between national culture, organizational culture, motivation, and incentive schemes. We will learn that different leadership types are effective in different environments with a strong acceptance of the transformational leader globally. The international project manager has to be able to adapt his or her leadership style to the situation at hand. Moreover, he or she has to be able to take the lead in projects characterized by geographical dispersion, cultural dispersion, organizational dispersion, and temporal dispersion. This environment requires so-called indirect leadership and virtual leadership skills.

Based on the outline of the leadership context, I will draw on the competences an international project manager needs to have in order to lead an international project successfully. We will distinguish between knowledge and skills on the one hand, and personal characteristics, traits and behaviours on the other.

I will then turn to the numerous tasks a leader of an international project needs to accomplish. Consequently, I will elaborate on activities which an international project manager needs to carry out in order to successfully create international project teams. Special emphasis will be put on measures to provide the international project team with structure and orientation.

CULTURAL IMPACT ON LEADERSHIP AND MOTIVATION

WHAT IS LEADERSHIP?

8.2 Among a plethora of existing definitions, I would like to use the term leadership in the same way as the GLOBE (Global Leadership and Organizational Behaviour Effectiveness) project defines it: 'The ability of an individual to influence, motivate, and enable others to contribute toward the effectiveness and success of the organizations of which they are members' (House et al., 2002: 5). The leadership processes of influencing, motivating, and enabling are based on leadership tasks such as communicating and trust building which I will discuss in Chapters 9 and 10 in more depth.

In Chapter 1, I stated that international project management needs to be viewed holistically, including the project context. Leadership in international projects also needs to be seen as a complex system. As a result, I will assume an integrative perspective on leadership in this chapter, considering leadership traits, behaviours, leaders and their followers, leadership processes and context (Mendenhall, 2008).

THE IMPACT OF NATIONAL CULTURE ON LEADERSHIP AND MOTIVATION

Due to their heterogeneity, leading international projects means influencing, motivating, and enabling project members from different national cultures. 'Influencing' is related to leadership and decision-making styles. 'Enabling' is related to feedback and also decision-making.

In contrast to the knowledge areas dealt with so far, there is no shortage of literature regarding the interrelations between leadership and national culture. One of the most comprehensive studies is the above mentioned project GLOBE. Among other things, they have found that the leadership styles and leadership preferences of each national culture will vary. However, there is also one preferred leadership style across national borders which we will discuss under transformational leadership.

For the leader of an international project this means he or she will first need to be aware of differences regarding leadership attitudes and behaviour. Based on a knowledge of these differences, he or she can self-reflect about his or her own leadership style and think about any adaptations that may be needed to lead in an international context.

Figure 8.1 depicts the most influential cultural dimensions and how they affect the behaviour of leaders and followers in the areas of leadership style, decision-making, providing feedback, and motivation.

Equality	Leaders from hierarchy cultures tend to act like 'benevolent autocrats' with absolute authority and decision-making power. Leaders from equality-oriented cultures may prefer a participative leadership style with shared responsibilities, including staff in the decision-making process.	Hierarchy
Individual	Leaders from collectivist cultures tend to prefer a patriarchic leadership style, giving their subordinates the feeling of (emotional) security. Incentives would be team or group oriented rather than given to single individuals. Leaders from individualistic cultures tend to assume the role of coaches developing their subordinates. They also tend to take decisions based on facts collected from the whole team. Leaders from group-oriented cultures usually take decisions based on the opinions of major stakeholders.	Group
Conflict	Leaders from conflict-oriented cultures tend to initiate open discussions on issues when providing feedback. They use brainstorming sessions for constructive conflict resolution. Leaders from consensus-oriented cultures tend to build up networks and use them to reach compromises. They may also tend to provide indirect feedback to give face.	Consensus
Task	For leaders from task-oriented cultures, the project team is only a temporary organization to accomplish the project task. For leaders from relationship-oriented cultures, good morale and close relationships in the project team are the sine qua non for task accomplishment and hence relationships in the team are more important. They would also support their subordinates on private issues.	Relationship
Achievement	Leaders from achievement-oriented cultures tend to measure themselves and their followers by the accomplishment of objectives. A preferred leadership style would be management by objectives. Leaders from status-oriented cultures tend to focus on networking with politically important players in order to safeguard their status and tend to manage rather subjectively.	Standing/ Status

FIGURE 8.1   Cultural dimensions and their impact on leadership style, decision-making, feedback, and motivation

As mentioned in the GLOBE definition, motivation is a crucial component of leadership. Therefore, I will outline the culturally-bound differences regarding motivation without underplaying the personalities of subordinates. However, it is close to impossible to categorize these due to their multiplicity. The international leader has to keep in mind that in rather collectivist cultures where employees' personal interests and goals typically are subordinate to the interests and goals of the organization, the project members are emotionally more dependent on the organization than persons from more individualistic cultures who will derive their self-identity from the self-pursuit of goals. Hence, project leaders need to provide a feeling of security and belonging to the collectivist staff. A Bulgarian project manager noticed that it was important for his Indian team members that he spent some time with them, to have lunch or dinner together. Project members from individualistic cultures usually appreciate more autonomy, working at arm's length provided clear project goals are established.

In the case of geographically dispersed teams, collectivist cultures pose a challenge to international project leaders because they have to establish close relations with their sub-teams and also establish a local leader who can continuously motivate and supervise staff even if the international project manager is not on site.

Motivation not only resides in leadership, but is also enhanced by adequate incentive systems. One size fits all systems do not exist. Project members from rather feminine cultures might appreciate some additional time off for their family, while people from rather masculine cultures may opt for a financial bonus, or, if paired with moderate or high uncertainty avoidance, some policies designed to protect job security (Hempel, 1998).

The project manager may want to use Maslow's (1987) hierarchy of needs and combine it with cultural dimensions in order to gain a rough orientation regarding incentive preferences by culture as shown in Figure 8.2. Physiological needs are universal to mankind and refer to sleep, hunger, and the like. Safety needs are related to security, the need for structure, protection, law and order. Social needs are also called belongingness or love needs. Apart from some who prefer to be loners, people need relations with other people. Esteem needs are connected with self-respect and the esteem of others. The latter could be called the desire for reputation, status, or fame. Self-actualization corresponds to the state where an individual is doing what he or she is personally fitted for, like an artist who has to paint.

As is the case for previously introduced management concepts, Maslow's hierarchy of needs is rooted in Anglo-American values and thus has to be used with care in different cultural settings where the hierarchy can be reversed or may at least be different.

Apart from preferences stemming from the national culture, the international project manager needs to consider the political, economic, and religious conditions in a country in order to design effective incentive systems. Best practice is a so-called cafeteria system which comprises incentives with approximately the same monetary value, tailored for the different needs of project staff. To give an example: while some US-American project members may regard it as indispensable to have convenient and luxurious accommodation in an American hotel chain in central Africa, some Indian team members may be happy with modest and functional accommodation and would appreciate being given the money they saved to take home to their families.

Mini Case 8.1 illustrates how diversity in leadership and motivation can turn into a big problem.

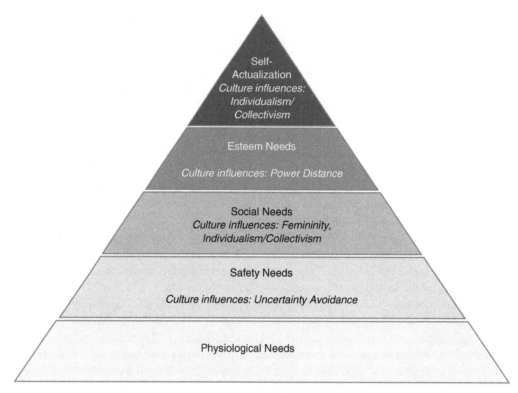

FIGURE 8.2 Hierarchy of needs combined with cultural dimensions
Source: Based on Maslow (1987)

Mini Case 8.1: Leading a purchasing project in Manaus, Brazil

A multinational corporation had to readjust its supply chain due to cost pressures. The project was quite complex comprising tasks such as an assessment of saving potentials, pricing negotiations, logistics, risk analysis and customs. The German project manager assigned the above mentioned bundle of tasks to one of his Brazilian team members. After having explained the details, he asked the Brazilian: 'Is everything clear? Do you think that you can do this by the beginning of next month?' The Brazilian seemed to be very confident answering: 'Sure, no problem at all. I will take care of this – don't worry.'

All the project members were sitting in a huge landscape office. Once in a while, the project manager had a look around and observed that the person with the re-sourcing task was working diligently at his desk and not talking to anybody else. Apparently, he did not even have any questions. Otherwise, he would have come to see him – after all, his desk was only a couple of metres away from the purchaser. At the agreed deadline, the team gathered together to report the status of the project.

When it was the purchaser's turn to update his colleagues and boss about the progress of his work, he said: 'I don't think that I have anything to report.' The project manager retorted: 'And why haven't you told me during the last three weeks that you had problems with the task? Now we have a real big problem because we have lost three precious weeks.' The purchaser did not reply. One day later, the project manager was called up by the head of personnel who told him that the purchaser had come to quit, stating: 'I have had enough. I am leaving.' The project manager then had an even bigger problem because it was quite difficult to get hold of qualified staff.

Source: Heiligtag (2008)

Question

What can you learn from this incident in terms of leadership and motivation in international projects?

LEADERSHIP TYPES AND REQUIREMENTS IN AN INTERNATIONAL CONTEXT

8.3

The GLOBE study has identified six global culturally endorsed leadership dimensions (Bass, 1985; House et al., 2004; Francesco and Gold, 2005):

1 **Charismatic/Value based leadership:** This leader is inspiring with his or her enthusiasm, acts like a teacher, is a role model, and creates conditions in the organization which motivate subordinates to actively contribute to the success of that organization.
2 **Team-oriented leadership:** This kind of leader is an integrative figure with a collaborative attitude. He or she is diplomatic and benevolent.
3 **Participative leadership:** Such a leader delegates as much as possible to his or her subordinates and encourages independence and autonomy. He or she also involves all subordinates in the decision-making process.
4 **Humane-oriented leadership:** This kind of leader expresses a lot of empathy and compassion, based on an attitude of modesty.
5 **Autonomous leadership:** Such a leader acts individualistically, independently, and autonomously.
6 **Self-protective leadership:** This kind of leader is status oriented and values formality and procedures. He or she is also conscious of the importance of face saving.

The GLOBE study concludes that the above mentioned leadership types differ in effectiveness between culture clusters. Hence, an international leader has to be able to adapt his or her style to the cultural script of his followers. Interestingly, the study identified the charismatic or so-called transformational or value based leadership type as most appropriate across geographical boundaries. In section 8.3, we will learn more about the competences that a transformational leader should possess.

LEADERSHIP CONTEXT

The international project manager does not only have to be aware of his or her cultural values and those of his or her subordinates. The manager of an international project also needs to create a project culture which is conducive to successful project delivery. I have already introduced frameworks from organizational culture that are supportive to international projects in Chapter 2.

The involvement of different organizational units and organizations not only brings different corporate cultures into play, but also typically entails geographically dispersed teams over which the international project manager might not have formal control. This means that the international project manager will have to manipulate project stakeholders to make them follow. We call this indirect leadership. Snapshot 8.1 provides you with an example of this.

SNAPSHOT 8.1

What is going wrong in Hungary?

The expansion into Hungary, one of the countries that has joined the European Union in 2004, had reached a standstill, although the potential of this market was very high. The project manager travelled to the local subsidiary in Hungary to find out the reasons for the stagnation. When confronted with direct questions, the local manager responsible for market development did not come up with clear answers. The project manager did not have any formal authority as the local manager reported to the director of the Hungarian subsidiary. Hence, the project manager could not reward or punish the local manager's behaviour. The project manager decided to accompany the local manager on on-site visits. He observed the behaviour of the Hungarian manager and found out after some visits that the local manager would not dare to talk to high-ranking people in local communities, for instance about permits or rental agreements. Asked for the reason why he did not talk to these people, the local manager said: 'They are too powerful.' Apparently, the status gap between him and them was too high. This refers to power distance as explained in Chapter 3. The challenge for the foreign project manager was to instil self-esteem, self-confidence and pride about his job and his (foreign) company in the local manager. The project manager took a lot of time to outline the importance of the company on the global market, and described at length what the company did for local communities around the world. Gradually, the self-confidence of the local manager increased, and the market expansion picked up speed.

The combination of leading across national and organizational boundaries is given in virtual structures as introduced in Chapter 6. These pose a special challenge to leadership in terms of the leader's role and presence, the processes and the technology. Most of the interactions in virtual teams are technology-based. Hence, leading virtual teams means working through electronic media, including relational development. The physical context and cues have to be replaced by other means, such as icons. Leadership is

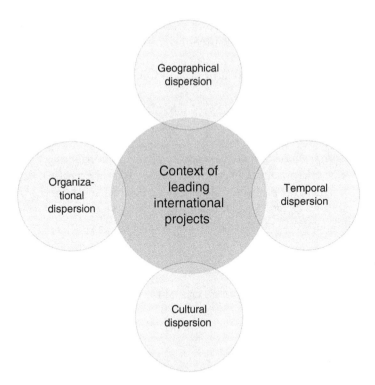

FIGURE 8.3   Context of leading international projects

characterized by the interplay of team members and technology which carries a tendency to shared leadership. Frequent and skilled communication from leaders to subordinates tends to be even more important than in traditional structures. As a result, I will dedicate a section to communication in virtual teams in Chapter 9.

To summarize this section highlighting the challenges of leadership in international projects: leaders have to span cultural, organizational, geographical and time boundaries.

Compared with traditional leadership, this makes leading international projects more difficult in their extent and type. Special competencies are required which we will analyse in the following section.

COMPETENCIES OF THE INTERNATIONAL PROJECT MANAGER

8.4 According to Spencer and Spencer (1993), competencies are consistent ways of behaving or thinking. They subdivide competencies into the following five characteristics:

1 Motives: what are the main drivers behind the activities of a person?
2 Traits: characteristics and consistent behaviour in certain situations, for instance empathy
3 Self-concept: an individual's attitude and values (strongly connected with national culture)
4 Knowledge: the information a person has in a certain content area
5 Skill: the ability to perform a certain task.

What kind of competencies should the leader of an international project have in order to successfully deliver that project? This certainly depends on the nature of the project and the industry. Yet, there are some critical competencies which any project manager should have. Many globally operating organizations will have developed their own competency standards and frameworks that are adapted to their needs (see further reading).

KNOWLEDGE AND SKILLS

What kinds of knowledge and skills are crucial for leading international projects?

Global organizing skills

Political awareness and strategic influence are extremely important to the successful delivery of international projects. A project manager needs to establish clout and convince the main stakeholders in a project about the importance of the project. Hence, he or she has to be able to create an excellent network within the organization, and will need to know in detail how the organization works. This also requires relationship development capabilities.

Technical skills

Many international projects are concerned with innovation. In new product development projects, the project manager needs to have knowledge about the technology used or about to be developed by the project. While he or she does not have to be an expert in each sub-field, he or she should have a sound basis enabling him or her to understand the problems of the project team and to take adequate decisions.

Cross-cultural skills

An international project manager needs comprehensive knowledge of different national cultures, and should have the skills to adapt to a different cultural script. Typically, this requires a longer work experience outside the domestic market. A study by Yasin et al. (1999) confirms a greater efficiency of project managers with international working experience in the construction industry when compared to managers without international experience.

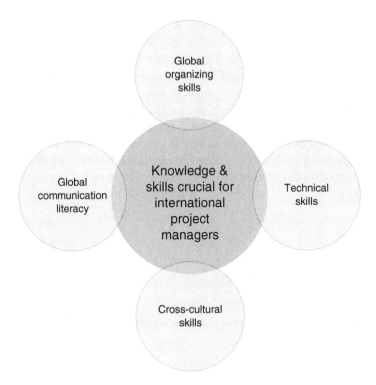

FIGURE 8.4 Knowledge and skills important for international project managers

Global communication literacy

An international project manager should be able to speak several languages and be capable of using contemporary communication technology. The minimal requirement is a proficiency in English if he or she is not an English native speaker. It helps to speak other languages, first in order to overcome language barriers, and second to earn the respect and goodwill of team members.

Figure 8.4 summarizes the knowledge and skill areas crucial for international project managers.

In general, an international project manager is more effective if he or she has used all these skills in the past. It speeds up decisions and increases self-confidence to have such references from experience.

PERSONALITY CHARACTERISTICS, ATTITUDES, AND BEHAVIOURS

Let us now proceed to the other group of competencies, namely motives, traits, and self-concept.

On the one hand, there are project management standards regarding the characteristics, attitudes and behaviours of project managers, typically without an international focus (Crawford, 2005). On the other hand, there is a comprehensive body of literature regarding the competencies of an effective global manager, albeit without any project management focus (e.g. Adler and Bartholomew, 1992; Gregersen et al., 1998; Mendenhall, 1999). Based on the existing body of literature and numerous interviews with experienced international project managers from different industries and countries, I suggest the following selection of characteristics, attitudes and behaviours which can be seen as prerequisites for successfully leading international projects. To some extent, they mirror the characteristics of the international project discussed in Figure 1.4. Please note that the order is alphabetical and does not indicate any ranking of importance.

Adaptability

An international project manager may be more effective if he or she adapts his behaviour to the local customs or needs.

SNAPSHOT 8.2

Recruiting the right people

A German project manager was assigned the task of building up a project team in a remote area of Brazil within a couple of weeks. He needed people who had a reasonable command of English, the corporate language, and were able to work under time pressures in an international set-up. In Germany, he had to go through lengthy procedures involving the personnel department to create job descriptions, publish ads, and conduct interviews according to a preset catalogue of requirements. In Manaus, he first lived in a hotel. When his laptop crashed, the hotel sent a lady to repair it. The project manager noticed that her English was extremely good, and that she was able to fix the problem quickly. So he asked her: 'What do you earn at the moment?' He offered to double her salary if she joined his team as a controller. She accepted the job. The project manager found and poached another project member from the sales staff of a boutique. Often, he recruited students who wanted to earn extra money. They tended to be very ambitious and became valuable project members. Due to the fact that most of their lectures took place in the evenings or weekends, they could still finish their studies.

Source: Heiligtag (2008)

Authenticity

At the same time, the project manager needs to come across as 'real' and credible, not as though they were an actor. While he or she has to be able to meet the expectations and demands of followers, the project manager needs to be consistent in his or her behaviour. It is important not to over-adapt to local cultures.

Empathy

Experience shows that people all over the globe want to be acknowledged as human beings and like to be taken care of, even if this is not a straightforward expectation towards a leader. A genuine attitude of caring for others can be expressed by a slap on the back, or by giving a piece of advice regarding a private issue, or by praising somebody for very good input. For people who are genuinely positive towards other people, this attitude is much easier to display and comes across authentically.

Context- and culture-sensitivity

An international project manager needs to be able to apply different approaches to establish trust as a basis to give and receive feedback.

A Japanese project manager shared his experience of managing European and Chinese sub-project teams: 'My European teams want to be included in the decision-making process. Without being asked, they will air their personal opinion in meetings, and they want me to share a lot of information. With my Chinese team members, it is totally different. Usually, they are reluctant to share their opinions with me because they are afraid of losing face. It is difficult for me to get to know exactly what they think. Therefore, I have taken some team members on a trip to a couple of local Chinese suppliers. After the visit, I have talked to them individually and asked them what they would improve if they were the supplier. After a while, they shared some ideas for improvement with me.'

Courage

Certainly, a project manager needs to balance the needs for context- and culture-sensitive behaviour against time pressures. We know that international projects are very dynamic. Typically, there is no time to lose in pondering about what decision to make, or to gather more details or hesitate. Obviously, individuals who are not afraid of taking a risk, who can analyse situations quickly, and who welcome ideas and suggestions from the team, even if they imply criticism, will be able to meet the requirements of moving forward quickly.

Enthusiasm

Whatever an international project manager does, if he or she does it with a lot of enthusiasm, displaying strong self-confidence and confidence in the attainment of the self-set goal, he or she may motivate staff and arouse more commitment then a 'normal' person.

Initiative and innovativeness

Coping with time pressures also means that an international project manager should avoid blame games. He or she should encourage all team members to work jointly on solutions. The international project manager should also take the initiative to cross-check the project status. An example is a South-East European project manager who travelled personally to remote areas in the Ugandan hinterland to gain first-hand impressions and to give direct advice to local people there. Innovativeness is linked with the courage to go for unique and creative solutions with all their implicit risk.

Personal stability

To break new ground also implies the danger of mistakes and criticism. An individual who is at ease with him- or herself will have more energy to weather the storm. Its uniqueness makes an international project highly stressful. The project manager will face a lot of uncertain situations and a lot of pressure from different stakeholders. Hence, he or she needs to have great stamina to function as a kind of shock absorber and to stay fair to his or her team even in tough situations.

Open-mindedness

The international project manager should always be willing to learn new things and must be prepared to revise his or her behaviour. Making the effort, like eating raw beef in Japan, knowing the national holidays in the countries your project members come from, and also being aware of personal details like birthdays, increases commitment towards the project. A US-American project manager recalled the positive reaction of his Chinese team members when he bought some moon cakes in Beijing and shared them with his Chinese team members at the mid-Autumn festival.

Patience and persistence

International project managers need to be very goal oriented. Otherwise, they would not be able to implement the project at all. However, many international projects tend to face a lot of issues and have a rather long duration. Therefore, the project manager should assume a long-term perspective and plan carefully. He or she needs to accept that international public holidays or religious festivities cannot be changed, nor can they be accelerated. The Muslim annual period of fasting called Ramadan takes one month, whether this fits in with the project schedule or not. Too zealous a goal orientation can be counter-productive if it offends local regulations or customs.

Patience, however, does not equal a lack of focus or commitment. Rather it has the connotation of persistence necessary to overcome numerous internal and external hurdles during the life cycle of a project.

Respect differences

A seasoned international project manager phrased his motto like this: 'We all are different. We have to learn from each other.' Everybody has certain strengths and weaknesses. It is important to acknowledge these differences. A US international project

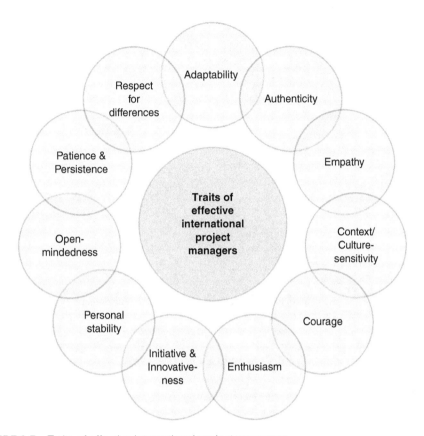

FIGURE 8.5 Traits of effective international project managers

manager with a quality assurance background, for instance, acknowledged that his Brazilian project member has more technical knowledge due to a Master's degree in electrical engineering. Therefore, he assigns the crucial task of selecting the right suppliers to this individual. Figure 8.5 summarizes the personal characteristics, attitudes, and behaviours which can help a project manager to deliver an international project successfully.

Each organization needs to develop the talent for leading international projects based on the requirement profile outlined above. Some organizational development programs refer to these traits as emotional and cultural intelligence, complementing rather traditional analytical intelligence (Alon and Higgins, 2005). The selection and development procedures for effective international project managers are beyond the scope of this book.

Now that we know what competencies a project manager needs to have in order to effectively deliver an international project, we will turn our attention to a description of the tasks an international project manager has to accomplish.

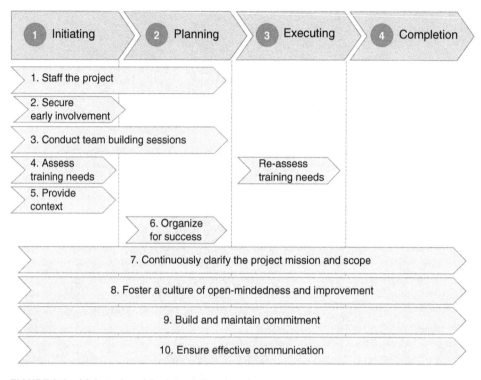

FIGURE 8.6 Main tasks of the international project manager

MAIN ROLES AND TASKS OF THE INTERNATIONAL PROJECT MANAGER

8.5

As you can see in Figure 8.6, the roles and tasks of the project manager will change in the course of the project life cycle. Let me now guide you through those tasks.

1 STAFF THE PROJECT

The project manager needs to have the right competences in his or her team. It is important not only to look at the skills set and performance of each individual but also to keep in mind that there are dynamics within groups which will have a strong impact on the performance of each individual. Hence, the project manager also needs to consider (cultural) diversity and personality. Obviously, an ideal member of an international project team will have similar traits to the project leader in the area of empathy, context- and culture-sensitivity, initiative and innovativeness, open-mindedness, and respect. But the chances are rather low that the project manager will find such individuals because he or she is competing for scarce resources with other projects and line functions. At a minimum, the key players should possess some of these characteristics along with the appropriate language, communication and technical skills.

It makes sense to have an internal application process. The core team with the key players will decide who will join the team and who will not in order to maintain harmony. This is especially important in situations where units of the organization will try to get rid of expensive or unqualified personnel by allocating them to projects.

Moreover, the project manager has to think about the adequate size of the team (see Chapter 6). Staffing starts with the assignment of the project management team, namely the sub-team leader roles.

Snapshot 8.3 gives an insight into staffing principles that could be helpful for project managers leading international development projects.

SNAPSHOT 8.3

Staffing guidelines for international development projects

An experienced manager of international development projects has created the following process for staff selection which has proved to be effective in NGOs and the public sector:

- ☑ Agree upfront on the process of selecting staff in order to identify clear criteria with the stakeholders.
- ☑ Do not select personnel on your own as a project manager.

It is advisable to have a selection panel of at least two or three project members. The purpose here is to safeguard neutrality, and to allow the other team members to become better involved by including them in the selection process. This procedure also ensures transparency.

- ☑ Have detailed labour contracts or job descriptions.

In case of a potential conflict it is helpful to be able to refer to clear terms of reference in a labour contract or task description. This kind of transparency can help to avoid quarrels about tasks and responsibilities later in the project.

---

2   SECURE THE EARLY INVOLVEMENT OF MAJOR STAKEHOLDERS

Early on in the project, the project manager needs to focus on involving all the major stakeholders in project planning. The purpose here is not only to get the required information from experts in the team, but also to foster ownership and commitment at a very early point in time.

3   CONDUCT TEAM-BUILDING SESSIONS

The project manager needs to make sure that all the individuals in the newly created team work together well. The basis for such good co-operation is trust. Especially in international projects, the chances are high that team members will not know each other at the beginning. On top of this, heterogeneity hampers collaboration. Thus it is important to provide a young team with opportunities to get to know each other better via social gatherings, to exchange experiences and brainstorm new ideas. More details will follow in section 8.6. In Chapter 10, I will dedicate a whole section to trust building which is not simply a leadership task.

4 ASSESS TRAINING NEEDS

When selecting the project members, the project leader has to assess the strengths and weaknesses of each individual, and above all of the sub-project leaders. The project manager needs to enable staff by providing training for missing competencies in terms of skills and knowledge. The attached costs must be input for budget planning as explained in Chapter 5.

However, the training needs assessment is not a one-off task. International projects are complex and full of risk. Chances are good that the team will encounter unforeseen difficulties. The project manager should re-assess training needs in light of the issue log. If we think of the Chapter 7 End Case, such additional training could be on tariffs and export-import regulations. These training sessions can be combined with a midway milestone review meeting.

5 PROVIDE CONTEXT

Due to the heterogeneity of the international project, the project manager needs to make sure that the local sites and major stakeholders of the project have a common understanding of the main approaches and procedures used. This also includes the use of technical terms.

6 ORGANIZE FOR SUCCESS

In the planning phase, the project manager needs to ensure transparency and accountability in terms of goal clarification, responsibility and authority. Tools discussed in previous chapters like a scope statement, a project organization chart, a responsibility matrix, and job descriptions can support these objectives.

7 CONTINUOUSLY CLARIFY THE PROJECT MISSION AND SCOPE

Heterogeneous international teams especially need an anchor they can rely on. This is the project objective. The project leader has to explain clearly how the project result is linked to the overall strategy of the organization. This endeavour can be supported by senior management who should personally explain the purpose of the project and stress its importance. In fact, many international projects will be of strategic importance for an organization. The project members should internalize this feeling from the beginning of the project. Especially for projects with a longer duration like big infrastructure projects, it is necessary to reiterate the project objective during the planning and implementation phase in order to keep the team focused. The project manager also needs to cross-check at the beginning of each project phase with the customer whether the project objectives are still valid, or whether some minor or major changes have perhaps even rendered the project obsolete.

8   FOSTER A CULTURE OF OPEN-MINDEDNESS AND IMPROVEMENT

Project effectiveness is based on a project culture which encourages open-mindedness, empathy, and the creative use of differences. The project manager needs to promote such a culture by living it. He or she has to function as a role model. These efforts may be constrained by the corporate cultures of the organizations involved in the international project. It is the task of senior executives to ensure consistency between the organizational strategy and its culture.

9   BUILD AND MAINTAIN COMMITMENT

The personal characteristics of the project manager will have a big impact on commitment. A great deal of enthusiasm brought across from the project manager can be kind of contagious. It can spark the commitment of team members. The project manager can further strengthen this commitment by using skills and knowledge. For instance, managing risks well reduces insecurity and anxiety which otherwise could paralyse team members and weaken commitment. Commitment is also furthered by being vigilant regarding emerging conflicts that will waste energy. How can the project manager find out about latent conflicts? Part of the effort is to have short interviews with key project members at face-to-face meetings, for instance at a milestone review meeting. For longer lasting projects, questionnaires mentioned in Chapter 7 for checking on tensions and conflicts should be done at six-monthly intervals. Special attention needs to be paid to differences in language proficiency, an unequal national status, and burn-out syndromes.

Another measure of maintaining commitment is the communication of interim achievements. One purpose is to keep the sponsors informed and involved. Reinforced support from the project sponsors, in turn, will motivate the team members. Another purpose is to instil pride in team members.

Commitment is also strengthened by celebrations of interim successes. Especially in the case of longer projects, stakeholders will need to feel that they are heading in the right direction. A form of celebration could be big parties at the main project sites, where project members and other stakeholders can interact informally with each other and just have fun together.

A party by itself, however, is insufficient to keep up good morale. Praise communicated to project-external parties regarding team contributions or individual contributions is very effective. Acknowledgement needs to be complemented by other incentives, such as additional days off or bonus payments. This is what we discussed in Section 8.2.

10   ENSURE EFFECTIVE COMMUNICATION

The project leader needs to make sure that a common language is spoken and has to enable the project members to do so. He or she also needs to establish clear communication rules and channels, with a clear reporting governance. I will discuss more details on this in Chapter 9.

You can cross-check your understanding of the competencies and tasks of an international project manager using Mini Case 8.2.

Mini Case 8.2: International SAP roll-out

A US company in the semiconductor business decided on implementing the enterprise resource planning system SAP in its global operations. This huge undertaking was divided into several sub-projects. One of these sub-projects had the objective to roll-out the SAP Sales and Distribution module (SD) to five factories and 15 sales offices world-wide. Approximately 400 employees would be affected by the change.

The sub-project leader was a US-American from headquarters. He had excellent qualifications and a consulting background, with a track record of successful projects in the USA. The rest of the team were recruited from the Austrian, French, British and German sites of the company. For nine months after the project kick-off, the team travelled backwards and forwards between the different main sites. This period resulted in the team bonding together which meant they got to know each other very well. For cost reasons, regular travelling was then stopped, and the team was transferred to one central site where they mainly worked out of a war room (cf. Chapter 6). From the beginning of the project, tensions were discernible between the team on one hand and the team leader on the other. These stemmed from discussions between the team members and their leader about legal and fiscal requirements in European countries which differed heavily from the USA. As all targeted company sites were legally independent and needed to do their own annual statements, the Sales and Distribution module of SAP needed to be customized to meet local demands. The team leader considered the change request from his team as displaying obstinacy. In his opinion, the company had a certain enterprise model, which needed to be implemented in the same way wherever the company was operating. He tried to put an end to these customization discussions by ordering his staff to follow his guidelines and his project master plan. The situation escalated after more than a year, slowing down the whole project until the team members complained to senior management about being forced to implement an illegal ERP system. Consequently, the team leader was sent back to HQ and the team continued to work for another six months on the project completion without a project leader. What had been planned to take one year was finally completed after two years.

Question

Why did the team leader fail? Base your answer on the competencies and tasks of an international project manager as outlined in this chapter.

Let us finish this chapter with a more detailed discussion of the main responsibilities related to leading an international project team, focusing on the initiating and planning phase of the project. As we learned in Chapter 3, the start of an international project is of paramount importance. This is true for planning the costs and timescale, and it is also true for leading people. If the scene is not properly set at the beginning, the international project team may become dysfunctional. Consequently, the project manager needs to put a lot of effort into providing orientation and structure at the beginning of the project.

BUILDING THE INTERNATIONAL TEAM AT THE PROJECT START

8.6

Effective leadership is always a challenge. However, it is a particularly demanding task to bond an international project team together and to influence, enable and motivate team members towards a successful project completion.

WHAT IS AN INTERNATIONAL PROJECT TEAM?

This is a number of people from different cultures, ideally with complementary skills, who will have a common goal that they will pursue together. International project teams will have a structure, a pattern of development, social processes, and decision-making styles that are affected to some extent by national cultures.

It is the task of the project manager to set the scene for the international team by determining the structure and influencing the development patterns and social processes in order to enable that team to work productively.

WHAT IS A SUCCESSFUL INTERNATIONAL PROJECT TEAM?

The goal of the international project manager is to influence his or her international team in a way that makes its outputs as efficient as possible. What are the indicators for the international project manager that he or she has achieved this goal? According to Nurick and Thumhain (2005) successful international teams will display behaviours and traits such as:

- commitment
- high morale and team spirit
- fun at work
- a pressing need for achievement
- self-direction
- a change orientation
- a quality orientation
- effective conflict management
- effective communications.

Communication and conflict management will be discussed in detail in Chapters 9 and 10 because these areas will affect all the stakeholders in an international project. These are not solely the responsibility of the project manager.

The following will outline in greater detail the most important activities a project manager has to perform in order to lay the foundations for effective team work. Plans can be modified during the course of the project, although at extra cost. When an international project team becomes dysfunctional, though, the project manager has a problem which can scarcely be solved. You cannot reboot people like you can reboot a personal computer or redraw a plan. Sour relationships are extremely difficult to repair. Hence, the project manager needs to prepare his or her actions very thoroughly in order to mitigate this serious risk.

PREPARING THE FIRST TEAM MEETINGS

Davison and Ward (1999) suggest the following steps that a project manager should take to lead an international team to success.

1   Interview the key players

Especially in organizations with a history of project failure or other pent-up frustrations, the project manager should interview his or her key team members prior to the first group meeting. Thus, he or she gains information about past problems that can be used to differentiate the new project from the past. At the same time, the project leader can signal to the key players that their input matters. The project manager can also learn about the sub-organizations the key players come from and brace him- or herself for any tensions that might exist.

2   Plan the first meeting

It is important to carefully select the venue and the team-building measures. The first meeting is like a harbinger. To put it somewhat polemically: if everything goes smoothly, the project is right on track for success; if the first meeting is already disrupted by tensions or bad administration, the course for a project failure is set.

3   Decide on the content of the first set of meetings

Experience shows that many international projects fail because the scope of the project was not explained or understood properly. Due to diversity in international projects, the participants and stakeholders may interpret objectives differently. Hence, the project manager and sponsor need to use the first set of meetings to ensure a common understanding of the scope. Issues need to be addressed such as: Why is this project important? Who is against it? What are any interrelated projects in the organization? Providing the context also refers to clarifying the key terms used, like commitment, goals, and scope (see Chapter 9). The project sponsor, manager, and the core team have to agree on the sub-goals and key success criteria of the project.

Sufficient time needs to be planned for. Remember: it does take longer to lay the foundations for successful international projects.

4   Focus on building interrelationships when together face-to-face

As I will explore further in Chapter 10, trust is the basis of effective co-operation. Most national cultures are relationship oriented. People will not tackle any task seriously without knowing each other more closely. For task-oriented cultures like the Anglophone world, or the Scandinavian or German, taking time to build trust first easily is felt as

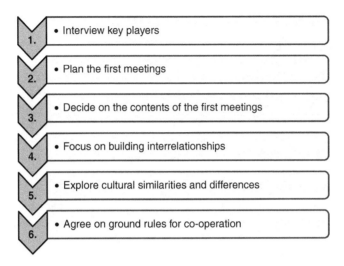

FIGURE 8.7   Leadership activities to build the international project team

wasting time and postponing tasks. However, international teams work best when trust is properly established. Such days at the beginning of the project are a good investment.

5   Explore the cultural similarities and differences of the international team

A cultural gap analysis as introduced in Chapter 3 has to be conducted at this stage to sensitize all team members towards their cultural differences. All team members present at the meeting should have the opportunity to explain the particularities of their cultures as they perceive them. The purpose of the cultural gap analysis tool is to raise cultural awareness. Furthermore, it ensures that feedback on cultural differences can be given without things becoming personal. The project manager needs to be careful to keep the balance and make sure that no single dominating culture will impose their own norms on the others. A culturally savvied facilitator might be useful to carry out those sessions.

6   Agree on the ground rules for co-operation and communication systems

At the end of the first meeting, all the participants should have agreed on common ground rules in the areas that are most relevant for an effective collaboration in an international team. I will explore the ground rules further in Chapter 10, as it is the responsibility of all project members to develop and follow them. Figure 8.7 gives an overview of the main leadership tasks at the start of an international project.

Let us close this section with Snapshot 8.4, illustrating the importance of the leadership tasks outlined above.

SNAPSHOT 8.4

Creating an international project team

A multinational company introduced a new software to the production planning and logistics functions in their sites in Asia and Europe. The team were recruited from all relevant sites and consisted of a Chinese person, a Filipino, two Austrians, two Germans and a Belgian person who was also the team leader. To bond the team together, the project manager decided to start with a three-day workshop carried out by a consulting company specializing in applied creativity. The workshop was a mixture of team-building measures like outdoor activities, and a training course on creativity tools such as mind-maps, and moderation. It also included one day where all the team members got the opportunity to explain taboos in their national cultures. Thus, the workshop contributed to a mutual understanding of the cultures of all team members. It also enabled the participants to use tools and techniques for leveraging their (joint) creativity and to come up with new ideas. This investment in the workshop proved to be successful. The team managed to develop a prototype of the SW module within three months compared to another team in the organization that worked on the same module for another divisional system. They needed six months to achieve their objectives.

SUMMARY

An effective international project manager needs to be aware of cultural differences regarding leadership and motivation. He or she must be able to adapt his or her leadership style to meet the expectations of the followers. Globally, a so-called value based or transformational leader is most accepted. An international project manager needs to lead in a context of geographical, temporal, cultural, and organizational dispersion. Apart from a global organizing expertise, technical skills, cross-cultural skills and global communication literacy, he or she should have such traits and behaviours as adaptability, authenticity, empathy, enthusiasm, context- and culture-sensitivity, courage, initiative and innovativeness, personal stability, open-mindedness, patience and persistence, and respect. The international project manager is responsible for staffing the project, involving all the stakeholders at an early stage, conducting team-building sessions, assessing training needs, providing context, organizing for success, continuously clarifying the project mission and scope, fostering a culture of open-mindedness and improvement, building and maintaining commitment, and ensuring effective communication. Building the international team at the project start is crucial. The project manager has to prepare the first team meeting thoroughly, interviewing key players, building trust, and allowing for an interpersonal and intercultural exchange.

 # KEY TERMS

Cafeteria system, charismatic leadership, value based leadership, transformational leadership, team oriented leadership, participative leadership, humane-oriented leadership, autonomous leadership, self-protective leadership, indirect leadership, competencies, global culture-sensitivity communication literacy, emotional and cultural intelligence, adaptability, authenticity, empathy.

REVIEW TASKS

Questions

1 Where do you see the link between national culture, organizational culture, leadership, and motivation?
2 What do you consider as the main challenges in leading an international project?
3 In your opinion, what kind of competence is most important for an international project manager in order to successfully deliver an international project? And how could those competences be developed?

EXERCISE

- Work in groups of five people.
- Each group member goes through the 11 characteristics and behaviours of an effective project manager outlined in Figure 8.5, assessing him- or herself against each trait.
- Each group member asks the group for their assessment of him or her against the traits. If there are deviations between self-assessment and the assessment by the group members, discuss the reasons for the differences.

CHAPTER END CASE: TOWARDS MANAGEMENT MATURITY PROJECT

Organizations which are heavily dependent on projects, mainly international projects, need to build up competences by fostering the successful management of international projects in developing unique resources and strategic capabilities in international project management.

A large multinational corporation with numerous international projects in new product development has introduced a process underpinning the successful delivery of international projects called PACT. PACT stands for Project Acceleration by Coaching and Teamwork. It is a hands-on workshop methodology aimed at increasing the efficient delivery of projects, mainly large-scale projects with 200–300 core members distributed across ten or more locations.

WHY DID THE GLOBAL ORGANIZATION INTRODUCE THIS APPROACH?

Although the organization possessed a full array of project management processes for product development, risk assessment, project completion and other areas, senior management were aware of the fact that the processes were not fully implemented and followed. The evaluation of completed projects also showed that project teams were staffed incompletely and sometimes at a late stage. Bearing in mind that international projects require additional time for preparation in the planning phase and for team building, the staff shortage at the beginning of the project resulted in issues in the implementation phase. Another finding from the analysis of past projects was the fact that project managers typically had an engineering background. They were specialists in writing software codes or designing mechanical components. However, they did not know how to lead people, or how to cope with conflicts. This caused problems or even project failures. Project managers were not able to keep inter-functional conflicts at bay. Milestone meetings with different functional representatives accusing each other of causing project delay or cost overruns were not the exception. Hence, there was clearly a need to train experienced engineers for project management roles combining technical expertise with interpersonal and intercultural competences. Such a new role should improve the management of international projects, and simultaneously offer a career track to engineers with leadership ambitions within project management.

WHAT DOES PACT CONSIST OF?

The approach can be divided into two: first, the methodology, and second, the facilitators or coaches applying that methodology.

These facilitators are experienced project managers, typically with an engineering background, who have obtained special training in the following areas:

- basic training for facilitation skills
- communication and presentation techniques
- team development tools and techniques
- conflict moderation tools and techniques
- approaches for efficient intercultural and virtual teamwork.

The organization recruited its PACT facilitators from all over the world. The majority of these came from locations where the organization had long experience of product development, such as the USA, Mexico, Brazil, France, Spain, Germany, and Australia. An increasing number of coaches originated from Singapore, Japan, or South Korea. The organization aims at using facilitators within their regions to minimize cost and to benefit from local market knowledge and cultural proximity. Over time, roughly 130 facilitators were trained who support the most important projects.

The method is rather simple and hands-on. The new product development project usually starts after Sales has done an opportunity evaluation, selected an opportunity and acquired a customer. It begins with Conception Creation, followed by Development/Integration, Prototype Verification, and Design Verification, and ends with Production Ramp-up. At this stage, the new product development project is handed over to the line organization again, namely to Manufacturing.

The PACT facilitators accompany the new product development project from cradle to grave over the entire project management life cycle. They mainly support the project manager with his or her main tasks as outlined in Chapter 8. This support is usually well accepted due to the long professional experience of the facilitators. Typically, the facilitators will attend project milestone meetings, which are also called intervention points. The facilitator or coach joins the project team at strategically important points in the life cycle of the project, focusing on the early phase of the international project which bears particular significance as explained in section 8.6.

As a side effect, the facilitators then disseminate intangible knowledge on international project management within the organization (see Chapter 11).

WHAT ARE THE PACT WORKSHOPS?

At the PACT workshops, all core team members of the project come together. In these, quick knowledge transfers are carried out by learning by doing. The facilitator enhances the qualifications of project managers and their teams, for instance regarding project management methodology and project procedures. In other words, the facilitators aim at fostering corporate project management standards within the respective project teams. Showing how the standards help to manage the project better on the job is much more convincing than sending around project management manuals. A systematic project management approach in a global organization not only increases project management efficiency but also functions as a common reference frame for all project managers and team members of the organization across the globe, providing them with a common language and methodology. This helps to bridge differences and ensures sustainable success in managing international projects. Of course, there needs to be sufficient room for adaptations to local requirements.

Another purpose of the PACT workshop is more related to the interpersonal side. The facilitators support the project manager in dealing with criticism and tensions within the team, and overcoming big divides between functions and local cultures. To give an example: in new product development, the risk is high that materials to be used for a certain component are not suitable. These technical issues can result in delays and cost increases. The project manager gets put under pressure from senior management, and the functions involved in the project will appear at milestone meetings with mutual accusations like: 'If procurement is running the show here, we will never be able to attain our quality goals.' Procurement accuses engineering of always thinking about what is possible, but never what is really needed. The German engineers accuse the French of spending all their time on extended lunch breaks, and the Brazilians reproach their German colleagues for wasting time with over-specifications. In such a tense atmosphere, a PACT facilitator will try to turn the discussions away from finger-pointing and towards a constructive search for solutions.

Depending on the severity of the situation, the facilitators may spend up to two days on conflict resolution, or only a couple of hours on a team building exercise.

The methods applied by the facilitator will vary between national cultures and will depend on the degree of maturity within the industry the customer comes from. If the majority of workshop participants are US-Americans or Germans, brainstorming techniques will prevail. In a Chinese context where industry experience is still developed, the facilitator tends to assume a role of a trainer to provide all workshop participants with the required background knowledge and context. For instance, the facilitator explains what exactly a milestone is.

WORKSHOP METHOD 'METAPLAN'

Typically, the facilitators work with the so-called 'Metaplan'-technique which is especially helpful in facilitating international project management teams. 'Metaplan' is a brand name for a low technology group brainstorming technique. It uses pin-boards, large sheets of paper and differently shaped and coloured cards and templates. According to Davison and Ward (1999), 'Metaplan' has the following advantages:

1 People need to write before they talk which is conducive to people who are more introverted, reflective, or have language difficulties.
2 At the same time, it prevents more dominant team members or native speakers from running the show.
3 A lot of ideas can be gathered in a short time-frame.
4 The technology is simple and can be used at all kinds of venues.
5 Participants at the workshop have to walk around to pin their contributions to the 'Metaplan' boards and thus look at what others have put there, which keeps people involved.
6 The group gets together physically around the 'Metaplan'. This overcomes the near automatic creation of sub-groups who share the same language and cultural background and who tend to cling together.

Overall, PACT has improved the efficiency of new product development projects over the years. An increasing number of facilitators now support more and more projects with the PACT method.

Questions

1 In your opinion, why is a process like PACT especially important in the context of international projects?
2 What are the prerequisites to developing as an effective facilitator?
3 How do the tasks of the PACT facilitator differ from the tasks of an international project manager?

FURTHER READING

Connerley, Mary L. and Pedersen, Paul B. (2005) *Leadership in a Diverse and Multicultural Environment: Developing Awareness, Knowledge, and Skills.* Thousand Oaks, CA: Sage. (This book focuses on methods to develop cultural awareness and skills for leading in a multicultural environment. However, there is no focus on project management.)

House, R.J., Hanges, P.J., Javidan, M., Dorfman, P.W. and Gupta, V. (eds) (2004) *Culture, Leadership, and Organizations: The GLOBE Study of 62 Societies.* Thousand Oaks, CA: Sage. (Provides the reader with a comprehensive overview of the GLOBE study, ranging from national cultural dimensions to the single country cluster scores of identified leadership behaviours.)

Köster, Kathrin (2007) 'Inter-relationship between organizational leadership, societal cultures, and organizational cultures'. In Seshagiri, S. and Gajendra, J.R. (eds), *Effective Leadership: Lessons in a Cross Cultural Context.* Hyderabad: The Icfai University Press, pp.9–28. (This article provides the reader with a concise overview of the relations between leadership, national culture and organizational culture. There is no focus on project management, however.)

Wong, Zachary (2007) *Human Factors in Project Management: Concepts, Tools, and Techniques for Inspiring Teamwork and Motivation.* San Francisco, CA: Jossey-Bass. (Chapter 7 explains team development stages, Chapter 8 provides a concise introduction in the main facilitation techniques.)

COMMUNICATING IN INTERNATIONAL PROJECTS

9

LEARNING OBJECTIVES

After studying this chapter, you will be able to:

- understand the basics of the communication process
- analyse how national culture is related to communication styles
- explain how language diversity impacts on communication
- switch between communication styles
- understand cultural impact on the negotiation process
- conceive relevant communication modes in international projects
- elucidate relevant communication technology
- analyse characteristics of communicating in purely virtual teams
- draft a communication governance system
- apply guidelines for minimizing communication hiccups in international projects.

INTRODUCTION

9.1 In the seventeeth century, the famous British philosopher John Locke had already stated how important it was for a community to attach the same meaning to words. Only then can language facilitate communication. And with communication we develop our knowledge further (Uzgalis, 2007). Brought forward to project management communities in the twenty-first century, the message remains the same: communication is the key to increasing value – in all types of projects. Heldman (2005: 20) points out, that 90 per cent of the time of a project manager is spent with communication: 'I can't think of any other element that has a greater impact on your project's success than good communication'. This statement was made for a 'standard' project. It certainly is even more valid for an international project. But what is 'good communication'? Depending on the national culture and the natural language, good communication can imply different behaviour as we will learn in this chapter. The challenge is to bring the communication process to an individual's attention, as we usually communicate unconsciously. Hence, we will first learn more about what happens in (intercultural) communication. We will then explore the role of language in the communication process. Cultures can be clustered together based on their communication styles into high-and low-context cultures, with one cluster favouring a more indirect communication style, and the other tending towards a direct communication style. Based on our knowledge regarding differences in intercultural communication, we will turn to other particularities of communication in international projects. From face-to-face communication to chats or databases, there is a wide range of modes which can be used to get a message across. I will introduce the most relevant communication modes and discuss their advantages and disadvantages in international projects. We will dwell on communication in purely virtual projects because of the special requirements this communication situation demands. As communication is essential in international projects, it is of the utmost importance to plan this well. For this purpose, we need a communication matrix which we will discuss within the frame of a comprehensive communication governance system. I will close this chapter with some recommendations on how to configure communication in international projects in the most effective way.

COMMUNICATION IN INTERNATIONAL PROJECTS

9.2 Communication is usually modelled as a process where an idea travels from the sender through a channel to a receiver. The sender encodes the idea into a message in verbal or non-verbal language, and the receiver decodes the message. The receiver typically reacts to the message of the sender in the form of feedback. Some noise interferes with the transmission. This process is embedded in culture, be it national, organizational, professional, or all of these. When the sender and receiver operate within different cultures, their meanings are probably different, too (Varner and Beamer, 2005). Figure 9.1 illustrates the basics of an intercultural communication process.

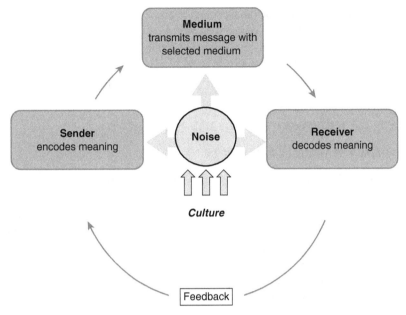

FIGURE 9.1   Intercultural communication model
Source: Gudykunst and Ting-Toomey, 1988

While the communication process as illustrated above looks straightforward, we are usually not aware of it. In other words, we communicate unconsciously. We are not aware of the fact that we all bring associations to the communication process based on our values and norms This is true for verbal communication using language and non-verbal communication using for instance voice pitch.

In Chapter 8 I highlighted the sensitivity of people management because of the fragility of interpersonal relations. This especially applies for the process of communication epitomizing interpersonal interactions. The (intercultural) communication process is irreversible because the receiver may not change his or her reaction to a communication the sender wants to 'take back' and edit.

What does this mean for international projects? All stakeholders have to be sensitized about the importance and cultural embeddedness of communication. This is especially true for the leader of the international project who has to turn his or her special attention to planning for smooth communication including the assessment of communication training needs of his or her project members (see Chapter 8).

LANGUAGE AND COMMUNICATION

9.3

Communication does not take place in a vacuum but needs a vehicle. This is language. It is obvious that the heterogeneity in international projects results in variations in natural and functional languages. Much to the dismay of many international project managers and team members, Douglas Adams's babel fish remains a piece of fiction in the *Hitchhikers' Guide to the Galaxy* (1980). An automatic translation machine that lets us ignore differences in language has still to be invented, although Google tries its best. For the time being, we have to face the reality of language diversity.

CAVEATS OF NATIONAL LANGUAGE DIVERSITY

1   *Insufficient project feasibility*

Very often, it is taken for granted that all the stakeholders involved in an international project will share a common language, usually English. In many countries, however, one should not assume that the majority of the workforce speaks English fluently. We only have to think of Latin American countries, Arab countries, Eastern European countries, Southern European countries, or Japan and South Korea to find cases in point. A possible remedy is language training or a multilingual project management team. If this is too time consuming or no resources are available, the organization will have to fall back on professional translation services.

2   *Loss of speed*

If major important stakeholders do not speak a common language to a reasonable level, professional interpreters will have to be used. The disadvantage, of course, is cost and a slowing down of the communication process. In addition, the loyalties and competences of the interpreter have to be closely scrutinized before extending full trust to him or her. And as regards planning: if an interpreter is used everything takes more time, which is often underestimated.

More time is also needed if decisions are taken in project team meetings with participants who are not proficient in the shared language. Usually, a lack of understanding will not be owned up to in public. After the project meeting, decision implementation or corrective actions may be delayed because people do not feel part of the decision as they have not understood the discussion that has just taken place. They might also request additional information and explications, which stalls activities (McDonough et al., 1999).

3   *Loss of creativity*

Another aspect to consider is that the brilliance of ideas and nuances tends to get lost when non-native speakers exchange thoughts in sub-standard English.

Therefore, it might not always be the best solution to have English as the mandatory shared language for all project communication. Sometimes, it might be more efficient to let people converse in their native languages with only parts of this being translated. We also call this code-switching. Another option is to establish English or any other common language as mandatory for written documentation, but to allow for an oral information exchange in other languages.

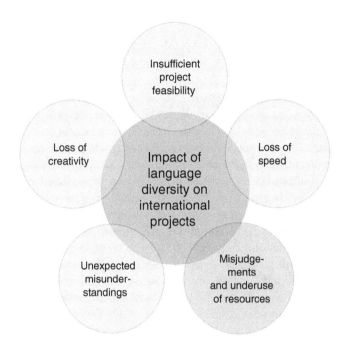

FIGURE 9.2   Impact of language diversity on international projects

4   *Misjudgements and underuse of resources*

People will judge others from their looks and their capability of expressing themselves. If the common language in a project is English, it is extremely premature to judge the intelligence and competence of non-native speakers from their language proficiency. In many international projects, there will be specialists and experts in the team who will tend to struggle with English, but can contribute a lot to technical or other areas. Hence, it is important not to frustrate these people, to leave them sufficient time to express their ideas, and not to be prejudiced against them. ABB's former CEO said that his company's official language was 'poor English' to make the point that no one should be embarrassed to forward an idea because of a lack of perfection in using English (Govindarajan and Gupta, 2001).

5   *Unexpected misunderstandings*

International projects where English is used as the lingua franca in a professional way will also experience a few or more hiccups. All project members will have to be careful about the language they are using. An example would be when a French English speaker says: 'I demand a meeting with you.' His British colleague may not feel too amused about the offensive language. The French person, however, won't notice the faux pas because he has directly translated the French word *demander*. These false friends may do some damage in a conversation, especially in a written conversation.

Figure 9.2 summarizes the impact language diversity may have on international projects.

Given all the challenges non-native speakers have with a common language, wouldn't it be better to assign tasks that involve a lot of communication to native speakers only? Typically, this would be native English speakers. The answer must be 'no' for the following reasons.

1   For many non-English native speakers, US-American English, Australian English, or English with an Irish, Welsh or Scottish bent is very difficult to understand. The reason often lies in the speed of the native speakers, their local accents, but also in the proverbs and colloquialisms they are using. An example would be US-project members who may integrate a lot of terminology originating from baseball or football into their communication without realising that their counterparts not being familiar with these games will mean they do not understand the meaning, say, of 'Send him down to the minors' (Varner and Beamer, 2005).

2   English native speakers tend to be mono-lingual. This means they will have difficulties putting themselves in the shoes of someone who communicates in a foreign language. This often results in a lack of sensitivity regarding the special needs of non-native speakers.

The only way out of the language diversity dilemma is to upgrade language skills continuously. This is the responsibility both of each individual and of globally operating organizations.

TECHNICAL AND FUNCTIONAL LANGUAGES

International projects, especially those with an internal focus like new product development projects, are often global and cross-functional which means that there are not only different national languages involved, but also different functional languages as well. For a finance person, the customer owes the company money, thus, the customer is called 'the debtor'. For a sales person, the customer issues an order, and therefore is referred to as the 'payer'. Both parties, however, might not be aware of these different perspectives. Engineers may use technical expressions that marketing people will have difficulty in understanding, and vice versa.

Functional or technical language is usually loaded with abbreviations that are not commonly used or understood. In addition, they might be rooted in the local language used by the headquarters of an international organization. Transferred to non-domestic sites, those acronyms lose their meaning, or get a new meaning. An example would be 'PP'. In German headquarters, it stands for 'Projekt-Prüfung' (project evaluation), whereas it stands for 'Project Planning' in many Anglophone subsidiaries. To avoid misunderstandings and to create a common base of understanding, the use of abbreviations should be minimized.

DIFFERENCES IN ASSOCIATIONS DUE TO NATIONAL, ORGANIZATIONAL, AND FUNCTIONAL CULTURE

As we have learnt in Chapter 8, one of the important tasks of the project manager is to provide the context that will reduce misunderstandings.

A study by Chen and Partington (2004) stressed the issue of the different associations people from different cultures might have with key terms used in the management of international projects. For instance, what do Chinese and UK project managers understand by 'good relationships with the customer'? For the Chinese, it means following each and every instruction from the customer to keep him happy. For the British, it means keeping the customer constantly informed to provide sufficient input for business decisions on the customer's side. 'Commitment' is a similarly difficult word which is often used, but is often interpreted by culturally diverse team members in different ways. Snapshot 9.1 illustrates how different meanings attached to the same word can cause project trouble.

SNAPSHOT 9.1

What is 'implementation'?

A US information technology multinational discovered only after a project was in trouble that an African local supplier had a different understanding of the word 'implementation'.

For the local partner it meant delivering the equipment and installing it with a basic configuration. For the IT multinational it comprised design, installation, configuration, training, acceptance testing and documentation.

The local contractor was selected due to his competitive offer. Too late in the project aid the US multinational understand the reason for the low quotation.

As a result, it is important to cross-check as to whether your communication partner can understand you at all. Always explain expressions which are embedded in your organizational unit's way of doing business or which may have other cultural connotations. Examples of terms that tend to cause communication disruptions are:

- accountability
- commitment
- deadline
- due date
- feedback
- issue
- process
- specifications
- responsibility.

Language related communication issues are only one side of the coin. Differences in communication styles are the other side. The same message can be expressed in different ways, even if the speakers use the same national, organizational or functional language.

CULTURAL DIFFERENCES IN COMMUNICATION STYLES

9.4 These differences in style were analysed by Hall and Hall (1987) who categorized cultures into high-context and low-context cultures. In high-context cultures, feelings and thoughts are not explicitly expressed in order to maintain harmony and to not cause any offence to the receiver. The communication receiver has to read between the lines and interpret the meaning from the context (Haywood, 1998). This can be:

1 The physical context, for example reading the facial expression of the communication partner. We can also talk about non-verbal language (see the companion website).
2 The social context, for instance the status of the communication partner or general values and norms.
3 The situational context, referring to the events surrounding the person or issue.

In low-context cultures, where personal and business relationships are more separate, communication will be explicit. Feelings and thoughts are clearly expressed in words, and information is given in a comprehensive way. The communication ideal in low-context cultures is to express oneself as unambiguously as possible, and also to be as succinct as possible. The context in which it is necessary to understand the message should be part of that message.

We said that high-context communication aims to avoid a loss of face. Hence, the blunt word 'no', directly thrown into the face of the communication recipient, tends to be replaced by the softer versions depicted in Snapshot 9.2. Individuals from low-context cultures, especially, should familiarize themselves with these expressions in order to recognize where a negative message can be hidden.

SNAPSHOT 9.2
Different ways of saying 'no'

Low-context communicators may have difficulties interpreting the following words or phrases as a clear 'no'. And indeed, depending on the context, it can also mean something more positive. This is the issue of high-context communication – the meaning is hidden in the context.

- We have to check this.
- We will think about it.

- Maybe.
- Maybe it's not so convenient now.
- Maybe this is inconvenient for you.
- We will do our best.
- This is a very interesting suggestion.

A 'yes' from an indirect communicator can mean agreement, but also can signal 'I am listening to you (and will decide later, whether I agree or not)'.

Usually, low-context communicators and high-context communicators will only notice that there are differences in communication styles when they interact with somebody from the 'other' world. Typically, the biggest misunderstandings or offences will occur when a person from one extreme, like a German, communicates with someone from another extreme, like a Japanese person.

Experience shows, however, that it is easier for high-context persons to understand low-context communicators than vice versa.

Hall and Hall's model as depicted in Figure 9.3 simplifies the world, and is certainly not comprehensive. Like the cultural frameworks introduced in Chapter 3, you should

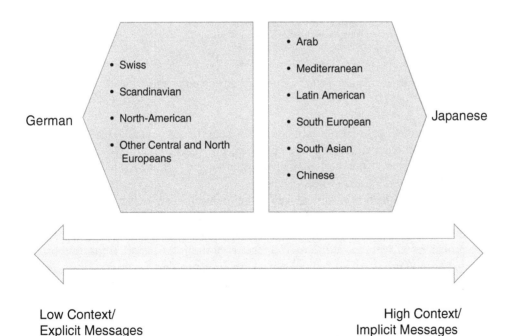

FIGURE 9.3 High-context versus low-context cultures

Sources: Hall and Hall (1987); Moran et al. (2007)

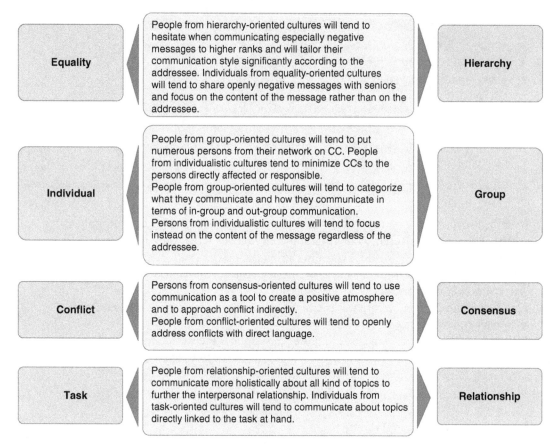

FIGURE 9.4   Cultural dimensions with an impact on communication

use this as a rough orientation only. Yet, it can help the international project manager and the project team to identify and anticipate potential communication issues. This awareness forms the basis of planning for smooth communication which is one of the main tasks of international project managers.

How can we explain those differences in communication style? Figure 9.1 depicts the influence of national culture on the communication process. Cultural dimensions can indeed have an impact on the content of a message and how it is communicated. Figure 9.4 provides you with an overview of the main cultural dimensions impacting on the communication process. This cultural gap analysis helps to alert the project manager and the whole team regarding potential communication issues. Based on this awareness, training needs to be planned and conducted and communication guidelines created.

As Hall's categorization into low-context and high-context cultures may appear slightly abstract, I will introduce more concrete communication styles that reflect high-context and low-context cultures.

1   DIRECT VERSUS INDIRECT

High-context cultures tend to use an indirect style of communication which is rather implicit. The sender does not verbally reveal his or her true intentions. People from low-context cultures tend to express themselves very directly. Their verbal message is explicit and embodies their true intentions (Gudykunst and Ting-Toomey, 1988).

A typical message by a representative of low-context could be:

'Please modify the plan based on last week's changes.'

This would leave the receiver of the communication with two options: he or she can modify the plan or start an argument with the sender about the reasons as to why a modification of the plan does not make sense. The advantage of direct communication is clarity. However, this can be a disadvantage at the same time because it might cause offence. In addition, the options to react to direct communication are limited.

An indirect communicator could express the same message as above like this:

'It is so important to always have the latest figures' or 'Maybe we should have some new figures … '

The implicit way of getting the message across lacks clarity which can be positive and negative. On the one hand, misunderstandings can easily occur; on the other hand, there are a variety of options that the receiver can choose from to react to the message. He or she can ignore the message, or ask somebody for updated figures, or confirm that the plan does indeed need actualization, or ask the sender where they can get the updated input from, etc. The receiver can then pick an option which does not cause any awkward feelings.

Mini Case 9.1 exemplifies some differences in communication styles and how these can cause trouble in a project.

Mini Case 9.1: A US-Japanese project team

A US-American manager was leading a project to build an interface for a US and Japanese customer-data system. During the implementation phase she worked closely on site with the Japanese team and discovered several problems in the system which could have a severe impact on company operations. Due to the severity of the issue, she quickly informed her superior in the US via e-mail, copying this to her Japanese team members. While her boss was happy about the early warning, she could feel that something was wrong between her and her team members in Tokyo. She had the impression that information was being withheld from her. Some documents were not translated into English, and people tried to avoid her.

Source: adapted from Brett et al. (2006)

Question

What was the problem? Base your answer on the communication style as well as its underlying cultural dimensions explained in Figure 9.4.

Another way of differentiating between communication styles is to categorize them into the extent of information volume combined with the degree of facts versus emotions. This results in three categories, namely elaborate, exacting, and succinct (Gudykunst and Ting-Toomey, 1988).

2 ELABORATE VERSUS SUCCINCT

A communicator using an elaborate communication style tends to use a lot of words full of emotions, metaphors, and exaggerations. An example of a typical message that a contractor would send to his customer could be: 'I am most delighted to see this wonderful, modern, fantastic high-tech terminal with all these beautiful shops and luxury lounges. I felt like I was in paradise. It broke my heart when my flight departed and I had to leave this exciting place behind me.'

An exacting communicator would try to express the same meaning by using less words and being as precise as possible: 'I like your new terminal which is both technically up to date and has a really nice atmosphere.'

Finally, a succinct communicator stands out because ideally he or she avoids big words and uses understatements and silence instead: 'Not bad, your new terminal.'

You can easily imagine how a communicator used to an elaborate style, like an Arab, will feel when he or she is confronted with a succinct communicator, for instance a Finnish person, whose comment is like a slap in the face rather than what it was meant to be: a compliment.

But we do not have to go to such extremes to find causes for irritation. At a status report meeting, a US-American project manager may hear a lot of 'Don't worry', 'No problem', 'I guarantee with the honour of my family', 'I give you my word' from his Mexican subordinate. Instead of feeling at ease, he or she should get the message that things are not going well on the side of the elaborate Mexican communicator who might be using such expressions to gain time or to cover up mistakes and thus save face.

3 PERSONAL VERSUS CONTEXTUAL

A third way of differentiating communication styles is by contrasting a verbal style which is individual-centred with a role-centred style. The personal style uses expressions that enhance the sense of 'I'-identity (Gudykunst and Ting-Toomey, 1988). Typically, people from individualistic cultures will apply a personal communication style. An example of a project manager talking to his subordinate could be: 'I would like you to achieve this.' For a contextual communicator who emphasizes his role or relation with others, the personal style could be much too aggressive potentially making the receiver lose face. A contextual-style person would phrase the same message as follows: 'There is a requirement that this has to be achieved.' In general, a contextual communicator will use different degrees of formality and different words depending on the addressee's status, gender, age, etc.

At the end of this section, we have learned that it is important to not just have reasonable command of the common project language. Even within the same national language, messages can be expressed in different ways. Interpretation is needed to avoid misunderstandings. It is recommended that the project manager adds differences in communication style to his or her cultural gap analysis in order to be able to plan for bridging those differences.

NEGOTIATIONS AS A SPECIAL COMMUNICATION SITUATION

9.5

In section 9.4 we discussed general communication styles which are the basis of the communication process. Project work is always a group effort based on efficient interactions with all team members. We could also call these interactions negotiations in the following sense: 'Negotiation is a process in which participants employ communication to identify behavioral alternatives and attempt to move toward outcomes that are individually and mutually beneficial' (Nadler et al., 1985: 90). Negotiations are ubiquitous in any international project. Informal negotiations are dialogues between the project leader and line managers about the release of resources. It can be a conversation between the contractor and the customer regarding the project scope change. On a more formal level, negotiations will relate to procurement tasks. These take place between signatories to the project contract. As a special form of communication, negotiations are culture bound and require special skills.

What factors have project leaders and members to consider for successfully negotiating in international projects, apart from differences in communication styles as discussed in section 9.4?

1 The relative emphasis on tasks versus interpersonal relationships:

- How much time do I have to spend on establishing a relationship with my negotiation partner? This is linked to the cultural dimension specific versus diffuse (task-versus relationship orientation).

2 Nature of persuasive arguments:

- How do the parties attempt to influence each other? Do they rely on rational arguments and facts, like many people from the Anglophone world, or accepted tradition, like East Asians, or on emotion, charisma, and subjective opinions, like for instance South Europeans, many Africans, or Latin Americans?

3 Use of time: I have explained cultural differences in the use of time in Chapters 3 and 5:

- What is my negotiation partner's attitude towards time?
- How fast should the negotiations proceed?

Obviously, time-conscious people and cultures can be taken advantage of by less time-dominated people or cultures with various delay or stalling tactics. This game is often played against US-American or central European negotiators.

4   Decision-making style:

- Is my negotiation partner as an individual in a certain hierarchical position able and willing to take a decision?
  The Anglo-Saxon world tends to prefer the delegation and empowerment of individuals. This means that the majority of individuals as negotiation partners are able and willing to take decisions, whereas for instance in Southern Europe, Asia, or Latin America a centralized decision-making style at the top of the organizational hierarchy will prevail.

I will conclude this section on negotiation styles by turning the spotlight on typical negotiator profiles of some important regions and cultures, namely the USA, Russia, and the Arab region (Pearson and Stephan, 1998; Loosemore and Al Muslmani, 1999; Gesteland, 2000; Al-Omari, 2003; Matveev and Nelson, 2004). Let us start with a typical US-American negotiator. How does he or she conduct a negotiation?

US negotiator profile:

- states his or her position as clearly as possible in a low-context style ('say it like it is')
- is fact focused ('let's get down to business')
- follows a linear agenda
- prepares to make concessions only if an equivalent is returned by the negotiation partner
- tends to take quick and pragmatic decisions
- prefers informality ('Call me John') to establish a warm atmosphere
- is very concerned with time ('time is money'), and sometimes nearly obsessed with time.

Arab negotiator profile:
As we are covering here not only one country, but a whole region, the reader has to be aware of local differences and deviations.

- uses an elaborate communication style with a display of emotions
- bases the negotiation on reciprocity assessed by equality, equity, or responsibility, depending on the situation
- avoids direct confrontation between opponents
- uses references to people who are highly respected by the negotiation partner to persuade them to change their mind on some issues
- is less concerned with time.

Let us finish with an analysis of a typical Russian negotiator.

Russian negotiator profile

- primary focus is on the relationship, not on the issue
- assesses the negotiation partner depending on how well he or she is connected with powerful people and has good connections (in Russian '*blat*')
- displays emotions
- uses a direct communication style
- is competitive and assertive with occasional threats
- believes that making compromises is a sign of weakness
- is reluctant to take any decisions if he or she does not reside at the top of the organization
- is less concerned with time.

May I remind the reader that such profiles do contain stereotypes and generalizations but can still offer a good orientation as to what kind of differences to expect from a formal or informal negotiation partner in an international project.

Mini Case 9.2: Persuading Scandinavian team members

Juan, the new Latin American project manager, was leading a change management project which targeted a new sales approach. When he met his Scandinavian team, he spontaneously decided to introduce this new concept without having prepared any slides. He was still fired up with a lot of new ideas he had come up with during his discussions with senior management. Of course, the concept had to be developed further and more systematically. Instead, he just shared his ideas with the team and colourfully pictured the great results that could be achieved with the new concept, agitating wildly. As he did not get any questions or comments, he raised his voice and described how happy and enthusiastic the customers will be with the new approach that was best in class, unheard of, and just great. Speaking freely and using all his best rhetoric, he was puzzled by the Scandinavians who continued to listen with stony faces, showing no reaction to what they were hearing. The Latin American project manager was desperate: why did his team ignore him? What an awful project start ...

Source: adapted from Gates (2007)

Task

Analyse the root cause of the problem from two perspectives: verbal communication styles and negotiation styles. Additionally, you can refer to non-verbal language (cf. the companion website).

So far, we have discussed the impact of culture on communication, differences in communication styles, and negotiation as a special communication situation. It is important to be aware of these differences and to be able to switch between communication styles.

Mini Case

THE CHOICE OF COMMUNICATION MODES

9.6 However, it is at least just as important, to have an understanding of different communication modes. Why? Because international projects will span not only cultural boundaries, but also organizational, geographical, and temporal boundaries. This means that for communication great volumes of information will need to travel across the globe at high speed (McDonough et al., 1999). Traditional communication methods like sitting in the same office and casually talking with each other cannot meet these new requirements. International projects are highly dependent on the use of computer-mediated communication.

Traditional communication modes and communication technologies respectively have advantages and disadvantages. There is a whole array of communication modes that the project manager and the project team can chose from. For effective communication in international projects, this choice needs to be made systematically in an informed way.

Let us therefore categorize communication modes according to the following criteria: communication can be verbal or in writing; it can be personal or virtual; and it can be aimed at mainly informing people (one way), or at interacting with people and leading a dialogue (two ways). Verbal communication is per se synchronous which means that all the parties involved are engaged in the communication simultaneously. Due to technological advances, even written communication can be synchronous.

Table 9.1 provides you with an overview of the communication modes facilitating the choice of suitable media for the respective communication purpose.

Another aspect in which communication modes or media will differ from each other is so-called media 'richness', which is determined by the following factors (Zigurs, 2003):

- Does the medium convey multiple cues?
- Does the medium support ambiguity?
- Does the medium require the co-presence of sender and receiver?
- Does the medium allow for personalization?
- Does the medium offer language variety?

Critics point out that richness not only depends on the medium but also on the context in which it is used.

The project manager has to combine insights from the communication mode with a media richness assessment, and with the culture gap analysis we have discussed in Chapter 3, to obtain the full picture regarding the suitability of media.

What insights are revealed? Relationship-oriented cultures tend to be high-context cultures. These are more oriented towards oral communication and prefer face-to-face meetings because they provide more context (physical, social, and situational). Moreover, personal meetings are better suited to establishing relations of trust (Rice et al., 1998). Task-oriented, low-context cultures tend to prefer fast, explicit communication style and modes.

TABLE 9.1 Categorization of communication modes

	Verbal traditional	Written traditional	Verbal virtual	Written virtual	
				Synchronous	Asynchronous
1-way active					
1: Many	Conference (Project) Roadshow	(Project) Magazine, Manual, Procedures, Newsletter, Memo	Webcast Internet Video		Internet video Mass E-mail Webcast Screensaver Attitude survey
1: Few	Team briefing	Fax			
2-way active					
1 : 1	Dialogue	Letter	Tel. conversation (fixed line/mobile) VoIP	Chat	E-mail Bulletin board
Few: Few	Workshop FTF Meeting 360 degree feedback	Flip chart Metaplan	(Multi-point) Video conference Audio conference Telepresence		
Few : Many or Many: Many	Project party				Intranet/Extranet Internet Web discussion groups

The reality of an international project, though, poses constraints on the choice of communication modes. Due to the time differences from one project site to the other, the opportunity for real-time interaction can be sharply reduced. Moreover, high travel costs can inhibit frequent traditional communication in the form of personal meetings. Virtual communication cannot be circumvented, although it offers fewer options to convey context and thereby cannot fully replace traditional communication modes.

As communication technology is crucial to communicating in international projects, we will discuss the pros and cons of the main telecommunication media in the following section.

THE USE OF COMMUNICATION TECHNOLOGY

9.7 The aforementioned categorizations can help us with the selection and use of the adequate telecommunication technology. It is beyond the scope of this book to explore all the kinds of different media from a simple telephone call to sophisticated collaborative project management planning and implementation software. Certainly, international projects require simple groupware tools such as Lotus Notes or MS Outlook/Exchange for communication support. Ideally, groupware should support process structuring with features likes agenda setting and facilitation, which make the task of project managers and sub-project managers easier. Features like the classification of message types, reply required or identification of role of sender may also be helpful (Haywood, 1998; Zigurs, 2003).

Whatever groupware is used, the project manager has to ensure that the same software solution is available across the sites involved in the project. Inter-organizational stakeholders who need to be included in the communication loop pose a special challenge as they may have different software solutions. Yet, it is important to work out of one single master document: either, the project leaders will have to go for a manual solution, or they may try to convince all parties about the advantages of global standard software like PRIMAVERA, which we have discussed in Chapter 5.

In the following, I will limit the discussion of media to a list of the most common and useful communication modes and tools with the main advantages and disadvantages for communicating in international projects.

TELEPHONE CONVERSATION

A phone conversation has the advantage of being interactive and providing context. The communicators can exchange their views and information instantly. Experience shows that phone calls are the second best way to discuss heated issues, if face-to-face meetings are impossible. The pitch of the voice, hesitations and other non-verbal cues can provide the communication recipient with a valuable context for interpreting what is said. A disadvantage, especially in international projects, is language constraints. Those of us who speak more than one language will know that a phone conversation can be one of the most difficult communication challenges, particularly if you have to switch languages unexpectedly, without knowing who is calling you.

Native speakers should be aware of such difficulties and speak clearly and slowly. In the case of important discussions, the sender should co-ordinate with the recipient as to a convenient time to talk, including the rough topic of the phone conversation. Such a procedure allows the recipient to prepare mentally and maybe also linguistically for the conversation.

A cost-conscious international project manager should remind his or her team to use fixed lines where possible. Usually, the quality is also better. Technology can also turn into a curse when you are available round the clock. To protect project members and allow them a good night's sleep, the project manager should remind people about different time zones and create time corridors in which a certain region or country can be called. The same goes for weekends or public holidays.

In Chapter 5, I introduced a calendar with the major public holidays worldwide. All project members should know about the most important breaks their colleagues have around the globe and respect differences in weekends, which might be Saturday/Sunday, or Thursday/Friday, or other days depending on the prevailing religion in the country the project members work in.

TELE-CONFERENCE OR AUDIO-CONFERENCE

For phone conferences, the same basic advantages and disadvantages as for phone conversations apply. The project manager will have to decide whether to use the tool as an interactive one, for instance to conduct brainstorming sessions across space. Let me raise a word of caution here: usually, only team members who know each other personally, and who have an extreme good command of the common language, will be happy to put forward their ideas in a phone conference. Power distance plays a role as well. High power distance people will typically volunteer their ideas only if no higher level people are listening in – and this is difficult to control with phone conferences. If these prerequisites are not given, phone conferences are better used for team briefings, allowing for direct interruptions in case of questions on the side of the communication recipients.

If the international project spans the whole globe, the timing of phone conferences poses a challenge. Either the Asian members have to work late, or the American members have to get up in the middle of the night. Typically, the Europeans are privileged being located in the middle. If hardship cannot be avoided, the project manager should make it a point to rotate schedules around the globe in order not to discriminate against the project members of one region.

E-MAIL

As both sender and receiver will have something in writing to refer to, e-mails are good tools for information exchange. They facilitate project documentation and increase transparency. Non-native speakers will have the opportunity to take their time in reading them at their own pace and looking up unfamiliar expressions in the dictionary. Information can be easily shared by forwarding the e-mail or putting team members on carbon copy. However, the differences in communication styles (high context versus low context) still need to be taken into account.

In longer projects with a lot of fluctuation among the members, it can be very time consuming and tedious to update the e-mail distribution list. It can also be counter-productive if any individual has been forgotten on the e-mail list (Eriksson et al., 2002). As e-mails are easily written and distributed fast, they can result in information overkill. Urgent matters should be followed up verbally, and to make sure also that the e-mail was indeed received.

GROUP VIDEO-CONFERENCE

Video-conferencing is an interactive communication mode which transcends a lot of non-verbal cues making it suitable for high-context communicators. If a face-to-face meeting is not possible, a video-conference is certainly a good alternative to bridge continents and to smooth and facilitate co-operation in international projects. However, reality has shown that there are a lot of technical hurdles to overcome, as all sites involved need to have the required technical equipment and need to be able to use it. Also video-conferencing facilities tend to be overbooked. Hence, no spontaneous video-conferencing is usually possible. The participants may also need training. For instance, they will have to talk in turns, not simultaneously.

DESKTOP VIDEO-CONFERENCE

Compared to group video-conferencing, this is more spontaneous and less high-tech. Costs are very reasonable for an interactive communication tool which transmits visual cues.

'TELEPRESENCE'

A new form of distant communication has been developed, the so-called 'telepresence'. It is basically a technically improved version of video-conferencing. Users still communicate via live audio and video feeds, but the speed and quality of transmission have increased, and the screens have grown and multiplied in order to create the illusion that the two parties to a conversation are at opposite ends of the same table. Participants of 'telepresence' meetings should behave as if they were in the same room. Unfortunately, this is still rather expensive (*The Economist*, 2007e).

WEBCAST

In a webcast, audio or video content is transmitted over the internet. The distributed information may be either live or recorded. Essentially, webcasting is a kind of broadcasting over the internet. A Dutch project manager with his team members located in

China, Japan, India, Sweden, and the USA used live webcasts to deliver motivational speeches. He tried to convey the common values all project members should display. While the Europeans and Americans liked these speeches, the Asians mostly felt bewildered. They did not understand their purpose. The experience of the Dutch project manager shows that the use of a one-way communication tool may have limited efficacy in high-context cultures, although the visual cues are transported. However, it is low cost and certainly a good supplement to other communication modes.

SHARED DATABASE

In the ABB project described at the end of Chapter 6, a database was created which contained the most relevant information for the project: functional design specifications; delivery plans; time schedules; notes from meetings; project related decisions; project diaries; and project weekly reports. The database was built in Lotus Notes, the software used in the entire organization. The main purpose of the database was to ensure that all the project members were following the same goals, and were fully informed about the latest status of the project. The database smoothed out the different national communication styles (Finland, Germany, Italy, Sweden, Switzerland, and the USA) and ensured the free flow of information (Eriksson et al., 2002). The project manager has to plan for resources to support database activities.

Now that we have obtained an overview of the array of communication modes and technology-based media, we will turn to the most challenging communication situation encountered in international projects, namely communication in a purely virtual team.

COMMUNICATING IN PURELY VIRTUAL TEAMS

9.8 The members of purely virtual teams will be geographically distributed. This means a great diversity of team members who – by definition – do not know each other personally. The number of international projects that rely solely on highly virtual teams is increasing steadily. Special communication guidelines and protocols are needed to secure efficient communication in this context.

Distant communication between strangers who are vastly different from each other presents the challenge of asynchronous communication due to non-overlapping time zones. In synchronous communication, the sender controls the information exchange. In asynchronous communication, the receiver controls the exchange without being able to rely on the visual cues he or she is used to from synchronous communication. An e-mail does not convey physical appearance, clothes, gestures and body language, which could greatly amplify meaning. In the case of unfamiliar languages and cultures, the receiver cannot even identify a sender's gender. Therefore, non-verbal language has to be replaced by cues which can be conveyed through writing. This could be computer literacy, e-signature, or emoticons, for instance a smiley with different facial expressions.

In addition, the sender has to find ways to incorporate context into his or her asynchronous communication. An alternative is to switch to synchronous communication every now and then. Haywood (1998) proposed the following guidelines for effective communication in purely virtual teams:

1 Team members must identify when they are available for receiving and responding to communication. These rules must be respected by team members.
2 Team members have to explicitly state the context of their communication in relation to intent, relevance, situation, and purpose.
3 Team members should strive to meet regularly in cyberspace, on a synchronous basis, to maintain rapport and continuity.
4 Senders must take responsibility for prioritizing communications as urgent, important, routine or informational only.

These rules should be considered in the various communication modes the virtual team will adopt. Based on these generic guidelines, the team should develop particular protocols for online team meetings, the indexing of meeting minutes, or other modes in parallel to what I will discuss in the next section.

COMMUNICATION GOVERNANCE

9.9 Due to geographical, organizational, and temporal dispersion, there are relatively few opportunities for an informal exchange of information in international projects. Therefore, the project management team has to decide at the beginning of the project how it will aim at securing the information flow between the various parties involved. There is a danger that either insufficient information is shared, or that it gets twisted and turned before it reaches its recipients. The situation is usually aggravated by different communication styles, insufficient language capabilities, and different uses of the common language.

Planning for smooth communication means the creation of a so-called communication governance system. This consists of the following activities:

1 Mapping the communication partners (stakeholders).
2 Defining communication content and structure.
3 Selecting the communication modes.
4 Defining communication frequency and timing.
5 Creating a communication matrix.
6 Agreeing on basic communication guidelines.
7 Determining communication protocols for the main communication modes.

While steps 1–5 build a process that needs continuous updating and cross-checking within a changing project context, activities 6 and 7 form the foundation for communication in the international project. All project members will have to adhere to these guidelines

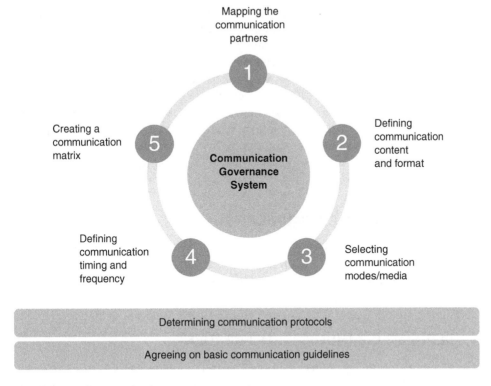

FIGURE 9.5 Communication governance system

and protocols during the duration of the project. This is crucial in an international context because guidelines and protocols must function as a common reference frame. Figure 9.5 illustrates the activities related to a communication governance system.

Let me briefly guide you through each activity.

1   MAPPING THE COMMUNICATION PARTNERS

The communication partners are all stakeholders of the international project. In Chapter 3 we discussed how to identify and manage the stakeholders. We can base the communication partner mapping exercise on Table 3.1 which provides us with an overview of all stakeholders. At this stage, it is important to categorize stakeholders in light of their communication needs. The communication partners map is the first component of the communication matrix illustrated in Figure 9.6, filling the column 'who'.

2   DEFINING COMMUNICATION CONTENT AND STRUCTURE

Communication content will vary during the project management's life cycle. In the initiation phase the emphasis will be on the project proposal, mainly on project scope and project objectives. At that stage, the context of the project needs to be communicated well. In the planning phase, the communication will focus on the input needed to create the project master plan. In the implementation phase, communication will need to revolve around project status. Project status is 'routine' communication, project risks or problems are 'issues'. Communication content is input for the next column of the communication matrix in Figure 9.6 where it is listed under 'what'.

In an international project with great diversity, templates for reporting concretely defined information are useful as a common reference frame. For instance, the project manager should create a one-page template for a weekly status report from his or her sub-team leaders. Such a template indicates clearly what kind of information the project manager needs.

3   SELECTING THE COMMUNICATION MODES

In sections 9.6 and 9.7 we have discussed the criteria for communication mode selection (see Table 9.1) as well as the advantages and disadvantages of the main communication modes. The selection of the appropriate communication mode is put into the communication matrix in the column 'how'.

4   DEFINING COMMUNICATION FREQUENCY

The project manager has to decide how often and at which intervals to inform each stakeholder. Routine content can be communicated in planned intervals, for example, weekly, monthly, or quarterly, depending on the nature and duration of the project. Issues should be communicated when they occur. It is worthwhile to conduct a monthly information exchange meeting with the customer where an alignment of the open issues list between the customer and the contractor is done to make sure that all the major parties involved are working to the same page. We have discussed the details of the structure in Chapter 6. Communication frequency information is incorporated into the communication matrix under 'when'.

5   CREATING A COMMUNICATION MATRIX

In the communication matrix, all relevant information for smooth stakeholder communication is compiled and visualized. In addition to the aforementioned input, the matrix contains information about the person in charge for the respective communication activity. It is a sub-part of the responsibility matrix and role descriptions dealt with in Chapter 6. To sum up, the communication matrix contains elements of the stakeholder map or matrix, the risk register, the issue log, and the responsibility matrix. It combines them with details on communication modes and timing. Figure 9.6 provides you with a sample of a communication matrix related to a global plant standardization project. The sub-project leaders are referred to as cluster leaders.

Stakeholders (WHO)	Topic/Issue (WHAT)	Method (HOW)	Timing (WHEN)	Who is responsible?
Project owner	Time overrun	Routine report	Monthly	Cluster Leaders
Senior Management	Time overrun	Routine report or face-to-face status meeting	Quarterly	Project Manager
Local Management	Equipment changes	Face-to-face meeting	Monthly	Plant Managers
Project Members	New project members, changes of responsibilities	Video conference/Webcast	Weekly	Project Manager
Support Units	e.g. IT: System modifications needed	Phone conference	Monthly or when needed	Cluster Leaders

FIGURE 9.6   Sample of a communication matrix

6   AGREEING ON BASIC COMMUNICATION GUIDELINES

In Chapter 8, we learned that the first series of project meetings has to be used for team building and the establishment of ground rules. Communication guidelines are part of this package and should be an outcome of the first project meeting. The following points are derived from experience. They highlight those areas which are crucial for communicating across cultural, geographical, and organizational borders.

- **Never take anything for granted.** What might be common sense in your own communication context might be nonsense for your communication partner; therefore, unearth your basic assumptions and continuously put things into perspective.
- **Face-to-face communication is most powerful,** especially for the establishment of trust and the discussion of controversial issues. The best replacements are phone conversations or video-conferences.
- **Be reluctant to reply immediately to negative e-mails.** A written reply when under emotional distress can easily escalate an issue and may lead to irreparable damage in interpersonal or intergroup relations. Wait until the following day at least before you answer. Preferably do this via an oral communication mode. If you are not familiar with your counterpart, do not use capitals, many colours or exclamation marks in e-mails as these can be interpreted differently across cultures.
- **Try to practise 'active listening'.** Show genuine interest in the speaker by using adequate non-verbal communication such as nodding and 'hmming'.

- **Be patient and willing to paraphrase.** Never assume that your counterpart has understood what you intended to say. If the communication partner doesn't understand, don't just repeat but rephrase what you have said using different words. This is called paraphrasing.
- **Consciously provide and ask for feedback.** You can do this by asking your counterpart (verbally or in writing) to repeat the conversation in his or her own words in order to make sure that he or she has really understood what you were saying. If you can't understand what is being said on the phone, delay by asking for an e-mail and think about it for a while. Remember the difference between direct and indirect communicators. Don't take polite indirect answers at face value. Conversely, try to buffer negative feedback and formulate it more indirectly.

  Davison and Ward (1999) suggest a colour coding system enabling people to provide feedback in a face-saving way alluding to cultural and personal particularities.

  > People = green
  > Action = red
  > Ideas = blue.

  Feedback from Mr Smith to Mr Jaworski could be 'Excuse me, could you be a little bit less green and a bit more red?', to let him know in an inoffensive way that the required action was quite urgent.

- **Determine response times for written communication.** When urgent decisions are needed, the response time should not exceed 48 hours. A visual code attached to correspondence as discussed in section 9.8 might be helpful for the recipient to immediately detect urgent issues. Such a code may also avoid misunderstandings, because recipients on different parts of the globe may prioritize a message differently. There also should be a clear rule about non-answering. It could say for instance: 'If the contractor does not receive an answer within 28 days, it will go ahead taking its own decisions.'

Figure 9.7 summarizes the basic guidelines which can enhance communication in international projects.

The last set of activities related to the creation of a communication governance system is the establishment of communication protocols.

7   DETERMINING COMMUNICATION PROTOCOLS FOR THE MAIN COMMUNICATION MODES

Communication protocols serve as a common reference frame for all heterogeneous stakeholders of the international project. They aim at enhancing a common communication style and creating common sense. At the same time, they are the reflection of a certain project culture. An abstract project culture needs to be 'materialized'. It is transformed into business practice in the area of interaction between all project members and stakeholders.

Basic communication guidelines for international projects

1. Never take anything for granted

2. Face-to-face communication is most powerful

3. Be reluctant to reply immediately to e-mails that cause offence

4. Practise active listening

5. Be patient and willing to re-phrase and paraphrase

6. Consciously provide and ask for feedback

7. Determine the response times for written communication.

FIGURE 9.7   Basic communication guidelines for international projects

This is done via communication. Communication is crucial for project success, and so is the effective implementation of communication protocols.

Snapshot 9.3 sets out communication protocols used by a multinational mobile phone manufacturer.

SNAPSHOT 9.3

Sample of communication protocols

General mindset:

- The quality of your communication impacts the response you get.
- Share information.
- Don't use acronyms and abbreviations.
- Establish personal contact especially for heated issues.

Face-to-face meeting:

- Have a clear purpose and agenda.
- Be focused, be prepared, be punctual.
- Summarize decisions and actions in a simple way.
- Switch off the mobile phone during meetings.

Phone conferences:

- Have a chairperson or facilitator.
- Identify the participants by their names and roles.
- Speak slowly and clearly.
- Confirm decisions by e-mail.
- Be aware: speaking on the phone in a foreign language is a difficult communication situation.

(Cont'd)

E-mail:

- Introduce yourself in the case of first contact.
- Be short and concise.
- Communicate in English for the sake of transparency only.
- Address the responsible person(s) only and minimize CCs.
- Think twice before sending confidential information.

SELECTED SPECIFICS OF COMMUNICATION IN INTERNATIONAL PROJECTS

THE IMPORTANCE OF VISUALIZATION

9.10 We started this chapter by talking about the language barrier in international projects. Replacing words with pictures, icons, diagrams or charts is a simple way of reducing this barrier. Of course, this is no guarantee against misunderstandings or misinterpretations. Yet, empirical evidence shows that visualization can facilitate communication across national, organizational and functional borders.

Individuals from national cultures with complicated scripts like the Chinese or Japanese are extremely well versed in quickly memorizing anything visual. So are people who are trained in professions related to information technology, engineering or other sciences where abstract interrelations often are visualized or condensed into formulas.

RAISING AWARENESS OF CONFIDENTIALITY

In globalized markets, competition is fierce. Hence, it is of great importance to protect the proprietary knowledge of the organization. This can be commercial or technical data. When travelling, the chances are high that project managers or members can be overheard on the phone, or that a neighbour will have a clear view of the screen of a laptop. In some industries, organized espionage carried out by competitors or by governments is the order of the day. Therefore, members of international projects need to be aware of this latent danger. They should also be careful when sending sensitive product drawings or price information as e-mail attachments cross-border. If they must do so, they should use encryption software. However, you will have to check which encryption software is allowed in which country.

SUMMARY

Communication and negotiation are processes that are vastly influenced by language and culture. Language diversity impacts on the international project. Visualization helps to overcome the language barrier. Even within the same language, messages can be expressed differently. High-context cultures tend to use indirect, elaborate, or contextual communication styles, whereas low-context cultures tend to revert to direct, exacting, succinct or personal communication styles. Complex international projects rely on the fast transmission of a huge amounts of information. Ideally, physical, social and situational contexts need to travel along with the information. Various communication modes fulfil these requirements to a different extent. These can be categorized as verbal or written, personal or virtual, one way or two way, synchronous or asynchronous. Telecommunication media such as telephone conversations, audio-conferences, e-mail, video-conferences, 'telepresence', webcasts and shared databases are indispensable in international projects. Purely virtual teams need special communication rules. At the beginning of an international project, the project manager has to set up the communication governance system consisting of mapping the communication partners, defining the communication content and structure, selecting the communication modes, defining the communication frequency and timing, creating a communication matrix, agreeing on basic communication guidelines, and determining communication protocols for the main communication modes.

 KEY TERMS

Communication process, verbal, non-verbal, direct, indirect, elaborate, exacting, succinct, personal, contextual, communication modes, synchronous, asynchronous, one way, two way, media richness, visual cues, communication governance, communication matrix, communication guidelines, communication protocols, paraphrasing, visualization.

REVIEW TASKS

Questions

1 How does language diversity affect international projects?
2 Why and how do communication styles differ from each other?
3 What do you consider important regarding the planning of effective communication in international projects?

EXERCISE 1 (WORKS BEST WITH CULTURALLY MIXED CLASSES)

Work in groups of five or six people in your class. The tutor reads 5–10 expressions to the groups. Each individual writes down a sentence, feeling, or any other association he or she spontaneously has with each expression. Do not talk to your group members during this process and try to be as fast as possible without thinking twice. After the tutor has finished, discuss your associations with your group members. Which expressions did you have difficulties with? Where do you have different associations? What could be the reasons for those differences? Write down your discussion results on a flipchart and after 30–45 minutes present it to the entire class. What implications do you see here for international project management?

EXERCISE 2

- Think of a typical situation in an international project. Now try to write a conversation between a low-context project leader and a high-context project member which plays out the imagined situation. The conversation can be via e-mail or face-to-face. Both parties will have to apply their typical communication styles. The communication must end with a misunderstanding. It should comprise 5–10 lines.
- Team up with one of your classmates and play out your own and his/her communication situation.
- Now try to change the communication course in a way whereby both parties understand each other correctly. Re-write your own and your classmate's communication situations accordingly.

CHAPTER END CASE: THE SOFTWARE DEAL

The following case focuses on negotiations. The Chapter End Case of Chapter 10 includes other communication related issues. Please refer to Questions 1 and 2.

A US-based high-tech company saw great potential in an idea brought up by an Israeli software firm and decided to contract the company with the advancement of that idea into a new software product. The contractor was allowed to work on two parallel versions, one for their own use to be marketed freely, and one for the American client who hoped that this special software could upgrade one of their products to make it more profitable.

After four years, the loosely controlled contractor–client relationship produced higher costs than expected. For each function that the customer wanted to have, the contractor charged extra because it was outside the scope, or so they said. After five years, the client decided on curbing the cost for that expensive project by assigning a British project manager to the project. He had the objective to negotiate a deal to cut costs. The contractor, however, had it in mind to be acquired by their client. They therefore put themselves up for sale.

The project manager prepared himself mentally for what to expect from the contractor's side by thinking along the lines of: 'I am an Englishman living and working in France. Both nations have gone to war with each other for one thousand years. And I know how difficult sometimes the co-operation between me and the French is. The Israelis are people that have quarrelled with the rest of the world for a much longer period – so I do see a tough time ahead … '

And indeed, the negotiation offered a couple of challenges. Firstly, the seasoned project manager had a clear plan as to when to finish the negotiations: he had identified the milestones outlining the discussion topics. Secondly, he had a clear agenda for each meeting; after all, he was under pressure from management to finish the negotiations with a positive result as quickly as possible.

One of the milestones was passed after a meeting on a Friday afternoon. Happy to have closed an issue which had been dragging on for quite some time, the project manager spent the weekend with his family. Much to his dismay, though, the contractor came back to him the following week to reopen the negotiation on that same point. They requested better conditions. This was even more embarrassing in light of the fact that the project manager had reported to the project owner that the milestone had been reached.

Apparently, the Englishman had to plan for another meeting. The Israelis, however, had their own negotiation pace in mind. They gathered information about the schedule of the project manager and followed him to India. Indeed, the project manager was most irritated to bump into one of the contractor's managers at a hotel in Bangalore where he was staying to attend to other business. The contractor's manager insisted that he needed to continue with the talks – immediately! The project manager got more and more frustrated, particularly in light of the fact that the contractor now ignored the negotiation plan along with the meeting agendas initially set. Instead, he got bombarded with constantly changing ideas and new items for discussion.

When the contractor saw that a stalemate had been reached, they circumvented the project manager and brought in the higher ranks of the American client. Due to continuous networking, the Israelis had good connections with the American client.

Hearing about this move, the project manager got really annoyed as he felt he was being ignored. He responded with the following countermeasures:

1 He closely involved his internal customers, two members of the senior management. In parallel, he found out who it was in his organization that the contractor was networking with. He made appointments with these people for a phone conversation where he could explain the purpose and background of his project, focusing on the cost-saving target of the project.
2 In addition, he plotted with the project owner, his direct superior. At one of the meetings, the project manager threatened the manager of the contractor by telling him that his company was looking for an alternative and intended to stop the negotiations. The Englishman expected that the contractor would react to this threat by appealing to the project owner. The project owner, however, was already prepared for this move. He had agreed with the project manager beforehand that he would reply to the contractor: 'My project manager is in charge, and whatever he thinks is right will be done at the end of the day – unfortunately … '

This statement restored the authority of the project manager and put all the pressure back on the contractor. Finally, a compromise was reached: the American client purchased the Israeli contractor, but at a substantially lower price than had been initially requested by the contractor. Part of the agreement was also the contractor's willingness not to charge for two years of work that had been done on extra features.

Questions

1   What negotiation tactics were used by both parties (see section 9.5)?
2   Do you see any communication and negotiation patterns related to the national cultures of both negotiation parties? You can draw on additional literature to supplement any missing information in the case.

FURTHER READING

Gallois, Cynthia and Callan, Victor (1997) *Communication and Culture: A Guide for Practice.* Chichester: Wiley. (This book offers a comprehensive overview of the interrelations between culture, language and communication with a direct business application.)

Lewis, Richard D. (1999) *When Cultures Collide: Managing Successfully Across Cultures.* London: Nicholas Brealey.

(This book offers easy to read pointers to verbal and non-verbal communication, structured by regions.)

Rad, Parviz F. and Levin, Ginger (2003) *Achieving Project Management Success Using Virtual Teams.* Boca Raton: J. Ross. (Provides the reader with very hands-on guidelines and insights on what to do when successfully setting up and running virtual teams.)

CO-OPERATING IN INTERNATIONAL PROJECTS

10

LEARNING OBJECTIVES

After studying this chapter, you will be able to:

- conceive the impact of national culture on co-operation in international projects
- analyse how diversity impacts on the creation of trust
- apply different measures to create trust
- discuss the ground rules for effective co-operation in international projects
- explain conflict and its influencing factors in international projects
- understand different strategies of conflict resolution
- explain these strategies to manage diversity in international projects.

INTRODUCTION

10.1

Co-operating efficiently and effectively in any project and with any team is charged with difficulties. However, it turns into a paramount challenge for international projects and their diverse stakeholders because co-operation has to overcome geographical, cultural, organizational, and temporal boundaries. In a study Govindarajan and Gupta (2001) conducted on global business teams working in international projects, only 18 per cent of the 70 teams under scrutiny categorized their performance as 'highly successful'. One third assessed their output as 'largely unsuccessful'. Although this study only concerned international teams within one organization, it cast light on the immense challenge that was posed on the international project manager and the major stakeholders involved. The project manager has to lay the foundations for smooth co-operation by successfully accomplishing the tasks discussed in Chapter 8. This responsibility, however, does not solely lie with the project manager. In geographically dispersed teams with several hundreds or even thousands of (multicultural) team members, every single project member has to be willing and able to co-operate further within an international project. The challenge starts with the creation of trust. You can only accomplish tasks under great resource constraints, time pressures, and uncertainty, if you believe that all your colleagues are doing their best and jointly are working towards the common project goal. Therefore, I will start with the meaning of trust and the different methods available to establish trust in international projects.

However, even with the best intentions, heterogeneity makes it difficult at times to co-operate smoothly with your colleagues or other stakeholders towards the project goal. There might be language problems as discussed in Chapter 9, or just 'strange' behaviour. Ground rules aim at minimizing such irritations right from the project start. We will discuss these as a reference framework for co-operation, especially within the project team, but also with the major stakeholders outside the project team.

Co-operation in international teams means dealing with differences. In business practice, differences can often lead to misunderstandings or conflicts. And conflicts, in turn, can be resolved in different ways, depending on the context, the national cultures involved, the organizational culture, and the personality of the individuals involved. Hence, project members have to recognize conflicts and know the different approaches to solve them. Ideally, a trained mediator in addition to the project manager should be available for conflict resolution. Escalation procedures also need to be established. Only if the number of conflicts is minimized can co-operation in an international project work smoothly. Therefore, I will dwell on conflict resolution approaches. The chapter will finish with casting a spotlight on strategies on how to overcome the difficulties caused by heterogeneity in international projects, and how to turn these into strengths.

CULTURE AND CO-OPERATION

10.2

Co-operation refers to a common effort or an association of persons for a common benefit. In international projects, these persons are typically of different descent, will have a different educational

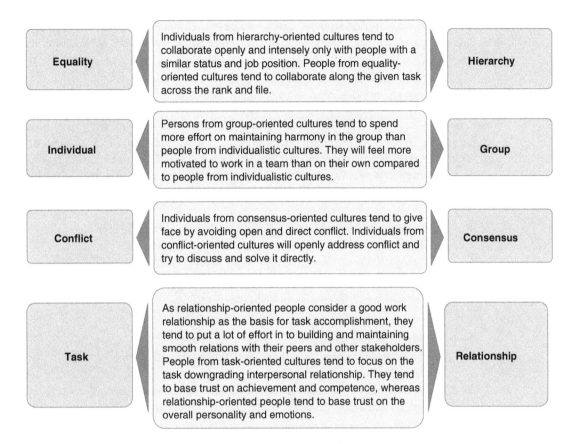

FIGURE 10.1   Cultural impact on co-operation in international projects

background, do not share the same natural language, etc. Therefore, their under-standing of the common project benefit and the nature of effort they take to pursue it may differ. Figure 10.1 provides you with an overview of the most important cultural dimensions relevant in the context of co-operation in international projects. As usual, this cultural gap tool aims at raising your own and the project manager's awareness of the major differences in order to deal with them effectively.

I will explore the main aspects resulting in effective co-operation in international projects in the following sections focusing on trust, communication ground rules, and conflict resolution styles. Let us first turn to the basis of any fruitful interpersonal inter-action, namely trust.

ESTABLISHING TRUST

10.3
For an effective co-operation, the project manager needs to trust the major stakeholders, and the stakeholders like the project team need to trust each other and the project manager. According to the

above mentioned empirical study of Govindarajan and Gupta (2001), cultivating trust is one of the most difficult yet one of the most important prerequisites for successfully managing global teams. This is also true for managing international projects in general.

WHAT IS TRUST?

For the purpose of this book, I will use the term in the narrow sense as 'the expectation that a partner will not engage in opportunistic behaviour, even in the face of opportunities and incentives for opportunism' (Nooteboom, 2006: 252). It is the belief by one person that another's motivation towards him or her is benevolent and 'honest'. Trust is fed by different sources (Kühlmann, 2008):

1 General context-related knowledge related to cultural norms and institutional rules of the partner.
2 Specific knowledge about the behaviour of the partner in different situations.

Trust works as an assumption and developer of co-operation. Whether people trust each other is determined by three factors (CULTPLAN, 2007):

1 Individual characteristics: do they share similarities?
2 Quality of communication: do they communicate frequently and with a minimum of misunderstanding?
3 Broader institutional context: do they operate in a common cultural context where behaviour leading to mistrust is negatively sanctioned?

In international projects, knowledge of the collaboration partner tends to be low. This is due to the high degree of multiculturalism and virtuality. Similarities are few and often unknown. Communication is charged with misunderstandings and institutional settings are heterogeneous. This is a very difficult starting point for the establishment of trust.

HOW TO ESTABLISH TRUST IN INTERNATIONAL PROJECTS

The challenge for the project manager is to establish trust within a very short timeframe, compared for instance with the more gradual development of trust between colleagues in an operational department. However, the development of trust does need some time. It is not a one-off event, but a reiterative process that is especially important for teams with a majority from relationship-oriented and diffuse cultures. These people prefer to work with 'friends', not only with 'colleagues'. Figure 10.2 depicts the measures contributing to the establishment of trust which I will discuss in more detail in the following paragraphs.

1 Overcoming prejudices

Prejudices and uninformed stereotypes will create a major barrier on the road to cultivating trust in international projects. Uninformed stereotypes are counter-productive and

Trust-building activities in international projects
1. Overcoming prejudices
2. Providing informal interaction opportunities
3. Exploring similarities
4. Bonding the international project team
5. Providing context

FIGURE 10.2   Trust-building activities in an international project

different from the informed stereotypes introduced in Chapter 3. If the heterogeneous stakeholders of an international project are to co-operate efficiently with each other, they have to overcome their mutual prejudices. But how?

As part of the kick-off event of an international project, the project manager could initiate a workshop where the main groups representing a national culture or sub-culture can have the opportunity to introduce themselves to their new colleagues each with a cultural hat on. They could even address the existing prejudices against them and explain to what extent there is a grain of truth in these, or where they come from.

The advantage of such a workshop is twofold: it addresses cultural differences directly and proactively, avoiding a climate of brewing discrimination and hidden barriers; it also enables all participants to learn first-hand about their new colleagues' cultures with training effects. Knowledge that is shared at such workshops could also be captured to make it accessible by other parts of the organization, thus contributing to project learning (see Chapter 11).

Experience shows that prejudices can be dealt with effectively by using them on your own culture: 'Here you go. As a typical German I cannot help it. I need to structure this pool of customers.' To laugh about the prejudices against one's own culture, which might be to some extent true, can help others to understand you better. In general, such an attitude contributes to an open and non-aggressive atmosphere which in turn can support overall project management efficiency.

But there are not only prejudices against people from different national cultures. There can also very well be reservations against team members from another unit of the same organization. Especially in big multinational corporations, there is a lot of bias against other business units, particularly if these were acquired from another organization. Prejudices can also exist between different functions like Marketing and Research and Development.

To understand each other better is essential, and a prerequisite is the acceptance of cultural differences. Mini Case 10.1 exemplifies what happens if cultural differences remain unnoticed and biased behaviour prevails.

Mini Case 10.1: The heartland of the European Union – worlds apart?

A team of Italian and German consultants started to work in Italy for an Italian customer on a new software solution for the service industry. The German consultants, commuting between Italy and Germany, were experienced in managing international customers, but did not have first-hand experience in Italy. For the Italian colleagues and customer, it was the first time a non-domestic party had been involved. Following the company policy, the local Italian colleagues took the lead. They assigned an Italian project manager and were responsible for all customer contacts.

The differences within the team showed up at the project start where the rough cost estimates of the German side turned out to be nearly 40 per cent higher than the fixed price that the Italian side of the team had quoted to the customer. They argued that they needed to get the customer on the hook, first, and then later on could add in some costs in further negotiations. The Italians seemed to prefer fixed-cost agreements, which they also negotiated internally with their German colleagues regarding travel costs.

During the implementation phase, the Germans reported their travel costs to the Italian project manager in the form of Excel files containing all details. They got a bit irritated when they noticed that a local internal controller was going through all the figures in detail to cross-check them, asking for invoices and more details.

To establish trust, the Germans showed their invoices and explained the arrangements with the travel agent. But nothing would convince their Italian colleagues who still assumed that the Germans were not honest.

Tensions within the culturally mixed team augmented. The Germans got aggressive because they could not understand what they had done wrong. In return, the Italians found the Germans to be extremely rude and non-co-operative – one more reason to distrust them.

Task

Explain the reason(s) for this mistrust in light of diversity.

2 *Providing informal interaction opportunities*

The kick-off workshop is only the first stage in the process of trust building. During the life cycle of the international project, the stakeholders need to have time to socialize and get to know each other better. Good opportunities for this apart from the kick-off meeting are planning workshops and review meetings at major milestones as described in Chapter 7. They should always be combined with team-building activities, such as doing sport together, or dining out at a nice place. With geographically dispersed teams, the project leaders should be considerate regarding the venues for such gatherings. Of course, cost plays a big role here. Still, the venue should not prefer one country or region over another. If feasible, it is best to rotate the venues across different regions, especially if the team is made up of equal numbers of people from those regions.

Here is one example of such a socializing opportunity: a US-American project manager invited his Asian team members to where he was located in the USA on the East Coast. Instead of dining out with them in a high-class restaurant, he took them along to hockey and baseball games where they all had hot dogs and beer. For the team members, this was a unique experience that they enjoyed very much. They could observe their team leader in a totally different environment and thus got to know him a bit better.

3   Exploring similarities

Trust, however, can be created through similarities which are not obvious in heterogeneous international projects. As a result, they need to be actively explored as a starting point to building a relationship. What could such diverse stakeholders have in common?

- shared hobbies, for instance sport, cooking, culture events, travelling
- the experience of raising a family, mainly the issue of education
- an academic education in a certain subject, like software engineering
- ancestors or family from the same country, region, or city.

4   Bonding the project team

Trust also emerges with a sense of belonging and feeling protected. Experience shows that members of international projects, regardless of their background, appreciate it if their project manager protects the team against conflicts with superiors, for instance line managers or the steering committee. By assuming the role of a 'shock absorber', the project manager takes the criticism from superiors and channels this in a modified and tailored way to the people in charge in the project team. On the one hand, such an attitude typically increases loyalty to the project manager. On the other hand, it enhances a 'we' feeling and fosters trust within the project team. It goes without saying that the project manager has to have the right skills to perform such a role effectively (see Chapter 8).

5   Providing context

Another approach to fostering trust is via an awareness of the importance of context and the willingness of providing background information. Anybody will have more trust in given tasks when he or she knows the reason for and background to this task. You can only expect people to do certain things or to follow certain guidelines when they understand the reasons why they should do this. Only then will they have confidence in the outcome of the task. Providing context not only contributes to faithful relations in the international project, but also simultaneously increases efficiency by helping to avoid misunderstandings.

Let me finish this section with an outline of a general attitude conducive to fostering trust in a culturally diverse environment.

Trust among international stakeholders is endorsed by:

- acknowledging differences and respecting them
- believing in the goodwill of all stakeholders to work toward a common goal
- establishing transparency
- being prepared to strike compromises
- admitting failure (in a culturally adequate way).

A seasoned international project manager once stated: 'Purpose is the glue, trust is the grease', when commenting on the most important factors that will lead international projects to success. Snapshot 10.1 provides you with an example of how to establish trust with a culturally diverse customer.

SNAPSHOT 10.1

Does your customer trust you?

Recalling his experience with a Ugandan customer, a project manager summarizes: 'You should show the customer that you are not egoistic in the sense that you only care for your company and the company's benefits. Show them that you will do anything possible to make the project a success – for the benefit of all parties involved.'

The specifications regarding the new IT infrastructure issued by a Ugandan ministry were quite comprehensive. When the project had reached the stage to implement these requirements, the above mentioned project manager representing the contractor told his customer: 'Well, you want this, but I have gone through the specs and discovered that they are redundant due to the fact that they had been developed years ago. You need something else, and although this is not in the project scope, we will deliver it to you at our own expense.' Faced with that offer, the customer felt taken seriously. It convinced the customer about the integrity of the contractor which established trust between both parties. Of course, the project manager had carefully calculated before making this offer. The additional costs were minimal compared to the intangible gain he had made by fostering the trust with his customer.

After a while, the same customer complained about the fact that the project manager was not permanently on site in Uganda but managing a lot of tasks out of South-East Europe. The customer was again losing confidence in the commitment of the contractor. The project leader managed to re-establish trust by highlighting that his presence in Uganda was not needed so much any more because he had transferred some responsibilities and skills to local Ugandan people thereby enabling them to carry out future projects on their own. The customer was happy to hear this and accepted the remote working style of the project manager. However, this only worked after the project manager had been on site in Uganda for quite a while in order to establish trust via face-to-face meetings and other events.

Analogous to a playground which is the prerequisite for playing a game, trust is the basis for effective co-operation in international projects. For playing, a playground is not sufficient, though. We need some rules of the game. Analogically, we need co-operation rules to make diverse stakeholders work efficiently within an international project.

GROUND RULES FOR CO-OPERATION

10.4

Common ground rules need to be established at the beginning of the project. The ground rules, however, can only contribute to greater efficiency in the international project if the overall project direction is well defined and communicated. In addition, the project manager has to have the necessary competences and authority to implement them. Moreover, they have to be embedded in a project culture of open-mindedness, flexibility and responsiveness (see Chapter 2). All project members have to display these attitudes. The following checklist comprises areas that need to be covered to lay the foundations for efficient co-operation (Davison and Ward, 1999; Longman and Mullins, 2005). You will notice that I have explained most of the areas in previous chapters. Instead of repeating content, I have added the numbers of the chapters in brackets where you will find more details on each area of co-operation. Still, it makes sense to have this overview in order to have all the fields contributing to smooth co-operation within an international project on the radar screen.

- ✓ What constitutes effective performance for us? (3, 7)
    This point is closely related to the project scope and goals. It needs to be clarified within the project team and between the project manager and project owner.
- ✓ How will we evaluate our performance? (1, 3, 7, 8)
    The team has to decide how feedback on the performance of individuals or the whole team will be measured (Key Performance Indicators) and communicated. The project manager needs to understand this according to which criteria his or her project will be evaluated by the project owner.
- ✓ How do we communicate across geographical, organizational, and cultural boundaries? (6, 9)
    Who communicates with whom and how?
- ✓ How do we design and conduct our meetings? (9)
    This point refers to communication protocols.
- ✓ How do we give feedback to each other? (9)
    Should it be direct or indirect, personal or impersonal, to individuals or groups?
- ✓ Do we fully understand the responsibility matrix and adhere to it? (6)
    It is important that each team member understands where the limits of his or her authority are. Each team member also needs to understand his or her duties regarding reporting information.

✓ How do we report project progress and communicate owner feedback? (6, 7, 9)

This refers to the methods for data collection and reporting. The content and report technique has to be incorporated into the communication matrix.

✓ How do we handle new ideas and inputs? (4, 6, 7)

This point deals with innovativeness, risk and change management. Should new ideas or suggestions be included in a weekly or monthly routine report, or should they be forwarded immediately to the project manager or project owner?

✓ How do we pass conflicts up to higher mangement? (10)

Typically, there are different escalation steps. Not all issues should be immediately reported to the project manager. International projects especially with such cultural diversity need to be very clear about escalation to make sure that issues are raised on the one hand, but must also avoid overloading the project manager with fighting small issues on various global sites. Which issues should the project manager flag up to the project owner, and when?

✓ How do we resolve conflicts? (10)

Should the project manager openly address those issues he or she gets to know? Should the team openly address and discuss problems?

The last two entries refer to a new topic, namely friction. What happens if co-operation is sub-optimal and a conflict occurs? Incorporating conflict management procedures into the ground rules means that conflict resolution is planned for. As we have discussed in Chapters 4 and 5, planning serves as an early-warning system and facilitates quick action in case a problem occurs. This applies to risks and conflicts which can be seen as a special category of risk.

EFFECTIVE CONFLICT MANAGEMENT

10.5
International projects are complex, full of uncertainty, with diverse stakeholders who will often have opposing interests. You can easily imagine that this is fruitful ground for conflicts.

WHAT IS A CONFLICT?

For the purpose of this book, I will use Ting-Toomey's definition (1985: 72) stating that 'conflict ... is conceptually defined as a form of intense interpersonal and/or intrapersonal dissonance (tension or antagonism) between two or more interdependent parties based on incompatible goals, needs, desires, values, beliefs and\or attitudes'. The reason for selecting this definition lies in the fact that it is very broad in scope. It also considers culture which is an important aspect when we talk about conflicts in international projects.

WHAT ARE THE MAIN REASONS FOR CONFLICTS IN INTERNATIONAL PROJECTS?

With the huge variety of international projects, there is a plethora of reasons why conflicts can occur. In general, all those sources of conflict also apply to 'standard' projects. In all project types, the most frequent sources of conflicts are (Kerzner, 2006):

1   Ambiguity of project objective
2   Insufficient authority of project manager
3   Manpower resources
4   Equipment and facilities
5   Costs
6   Technical opinions
7   Priorities
8   Administrative procedures
9   Scheduling
10 Responsibilities
11 Personality clashes.

We have discussed the conflict sources numbers 1–10 in Chapters 2 to 8. For instance, priorities are clarified within a project portfolio management system which categorizes projects according to their importance for strategy implementation. Responsibilities are clarified in a responsibility matrix that reduces the likelihood of disputes about who will do what in a project.

With the application of proper project management tools and techniques, we can pre-empt the occurrence of many conflicts and hence increase project efficiency and effectiveness. Yet, we have to acknowledge that conflicts are ubiquitous as they are part of the human condition. Personality clashes do happen everywhere regardless of how professionally we manage a project.

In this chapter, we will learn more about the conflict sources that are innate to international projects. These deserve special attention within the context of this book.

HIDDEN AGENDAS

A frequent source of conflict in international projects is a hidden agenda or a diverging self-interest within the multitude of stakeholders involved. Snapshot 10.2 will illustrate this point.

SNAPSHOT 10.2

Do we share the same goal?

Let us go back to the IT infrastructure project of the Ugandan ministry introduced in Snapshot 10.1. An international consortium headed by a US-based company was contracted to develop a

(Cont'd)

specific solution for the ministry. The whole project was behind schedule when a new project manager was appointed to lead the consortium. After the project recovery seemed to be successful and the project was on track again, another standstill occurred. The project manager, frustrated about this new problem, investigated the reason for the delay and found out that it was caused by a local East African contractor. When talking to this contractor, he discovered that this project was the only business the contractor had. Hence, employees of that subcontractor wanted to prolong the work in progress for as long as possible. The project manager offered high bonuses to the employees of the subcontractor based on completed work. This gave them an incentive to expedite the work. Thus, the self-interest of the employees of the local contractor was re-aligned to the overall project goal.

While Snapshot 10.2 depicted diverging goals between inter-organizational stakeholders, Mini Case 10.2 shows how conflicts can easily occur due to diverging intra-organizational self-interests.

Mini Case 10.2: Who 'owns' the customer?

In many global organizations, there will be an ongoing political struggle between the local subsidiary and headquarters regarding the responsibility and authority of customer relation management. This tension is frequently reflected in international projects dealing with the development of new products for a customer headquartered in the subsidiary's country.

The local subsidiary sees its main competences in knowing the customer's needs best, speaking the customer's language, knowing the market and sharing the same culture. Hence, the local subsidiary claims that all contacts and final authority for delivering satisfactory results should reside with the project team of the local subsidiary. However, the local subsidiary usually lacks the resources to deliver the product or service the customer requires. Therefore, it has to draw on other units including headquarters for support. Headquarters, in return, prefers to have direct contact with the customer citing speed and ease of direct communication. Although both parties belong to the same organization and pursue the same project goal, namely fulfilling the customer's needs at a competitive cost and time, the two organizational units often oppose each other and have difficulties with smooth co-operation, impacting on the overall results of an international project.

Question

What would you suggest in order to solve this intra-organizational conflict? Base your answer on the structural topics discussed in Chapter 6 and communication as discussed in Chapter 9.

MISUNDERSTANDINGS

In general, conflict is a social construct and has to be considered within the context it occurs. Part of this context is culture (Ting-Toomey, 1985). Conflicts will typically start with a misinterpretation or a misunderstanding which can be due to ambiguous information, or differences in communication styles which we have discussed in Chapter 9. People will usually act as if they were in their own domestic environment, their own organizational units, or in their own function and discipline. They then take things for granted, causing confusion or friction, often without being aware of it.

DIFFERENT VALUES AND NORMS

The root cause of a conflict can be even deeper, originating from different values and norms among diverse stakeholders. People with different values and beliefs will have different judgements regarding adequate behaviour which can be illustrated in Snapshot 10.3.

SNAPSHOT 10.3

Can you drive me to the airport?

A British project manager was working with an international team in the Middle Eastern Gulf State of Qatar. Among his team members were local Qatari. Having worked on site for the project for two years, he felt quite comfortable in Qatar and got along with his team members very well. One day, he got a phone call from the UK with the bad news that his mother had had a serious accident. Totally upset, he asked one of his Qatari team members to drive him to the airport as quickly as possible so that he could catch the next flight back home. Unfortunately, his Qatari team member happened to be a woman whose family did not appreciate at all the fact that her boss had asked her to be alone with him in a car. The family forcefully complained to the senior management of the company running this international project about the unethical behaviour of the British project manager. At the end of a week of conflict escalation, including serious threats concerning the health of the project manager, the company decided to exchange him. The whole conflict resulted in expenses for the company as it had had to quickly find a replacement to carry on with the project.

PERCEIVED DISCRIMINATION

Another frequent source of conflict can be the feeling of discrimination. Project members may feel they are not being taken seriously because they belong to a cultural or ethnic minority, because they come from a subsidiary disregarded by headquarters, because they are not that eloquent in the dominant project language, because they feel stereotyped, or because they work in the same organization but under different conditions due to diverse jurisdictions. The latter case is depicted in Snapshot 10.4. Cross-border differences in salary levels on one side, and travel costs on the other side, can be frequent causes of friction between the stakeholders of international projects.

SNAPSHOT 10.4

Treated unfairly?

An international project with German and Chinese partners divided the areas of responsibility as follows: new product development was done in Germany, while production was carried out in

(Cont'd)

China because of competitive wages. Due to technical problems in the ramp-up phase, German engineers and technicians needed to fly to China frequently to solve these issues together with their Chinese partners. According to internal company policies, each employee flying more than six hours was entitled to a business class ticket. Thus, each trip cost around 4,000 Euros per person. The Chinese counterparts, earning approximately 300 Euros per month, were outraged by that kind of expense. Stating that they also had to pay for high travelling expenses as members of the consortium, they requested a permanent presence of technical experts in China. Word of the 'rich' Germans spread across the team, affecting the working morale. The Chinese had the impression that the German company was 'rich'. Therefore, it would not do any harm to try to charge them extra. This again caused some level of frustration on the German side.

Figure 10.3 summarizes the most typical reasons for conflicts in international projects.

In international projects, it can be a challenge to assess the root causes of conflict. Is it influenced by cultural socialization, by the personal factors of the individuals involved such as gender or personality, or by the context, or by everything together? Typically, the root causes for conflicts will be multi-faceted, with national culture and organizational culture playing a vital role. Therefore, I will explain in more detail how cultural differences can influence conflict management.

VIEWS ON CONFLICT

According to Augsburger (1992), conflicts can be seen as belonging to the group that needs to solve them, or as an individual issue with the persons involved having the responsibility

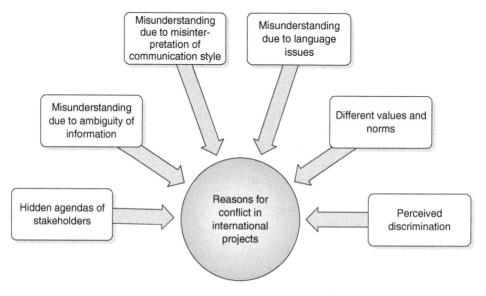

FIGURE 10.3 Typical reasons for conflicts in international projects

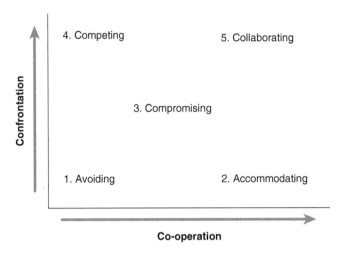

FIGURE 10.4 Conflict orientation patterns
Sources: Thomas (1976); Nadler et al. (1985), McKenna (1995)

of solving the dispute. Conflicts can be regarded as something creative, bonding people together and leading to new structures. They can also be assessed as destructive, alienating the conflicting parties from each other, leading to stalemate or denial. Some cultures view conflict as situationally defined and are open to all kinds of conflict resolution options depending on the situation at hand. Other groups or societies will have a culturally pre-scribed way of solving issues that is deeply embedded in their norms and values. Last but not least, conflict can be solved in an indirect, triangular way, based on a third party, or conflict can be tackled directly, in a one-on-one process between the persons involved.

ATTITUDES TOWARDS CONFLICT

The different views on conflict lead to different attitudes towards conflict. According to Thomas (1976), there are principally five basic orientations to approaching con-flict. These differ according to their desire to satisfy one's own concerns versus the concerns of another.

Let me briefly discuss the five patterns in light of cultural differences, keeping in mind that the orientation towards conflict depends on much more than cultural factors such as the personality of the individual:

1 *Avoiding*

A person practising conflict avoidance will refuse overt recognition of the conflict and will take no action to actively push for conflict resolution. He or she wants to stay out of the conflict. We can also talk about passive mitigation, or withdrawal. This attitude seems to be culturally prescribed in high-context cultures rather than in low-context cultures. It can be used for various reasons: maintenance of relationship; prevention of conflict escalation; no solution readily at hand; sharing responsibility for the situation at hand; non-seriousness of the conflict; or for other reasons, partly personality related. The stronger the group pres-sure for harmony, the likelier the use of the avoidance style (Ohbuchi and Takahashi, 1994).

2 Accommodating

An individual will select an accommodating style if he or she is concerned about the interests or the power of the other conflicting party, but has less concern for his or her own interests. This attitude may be common in high-context cultures with high power distance and strong collectivism.

3 Competing

This style is characterized by the strong assertiveness of the individual whose concern for his or her own interests is much higher than any concern for the interest of the conflicting party. We can also talk about a win–lose attitude. This attitude may prevail in cultures with strong individualism and/or masculinity.

4 Compromising

This style is used when both conflicting parties are prepared to give up part of their interests in order to come to a mutual agreement. In cultures like that of Russia, compromising has a negative connotation.

5 Collaborating

Individuals choosing this conflict interaction style are creative in offering additional incentives or topics they can discuss and include in their effort to find a solution to the conflict which usually results in a win–win situation for both conflicting parties. Typically, this orientation is found with people from individualistic, low power distance, low uncertainty avoidance, and rather feminine cultures.

For international projects, this means that all stakeholders have to be aware of the differences concerning attitudes towards conflicts. Those differences have to be acknowledged and managed actively in order not to turn into issues. A project manager, for instance, has to know that team members from high-context cultures may tend to adopt conflict avoidance. This could have a direct implication for project monitoring as discussed in Chapter 7. If there is bad news to be reported, like a delay or additional unplanned costs, those individuals may prefer not to report anything in order not to run into conflict with the project manager. The project manager, in turn, may lose precious time by not probing further. It is wothwhile talking about differences in conflict management early on in the project, for instance in a kick-off workshop as discussed in Chapter 8. The team needs to find a way to jointly handle conflict. This should be documented in the ground rules. The initiative needs to come from the project manager who has to raise awareness and train his project team, at least the core team, in effective conflict handling in a complex and culturally diverse environment.

   As there are different orientations towards conflict, there are a variety of options for resolving conflicts which I will now discuss.

CONFLICT RESOLUTION STRATEGIES

Depending on the context, the people involved and the cultural diversity, individuals can choose between various strategies that will help them to solve a conflict. These can be categorized according to two dimensions (Falbo and Peplau, 1980):

1   A direct or indirect approach to conflict resolution is taken.
2   Conflicts can be solved in a bilateral process, with the parties involved exchanging their views, or unilaterally, with typically the more powerful party trying to impose their solution on the other people involved.

Let me now comment on some selected conflict resolution strategies which are often used in international projects, depending of course on the context and who is involved.

Bilateral and direct: persuasion (through experience)

Many relationship-oriented, high power distance and ascription based cultures will attach a lot of importance to experience. In an argument, a good way to convince project members or customers is to make a reference to experience. Persuasion in the form of scenarios or cases is usually also very helpful; in other words it is best not to be too abstract but to tell people a story they can relate to.

Bilateral and direct: open and direct discussion

All the people involved must directly confront each other and openly discuss the issues. This strategy is typically applied by low-context cultures or by organizations headquartered in low-context cultures. Snapshot 10.5 provides you with an example of this strategy.

SNAPSHOT 10.5

The wrong project manager?

An African customer of a US contractor did not seem to be too pleased to work with a new project manager sent by the contractor. After a Swiss, German, and UK project manager had each admitted defeat, the Bulgarian project manager was sent to recover the project. When he noticed a certain reservation towards his abilities – there was this notion about a 'low-cost-person not being up to scratch – he faced the customer's reluctance to co-operate by quite straightforwardly giving the customer two options: either they could give it a try and co-operate to make the project a success, or he could go home immediately and ask for a replacement. If the latter case, however, the customer would still have the problem of a project stuck in the implementation phase and yet another significant delay.

Unilateral and direct: coercion or threat

The problem resolution is carried out by a generally respected authority which can be an institution such as the steering committee or the project manager. The effectiveness of this strategy depends on what is at stake, how widespread the acceptance of authority is in the organization, and whether the authority has credibility regarding potential punishment in the case of disobedience. Typically, acceptance is stronger in high power distance cultures with autocratic leadership styles. As explained in Chapter 8, the great complexity of international projects endorses shared responsibility and co-leadership which means that this strategy should be applied only where deemed as absolutely necessary. Snapshot 10.6 illustrates what can happen if an open discussion style collides with a coercion style.

SNAPSHOT 10.6

The autocratic Italian customer

The CIO of an Italian corporation was used to giving orders. He expected absolute obedience from his employees and of course from his contractors. Nobody dared to openly criticize him. The international contractor wanted to offer the best solution available with some upgrades, trying to convince the CIO with arguments and facts and figures about the advantages of the new add-on. The CIO, however, not fully grasping all the details of the proposal, disapproved of the proposal. When the team from the international contractor approached him again, he became furious and threatened to stop the whole project only one month before the go live date. Nobody on the contractor's side really took the threat seriously, as it would have meant a loss for the customer of several million Euros. The CIO, however, attached more importance to this demonstration of his power than to a financial loss. He ordered the staff of the international contractor to leave immediately and cancelled the whole project.

Bilateral and indirect: third-person intermediary

A third party respected and known by the involved conflicting parties is used to mediate between the two individuals or groups that have a conflict. Mediation differs from negotiation as a third party is involved in the process. This strategy is also referred to as 'shuttle diplomacy' because the mediator oscillates between the conflicting parties to avoid a direct confrontation between them. The mediator explores the reasons for the conflict and tries to find an acceptable solution for both parties. The advantage is that a loss of face can be avoided through this indirect approach which typically is applied in high-context, high power distance, high risk avoidance and collectivist cultures.

Let us finish this section on conflict management with an example from an international project where conflicts occurred right at the start of the project endangering the whole undertaking (Mini Case 10.3).

Mini Case 10.3: Starting off on the wrong foot

Racy (name disguised), a multinational automotive supplier, won a tender to supply components to a US-based auto manufacturer. Local production of parts in Brazil, South Africa, and Thailand was requested. Racy had facilities in the first two countries but the Thailand plant had to be built up. Racy had a facility in Malaysia and planned to use Malaysian resources to the improve Thai facility.

The US client handled the project through its purchasing department in Australia. To be close to the customer, Racy decided to locate the project base in Australia as well. Australia has the additional advantage of sitting 'right in between' Malaysia and Brazil from a time zone perspective. As Racy was short of qualified staff in Australia, it transferred a project manager from India to Australia.

The new project started with a kick-off meeting in Australia. At Racy, such a meeting typically takes two days. The Malay project members, however, left prematurely complaining to a corporate project management facilitator about the project manager. What had happened?

The Indian project manager, technically highly capable, but without any international leadership experience, introduced himself with: 'I am the king. In my local language, my name stands for king. I stem from the highest caste in India.' Then he requested input from the Malays in a brainstorming meeting that the Malays were not prepared for. The Malays had the suspicion that the project manager had deliberately not briefed them before the kick-off meeting to make them look dull in front of their Australian colleagues. They were afraid of getting fewer tasks assigned at the kick-off workshop than the other sites. Fewer tasks meant a lower income for their local site, translating into less importance and fewer jobs.

The Malays wanted to discuss their concerns with the Indian project manager. However, they had the impression that he was too arrogant to listen. So the Malays gave up and returned to their subsidiary, leaving the project manager puzzled. What was going on? Certainly, this was the worst project start one could imagine.

The external facilitator who the Malays had turned to suggested a second kick-off meeting, this time facilitated by her.

Question

If you were the facilitator, what would you do to get the project back on track?

We have seen in this chapter that co-operation in international projects is closely related to dealing with diversity. While previous chapters have touched on diversity in its full breadth including context diversity (e.g. jurisdictions), I have focused in this chapter on diversity in a narrower sense, mainly cultural and educational diversity.

All project members are different, and the project manager has to set the scene for successfully dealing with these differences. As diversity is one of the main characteristics of an international project, its efficient management is critical for project success. Therefore, I will close this chapter with suitable strategies to manage heterogeneity or diversity.

MANAGING HETEROGENEITY

10.6

Diversity adds to complexity, another trait of international projects, making their management a challenging task. Can we conclude then that the target is to minimize the damage caused by diversity, or are there even advantages in diversity? According to Parker (2009), differences are opportunities. Combining different perspectives can lead to a richer set of experiences and better solutions. Brett at al. (2006) suggest the following strategy to deal with diversity.

ADAPTATION OR FUSION?

Teams with diverse stakeholders are more efficient if they can mutually acknowledge their differences. This requires, however, knowledge about other norms and values, an attitude of open-mindedness and flexibility, and the willingness to adapt or create something new.

Adaptation means that project stakeholders are flexible in their attitudes and behaviours and can adapt themselves to the necessities of the situation in an international project. This could be an adaptation to the cultural script of the external customer.

A stronger approach is fusion where all members try to cherry pick what works best in their traditional ways of doing things and to fuse these styles. In other words, synergies are created from diversity.

A good example would be a US-German mixed team in the area of decision-making. In the USA, decisions tend to be taken very fast, due to the individual's willingness to take risks and a general impatience with and appreciation of time being limited and precious, as highlighted in the US-American negotiator profile in Chapter 9. The downside of this behaviour is that not all relevant factors might be taken into account. In Germany, decisions tend to take some time. Individuals first like to assess all the relevant pros and cons before they take a decision. To some extent, this is based on risk aversion and the mentality of being precise and detail-oriented. The clear disadvantage here is that decisions may take too long and invite pre-emptive initiatives by internal or external rivals. If both sides mix their approaches, though, they can arrive at faster decisions which are of better quality.

Another example of creating synergies out of differences is a Chinese-German mixed product development team. In China, product developers like mechanical or electrical engineers tend to have a pragmatic view of what the customer needs and how to design it in a simple, fast way which leads to quick and cost-efficient product development. The pitfall might be that products will tend to be more difficult to repair due to a non-transparent development process and the lack of a proper conception phase. In Germany, product developers tend to be painstakingly correct with their product conceptualization and documentation, obsessed with optimization and further high-tech developments with a high degree of innovativeness. The downside is that new products may be over-specified and thus too expensive with too lengthy development cycles. If the differences are acknowledged and used well mixed teams can develop new products faster, at the appropriate level of specification demanded by the customers with proper documentation to facilitate after sales service.

A fusion strategy is certainly ideal but difficult to achieve under time pressures, especially in very complex settings, and with people who are typically not that experienced with international projects. Yet, it is a strategy to strive for in order to benefit most from diversity.

ELEMENTS OF EFFECTIVE CO-OPERATION

10.7

Let me wrap up this chapter with a summary of the key factors that are critical to managing the 'soft side' of an international project successfully. Based on a project culture of strong internal integration, strong autonomy and involvement, great adaptability, strong orientation

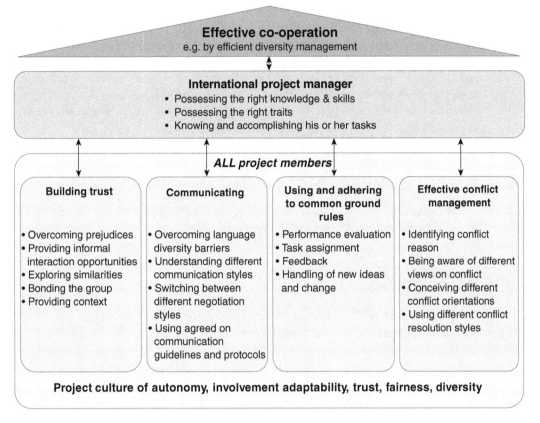

FIGURE 10.5   Components of effective co-operation in international projects

towards fairness and trust as well as open-mindedness towards differences, the project manager lays the foundations of trust among internal and external stakeholders. It is important that the project manager lives up to the values of the project culture. All project members are sensitized and trained towards coping with language, communication, negotiation, and conflict resolution style differences. They have been involved in the creation of communication guidelines and protocols which are part of the ground rules.

The international project manager has suitable knowledge, skills, and traits to establish the basis for effective co-operation. One important element of effective collaboration in international projects is the management of diversity, as diversity is a main characteristic of international projects. Figure 10.5 illustrates the key components for effective co-operation in international projects.

SUMMARY

Effective co-operation in international projects is a paramount challenge mainly due to diversity. Trust is the basis for co-operation and needs to be established by overcoming prejudices and stereotypes, providing informal interaction opportunities, exploring similarities, bonding the project group, and providing context. Based on trust, the international project needs to be governed by ground rules for co-operation from its start. Special attention needs to be drawn to conflict management. Typical causes of conflicts in international projects are the hidden agendas of stakeholders, misunderstandings due to information ambiguity, communication styles or language, differences in norms and values, and perceived discrimination. Possible attitudes towards conflict are avoidance, accommodation, compromise, competition, and collaboration. Conflict resolution strategies can be direct or indirect, bilateral or unilateral. For effective co-operation in international projects, it is important to have a project manager fostering a project culture of autonomy, involvement, adaptability, trust, and fairness. To sum up: trust building, communication across organizational, geographical, and cultural boundaries, allegiance to ground rules and active conflict management are crucial elements for effective co-operation in international projects.

 KEY TERMS

Co-operation, trust, conflict, avoiding, competing, compromising, accommodating, collaborating, unilateral, bilateral, adaptation, fusion.

REVIEW TASKS

Questions

1   In your opinion, what roles does trust play in international co-operation?
2   Where do you see the impact of culture (national, organizational, functional) coming on attitudes towards conflict and conflict resolution strategies?
3   Suppose you are an international project manager: how do you cope with diversity?

EXERCISE 1 (WORKS BEST WITH CULTURALLY MIXED GROUPS)

Work in groups of five or six people.

- Each group member writes down five words they associate with mistrust.
- Compare notes within the group.
- In the group discuss the measures to be taken in order to reduce mistrust. Can these measures be transferred to a project management context?

EXERCISE 2

Work in groups of five or six people.

- Think of a situation (individually) where you experienced tensions with your family, with a business partner, or with a colleague at work. Reflect on the attitude you had towards this conflict, and how you solved it.
- Present the situation and your reflection to the group.
- Discuss in your group the reasons for the conflict and the reasons for the chosen conflict resolution strategy. Can you detect any conflict handling patterns within your group?
- If time allows, present your group analysis to the whole class.

CHAPTER END CASE: TWO CONTINENTS – TWO WORLDS?

The following case also touches on communication issues discussed in Chapter 9.

THE STRUCTURE OF THE COMPANY AND ITS INTERNATIONAL PROJECTS

This manufacturer of electrical parts ('contractor') produces customer specific components for clients all over the world, with main markets in Japan, Europe, and North America. When a customer approaches the contractor with specifications regarding a tailor-made component, the manufacturer initiates a project. The manager of the project is co-located with the Research and Development facilities of the customer. This means if the customer's development people remain in the USA, as in our case, the contractor also locates his project manager in the USA. The contractor manufactures complicated products. Hence, the project is broken down into various sub-projects focusing on special technical areas. The sub-project managers are responsible for the technical development of their respective sub-component. The customer is in contact with the overall project manager. In our case, the sub-projects are located either in the USA or Germany. They report to the project manager in the USA. In each sub-team, there are application engineers working on the new technical

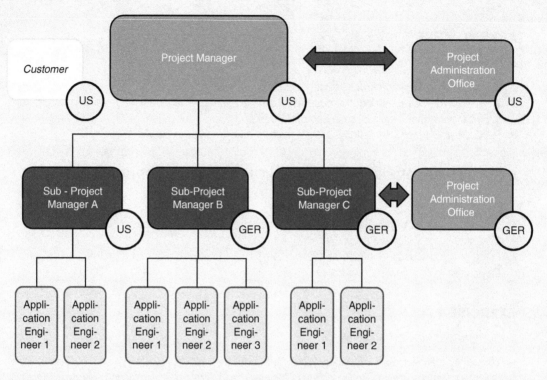

Project organization

solutions. The application engineers also directly communicate with the customer to verify and clarify technical data. The project is supported by a project administration office in the USA, and by a project administration office in Germany respectively. This project organization is illustrated in the figure above.

PROBLEMS IN INTRA-ORGANIZATIONAL CO-OPERATION

One day, the project manager is summoned by the American customer who is becoming increasingly worried by frequently occurring delays and a general lack of attitude to customer service. He feels that he is not being supported well enough and even starts considering other sources of supply if the contractor's attitude and performance do not improve.

Alarmed by that situation, the project manager loses no time in investigating what made his customer unhappy. Especially in difficult markets and times, they definitely could not afford losing such an important client. What a nuisance, he thought, to waste time on issues like that instead of updating the plans, monitoring progress and looking after the customer. As if he did not had enough on his plate with a steep downturn in the world economy. And after all, he wasn't paid to chat with colleagues around the world, but to deliver projects on time, within budget, and meeting customer's expectations. But there again, that was exactly the issue …

THE AMERICAN PROJECT ADMINISTRATION OFFICE

OBSERVATIONS

The project manager first visits the admin office in the USA. He is really surprised to hear from his customer about the lack of support because he has had the impression that his team members in the project admin office are extremely customer and service oriented. Usually, their motto is: 'The customer is always right.' Of course, the office's workforce is very heterogeneous with more than half of the team from outside the USA, mainly from Asia and Latin America. Does the problem stem from diversity? Observing how people work, he feels that deadlines are absolutely adhered to and are regarded as even more important than quality. Employees are pragmatic and take decisions fast. No complicated procedures are slowing down customer support. They do not even bother with lengthy kick-off meetings for new projects. The head of the office seems to be very approachable and easy going – and again swift in taking decisions and action. So he is really puzzled at what may cause the customer's dissatisfaction.

STATEMENTS

When he confronts the head and employees of the US project admin office with the customer's complaints and asks for an explanation, they come up with things like: 'We don't have access to information in Germany which we urgently need to advance local activities for our customer.' They complain about their counterparts in Germany who, instead of co-operating, seem to be competing with them. 'When we have a technical issue here, we need support from our German colleagues. We call them describing the situation. Without hesitating, our German counterpart just answers, "This is technically impossible." He does not even give it another thought or try. We often get e-mails from Germany simply saying, "No, I can't do that", or "It's like that here." Another day, we got a call from Germany blaming us that we had done something the wrong way. We feel that they don't want to support us. They are pretty stubborn and always wave the rules at us. But what can we do if the customer doesn't stick to "their" rules? They give us the impression that we are bothering them. And they are so slow. Sometimes, you only get an answer after one week or even two – what are they doing the whole day? At the end of the day, it is the customer, OUR customer, who pays our salaries. And if we don't find a good solution for the customer, we won't get any more orders. Shouldn't we all know this and act accordingly?'

The project manager is quite irritated and astonished at the frustration level of the American project admin office staff. He also can't believe that his team members in Germany really did what their American colleagues have complained about. Why should they 'sabotage' their own project?

THE GERMAN PROJECT ADMINISTRATION OFFICE

OBSERVATIONS

Hopeful that the whole situation would eventually be clarified, the American project manager travels to the German admin office. At first sight, he is a bit confused because he does not understand a word. Apparently, it is only Germans working in that office, speaking German to each other. Isn't the company language English? They also seem to be quite young and inexperienced. Human Resources tell him that their average tenure is 1–2 years. It is striking that they sit in their office working diligently, mostly in silence. The office walls are full of long process flow charts. A large manual on procedures and guidelines lying in the middle of the landscape office seems to be very popular. Supported by a young employee who translates for him, he overhears people getting upset and telling each other stories about unreasonable customer requests: even after a design freeze one customer came with an urgent change request as if nothing had happened, although the customer knew the processes and had been warned that, after that particular milestone, no further changes were possible. In another conversation, an employee prides himself of having clearly said 'no' to the customer who always comes up with crazy suggestions. How can one secure a top-quality level with last minute changes? When he talks to the local Human Resource representative, he is surprised to hear that the members of the German project admin office – like all other non-managerial employees located at the German sites – are entitled to overtime allowances. On top of that, they have several weeks of paid holidays per year, something he could only dream of.

STATEMENTS

He talks to the staff in Germany by asking the same questions as in the USA. He explains the reason for his visit, summarizes the issues their American counterparts had described to him, and asks the Germans what they think about the situation.

The Germans bring up the following complaints: 'Each day the phone rings and our American colleagues request us to do this or that or something else. We have company standards, but they never use them. They say that the customer wanted something special that we have to deliver. Why do we have corporate standards if our colleagues keep on ignoring them? They create a lot of extra work for us, and they always want it to be done yesterday. Moreover, they are asking for commercial information we are not entitled to disclose without the approval of top management. Why do they have to have it anyway? And what are they doing with this kind of confidential information? Due to different time zones, we always have to stay on late in the office which causes trouble at home. Our spouses don't understand at all why we always have to work late. And on top of that, it is very tiring to understand those strange American accents. Nobody over there even tries to speak a bit of German. They chit-chat right away without thinking twice that we are sitting in Germany and are not Americans.'

This sounds quite different from what he has heard in the USA. He has never looked at things from that perspective. But what should he do with all these negative feelings, frustrations and anger? No wonder that the co-operation deteriorates weekly resulting in more and more delays. Apparently, there is a lack of support and understanding on both sides of the Atlantic.

PROJECT MANAGEMENT TOOLS AND TECHNIQUES

Apart from talking to the people in both project offices, the American project manager has a second look at the project management system and processes. So far, he has not been concerned about them trying to drive down 'bureaucracy', as he sees it, to a minimum. But then again, a common system or approach might be helpful to align his international team: One thing that strikes him is the fact that the component sub-teams have their own little databases to which other sub-teams from other sites have no access. Apparently, the sub-teams think they have to protect their technical knowledge from externals. And some sub-teams regard all other organizational units on different international sites as 'external'. He cannot find any procedure identifying which kind of information was classified as being confidential, nor can he find any rules regarding intra-organizational knowledge sharing among globally working sub-projects of the organization. Browsing through the databases, he finds some of the information really difficult to understand. A lot of incomprehensible acronyms are used, without any context. Sometimes the information is only available in the local language of the respective site. Then he has a look at the organization's intranet for common project procedures. He notices that the US-based teams were using an outdated version – apparently, somebody has updated the methodology, but not notified any-body about it. Last but not least, he discovers that only sub-project managers are entitled to change data in the local project database. The application engineers only have reading rights. When the application engineer dis-cusses a technical issue with the customer resulting in a change, he has to inform the sub-project manager to update the database accordingly, an additional step in the process that is often forgotten. This results in con-flicts between interdependent sub-teams because their own product development is dependent on up-to-date input from other sub-teams. Work that is based on outdated specifications also means a loss of time resulting in further project delays.

CONCLUSION

What should he do now? Apparently, his international team was dysfunctional. Co-operation needed to be improved. If not, the organization could face serious consequences, in the worst case losing a customer. But where should he start? The situation looks quite complex and confusing …

Questions and tasks

1 Where do you see the differences in communication style between the US-Americans and Germans?
2 Create a suitable communication governance system (cf. Figure 9.5) on behalf of the American project manager. You are free to add information not given in the text based on your own assumptions.
3 What reasons for the conflicts between the US and the German project administration offices can you identify?
4 Outline the ground rules for efficient co-operation in the transnational development team that could have avoided the conflicts.

FURTHER READING

Avruch, Kevin (2002) *Culture & Conflict Resolution*. Washington, DC: United States Institute of Peace Press. (This book explores in detail the relation between culture, negotiation, power, and different conflict resolution styles.)

Ting-Toomey, Stella and Oetzel, John G. (2001) *Managing Intercultural Conflict Effectively*. Thousand Oaks, CA: SAGE.

(This book provides the reader with a comprehensive overview of all aspects of intercultural conflicts. It gives hands-on recommendations for effective conflict manage-ment in diverse work groups and for conflicts between managers and employees.)

LEARNING IN AND LEARNING FROM INTERNATIONAL PROJECTS

11

LEARNING OBJECTIVES

After studying this chapter you will be able to:

- assess the importance of organizational learning

- understand knowledge and knowledge management

- know the knowledge creation circle and the knowledge management circle

- explain the interaction between culture and knowledge creation and transfer

- discuss the main impediments to learning in and from international projects

- apply methods to capture knowledge in international projects

- elucidate the main tasks, methods and output of the project completion phase

- deal with measures to enable and foster project learning in an international context

- understand the link between project learning and the learning organization.

INTRODUCTION

11.1 Due to their time limitations, resource constraints, great complexity, diversity, and risk propensity, projects in general and international projects specifically are extremely suitable for learning. In Chapter 2, I introduced programs consisting of several projects contributing to the same purpose, for instance the Framework Programs of the European Union. Obviously, information sharing and experience exchange within such programs are helpful for the realization of synergies, as all projects within the program will pursue the same purpose. Single projects can be accelerated because the wheel does not have to be reinvented. Yet, in many organizations, knowledge and experience gathered in different (international) projects are not systematically integrated into the organizational learning base. Research indicates that organizations have difficulties in tapping this source of innovation and learning. Project documentation is normally limited to standard figures and reports, but also tends to omit the wealth of experience which was collected during the project. The end of the project, therefore, often constitutes the end of the learning.

In a new project, mistakes may be repeated, and some efforts may be redundant. And above all, the organization cannot operate as effectively as it could if it used all the knowledge it possesses. Some authors speak of the phenomenon of 'project amnesia' costing the organization dearly (Schindler and Eppler, 2003). Such an organizational blindness is difficult to understand in light of increasing global and competitive pressure. By systematically documenting its most effective problem-solving mechanisms and the most serious mistakes it made in the course of projects, the organization can reduce project risk, develop project competencies and build up sustainable innovativeness and competitive advantage. Rearchers like Bartlett and Ghoshal (1989) as well as Doz and Prahalad (1991) have already argued two decades ago that a global enhancement of learning levels is the most important competitive source of today's organization.

This chapter first discusses what we understand by organizational learning, knowledge, and knowledge management in the context of projects. Then we will cast light on why organizations are apparently lagging behind when it comes to the efficient use of experience in and from international projects. Various impediments to project learning will be identified, among them national culture and intercultural communication. Based on the elucidation of project learning problems, we will delve into the range of methods that are appropriate in order to learn from international projects. While it is obvious that learning should take place continuously during the course of projects, it typically occurs – if at all – at the end of projects in this phase. Hence, I will explain the main tasks and outputs of this phase, before I will give an outlook on what an organization can and should do in order to create an effective learning environment. As our focus is on international projects, we will pay special attention to the impact of diversity on organizational learning from projects.

ORGANIZATIONAL LEARNING AND KNOWLEDGE MANAGEMENT

WHAT IS LEARNING?

11.2 For the purpose of this book, the definition of learning will be integrative. We will look at learning as an experience of cognitive refinement through the acquisition of knowledge and skills, but also as an exercise of continuous behavioural adjustment (Cyert and March, 1992).

WHAT IS ORGANIZATIONAL LEARNING?

Learning is an activity performed by individual organizational members who facilitate organizational learning. Individual learning is a prerequisite for organizational learning but does not automatically lead to organizational learning. The prerequisite for group and organizational learning is effective communication between the individual learners that is embedded in the organization's culture as well as the organizational structure. I will further comment on these points at the end of this chapter. As learning creates knowledge, I will use learning and knowledge interchangeably.

WHAT IS KNOWLEDGE?

We have to distinguish between data, information, and knowledge. When unstructured, isolated, context-independent data are patterned in a certain way, these are transformed into information. If a certain structure, cognitive behavioural patterns, or heuristics (rules of thumb) are applied to this information, knowledge is created (Chini, 2004). In a project management environment, such rules of thumb can add two times the estimate to the original time estimate to build a diverse project team in contrast to a homogeneous project team (see Chapter 8).

Traditionally, project learning focuses on knowledge that is relatively simple to document, such as figures on costs, estimates on time, or technical test data. Numerical data give important input for learning. However, these do not provide insights regarding cause-and-effect relationships. This is more complex knowledge that often resides in the heads of project managers or project members and thus is rather difficult to document.

In the world of knowledge management, we have two technical expressions for the different knowledge explained above. As Takeuchi and Nonaka (2004: 3) put it:

> Explicit knowledge can be expressed in words, numbers, or sound, and shared in the form of data, scientific formulas, visuals, audiotapes, product specifications, or manuals. Explicit knowledge can be readily transmitted to individuals formally and systematically. Tacit knowledge, on the other hand, is not easily visible and expressible. Tacit knowledge is highly personal and hard

to formalize, making it difficult to communicate or share with others … Tacit knowledge is deeply rooted in an individual's actions and bodily experience, as well as in the ideals, values, or emotions that they embrace.

The authors state that tacit knowledge consists of two parts:

1 A technical dimension encompassing know-how, for instance that of an experienced aerospace engineer.
2 A 'cognitive' dimension consisting of values, beliefs, and emotions. This dimension is subjective and builds a framework for individual perceptions.

In Chapters 3 and 9, we discussed culture and communication, their interrelatedness, and how they impact on the things we perceive. The same is true for tacit knowledge. In other words, we have cultural impact here as well in terms of national, organizational, and above all functional culture. Therefore, Takeuchi's and Nonaka's definition, although disputed (see Glisby and Holden, 2003), is most suitable in the context of this book.

HOW IS KNOWLEDGE CREATED?

According to Takeuchi and Nonaka (2004), tacit and explicit knowledge need to be viewed as interdependent. One creates the other and vice versa. This process is also called the SECI-spiral:

1 Knowledge creation starts with socialization. An individual shares knowledge with another individual and creates tacit knowledge through direct experience. In organizational theory, this is similar to group processes and organizational culture (see Chapter 2).
2 In the externalization phase, the individual articulates tacit knowledge through dialogue and reflection turning it into explicit knowledge of the group. This is a very crucial step. Metaphors and analogies might be helpful tools for replacing the context which otherwise will only reside in the individual.
3 In the combination phase, explicit knowledge is systematized and applied which means that knowledge moves from the group to the whole organization.
4 The last phase, internalization, sees individuals learning and acquiring new tacit knowledge from explicit knowledge provided by the organization. In organizational theory, this phase is discussed in the context of learning organizations.

Figure 11.1 illustrates the process of knowledge creation.

Now we know what knowledge consists of. We are also aware of the fact that knowledge constitutes a crucial strategic organizational asset. For this purpose, it has to be managed.

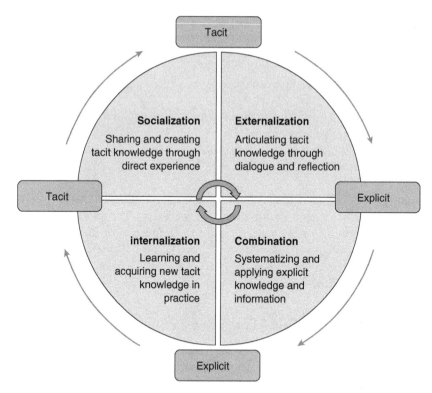

FIGURE 11.1   The SECI process

Source: Takeuchi and Nonaka (2004: 9) *0470820748/Hitotrubashi on Knowledge Management. © 2003 by Hirotaka Takeuchi and Ikujiro Nonaka. Reproduced with the permission of John Wiley & Sons: Asia.*

WHAT IS KNOWLEDGE MANAGEMENT?

According to Liebowitz (2005: 1): 'knowledge management refers to sharing and leveraging knowledge within an organization and outwards toward customers and stakeholders'.

   For our purposes here, knowledge management occurs in and between international projects. It is enabled by the organization's vision and strategy, its culture, its systems and processes, as well as the value set of the individual employees and other characteristics of the diverse workforce as depicted in Figure 11.2. Knowledge management, or in a broader sense 'learning', is not confined to an operational level within each project. It is also leveraged to the strategic level. The result of each (international) project needs to be fed back to the organization's senior management in order for them to review the validity and effectiveness of their chosen strategy. It is one thing to manage projects efficiently, another thing to decide on the right projects or the right portfolio of projects, or in other words to implement a strategy that ensures the organization's competitive edge (see Chapter 2).

   Explicit knowledge can be well managed with structural and systemic approaches, supported by computer-aided solutions. This type of knowledge management is based on a cognitive model. Following the vein of the increasing availability of information technology based tools, most knowledge management research focuses on cognitive models.

Tacit knowledge is better managed with human-centred approaches such as socialization, self-organizing teams, extended social interactions, personnel rotation, etc. (Davis et al., 2005). This type of knowledge management is based on a community model. In light of the characteristics of international projects, a community model seems to be more suitable to frame and shape learning in and from international projects. The main reason behind this argument is the importance of context.

Let us now look at learning and knowledge management in a project set-up.

HOW CAN PROJECTS CONTRIBUTE TO ORGANIZATIONAL LEARNING?

We learned in Chapter 1 that a project aims at producing a product or service. In the course of achieving this target, the following categories of knowledge are intentionally or unintentionally created (based on Kasvi et al., 2003):

1 Technical knowledge regarding the product together with its components or service, including its underlying technologies.
2 Procedural knowledge regarding manufacturing a product or delivering a service, including the application of a certain project management methodology.
3 Organizational knowledge regarding communication, leadership, and co-operation, in the case of an international project across organizational, cultural, temporal, and geographical boundaries.

From an epistemological standpoint, the first two categories can be subsumed as 'strong knowledge' which includes true beliefs backed up by a valid justification or warrant for that belief, and the systematic exclusion of alternative possibilities. The third category belongs to 'weak knowledge' which prefers consensus over strong verifiability (Davis et al., 2005). Weak knowledge tends to be 'sticky' or tacit and local in projects, whereas strong knowledge is easier to globalize and transfer across projects.

WHAT IS KNOWLEDGE MANAGEMENT IN PROJECTS?

The literature describes the knowledge management value chain as follows: (1) creation; (2) storage; (3) distribution; (4) application (Chini, 2004). Kasvi et al. (2003) break this knowledge management value chain down to the context of projects with the following activities:

1 **Knowledge creation**: gathering data, turning these into information and compiling them to knowledge as shown in the phases one to three in Figure 11.2.
2 **Knowledge administration**: storage, structuring and retrieval. These activities constitute the preparation for knowledge application, phase four in Figure 11.2.

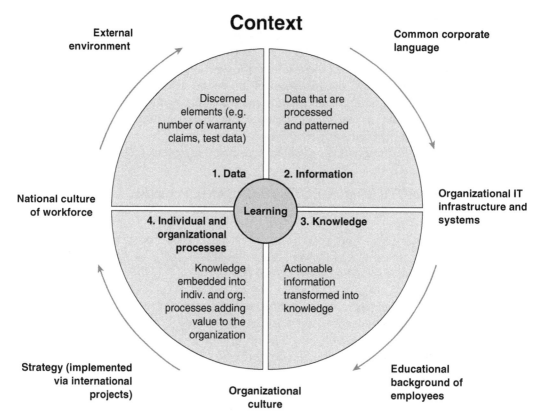

FIGURE 11.2 Knowledge management cycle in international projects
Source: Adapted from Liebowitz (2005)

3 **Knowledge dissemination**: within the project and between projects, internally and externally. This step occurs between phases three and four as depicted in Figure 11.2.

4 **Knowledge embodiment**: application of knowledge to improve technical, procedural and organizational competences of the whole organization. This step coincides with phase four of Figure 11.2.

Figure 11.2 provides you with an overview of the main phases of knowledge management in and between international projects. It also refers to the context that knowledge management is embedded in.

CULTURAL EMBEDDEDNESS OF LEARNING

11.3 Figure 11.2 illustrates how important context is for organizational learning. In this section, I will explain further one aspect of this context that is often neglected, namely the national or regional cultures

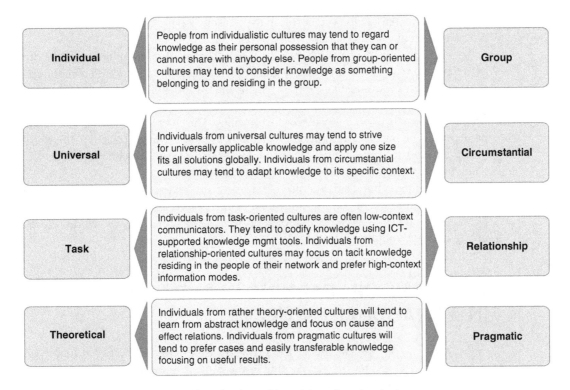

FIGURE 11.3 Cultural impact on learning in and from international projects

of the individuals participating in the learning process. As the famous anthropologist Geertz (2000) said, most local knowledge is constituted as complex and coherent wholes in the form of intricate webs of meaning. Put differently, tacit knowledge reflects culture and needs to be interpreted through a cultural lens. An international project manager, for instance, has to know that individuals in the Arab and Chinese world are socialized in networks, called *wasta* in the Arab world and *guanxi* in the Chinese world. These networks mainly span close family and kinship (Weir and Hutchings, 2005). They have their own rules that also apply regarding knowledge creation and sharing. Due to seniority, for instance, the experience of the elder is highly valued, and they are supposed to share their knowledge, while younger members of the networks will be more constrained in identifying the mistakes of seniors, for instance, or promulgating the knowledge they have acquired at school. This is especially true if it is contradictory to the prevailing wisdom.

It takes cross-cultural knowledge to understand these particularities, and cultural intelligence to use them in order to engender a suitable environment for creating and sharing knowledge in an organization.

Moreover, intercultural communication is needed to transfer tacit knowledge eventually into explicit knowledge: as depicted in the SECI-process, the individual communicates with the organization and vice versa. Be it tacit or explicit knowledge, whether it is transmitted between groups or individuals, or between the individual and the group, communication plays an important role in the transmission process. And communication is impacted on by national culture.

Communication is the basis for learning. The exchange of information or knowledge between culturally diverse individuals, therefore, is related to intercultural communication that we have discussed in Chapter 9 (Taylor and Osland, 2003). Figure 11.3 provides you with an overview of the main national cultural dimensions influencing the individual's attitude and behaviour towards project learning. The chart does not claim to be comprehensive. The purpose, as in previous chapters, is to sensitize you as an international project member towards cultural diversity in order to anticipate potential problems and contribute to a better understanding of diverse stakeholders.

Not only multiculturalism, but also other aspects of diversity such as differences in language, organizational culture, functional culture, or educational background complicate learning in and from international projects. In section 11.4, we will discuss the nature of these complications.

PROBLEMS OF LEARNING IN AND FROM INTERNATIONAL PROJECTS

11.4

We can cluster the problems that occur in intra- but mainly in inter-project learning in the context of international projects into four groups:

1 Problems related to the cultural diversity of stakeholders.
2 Problems related to the inherent characteristics of a project.
3 Communication problems impeding knowledge transfer.
4 Problems concerning the organization as a whole.

Let me comment on those problems in more detail.

1 ISSUES RELATED TO CULTURAL DIVERSITY

Diversity in terms of language, cultural and ethnic background, gender and professional affiliation can have a strong impact on knowledge management (Holden, 2002). As we have discussed diversity and its challenges in the management of international projects in previous chapters, I would like to focus on three main aspects that especially affect learning.

Avoidance of loss of face

Learning from projects also means learning from failures. Admitting mistakes is not easy for anybody. However, this poses a serious threat of loss of face to many high-context people. It is also a taboo in many Asian cultures. Latin Americans and people from the

Arab region, African countries and Southern and Eastern European countries are also receptive to the concept of face and hence reluctant to admit failure openly. The problem is that experience resides in people, and mistakes have been made by people. Hence, any discussion of mistakes is always implicitly linked to a discussion of some individuals' failures, a fact that is especially unacceptable if that discussion takes place in public such as a project workshop with customers as witnesses.

Impact of collectivism

Collectivist cultures, but also certain organizational cultures, tend to nurture a certain degree of competition between teams (in the literature often called co-option), in our case project teams. Therefore, the willingness of one team to pass on their experience to another team would be rather low.

Impact of multi-disciplinarity

Each discipline has its own way of thinking along with specific methodologies and their technical terminology. These may constitute a barrier for understanding the ideas or knowledge created by another discipline.

2 ISSUES RELATED TO THE NATURE OF A PROJECT

Discontinuities

Projects are self-contained, idiosyncratic and finite in nature. Hence, discontinuities occur within the flow of resources, especially people and information, across time and space.

Fragmentation

Bigger projects tend not only to be geographically dispersed, but also multi-disciplinary. Different functions, or within the same function different disciplines, will have different ways of codifying their knowledge. Often databases will not span functional boundaries or geographical boundaries either (see Chapter End Case 10).

Lack of time

Typically, project staff operate under huge time pressures. Under time constraints, learning is often low priority, especially with new assignments already waiting for the project team and manager due to notorious resource constraints.

Lack of transparency

In geographically dispersed project teams it is difficult to know who has done exactly what, if this is not reported to the project manager. Hence, negative or positive lessons learned are more difficult to compile in detail.

Focus on evaluation at the end

International projects are complex and often tend to have a long duration. You can easily imagine that over several years people will join and leave the project, and after it is finished, nobody will really remember all the details and incidents that happened in the meantime. Therefore, a recommendation would be not to wait until the end of the project to evaluate it.

3 ISSUES RELATED TO COMMUNICATION

As we have already discussed communication and intercultural communication in Chapter 9, I will pinpoint a few issues with special relevant to the learning process (Taylor and Osland, 2003).

Marginality of the sender

If the person contributing the experience of knowledge is seen as marginal to the organization, chances are high that his or her contribution will not be valued. Marginal people can be those who do not belong to the dominant coalition and decision-makers, for example, people with a non-headquarters background. These can also be individuals from smaller subsidiaries of the organization and this is also applicable for functions. People from IT, for instance, might be ignored as the 'tech guys'.

Stereotypes of and against the sender

The sender may belong to a nationality that decision-makers have stereotypes against and thus will dismiss the received information or knowledge. A Syrian project manager may not even listen to an optimization idea of his Israeli project member because of the political problems these two countries have. Again, stereotyping also applies to a cross-functional set-up.

Linguistic ability of the sender and receiver

Especially with complicated ideas or suggestions, it is important to be able to express oneself in sufficient detail. Otherwise, the knowledge will not be understood.

4 ISSUES RELATED TO THE OVERALL ORGANIZATION

Lack of support by the organizational culture

The organization as such, and not only a single sender and receiver, needs to endorse and foster values like open-mindedness and innovativeness in order to push for the continuous creation of new knowledge. It also needs to overcome the ethnocentric stage by moving towards ethno-relative attitudes such as acceptance, adaptation, and finally towards integration (Bennet and Bennett, 2004), as outlined at the end of Chapter 10 (see 10.6).

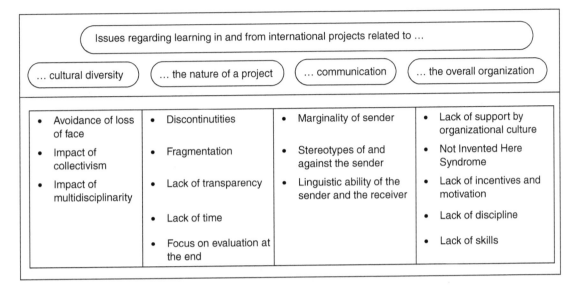

FIGURE 11.4 Impediments to learning in and from international projects

Not Invented Here Syndrome

Even if the project experience is captured and adequately accessible, we can observe reluctance on the part of other project managers or teams to tap this knowledge pool due to the fact that this is not their own experience. They will doubt the transferability of the knowledge and experience to their special circumstances: after all, their project really is unique – and as we have learnt in Chapter 1, projects are indeed unique, although there is plenty of room for knowledge transfer.

Lack of incentives and motivation

Even if any lessons learned are compiled, they will not necessarily be used in the organization. Therefore, their compilation might be considered a waste of time. If no special monetary incentives are granted to 'give away experience' to the organization, individuals or groups may decide to keep it for themselves to further capitalize on it to the detriment of the organization. This could only be counteracted by a positive organizational culture.

Lack of discipline

The existing processes requesting a final report on project experience are not enforced.

Lack of skills

Methods on how to learn and capture experience are not known.

The following case on the transfer of a production system from Japan to Taiwan illustrates some of the problems mentioned above on project learning in an international context.

Mini Case 11.1: Transferring valve production from Japan to Taiwan

With revenues of more than 18 billion US-dollars and a total workforce of 118,000 people in 2007, the US-based multinational Tyco International is a highly diversified company with a product range covering electronic security and alarm monitoring to fire-fighting equipment and flow control solutions.

After the flow control division had bought new companies in Japan in 2000 and in Taiwan in 2001, it aimed at transferring production knowledge from its new Japanese facilities to the newly acquired production sites in Taiwan in order to save money. The Japanese entity was known for its high-quality ball valves, whereas the Taiwanese unit showed its strength in the mass production of low cost valves. The project was initiated and planned by US-American staff in the regional headquarters in Singapore. The Asian regional HQ was responsible for the formulation and communication of project goals, for allocating responsibilities, and for allocating and assessing available resources within the overall framework of the Tyco Flow Control Project Management guidelines.

The task was to transfer the complete design and manufacturing knowledge from the Japanese to the Taiwanese factory.

Phase 1: The codified knowledge, namely relevant engineering documentation, was sent from Japan to Taiwan to be redrawn in the local system and where necessary to be translated from Japanese into Mandarin. Afterwards, the documents were sent back to Japan for verification. This process was supported by face-to-face meetings between the Japanese and Taiwanese engineers who, with the help of interpreters, discussed the background to the drawings to learn more about the documents. Although the language barrier between Japanese and Mandarin slowed down communication, both sides discovered that reverting back to drawings and their common functional language of 'engineering' would help them overcome the language barrier and exchange information without interpreters. Still, regional HQ requested all documents be translated into English due to company policies.

Phase 2: The suppliers of the Taiwanese manufacturers needed to be developed because the sourcing of major components would have to be done locally. Japanese engineers were assigned to visit Taiwanese suppliers and stay in Taiwan for a week or more. During that time, a lot of socializing activities in the evenings occurred between the Japanese and the Taiwanese who got to know each other better. Gradually, the Japanese came to understand why the Taiwanese put more stress on low production cost, and vice versa the Taiwanese understood the quest for quality of the Japanese. Upon their return to Japan, the Japanese engineers started to experiment with some of the newly learned Taiwanese methods in their production site. While they were happy to get something in return for their knowledge on high quality production, they felt that the Taiwanese had held back knowledge from and about their local suppliers. The

Japanese became worried about a lack of data flow from the Taiwanese suppliers. The Taiwanese site started to complain to regional headquarters that they felt increasingly bullied by the Japanese who requested all kinds of quality related documentation from their suppliers. As the Taiwanese had a long working relationship with their suppliers, they considered the documents requested from Japan as a sign of mistrust.

Phase 3: This concerned the assembly of the valves, pressure-testing, packing and shipping. Each assembly step had to be taught by Japanese workers who were dispatched to the Taiwanese factory to train their new colleagues. With more than 20 years of experience on average, the Japanese workers were highly qualified in their trades, but not able to speak any foreign languages. They instructed their Taiwanese counterparts with the help of interpreters and simply by demonstrating each step physically so it could be copied by the Taiwanese. Photos and checklists helped with the knowledge transfer.

Source: Kohlbacher and Kraehe (2007); Tyco International (2008a); Tyco International (2008b)

Questions

1 What kinds of problems impeding knowledge transfer in international projects can you identify?
2 How was knowledge created and transferred? (Base your answer on the SECI cycle.)

Now we know why it is so difficult to learn in and from international projects. Yet, for successfully managing an international project and international projects, project learning is a sine qua non if the organization wants to ensure its competitiveness. In section 11.5, we will learn about the tools and techniques that are suitable for capturing project experience.

METHODS OF PROJECT LEARNING

11.5 Basically, all approaches aiming at capturing knowledge and experience derived from international projects need to fulfil two requirements:

1 They must be able to link the knowledge with the context in which it was created in order to enable the organization to fully grasp and apply that new knowledge. The tools need to give insights into the reasons why certain knowledge emerged. Without this cause–effect relation, knowledge cannot be transferred across projects.
2 They must span geographical and organizational boundaries. This means that all approaches need to be supported by adequate information and communication technology in order to make the knowledge accessible across the organization and beyond the organization for other project stakeholders.

Under these premises, what methods are suitable in order to learn best from international projects?

HUMAN-CENTRED METHODS

There is consensus in the literature that tacit knowledge highly contributes to innovation. As this resides in the knower and the context where it is created, it is suitable to link those individuals together in order to achieve a cross-fertilization.

Knowledge networks

So-called knowledge networks are an important knowledge management tool. The literature distinguishes between formal or intentional knowledge networks, and informal or emergent knowledge networks that already exist in an organization. Knowledge networks can be self-managed or managed by the organization. They can primarily benefit the individual or the organization. In our context, we focus on the organizational benefit. Their main purpose is improved organizational efficiency, increased innovation, and as a side effect employee satisfaction. It is critical that knowledge networks do not get too big because strong personal ties tend to get weakened, a free-rider effect kicks in, and the development of a common language becomes more difficult (Büchel and Raub, 2002; Schönström, 2005).

A so-called community of practice is a special form of knowledge network. It targets sharing knowledge among experts or certain social groups, such as deep water drilling engineers or consultants specialized in strategic marketing. As tacit knowledge is shared, people in these groups or communities need to speak this same language and share the same vision and values in order to interpret this tacit knowledge adequately.

A way of sharing experience and knowledge between international projects could be to establish a community of practice made up of international project managers. The project management office or project support office introduced in Chapter 2 could assume the role of a knowledge activist driving the community of practice through its various steps of emergence, which are (Büchel and Raub, 2002):

1 Focusing on the knowledge network: at this stage it is important that the network activities are closely aligned with corporate strategy as reflected in (international) projects.
2 Creating its context: in the second phase, the same mechanisms apply as for efficient co-operation in international projects: ground rules need to be established based on mutual trust.
3 Routinizing network activities: in the third step, network roles are defined and processes fostered, for example, with websites and libraries.
4 Leveraging network results back to the overall organization: in this last step, the network needs to demonstrate that it can contribute to measurable improvements in the organization.

While the PMO should have sufficient resources for the third phase, it needs strong top management support with the first and second phases.

The potential issue with a community of practice consisting of international project managers is heterogeneity. Managers of international projects can have a technical or commercial background, and they can come from all over the world, namely from different organizational units and/or different countries, etc. Where is the common aspect that can provide the frame they need in order to share their knowledge among them?

The answer lies in the corporate strategy and organizational culture. The organization has to be actively promulgating its vision and mission, along with a set of core values that all employees can identify with. This constitutes a common platform for the participants in the knowledge network.

Snapshot 11.1 gives an example of one company that has established a community of practice for international project managers.

SNAPSHOT 11.1

Community of practice of international project managers

A global corporation, with roughly 1,200 international product development projects in the definition or implementation phase at any point in time, decided on building communities of practice to benefit from globally created knowledge. The target group were project managers who had participated in a company internal training program focusing on the development of emotional and cultural intelligence. Usually, these project managers would have a technical background. A common educational background and additional training would constitute a common base for understanding.

Knowledge management specialists established a computer-based system for sharing knowledge via shared drives, chatrooms etc. The bigger challenge, however, was to attract the target group. It took the specialists more than six months to feed the system with the information the group was looking for. When this threshold was overcome, the community of practice developed into a vivid network with 160 project managers exchanging tips and experience on international project management. Once a year, many of them will meet face-to-face to enhance their relationships.

Establishment of new roles dedicated to knowledge management

This is another human-centred method. A multinational organization in project driven industries such as construction or software may want to establish new roles to ensure the dissemination of knowledge across geographical borders. Such an initiative is easier if the new network of new roles stays within the boundaries of a given profession like application engineers or quantifiers, because shared meaning is given by the common function. In Mini Case 11.2 you can analyse the effectiveness of such an approach.

Mini Case 11.2: Knowledge management in an international construction company

A UK-based internationally operating construction company with an annual turnover of about 370 million GBP has three divisions (building work, civil engineering work, marine/water) and operates in four geographic regions. In the mid-90s the top management started a change project to improve the knowledge management of the company due to the insight that many severe problems within the organization stemmed from bad engineering. This initiative drew on the establishment of a new role, the so-called Regional Engineering Managers (REM). After several years, there were ten REMs in the company, two in each region and two in group companies. The REM had three main functions:

1 To contribute towards putting together tenders.
2 To value engineer tenders and ongoing projects.
3 To support the training and development of site engineers.

The REMs were expected to be the major conduit between the sites and the regions on one hand, and between the regions on the other hand. The new role was designed to enable learning between single sites and between projects in different regions.

The REMs created a network among themselves. If one came across a good idea, he would put it on a report sheet and distribute this to his colleagues, the other REMs, via email. Interestingly, they hardly used the internal register of expertise that the enterprise possessed, but instead relied heavily on their own personal networks within and outside of the organization. All REMs met every three months at 'engineering forums' to discuss a wide range of issues and to extend and reinforce personal contacts and networks. They also organized biannual conferences for site engineers who would meet to discuss project successes and failures, new jobs, current issues and so forth.

REMs were not very much involved in formal project progress meetings, but in value engineering workshops, pre-and post-contract meetings, and to some extent in project review meetings.

The REMs had no line authority over engineers. Hence, they had to rely on their persuasive skills and build up good relations with the site engineers in order to gain access to their knowledge, and to convince the engineers to apply the new knowledge the REMs had promulgated. Given the diverse cultures and personalities on the various sites, the REMs had to be more than experienced engineers.

Source: Bresnen et al. (2003)

Question

What are the key success factors of this knowledge management tool in order for it to work well?

Mentor relationships

Another method of disseminating mainly tacit knowledge is the so-called mentor or shadowing system. Typically, the mentor is an experienced employee, for instance a seasoned project manager with international experience. To grow future international project managers, an individual with high potential but a lack of experience could be allocated to the project manager for the course of a project, or at least for a stage of the project. It would be the task of the junior person to observe what the mentor is doing and to learn from him or her. The prerequisite here is a trusting relationship between both and the willingness of the mentor to share his or her experiences under a time pressure.

However, it is not only human-centred approaches that are suitable for knowledge creation and dissemination in an international project. Cognitive models that focus more on explicit knowledge can also play a role. The literature differentiates between process-based methods and content-based methods. The first family of methods puts an emphasis on the sequence of data collection, whereas the second family focuses on what content should be retrieved, and where it should be stored.

PROCESS-BASED METHODS

Project audit

Such an audit is performed at the end of the project by dedicated auditors. Typically the project manager is audited along with all the documentation available for the project. The main purpose is to analyse the reasons for deviations between estimates and actual results and to ensure compliance with organizational standards. Issue logs, introduced in Chapter 7, can be very useful at project audits as each problem encountered over the time-span of a project can be described and analysed there. This also contains any solutions. In order to be used for project learning, project audit reports need to be circulated or fed into the relevant databases. The issue log is a rich source for project learning. According to Lientz and Rea (2003), a typical issue log for an international project enlists 200 to 300 different issues that should be indexed in a database to make the information easier to re-use for other international projects. Snapshot 11.2 provides one example of the implementation of project audits.

SNAPSHOT 11.2

Project audits and databases

Sharing procedural knowledge between projects

The multinational corporation depicted in this snapshot has a central 'Academy for Project Management'. One of the tasks of the academy is to develop project management methodology and ensure its application throughout the company. In a cycle of two to three years, each company-internal certified project manager will be audited. He or she needs to explain the reasons for deviations from standard processes and policies in case of their occurrence. If the deviations prove to be an increase in efficiency, the project management methodology will be modified accordingly and disseminated to the whole organization during the following improvement and audit cycle.

(Cont'd)

Sharing technical knowledge between projects

The civil engineering division of this multinational has so-called reference architecture or models for constructing plants and equipment. All approvals are made for those reference models. The sales representatives will try to offer the reference plants mainly because no additional approvals and engineering need to be made. There is a company-wide accessible database with these reference plants in order to disseminate knowledge.

Structured project walkthrough

This technique was developed back in the 1960s by IBM. Its purpose is to encourage learning by giving the people who are being evaluated control over the process. An emphasis is laid on an environment of trust. The rules are (Frame, 2002):

1 The group being evaluated chooses its judge and jury. The aim here is to avoid political distortions and to create trust. In some organizations, the choice is limited to a list of candidates approved by a central project management authority.

2 The group under evaluation determines the rules of the evaluation process such as evaluation criteria and the agenda of the evaluation sessions. To avoid bias some organizations will limit the freedom here by using a framework of evaluation guidelines that the group has to operate within.

3 The group under evaluation conducts the evaluation meetings. There can be one or more of those meetings that constitute the actual walkthrough. Experience shows that some people will be missing the skills to run such meetings. In an international project environment, intercultural communication issues need to be considered. No upper level managers should participate in the evaluation meetings in order not to let the hierarchy interfere with the open feedback process. This rule supports the openness of people from high power distance cultures.

4 A thorough documentation of the evaluation process is necessary including action items with deadlines and responsible individuals in order to turn the lessons learnt during the structured walkthrough into organizational knowledge.

CONTENT-BASED APPROACHES

As explained above, these approaches provide a structure for the content of the learning that comes from projects. Let us have a look at two relevant formats.

Micro article

Willke (1998) proposes securing project experience by writing short articles of a maximum of one page on the main lessons learnt in an informal, journalistic way. In intercultural management, a similar learning tool is used in the form of so-called critical incidents. Both have in common that they provide the context which is essential for the learning experience. This is a light-weight approach providing authentic yet entertaining insights into what went wrong or well in a certain project. A micro article should contain a high degree of visualization and use various media, for instance video clips. It is important to disseminate micro articles via the intranet or other organizational databases. The richness on one hand and simplicity on the other hand make it a very suitable approach for learning in and from international projects.

Learning history

Another approach which is suitable in the context of international projects is the so-called Learning History Approach developed by a team at MIT. This strives to embed project experience in a context which is often lost when tacit knowledge is turned into explicit knowledge. The documents comprise between 20 and 100 pages and narrate the story of a project chronologically. To be as authentic as possible, they refer to many direct quotations from project members who will remain anonymous. These histories are structured in the following way: each page is divided into two columns, with the right-hand column containing the interview transcripts of project members, and the left-hand column comments by the 'historians' regarding project details or non-verbal cues provided by the interview partners. Additional boxes between the interviews will provide background information on the project at hand. The learning histories are validated with the project members before being shared with the organization in the form of workshops or group discussions revolving around the documented case (Schindler and Eppler, 2003).

Table 11.1 provides you with an overview of all human-centred, process-oriented, and content-oriented knowledge management tools as discussed above. It indicates the strengths and weaknesses of the various instruments that can be used to learn in and from projects.

Let me finish this section with two recommendations regarding learning in and from international projects.

1 Due to the great scope of international projects and their relatively long duration it makes sense to carry out periodic reviews to capture project experience and to learn directly from this as part of regular milestone reviews. Thus, the lessons learnt can already be used for ongoing projects, providing the stakeholders with a further incentive to learn and share their experiences.

2 Due to the diversity of international project management teams and stakeholders, it makes sense to have specially trained facilitators or 'debriefers' from outside the project team to accompany the learning

TABLE 11.1 Overview of appropriate knowledge management methods to learn in and from international projects

Name of Method	Description	Main Advantages	Main Disadvantages
Knowledge networks/community of practice (IPMs)	Individuals with the role of international project managers exchange experience via email or intranet and meet to maintain their networks personally at regular intervals	Tracit knowledge can be shared in face-to-face meetings but also easily via phone, email or intranet crossing organizational, cultural, and geographic boundaries	PMs of international projects may be too heterogeneous to create a common reference frame
New roles dedicated to knowledge management	New roles such as regional engineering managers who collect learning from projects and other relevant knowledge and disseminate this in their networks around the globe	External and internal knowledge is collected and disseminated; due to personal networks, tacit knowledge can be shared across organzational, cultural and geographic boundaries	Effectiveness of the new roles is dependent on the qualifications (including cultural intelligence) of individuals assigned to the new roles. Difficult to span functional boundaries
Mentor relationships	Experienced international project manager is shadowed by project manager to-be	Good tool to share tracit knowledge, also across organizational, cultural, and geographic boundaries	Time consuming, and effectiveness depends on the performance of the mentor and the relationship between the two
Project Audit	Project-external auditors sit down with the PM to check project documentation for compliance and deviations from the plan. Most adequate for learning if based on the issue log	Neutral view on evaluation; adequate for fostering project management methodology across organizational, cultural and geographic boundaries	Tends to focus on compliance issues at the expense of organizational learning

TABLE 11.1

Name of Method	Description	Main Advantages	Main Disadvantages
Structured Project Walkthrough	Method focusing on project team, face-to-face. Project team controls the evaluation process determining its own evaluators and rules	Atmosphere of trust leads to honest reflection; crosses organizational, cultural and geographic boundaries; effectiveness of sharing tacit knowledge depends on documentation of walkthrough process	Lack of intercultural skills may interfere with process; cost intensive to gather international project team together at one site
Micro Article	Short articles of a maximum of one page comprising key experiences or lessons learnt from a project: highly visualized, written in an entertaining way, and disseminated digitally	Sharing of tacit knowledge possible due to inclusion of context. Can be disseminated also as video clips, cartoons or other visualized forms travelling far across organizational, cultural and geographic boundaries	Takes time and resources to create articles. Strict anonymity required in case of negative lessons learnt due to potential loss of face for certain cultures
Learning History	Document of 20–100 pages narrating the history of the project chronologically quoting directly project participants anonymously. Distributed as hard copies at a special workshop	Through the direct input of the project participants these are very authentic and through the comments of editors very context rich. Good to turn tacit knowledge into explicit knowledge. If workshops are carried out in different locations, suitable for the whole organization	Takes a lot of time and resources. Only meaningful for strategic and big projects

process. This could be facilitators or mediators introduced in a different context in Chapters 8 and 10. Their task would include the preparation of interim or final review workshops, to carry out the workshops and to help disseminate the lessons learnt.

THE PHASE OF PROJECT COMPLETION

11.6

The process-oriented project learning methods especially are closely linked to the last phase in a project, the completion or termination phase which we discuss in this section. We have learned at the beginning of this chapter that evaluation based project learning is one of the main tasks of this phase.

Another important task is to hand over the product or service to the customer and make sure that they are satisfied. In this context, all necessary documents should be finalized, such as the signature on a project acceptance form by the customer. The planning of follow-up activities such as services to customer, warranty, etc. also belongs with this task.

Figure 11.5 gives you an overview of the main inputs and outputs of the completion phase.

As our focus rests on learning at the project completion, we will explore further the content of the project evaluation. The project manager or project auditor typically evaluates actual results versus plans and assumptions, focusing on:

- the project schedule (on time or delayed?)
- the accuracy of the resource estimates
- the impact of resource availability or shortages on the project.

This comparison is relatively easily done because of the availability of the data. It gets more difficult with the performance evaluation of so-called 'soft' areas such as:

- quality of communication
- quality of co-operation within the team and between the team and other stakeholders
- quality of project leadership
- timeliness and accuracy of feedback provided to the team by the project manager and sponsor
- resolution of conflicts.

Evaluations of the soft performance factors are facilitated by adequate quantification in the execution and monitoring phase as described in Chapter 7. In project reality, however, this area is often neglected. Especially in international projects, it is crucial to include hard and soft factors in the evaluation results which should aim at:

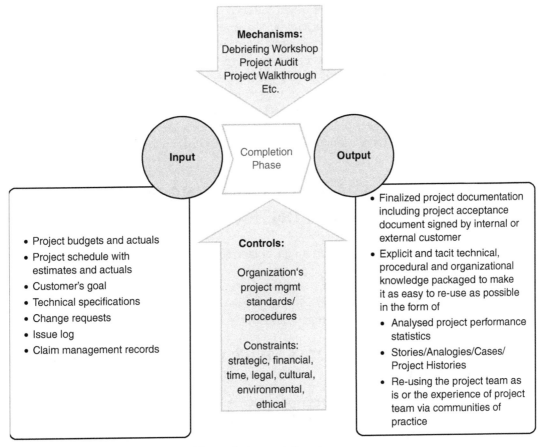

FIGURE 11.5 Inputs and outputs of the project completion phase

- securing and analysing experiences regarding technical, procedural, and organizational issues
- increasing organizational efficiency by making these experiences re-usable for following projects, for example, putting reference designs into a corporate database, or feeding the corporate database with project calculations and estimations
- continuing to use interpersonal experience, for example, to work with the team which was built on successfully, or at least to maintain relations in the form of communities of practice of other networks
- fostering smooth customer relations and securing follow-up projects with this same customer.

Although an evaluation of the project performance is of paramount importance for the future development of the organization, many organizations seem to have difficulty in professionally closing a project. This is certainly linked to the problems underlying evaluation as such. It carries always a subjective element, even if the evaluation criteria are made explicit at the beginning of the project. All criteria contain elements of interpretation done by the evaluator, for instance an auditor. Moreover, project members will tend to feel threatened by any form of evaluation, as it smacks of criticism. This is especially true for individuals from cultures where a loss of face is severe. Last but not least, an evaluation can be misused for political purposes causing destructive distortion. This can often be observed in bigger organizations in the case of international projects where political purposes and hidden agendas do play a major role, as I have pointed out in the first chapter of this book.

What can be done in order to improve the efficiency and effectiveness of the completion phase, and to enhance learning in and from international projects in general?

FOSTERING PROJECT LEARNING IN AN INTERNATIONAL CONTEXT

11.7 Learning on an organizational level is extremely important for successful project management and sustainable project success. In light of the problems linked to evaluation and issues linked to learning discussed in section 11.4, an organization will have to adopt the following measures in order to foster organizational learning.

INTEGRATING PROJECT LEARNING INTO PROJECT MANAGEMENT METHODOLOGY

Schindler and Eppler (2003) propose integrating the compilation of knowledge and transfer of knowledge into the life cycle management of the project. At each gate or milestone, time, cost, and output targets are checked. In addition, learning or knowledge targets should be included, such as:

- Are there checklists, or stories, helping to turn tacit knowledge into explicit knowledge?
- Have relevant insights been secured and documented?
- Have the reasons for failure been documented?

A concrete example could be a team glossary as proof of a common language that can be passed on to other project teams. Another example could be a report stating how certain know-how was transferred from headquarters to a foreign subsidiary.

Although it is important to include knowledge creation and management in the targets of all milestones, the most important phase regarding learning is still classically the project termination phase.

ESTABLISHING KNOWLEDGE ENABLERS

This is a whole set of activities that are directly related to the core values and systems of the organization. Consequently, a huge change initiative is necessary to develop the required enablers in the organization. It is outside the scope of this book to go into the details of such a campaign. Instead let me just mention the bare bones of what needs to be tackled.

Trust

In Chapter 10, you will have learned that trust is the basis for effective co-operation. For DeLong and Fahey (2000: 119) trust plays another key role: 'The level of trust that exists between the organization, its subunits, and its employees greatly influences the amount of knowledge that flows both between individuals and from individuals into the firm's databases, best practices archives, and other records'. In other words, trust among the members of the organization is an enabler for knowledge creation.

Motivation

Apart from trust, the motivation to create and share knowledge is another prerequisite for knowledge creation. This does refer to monetary incentives like a premium for a new entry into a database or the well-known prizes an employee can win for a good idea he or she has put into a suggestion box.

Motivation is also enhanced by linking the performance appraisal system with knowledge creation and sharing. Project managers, for instance, could have a learning related component in their personal annual performance targets and could do the same with their core team members.

Motivation also resides in the people seeking knowledge. A prerequisite of the willingness to learn is critical self-reflection and the perception of deficiencies. In the context of international projects, the project manager has to recognize that he or she can only gain by tapping the experience of other project managers or using project management databases. The motivation to use existing knowledge is also enhanced by the ability to quickly assess the credibility of knowledge, the ability to quickly assess the degree of fit of reusable knowledge to the problem at hand, and the ability to quickly assess the practicability of the knowledge. This leads us back to the project learning methods discussed in section 11.5.

Finally, the motivation to create and share knowledge is influenced by power and power sharing. People in an organization who are afraid of losing power when they share or transfer their knowledge will certainly be less inclined to do so. In international organizations, a typical dilemma is the transfer of manufacturing or research and development activities from high cost to low cost countries. If the project team members charged with transferring knowledge away from their sites are afraid of losing their jobs after they will have completed the project, they will be reluctant to finish the project successfully. The only way to reduce this barrier to knowledge transfer is to build up trust between all the parties involved as described in Mini Case 11.1.

Absorption capacity

Another enabler for knowledge creation lies in the continuous improvement of the qualifications of the workforce. This applies to technical knowledge, but in an international context also to interpersonal and intercultural skills. Concretely, the organization needs to sensitize its employees, especially its international project managers, towards cultural differences and how these show up in project management. In general, the organization needs to invest heavily in all its employees to reduce the language barrier.

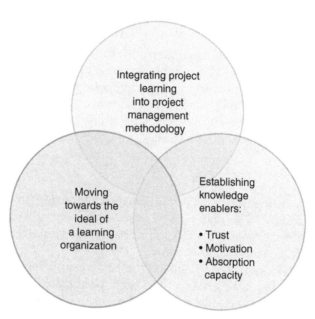

FIGURE 11.6   Areas to improve learning in and from international projects

MOVING TOWARDS THE IDEAL OF A LEARNING ORGANIZATION

It is certainly a very cumbersome and long path towards becoming a learning organization. Nevertheless, the requirements of today's world economy do mandate such a move. Hansen and Nohria (2004) have quite rightly stated that the new economies within scope within today's globally operating organizations are based on their internationally dispersed sub-units' ability to collaborate successfully by sharing knowledge and jointly developing new products and services.

What is the target? According to Senge (1990), a learning organization is an organization that learns not only in an adaptive way, but also in a way that enhances the organization's capacity to create something new. A learning organization will have embedded continuous learning on an individual, group, and organizational level in its culture. It builds an environment where synergies are created based on a shared understanding. For more details refer to the companion website.

Figure 11.6 summarizes the range of activities that contribute to the improvement of learning in and from international projects.

THE LEARNING ORGANIZATION AND INTERNATIONAL PROJECT MANAGEMENT

11.8

A learning organization provides all the prerequisites to effectively manage international projects. There is a lot of accordance between measures to deal with diversity, dynamics, risk, and complexity as explained in previous chapters and the ideal of a learning organization. Based on the ideal state envisaged by Senge (1990), a 'projectized' organization as introduced in Chapter 6 could work as a perfect open system as described in Chapter 1 – absolutely flexible, open to fast environmental change, and capable of integrating and using its diverse stakeholders in the most creative way. International projects can help to develop a learning organization, and vice versa: a learning organization is conducive to international project management.

We are now back to where we started: international project management and how it is interwoven with the overall organization, seen from an open system perspective.

SUMMARY

Organizational learning constitutes a competitive edge to today's organizations. It takes place within the frame of knowledge management, turning tacit knowledge into explicit knowledge. The nature of international projects, cultural diversity, communication and organizational issues impedes organizational learning. To enhance knowledge creation in and from international projects, there are human-centred approaches such as knowledge networks, special roles dedicated to knowledge management, and mentor relationships aiming at disseminating tacit knowledge. Process-based methods such as project audits and structured project walkthroughs, and content-based methods such as micro articles and learning histories also contribute to greater knowledge. Most of this learning is done in the form of project evaluation in the last project management phase, the completion phase of which another main task is the handover of the product or service to the customer. Due to subjectivity, lack of time, etc., such project completion is seldom done properly. To improve this situation and to enhance learning, the organization has to integrate project learning into project management methodology, strengthen the enablers of learning such as trust, motivation, and absorption capacity, and strive to become a learning organization.

 ## KEY TERMS

Organizational learning, knowledge, explicit knowledge, tacit knowledge, strong knowledge, weak knowledge, SECI process, knowledge management, cognitive model, community model, knowledge network, community of practice, mentor relationships, project audit, structured project walkthrough, micro article, learning history, project completion, learning organization.

REVIEW TASKS

Questions

1 Where do you see the greatest impediments to learning in and from projects?
2 What measures can be taken to enable project learning in an international context?
3 Where do you see the link between 'projectized' organizations, project learning, and the learning organization?

EXERCISE

- Think of a key learning experience you have made in the last two years (either related to your job or studies).
- Write up a micro article (maximum the size of one page of this book) focusing on providing sufficient context and using a high degree of visualization.
- Send your article via e-mail to a friend in another organization and/or another country and ask for feedback. The more diverse the receiver is from you, the better.
- If your friend understands your key experience, you have formulated the micro article well. If you get back a lot of questions in return, you should re-formulate your micro article and send it again.

CHAPTER END CASE: TWO CONTINENT – ONE WORLD

This case also touches on monitoring and controlling issues (Chapter 7).

Pfleiderer AG, founded in 1894, is a publicly listed company headquartered in Southern Germany. It is a global player in the areas of engineered wood, surface finished products and laminate flooring. With around 6,000 employees and production sites in Western Europe, Eastern Europe and North America, the Pfleiderer Group posted revenues of more than 1.8 billion Euros in the fiscal year 2007, 71.3 per cent originating from outside Germany. Since 2004, the company has embarked on an ambitious growth path with acquisitions in various countries. As of 2008, its 23 factories are located in: Germany (8), Canada (7), Poland (3), the USA (2), Sweden (2), and Russia (1). The multinational's strategic objective is to dramatically increase profits further by focusing on markets with a beneficial demographic structure and consumer behaviour, by committing to a market share of at least 15 per cent of each market it operates in, and by cost leadership through a full utilization of learning curve effects and economies of scale. The achievement of the strategic intent will result in challenges in the area of operations which highly depends on innovation and cost efficiency. High-speed growth – through acquisitions and organic development – requires the identification and realization of synergies, the integration of different organizational cultures, and close co-operation between employees from different geographical regions.

To pursue this strategy, the company has initiated an international project called 'Global Pfleiderer Production System (GPPS)' with the following targets:

1 Introduction of a worldwide standardized production system to reach a maximum of transparency to identify best practice globally.
2 Efficient and effective transfer of best practices between the different factories in order to maximize overall productivity.
3 Standardized production system as a management tool to support acquisitions by enabling decision-makers to identify potential synergies quickly and to speed up the integration process.
4 Speeding up knowledge transfer to new green field operations.

The first step in this international project was the creation of so-called production clusters. Factories using similar technologies for similar products were put in one cluster with the goal of information exchange and best practice sharing within the cluster. The second step was bolder: the different clusters are supposed to exchange information and try to use synergies wherever possible.

The main areas for improvement are the increase of uptime, i.e. the efficient use of machines, and the acceleration of output, i.e. the increase of output through faster production.

When the project was introduced in the organization, it was not met with great enthusiasm. On the contrary, there was a great deal of competition between the different factories that were not even willing to help each other out with spare parts in case of a machine break down. Even within the same country, factories were jealously hiding their know-how from each other, partially due to the fact the factories were acquired from different companies and thus had their own heritage and pride.

At the project kick-off meeting, the Chief Operations Officer, sponsor and manager of the GPPS project, explained the reasons underlying the cluster categorization and built the clusters. On the evening of the first kick-off meeting day, the representatives of each cluster were given the task of creating a dish together with the support of a professional chef. Communication was mainly non-verbal due to language barriers, but the menu was tasty. A second event followed the kitchen party one day later: in the afternoon, the different cluster groups were equipped with a backpack, a compass, supplies, and a map of the area. The task was to find a certain hut on the peak of a mountain. The different groups were 'abandoned' at different locations around this mountain. After they had reached the hut, each team had to pursue certain tasks like collecting fire wood. After that exercise, some people started to talk who had ignored each other previously.

Four weeks after the kick-off meeting, the clusters received their first technical and project related task: they were supposed to analyse the status of their production systems at each factory within the cluster. Following this analysis, they were supposed to identify best practices they wanted to share within the cluster. The timeframe given for this task was six months. There was a meeting planned after that period where all the clusters had to report on their successes.

In parallel, a central controlling function directly reporting to the COO started to monitor the production processes at all sites. The team consisted of five internationally experienced process and technology experts, from Canada, the USA, Poland and Germany. They used a matrix with the same parameters for all the different factories in order to systematically compare the performance of each site. A traffic light system was used to highlight the strong and weak performances for each parameter for each factory. Thus, the central controlling unit could easily identify those factories with a higher than average performance. Depending on the nature of the parameters monitored, the operations controllers informed the overperforming as well as the underperforming factories within the same cluster and encouraged an exchange of personnel and knowledge. Usually, the controllers travelled around the globe and gave support in identifying best practices. Typically, a team of technicians, operators and other relevant personnel was created, with members of good and bad factories. The group first went to the high-performing factory to analyse in detail the root causes of the good performance. This group was typically supported by a facilitator (first external, then mostly internal). The same group then met again in the underperforming factory and implemented improvement measures. By systematically analysing the situation and any room for improvement, the groups often even optimized the system of the outperforming factory thus leading to an overall efficiency increase in both factories. Depending on the nature of the issue, the manufacturers of the production equipment were also invited to the improvement team's brainstorming sessions.

After one year, there was another workshop where all the clusters gathered together. The event was used to lead the project into its next phase which was called 'To new frontiers'. The teams in each cluster were encouraged to overcome physical and eventually mental barriers. Once again, an event was organized to kick-off this phase. It was an abseiling exercise down a steep cliff. Each team member had to let him or herself down with a rope over 20 metres, only protected by his or her team members holding the rope at the top of the rock. Although many were scared at the beginning, all the team members achieved this challenging task. Back in the workshop room, all the clusters were encouraged to transfer their experience of overcoming barriers to the business world, to think outside the box and to find new ways of approaching problems and increasing efficiency. One of the results was an approach to proactively maintaining the machines in order to dramatically reduce downtimes, instead of repairing only in the case of a breakdown.

An in the first project phase, the teams were assigned a task. This time, they were supposed to implement any innovative approaches they had come up with across all clusters within the time-frame of 12 months. At the workshop, the COO increased the pressure on the team members who were reluctant to participate in the scheme by reading aloud their names. He also pointed out the strategic importance of the project, and the duty of all members to lead by example.

At the first kick-off event, language barriers were identified as the biggest single issue impeding the project to succeed. Hence, a lot of time and money was invested in language training, namely English. It was made clear that English was mandatory for all members of the project. The local human resource departments in each factory offered training measures and also controlled the learning success. Out of 50 members of the project, 20 had a sufficient command of English from the start, 20 people needed to brush up their English language skills and another 10 needed to start more or less from scratch.

In the project meetings, the project manager overheard comments like, 'This is typical of those German engineers.' Apparently, prejudices impeded fruitful co-operation within some clusters. This was true mainly for clusters where Germans had to closely co-operate with Polish colleagues, and clusters where Poles and Russians needed to collaborate intensively. External coaches were used to clarify the reasons for tensions which were mainly due to problematic historical ties.

The next phase of the project could be the introduction of an incentive system rewarding knowledge sharing.

Source: Hopperdietzel (2007); Pfleiderer AG (2008)

Questions

1   What type of project learning method does the GPPS constitute?
2   Is the knowledge management method handled well? Give the reasons for your answer.
3   What barriers needed to be overcome?
    General question referring back to Chapter 1:
4   What do you consider the key success factors (in light of the success criteria discussed in section 1.9) for implementing this special international project?

FURTHER READING

Love, Peter, Fong, P.S., and Zahir Irani. (eds) (2005) *Management of Knowledge in Project Environments*. Oxford: Elsevier Butterworth-Heinemann. (This is one of the few comprehensive readers on knowledge management in a project environment. Its articles cover different aspects of learning in a project context, from cross-functional learning to learning from project failure.)

Nonaka, Ikujiro and Toshihiro Nikshiguchi (eds) (2001) *Knowledge Emergence: Social, Technical, and Evolutionary Dimensions of Knowledge Creation*. Oxford: University Press. (This is a classical reader for students interested in knowledge creation as such, not focusing on the relation between knowledge and projects. It covers the domains of technology and cooperation, transnational knowledge creation, as well as inter-organizational relations concerning knowledge creation.)

GLOSSARY

A

Accountability – being responsible for the timely and correct execution of a certain task

Activity – task of a project which consumes time

Activity Duration – estimate of time (hours, days, weeks, months) necessary to complete a project task

Activity on Arc – see Activity on Arrow

Activity on Arrow – a technique representing the precedence and interdependence of activities in order to schedule projects

Actual Cost of Work Performed – the sum of the costs incurred for accomplished work packages

Attitude – a learned tendency to respond in the same way to the same situation, based on values

Authority – having the decision-making power

B

Balanced Matrix – a matrix structure in which the project manager and functional manager share roughly equal authority over a project

Balanced Score Card – approach to strategic management integrating four major fields: the financial perspective, the customer's perspective, the internal business processes, and the learning and growth perspective

Behaviour – is the action based on attitudes and values

Budgeted Cost of Work Performed – see Earned Value

Budgeted Cost of Work Scheduled – is the curve of the planned cost

C

Central and Eastern Europe – commonly, the following countries make up this area: Czech Republic, Estonia, Hungary, Latvia, Lithuania, Poland, Romania, Slovakia, Slovenia

Check Point – see milestone

Chunking – to break down activities according to their logic and sequence for a Work Breakdown Structure

Communication – is modelled as a process where an idea travels from the sender through a channel to a receiver. The sender encodes the idea into a message in verbal or non-verbal language, and the receiver decodes the message

Completion Phase – also called the termination phase or project closing; it is the fourth and last phase of the project management lifecycle

Conflict – form of tension between two or more interdependent parties based on incompatible goals, needs, values, or attitudes

Constraints – actions or decisions that limit the decision-making power of the project manager and team members

Context – the interrelated conditions in which something occurs or exists. Can be divided into physical, social, and situational contexts.

Contingency Plan – planning for alternatives and solutions should the risk occur

Contingency Reserves – additional project funds in terms of time, or resources, to offset any unavoidable threat that might occur to the international project

Contractor – organization (sub-unit, or individual) using the capital of the owner in order to produce the product/service or result the owner wants to have. Term is typically used for inter-organizational relations

Corporate Culture – see Organizational Culture

Cost Performance Index – as part of the Earned Value Analysis, the earned value is divided by the actual cost

Cost Plus Fixed Fee Contract – a special form of cost reimbursement contract. On top of the reimbursement for costs incurred with product or service delivery, the contractor is paid an additional fixed fee

Critical Path – the longest duration of tasks in the project network. It reflects the overall duration of the project

Culture – refers to functional, organizational and national cultures

D

Deliverables – pre-defined outcome of a project task (or a whole set of project tasks)

Diversity – differences in experience, age, gender, expertise, personality, culture (national, organizational, functional), background, etc., of stakeholders of an international project. But also differences in time zones, currencies, jurisdictions etc., within one international project

Dummy Activity – an activity which does not consume resources (including time). It is marked as a dotted arrow in the activities on an arrow network diagram. A dummy activity is used to ensure a unique identification for parallel activities and to maintain dependencies among activities on the network

E

Earned Value – the value of the work completed at a certain point of time based upon the planned or budgeted value for that work

Earned Value Analysis – is a method to evaluate more accurately the performance of a project in terms of both schedule deviation and cost deviation

Emergent Risk – risk that cannot be planned for

Emerging Market – this term is now more than 25 years old. Originally, it defined countries undergoing rapid economic change, typically fast growing economies in South-East Asia and Eastern Europe, later also in Latin America, China, India, and Russia. Today, a variety of countries are subsumed under this term causing it to lose meaning. There is no commonly accepted definition

Estimate – is a prediction of the time required to complete a task or activity. It could also refer to a cost estimate

Estimate Allowance – additional financial resources added to the total budget to cover oversights and unknowns

Ethnocentrism – the attitude of people who (unconsciously) operate from the basic assumption that their ways of doing things are best

Ethnorelativism – the attitude of people who accept cultural differences, and adapt to them or integrate them in their own behaviour

Event – a point in time when an activity is started or completed. Typically, it does not consume time

Explicit Knowledge – knowledge that is easy to formalize such as figures, words, scientific formulas, or product specifications. It can be transmitted to other individuals systematically

F

Fixed Price Contract – contractor is supposed to deliver a product or service at a fixed price, even if a loss is incurred

Float – buffer time between the earliest finish time and latest finish time of an activity which is non-critical for on time project delivery

Force Majeure – natural disasters such as earthquakes, volcanic eruptions, pandemics, but also man-made catastrophes like terrorist attacks

Functional Culture – refers to a certain methodology, standards, and ethics prevalent in a certain profession, like accountants, or organisational functions, such as Marketing & Sales

Functional Structure – also called traditional or classical structure, in which people are grouped by discipline and their level of authority in a top-down hierarchy

G

Gantt Chart – a graphic presentation of project activities shown as a time-scaled bar line (also called a bar chart)

Gate – see milestone

Goal – the end towards which effort is directed

H

Heterogeneity – in the context of this book used in the same way as diversity

HTS – Harmonized Tariff Schedule of the United States

I

Impact – the expected consequence of a risk on the project's objectives

Implementation phase – also called the execution phase. It is the third phase of the project management life cycle

Individualism – with regard to Hofstede's model this dimension refers to the relationship between the individual and the groups to which he or she belongs

Initiation Phase – first phase of the project management life cycle

K

Knowledge – if certain rules or heuristics are applied to information, knowledge is created

Knowledge Management – the process of creating value from an organization's intangible assets

Known-unknown – risk that can be anticipated and planned for

L

Learning – comprises cognitive refinement as well as behavioural adjustment. It is a process embedded in culture

Learning Histories – a learning history aims at capturing project experience with as much context as possible. It is a document comprising between 20 and 100 pages that narrates the story of a project chronologically

Local Culture – see national culture

M

Magic Triangle – to deliver projects on time, to budget and within scope with an agreed quality level

Management by Projects – managerial approach adopted by an increasing number of organizations. It extends project management to activities in the area of ongoing operations that are redefined as projects

Matrix Structure – any organizational structure in which the project manager shares authority over a project with the functional manager

Micro Article – a summary of approximately half a page of a special experience gained in a given project, distributed electronically or in an organization's magazines, with the purpose of learning from past project experiences

Milestone – an event which represents a significant, measurable accomplishment towards the project's completion

Mitigation – a risk response strategy that reduces either the impact and/or the probability of the risk

N

National Culture – in this book synonymously used with local culture. It is the set of values, attitudes, customs and beliefs of a group of people. Culture is learnt during the socialization process. There are various sub-cultures of one national culture due to regional differences

Negotiation – a process in which participants communicate to identify alternatives to move towards outcomes that are individually and mutually beneficial

O

OECD – organization with 30 member countries as of August 2007: Australia, Austria, Belgium, Canada, Czech Republic, Denmark, Finland, France, Germany, Greece, Hungary, Iceland, Ireland, Italy, Japan, South Korea, Luxembourg, Mexico, Netherlands, New Zealand, Norway, Poland, Portugal, Slovak Republic, Spain, Sweden, Switzerland, Turkey, United Kingdom, United States

Open System Theory – an organization is viewed as an open system getting input from its environment transforming it into throughout, which will be returned to the environment as output

Organizational Culture – system of shared values, norms, and beliefs held by an organization's members. It tends to be less deeply ingrained in an individual rather than national or local culture

Organization Breakdown Structure – shows all the people who are going to do the work in a project

P

Planning Phase – second phase of the project management life cycle

Power Distance – the degree to which a society accepts that power is distributed unequally

Probability – likelihood of the occurrence of a risk

Professional Culture – see Functional Culture

Program – is a bundle of projects serving the same purpose

Program Director – provides overall leadership and has ultimate responsibility for the successful implementation of the project program

Program Evaluation and Review Technique – also Project Evaluation and Review Technique. It is a tool to simplify the planning and scheduling of complex projects

Program Governance – the whole process of managing and directing the project program

Program Manager – individual responsible for a successful delivery of the program on the behalf of the project owner

Program Owner – individual responsible for ensuring that a program meets its objectives and delivers the projected benefits to the customer (internal or external)

Project – is a unique and time-limited endeavour to turn an idea into a result that is beneficial to the organization (under organizational constraints)

Project Charter – an official, written document acknowledging the existence of a project and authorizing the project manager to assign resources to the project

Project Governance – see Program Governance

Project Management – project management defines the process by which projects are initiated, planned, implemented, and completed in such a way that the benefits for the organization are delivered

Project Management Life Cycle – typically consists of four phases, namely initiating, planning, executing/controlling and completing the project

Project Management Maturity Model – model that describes the different levels an organization achieves on its way to effective project portfolio management

Project Management Office – central organizational unit which supports multiple project management on a high level with input and infrastructure

Project Management Team – group of sub-project managers who have their own areas of responsibility. They report to the project manager

Project Master Plan – plan that comprises all the details regarding the time, cost, quality, and structure of a project

Project Owner – provides the resources to deliver the project results

Project Phase – each phase within a project is separated from another by a decision-making point called the 'gate' or 'milestone'. The classical project management life cycle comprises four project phases, namely initiating, planning, implementing/monitoring, and completing

Project Proposal – also referred to as an investment proposal or business case. It functions as the basis for a go/no-go decision regarding project implementation

Project Scope – extent of the project outlining which activities are included in the project

Project Sponsor – typically a high-ranking manager who champions and supports a project. Often used synonymously with project owner

Project Stakeholder – see Stakeholder

Projectized Structure – describes a structure according to a product line, programme or project in which employees are typically collocated

Project Support Office – see Project Management Office

Project Team Members – all members of the project team. They are directly involved in the project and contribute to its completion

R

Responsibility Chart – a chart which shows the relationship between an activity or work package and the person or group being responsible for its completion – used synonymously with a responsibility matrix

Responsibility Matrix – a matrix which shows the relationship between an activity or work package and the person or group being responsible for its completion

Risk – an event which, if it occurs, can be a threat or an opportunity for a project

Risk Audit – a method to assess the effectiveness of the risk management process of a project at the end of the project

Risk Owner – a person responsible for the analysis and monitoring of a certain risk

Risk Register – list of identified project risks indicating the causes of risk and uncertain project assumptions

Risk Trigger – event that warns of impeding risk

S

Scope Acceptance – a document which is usually part of the scope statement signed by the project owner and manager to indicate their agreement on project objectives

Scope Statement – a document which clearly contains what is part of the project, and also what is not part of the project

Schedule Performance Index – as part of the Earned Value Analysis the Earned Value is divided by the budgeted cost

Sensitivity Analysis – often referred to as 'what-if-analysis, this aims to test how sensitive a predicted performance or outcome is to the assumptions made

Slack – the length of time an activity can be delayed by before the delay results in an overall delay of the project – see also Float.

South Eastern European Countries – commonly, the following countries: Albania, Bosnia and Herzegovina, Bulgaria, Croatia, the former Yugoslav Republic of Macedonia, Montenegro, Serbia

Stage – see Project Phase

Stakeholder – individual or organization that is actively involved in a project or that has an interest in the positive or negative outcomes of the project

Steering Committee – group of people, typically senior executives, who will form a platform or body of authority within an organization in order to take the final decisions on behalf of lower ranking units within the organization, like a project

Strategy – set of long-term goals of an organization and the plan as to how to achieve those goals

Strong Knowledge – includes true beliefs backed up by valid justification and the systematic exclusion of alternative possibilities. The focus is on strong verifiability, and super-objectivity. It tends to be explicit knowledge

Strong Matrix – a matrix structure in which the project manager has more authority over a project than the functional manager

T

Tacit Knowledge – knowledge that is deeply ingrained in an individual's actions and experience. It is highly context specific, not visible and hard to formalize

TARIC – ten digit code to be used in the EU for trade with third countries (customers and statistical declarations)

Trust – the belief by one person that another's motivation towards him or her is benevolent and 'honest'

U

Unbundling – see Chunking

Uncertainty Avoidance – is the degree to which a society is willing to accept and deal with uncertainty

Universalism – in a universalistic society it is the ideal to govern business relationships with contracts and clear rules which are applicable under any circumstances to anyone

Unknown-unknown – risk that emerges during a project and cannot be planned for. Also referred to as unk-unk

V

Value – beliefs deeply ingrained in an individual, such as the importance of seniority or freedom

W

Weak Knowledge – subjective knowledge focusing on consensus and the perceived use value. It tends to be tacit knowledge

Weak Matrix – a matrix structure in which the functional manager has more authority over a project than the project manager

Work Breakdown Structure – a hierarchy of activities or work packages which are grouped around the final deliverable or objectives of the project. It can be considered as the 'to-do list' of a project

REFERENCES

ABB (2008a) www.abb.com/cawp/abbzh252/9c53e7b73aa42f7ec1256ae700541c35.aspx, accessed 4 April, 2008.

ABB (2008b) www.abb.com/cawp/abbzh252/c2db8bbe34ab0961c1256aed003368b8.aspx, accessed 4 April, 2008.

Adams, Douglas (1980) *The Hitchhiker's Guide to the Galaxy.* New York: Harmony Books.

Adler, Nancy (2002) *Intenational Dimensions of Organizational Behavior.* 4th edition. Cincinnati: South-Western.

Adler, Nancy J. and Bartholomew, Susan (1992) 'Managing globally competent people'. In: *Academy of Management Executive*, 6 (3): 52–65.

Al-Omari, Jehad (2003) *The Arab Way: How to Work more Effectively with Arab Cultures.* Oxford: Howtobooks.

Alon, Ilan and James M. Higgins (2005) Global leadership success through emotional and cultural intelligences. In: *Business Horizons*, 48, pp. 501–12.

American Society for Quality ASQ (2007) Quality tools: Process analysis tools, http://www.asq.org/learn-about-quality/process-analysis-tools/overview/fmea.html, accessed 31 August, 2007.

Andersen, Bjorn; Henriksen, Bjornar and Aarseth, Wenche (2006) 'Project Management Office Establishment Best Practices'. In: *Project Perspectives.* Annual Publication of IPMA, Vol. XXVIII, 30–5.

AP (2008) Jakarta agrees to launch online bird flu database. In: *The Japan Times,* 16 May, p. 4.

Arenius, Marko, Artto, Karlos A., Lahti, Mika and Meklin, Jukka (2002) 'Project companies and the multi-project paradigm: a new management approach'. In: Selvin, Dennis P., Cleland, David I. and Pinto, Jeffrey K. (eds): *The Frontiers of Project Management Research.* Newton Square, Pennsylvania: Project Management Institute, pp. 289–308.

Artto, Karlos A., Martinsuo, Mii and Aalto, Taru (eds) (2001) *Project Portfolio Management: Strategic Management through Projects.* Helsinki: Project Management Association Finland.

Association for Project Management APM (2006a) *APM Body of Knowledge Definitions.* 5th edition, http://www.apm.org.uk/page.asp?categoryID=4&subCategoryID=27&pageID=0, accessed 30 March, 2007.

Association for Project Management APM (2006b) *Comparison of the APM Body of Knowledge.* 4th and 5th edition. http://www.apm.org.uk/page.asp?categoryID=4&subCategoryID=27&pageID=0, accessed 01 April, 2007.

Augsburger, David W. (1992) *Conflict Mediation Across Cultures: Pathways and Patterns.* Louisville/London: Westminster John Know Press.

AutoAsia (2006) Fiat may assist Tata Motors with low-cost car. http://www.auto-asia.com/viewcontentprem.asp?pk=10547&page=viewprem, accessed 18 December, 2006.

Avruch, Kevin (2002) *Culture and Conflict Resolution.* Washington DC: United States Institute of Peace Press.

Bartlett, Christopher B. and Ghoshal, Sumatra (1989) *Managing Across Borders: The Transnational Solution.* Boston, MA: Harvard Business School Press.

Bartlett, Christopher A. and Ghoshal, Sumantra (1990) 'Matrix management: not a structure, a frame of mind'. In: *Harvard Business Review,* July-August, pp.138–45.

Bass, B.M. (1985) *Leadership and Performance Beyond Expectations.* New York: Free Press.

Bate, Paul (2004) *Strategies for Cultural Change.* Oxford et al.: Butterworth Heinemann.

Benator, Barry and Thumann, Albert (2003) *Project Management and Leadership Skills for Engineering and Construction Projects.* Lilburn: The Fairmont Press.

Bennett, Janet M. and Bennett, Milton J. (2004) 'Developing intercultural sensitivity: an integrative approach to global and domestic diversity'. In: Landis, Dan, Bennett, Janet M. and Bennett, Milton J. (eds): *The Handbook of Intercultural Training.* Thousand Oaks, CA: Sage, pp. 147–65.

Benz, Rudolf (2005) Projektmanagementpraxis in der Raumfahrt. Entwicklung von Satellitenmissionen und Systemen. In: VDI (ed.): Projektmanagement Praxis 2005. Sechster praxisorientierter Anwendertag zum Projektmanagement. Expertenforum Hamburg.

VDI Berichte 1925, VDI-Verlag: Düsseldorf, pp. 17–31.

Bergman, Inger (2006) 'Ericsson and the Project Environment Maturity Assessment', In: Dinsmore, Paul C. and Cooke-Davies Terence J.: *The Right Projects Done Right*! San Francisco, CA: Jossey-Bass, pp. 111–17.

BHP Billiton (2008) Annual Report 2008, http://www.bhpbilliton.com/annualreports2008/2008-business-review-and-annual-report/ accessed 5 January, 2009.

Blasig, K. (2005) Produkt-Transfer innerhalb des Rolls-Royce-Konzerns am Beispiel der Triebwerke Tay 611-8/8C. In: VDI (ed.): Projektmanagement Praxis 2005. Sechster praxisorientierter Anwendertag zum Projektmanagement. Expertenforum Hamburg. VDI Berichte 1925, VDI-Verlag: Düsseldorf, pp. 9–16.

Brandon, Daniel M. Jr. (2004) 'Project Performance Measurement'. In: Morris, Peter W.G. and Pinto, Jeffrey K. (eds): *The Wiley Guide to Managing Projects*. Hoboken, NJ: John Wiley & Sons, pp. 830–51.

Bresnen, Mike, Edelmann, Linda, Newell, Sue, Scarbrough, Harry and Swan, Jacky (2003) 'Social practices and the management of knowledge in project environments'. In: *International Journal of Project Management*, 21: 157–66.

Brett, Jeanne, Behfar, Kristin and Kern, Mary C. (2006) 'Managing multicultural teams'. In: *Harvard Business Review*, November, 84–91.

Business Objects (2008) About Business Objects. www.businessobjects.com/company/overview/history.asp#, accessed 19 November, 2008.

Business Wire (2005) Samsung Corning Precision supplies first commercial quantities of Generation 7 Size Glass Substrates, Jan. 17, www.findarticles.com/p/articles/mi_m0EIN/is_2005_Jan_17/ai_n869481, accessed 01 April 1, 2007.

Büchel, Bettina and Raub, Steffen (2002) Building Knowledge–creating Value Networks. In: *European Mnangement Journal*, Vol. 20, No. 6, pp. 587–96.

Cadbury, Deborah (2003) *Seven Wonders of the Industrial World*. Accompanies the major television series, BBC. London: Harper Perennial.

Callahan, Kevin R. and Brooks, Lynne M. (2004): *Essentials of Strategic Project Management*. Hoboken, NJ: John Wiley & Sons.

Cameron, Kim S. and Quinn, Robert E. (2006) *Diagnosing and Changing Organizational Culture*. Revised edition. San Francisco, CA: Jossey-Bass.

Capels, Thomas M. (2004) *Financially Focused Project Management*. Boca Raton: J. Ross.

Cartwright, Susan and McCarthy, Simon (2005) 'Developing a framework for cultural diligence in mergers and acquisitions: issues and ideas'. In: Mark E. Mendenhall and Günter Stahl (eds): *Mergers and Acquisitions: Managing Culture and Human Resources,* Stanford: Stanford Business Books, pp. 253–67.

Chapman, Chris and Ward, Stephen (2002) *Managing Project Risk and Uncertainty: A Constructively Simple Approach to Decision Making*. Chichester: John Wiley & Sons.

Chen, Ping and Partington, David (2004) 'An interpretive comparison of Chinese and Western conceptions of relationships in construction project management work'. In: *International Journal of Project Management*, 22: 397–406.

Chini, Tina C. (2004) *Effective Knowledge Transfer in Multinational Corporations*. London: Palgrave Macmillan.

Christensen, Clayton M. (2000) *Using Aggregate Project Planning to Link Strategy, Innovation, and Resource Allocation Process*. Boston: Harvard Business School Press.

Cleland, David I. and Ireland, Lewis R. (2002) *Project Management. Strategic Design and Implementation*. 4th edition. New Jersey: McGraw-Hill.

Cleland, David I. and Gareis, Roland (eds) (2006) *Global Project Management Handbook. Planning, Organizing, and Controlling International Projects*. 2nd edition. New York: McGraw-Hill.

Commonwealth of Independent States CIS (2007) About us. http:// cis.minsk.by/main.aspx?uid=3390, accessed 27 August, 2007.

Conclaves, Marcus (2005) *Managing Virtual Projects*. San Francisco, CA: McGraw-Hill.

Connerley, Mary L. and Pedersen, Paul B. (2005): *Leadership in a Diverse and Multicultural Environment. Developing Awareness, Knowledge, and Skills*. Thousand Oaks, CA: Sage.

Cooke-Davies, Terry (2002) 'The "real" success factors on projects'. In: *International Journal of Project Management*, 20: 185–90.

Cooke-Davis, Terry (2004) 'Project success'. In: Morris, Peter W.G. and Pinto, Jeffrey K. (eds): *The Wiley Guide to Managing Projects*. Hoboken, NJ: John Wiley & Sons, pp. 99–122.

Cooper., Dale F., Grey, Stephen, Raymond, Geoffrey and Walker, Phill (2005) *Project Risk Management Guidelines: Managing Risk in Large Projects and Complex Procurements*. Chichester: John Wiley & Sons.

Corning Inc. (2008) www.corning.com/CMS/Overview Print.aspx?id=371&url=http://www.corning.com/about_us/inside_corning/index.aspx, accessed 13 November, 2008.

Crawford, Lynn (2004) 'Professional associations and global initiatives'. In: Morris, Peter W.G. and Pinto, Jeffrey K. (eds): *The Wiley Guide to Managing Projects*. Hoboken, NJ: John Wiley & Sons, 1389–402.

Crawford, Lynn (2005) 'Competencies of project managers'. In: Cleland, David I. and Gareis, Roland (eds): *Global Project Management Handbook. Planning, Organizing, and Controlling International Projects*. 2nd edition. New York: McGraw-Hill, pp. 8–3 to 8–20.

CULTPLAN Team (2007) Cultural differences in European cooperation. Learning from INTER-REG Practice. Pdf-file available on www.cultplan.org, accessed 10 August, 2008.

Cyert, Richard M. and March, James G. (1992) *A Behavioral Theory of the Firm*. 2nd edition. Oxford: Blackwell Publishers.

Davis, Joseph G., Subrahmanian, Eswaran and Westerberg, Arthur W. (2005) 'The "global" and the "local" in knowledge management'. In: *Journal of Knowledge Management*, 9 (1): 101–12.

Davison, Sue Canney and Ward, Karen (1999) *Leading International Teams*. London: McGraw-Hill.

De Meyer, Arnoud, Loch, Christoph H. and Pich, Michael T. (2006) 'Management of novel projects under conditions of high uncertainty'. *Working Paper Series 21*. Cambridge: Judge Business School.

DeLong, David W. and Fahey, Liam (2000) 'Diagnosing cultural barriers to knowledge management'. In: *Academy of Management Executive*, 14 (4): 113–27.

Demeulemeester, Erik L. and Herroelen, Willy S. (2002) *Project Scheduling: A Research Handbook*. Boston: Kluwer Academic Publishers.

Dengel, Birgit (2007a) McDonald's richtet Fokus auf Europa. In: *Financial Times Deutschland*. 164/34, 21 August, p. 1.

Dengel, Birgit (2007b) McDonald's verringert Zahl eigener Filialen. In: *Financial Times Deutschland*. 164/34, 21 August, p. 7.

Dinsmore, Paul C. and Cooke-Davies, Terrence J. (2006) *The Right Projects Done Right! From Business Strategy to Successful Project Implementation*. San Francisco, CA: Jossey-Bass.

Doz, Yves L. and Coimbatore Krishnarao Prahalad (1991) 'Managing DMNCs: a search for a new paradigm'. In: *Strategic Management Journal*, 12 (5): 145–64.

dpa (2008) Windows für den 100-Dollar Laptop. In: *Süddeutsche Zeitung* No. 114, 17./18 May, p. 26.

Duarte, Deborah L. and Snyder, Nancy Tennant (2006) *Mastering Virtual Teams: Strategies, Tools, and Techniques That Succeed,* 3rd edition. San Francisco, CA: Jossey-Bass.

EADS (2008) EADS at a glance, www.eads.com/1024/en/eads/eads_at_a_glance/eads_at_a_glance.html, accessed 24 December, 2008.

EADS Astrium (2008) The company, www.astrium.eads.net/company, accessed 16 December, 2008.

Ehmann, Markus (2007) Telephone Interview, conducted 24 June, 10.00–11.30.

Englund, Randall L., Graham, Robert and Dinsmore, Paul C. (2003) *Creating the Project Office: A Manager's Guide to Leading Organizational Change*. San Francisco, CA: Jossey-Bass.

Engwall, Mats (2003) 'No project is an island: linking projects to history and context'. In: *Research Policy*, 32: 789–808.

Ericsson (2006) Annual financial report 2006, www.ericsson.com/ericsson/investors/financial_reports/2006/annual06/summary_downloads/ar_en_complete.pdf, accessed 7 April, 2007.

Eriksson, Mikael, Jonsson, Narcisa, Lillieskold, Joakim and Novosel, Damir (2002) 'How to manage complex, multinational R&D projects successfully'. In: *Engineering Management Journal*, 14 (2) June, pp. 53–60.

European Union (EU) (2002a) New Framework Program launched – a fact sheet, http://ec.europa.eu/research/fp6/pdf/facts_en.pdf, accessed 6 April, 2007.

European Union (EU) (2002b) The 6th Framework Program in brief. http://ec.europa.eu/research/fp6/pdf/fp6-in-brief_en.pdf, accessed 6 April, 2007.

Evaristo, J. Roberto and Richard Scudder (2000) 'Geographically distributed project teams: a dimensional analysis'. *Proceedings of the 33rd Hawaii International Conference on System Sciences*.

Falbo, Toni and Peplau, Letitia Anne (1980) 'Power strategies in intimate relationships'. In: *Journal of Personality and Social Psychology*, 38 (4): 618–28.

Financial Express (2006) Fiat mulls joining Tata in low-cost car project, www.financialexpress.com/fe_full_story.php?content_id=139539, accessed 18 December, 2006.

Financial Times (2007) Jakarta refuses to give bird flu samples to WHO. 15 July, p. 5

Flyvbjerg, Bent, Buzelius, Nils and Rothengatter, Werner (2003) *Megaprojects and Risk: An Anatomy of Ambition*. Cambridge: Cambridge University Press.

Frame, J. Davidson (2002) *The New Project Management: Tools for an Age of Rapid Change, Complexity, and Other Business Realities,* 2nd edition. San Francisco, CA: Jossey-Bass.

Francesco, Anne Marie and Gold, Barry Allen (2005) *International Organizational Behavior,* 2nd edition. Upper Saddle River, NJ: Pearson Prentice Hall.

Galbraith, Jay R. (2002) *Designing Organizations: An Executive Guide to Strategy, Structure, and Process,* new and revised. San Francisco, CA: Jossey-Bass.

Gallois, Cynthia and Callan, Victor (1997) *Communication and Culture: A Guide for Practice.* Chichester: John Wiley & Sons.

Gardiner, Paul (2005) *Project Management: A Strategic Planning Approach.* Basingstoke: Palgrave Macmillan.

Gareis, Roland (2006a) 'Program management and project portfolio management'. In: Cleland, David I. and Gareis, Roland (eds): *Global Project Management Handbook. Planning, Organizing, and Controlling International Projects,* 2nd edition. New York: McGraw-Hill, pp. 7–1 to 7–24.

Gareis, Roland (2006b) 'Management of the project-oriented company'. In: Cleland, David I. and Gareis, Roland (eds): *Global Project Management Handbook. Planning, Organizing, and Controlling International Projects,* 2nd edition. New York: McGraw-Hill, pp.18–3 to 18–25.

Gates, Michael (2007) 'Communicating successfully across cultures'. In: *HR Director,* March, pp. 26–8.

Geertz, Clifford (2000) *Local Knowledge: Further Essays in Interpretive Anthropology.* New York: Basic Books.

Gesteland, Richard (2000) *Cross-cultural Business Behavior: Marketing, Negotiating and Managing Across Cultures.* Copenhagen: Copenhagen Business School Press/Handelshojskolens Forlag.

Ghemawat, Pankaj (2006) *Strategy and the Business Landscape,* 2nd edition. Upper Saddle River, NJ: Pearson/Prentice Hall.

Glisby, M. and Holden, N. (2003) Contextual constraints in knowledge management theory: the cultural embeddedness of Nonaka's knowledge-creating company. In: *Knowledge and Process Management,* Vol. 10, Issue 1, pp. 29–36.

Goldratt, Eliyahu M. (1997) *Critical Chain.* Great Barrington: The North River Press.

Govindarajan, Vijay and Gupta, Anil K. (2001) 'Building an effective global business team. In: *MIT Sloan Management Review,* summer, pp.63–71.

Greenpeace (2006) About Greenpeace, www.greenpeace.org/international/about, accessed 31 March, 2007.

Gregersen, Hal B., Morrison, Allen J. and Black, J. Steward (1998) 'Developing leaders for the global frontier'. In: *Sloan Management Review,* 40: 21–32.

GTZ (2006) Wassermanagement in der ägyptischen Bewässerungslandschaft. www.gtz.de/de/weltweit/maghreb-naher-osten/aegypten/13493.htm, accessed 31 March, 2007.

Gudykunst, William B. and Ting-Toomey, Stella with Elizabeth Chua (1988) *Culture and Interpersonal Communication.* Newbury Park: Sage.

Guillén, Mauro F. (1994) *Models of Management: Work, Authority, and Organization in a Comparative Perspective.* Chicago/London: University of Chicago Press.

Gullestrup, Hans (2006) *Cultural Analysis – Towards Cross-cultural Understanding.* Copenhagen: Copenhagen Business School Press/Aalborg Universitetsforlag.

Hall, Edward T. and Hall, Mildred Reed (1987) *Hidden Differences: Doing Business with the Japanese.* New York: Doubleday (Anchor Books).

Han, Seung H.; Kim, Du Y and Kim, Hyoungkwan (2007) 'Predicting profit performance for selecting candidate international construction projects'. In: *Journal of Construction Engineering and Management,* June, pp. 425–36.

Handy, Charles B. (1991) *Gods of Management.* London: Arrow.

Hansen, Morten T. and Nohria, Nitin (2004) 'How to build collaborative advantage'. In: *MIT Sloan Management Review,* Fall, pp. 22–30.

Harms, Rainer., Köster, Kathrin and Mikova, Violina (2006) Projektportfolio-Management – ein Thema für den wachstumsorientierten Mittelstand? In: *Zeitschrift für KMU und Entrepreneurship,* No. 4, pp. 249–65.

Harpum, Peter (2004) 'Project Control'. In: Morris, Peter W.G. and Pinto, Jeffrey K. (eds): *The Wiley Guide to Managing Projects.* Hoboken, NJ: John Wiley & Sons, pp. 5–29.

Harrison, Roger (1972) 'Understanding your organization's character'. In: *Harvard Business Review,* May/June, pp. 119–28.

Harzing, Anne-Wil et al. (under review) *Ranking versus Rating: What is the Best Way to Reduce Response and Language Bias in Cross-national Research?*

Haywood, Martha (1998) *Managing Virtual Teams: Practical Techniques for High-Technology Project Managers.* Boston/London: Artech House.

REFERENCES

Heiligtag, Bernhard (2008) Phone interview, 6 November, 9.00–10.00.

Heldman, Kim (2005) *Project Manager's Spotlight on Risk Management.* Alameda: Harbor Light Press.

Hempel, Paul S. (1998) 'Designing multinational benefits programs: the role of national culture'. In: *Journal of World Business,* 33 (3): 277–94.

Hillson, David (2004) *Effective Opportunity Management for Projects: Exploiting Positive Risk.* New York/Basel: Marcel Dekker.

Hoegl, Martin (2005) 'Smaller teams – better teamwork: how to keep project teams small'. In: *Business Horizons,* 48: 209–14.

Hofstede, Geert (1993) 'Cultural constraints in management theories'. In: *Academy of Management Executive,* 7 (1): 81–94.

Hofstede, Geert (1997) *Cultures and Organizations: Software of the Mind,* 2nd revised edition. New York: McGraw-Hill.

Hofstede, Geert (2001) *Culture's Consequences: Comparing Values, Behaviors, Institutions, and Organizations across Nations,* 2nd edition, Thousand Oaks, CA: Sage.

Holden, N. (2002) *Cross-cultural Management: A Knowledge Management Perspective.* Harlow, Munich: Financial Times Prentice Hall.

Hopperdietzel, Robert (2007) Interview with Dr Robert Hopperdietzel, COO of Pfleiderer AG, 13 December.

House, Robert J., Hanges, Paul J., Javidan, Mansour, Dorfman, Peter W. and Gupta, V. (eds) (2004) *Culture, Leadership, and Organizations: The GLOBE Study of 62 Societies.* Thousand Oaks, CA: Sage.

House, Robert J., Javidan, Mansour, Hanges, Paul and Dorfman, Peter (2002) 'Understanding cultures and implicit leadership theories across the globe: an introduction to project GLOBE'. In: *Journal of World Business,* 27: 3–10.

Huemann, Martina (2004) 'Improving quality in projects and programs'. In: Morris, Peter W.G. and Pinto Jeffery K. (eds): *The Wiley Guide to Managing Projects.* Hoboken, NJ: John Wiley & Sons, pp. 903–36.

IMPULSE (2005a) Impulse objectives. www.impulse-project.net/content.php?pageId=2593&lang=en, accessed 6 April 6, 2007.

IMPULSE (2005b) Towards innovative chemical production. www.impulse-project.net/content.php?pageId=2556&lang=en, accessed 6 April, 2007.

International Chamber of Commerce ICC (2008) Rules at the core of world trade. www.iccwbo.org/incoterms/id3045/index.html, accessed 12 August, 2008.

International Federation of Consulting Engineers FIDIC (2008): FIDIC new suite of standard forms of contract. www1.fidic.org/resources/contracts/which_contract.asp, accessed 6 March, 2008.

International Monetary Fund IMF (2006) World Economic Outlook. www.imf.org/external/pubs/ft/weo/2007/01/index.htm#ch1fig, accessed 1 September, 2007.

IntoAsia (2006) Suvarnabhumi airport. www.into-asia.com/bangkok/airport/, accessed 4 April, 2007.

Ireland, Lewis R. (2006) 'Project quality management in international projects. In: Cleland, David I. and Gareis, Roland (eds): *Global Project Management Handbook. Planning, Organizing, and Controlling International Projects,* 2nd edition. New York: McGraw-Hill, pp. 15–1 to 15–11.

Javidan, Mansour, Stahl, Günter K. and House, Robert J. (2004) 'Leadership in a global organization: a cross-cultural perspective'. In: Gatignon, Hubert and Kimberley, John R. (eds): *The INSEAD-Wharton Alliance on Globalizing. Strategies for Building Successful Global Businesses.* Cambridge: Cambridge University Press, pp. 78–103.

Jennen, Birgit (2008) Siemens-Affäre weitet sich aus. Behörden ermittelt nun auch gegen die Regierung. In: *Financial Times Deutschland,* 11 August, p. 3.

Jensen, Christian, Johansson, Staffan and Löfström, Mikael (2006) 'Project relationships – a model for analyzing interactional uncertainty'. In: *International Project Management,* 24: 4–12.

Johnson, Gerry, Scholes, Kevan and Whittington, Richard (2005) *Exploring Corporate Strategy. Text and Cases,* 7th edition. Harlow: Prentice Hall, *Financial Times.*

Jungkunz, Ralf Maximilian (2006) PDM-basierte Überwachung komplexer Entwicklungsprojekte. In: *Projekt Management,* 4, pp. 49–55.

Kaplan, Robert S. and Norton, David P. (1996) 'Using the balanced scorecard as a strategic management system'. In: *Harvard Business Review,* January/February, pp. 75–85.

Kasvi, Jyrki J.J., Vartiainen, Matti and Hailikari, Milla (2003) 'Managing knowledge and knowledge competences in projects and project organisations'. In: *International Journal of Project Management,* 21: 571–82.

Katz, D. and Kahn, R.L. (1969) 'Common characteristics of open systems', In: Emery, F.E. (ed): *Systems Thinking.* Harmondworth: Penguin Books, pp. 86–104.

Keller Johnson, Lauren (2004) 'Close the gap between projects and Strategy'. In: *Harvard Management Update,* June, pp. 4–5.

Kendrick, Tom (2003) *Identifying and Managing Project Risk: Essential Tools for Failure-Proofing Your Project*. New York et al.: AMACOM.

Kerzner, Harlod (2006) *Project Management: A Systems Approach to Planning, Scheduling, and Controlling*, 9th edition. Hoboken, NJ: John Wiley & Sons.

Kilpi, Matti, Palko, Sakari, Martinsuo, Miia and Aalto, Taru (2001) 'Renewing the corporate reserach porfolio through Nokia Research Center – Business Group Interaction'. In: Artto, Karlos A., Martinsuo, Mii and Aalto, Taru (eds), *Project Portfolio Management: Strategic Management through Projects*. Helsinki: Project Management Association Finland, pp. 145–52.

Knutson, Joan (2001) *Succeeding in Project-Driven Organizations: People, Processes, and Politics*. New York: John Wiley & Sons.

Kohlbacher, Florian (2007) *International Marketing in the Network Economy: A Knowledge-based Approach*. Basingstoke: Palgrave Macmillan.

Kohlbacher, Florian and Kraehe, Michael O.B. (2007) 'Knowledge creation and transfer in a cross-cultural context – empirical evidence from Tyco Flow Control'. In: *Knowledge and Process Management, 14* (3): 169–81.

Köster, Kathrin (2007) 'Inter-relationship between organizational leadership, societal cultures, and organizational cultures'. In: Seshagiri, Sarita; Gajendra and Rajul, Joshi (eds): *Effective Leadership. Lessons in a Cross Cultural Context*. Hyderabad: The Icfai University Press, pp. 9–28.

Kreiner, K. (1995) In search of relevance: project management in drifting environments. In: *Scandinavian Journal of Management, 11* (4): 335–46.

Kremer, S. (2006) $ 2,200 car in 2008? www.redherring.com/article.aspx?a=17847, accessed 18 December, 2006.

Kühlmann, Torsten (2008) Opportunismus, Vertrauen und Kontrolle in internationalen Geschäftsbeziehungen. In: Jammal, Elias (ed.): *Vertrauen im interkulturellen Kontext. Perspectives of the Other: Studies on Intercultural Communication*. Wiesbaden: VS Research, pp. 51–67.

Kumar, Kuldeep, van Fenema, Paul C. and Von Glinow, Mary Ann (2005) 'Intense collaboration in globally distributed work teams: evolving patterns of dependencies and co-ordination'. In: Shapiro, Debra L., Von Glinow, Mary Ann and Cheng, Joseph L.C. (eds): *Managing Multinational Teams: Global Perspectives:* *Advances in international management volume 18*, Amsterdam: Elsevier JAI, pp. 127–53.

Laptop.org (2007a) One laptop per child, www.laptop.org/index.shtml, accessed 27 January, 2007.

Laptop.org (2007b) Frequently asked questions, www.laptop.org/vision/mission/faq.shtml, accessed 27 January, 2007.

Laptop.org (2007c) Map, www.laptop.org/vision/progress/maps.shtml, accessed 27 January, 2007.

Larson, Erik (2004) 'Project Management Structures'. In: Morris, Peter W.G. and K. Pinto, Jeffrey (eds): *The Wiley Guide to Managing Projects*. Hoboken, NJ: John Wiley & Sons, pp. 48–66.

LEGO (2008) Annual report 2007 Lego Group. www.lego.com/info/pdf/annualreport2007UK.pdf, accessed 5 January, 2009.

Levine, Harvey A. (2005) *Project Portfolio Management: A Practical Guide to Selecting Projects, Managing Portfolios, and Maximizing Benefits*. San Francisco, CA: Jossey-Bass.

Lewis, Richard D. (1999) *When Cultures Collide: Managing Successfully Across Cultures*. London: Nicholas Brealey Publishing.

Liebowitz, Jay (2005) 'Conceptualizing and implementing knowledge management'. In: Love, Peter; Fong, P.S.W. and Irani, Zahir (eds): *Management of Knowledge in Project Environments*. Oxford: Elsevier Butterworth-Heinemann, pp. 1–18.

Lientz, Bennet and Rea, Kathryn P. (2003) *International Project Management*. Amsterdam: Academic Press.

Lim, C.S. and Mohamed Z. (1999) 'Criteria of project success: an exploratory re-examination'. In: *International Journal of Project Management, 17*: 243–8.

Longman, Andrew and Mullins, Jim (2005) *The Rational Project Manager: A Thinking Team's Guide to Getting Work Done*. Hoboken, NJ: John Wiley & Sons.

Loosemore, M. and Al Muslmani, H.S. (1999) 'Construction project management in the Persian Gulf: inter-cultural communication'. In: *International Journal of Project Management, 17* (2): 95–100.

Love, Peter, Fong, P.S.W. and Irani, Zahir (eds) (2005) *Management of Knowledge in Project Environments*. Oxford: Elsevier Butterworth-Heinemann.

Lucas, Chris (2005) *Risk Perspectives – Bringing Together Leading Risk Management Insights from the Banking Industry*. Pricewaterhouse-Coopers.

Marsh, Peter (2003a) 'Contracts and payment structures'. In: Turner, Rodney, J. (ed.): *Contracting For Project Management*. Aldershot: Gower, pp. 19–31.

Marsh, Peter (2003b) 'Managing variations, claims, and disputes'. In: Turner, Rodney J. (ed.): *Contracting for Project Management*. Aldershot: Gower, pp. 125–38.

Maslow, Abraham H. (1987) *Motivation and Personality*, 3rd edition. New York: Harper Collins Publishers.

Matveev, Alexei V. and Nelson, Paul E. (2004) 'Cross cultural communication competence and multicultural team performance'. In: *International Journal of Cross Cultural Management*, 4 (2): 253–70.

McDonough, Edward F. III; Kahn, Kenneth V. and Griffin, Abbie (1999) 'Managing communication in gobal product development teams'. In: *IEEE Transactions on Engineering Management*, 46 (4), November, pp. 375–86.

McKenna, Stephen (1995) 'The business impact of management attitudes towards dealing with conflict: a cross-cultural assessment'. In: *Journal of Managerial Psychology*, 10 (7): 22–7.

Mendenhall, M.E. (1999) 'On the need for paradigmatic integration in international human resource management'. In: *Management International Review*, 39 (2): 1–23.

Mendenhall, Mark E. (2008) 'Leadership and the birth of global leadership'. In: Mendenhall, Mark E., osland, Joyce S., Bird, Allan B., Oddou, Gary R. and Maznevski, Martha L.: *Global Leadership: Research, Practice and Development*. London/New York: Routledge, pp. 1–17.

Miller, Roger and Hobbs, Brian (2006) 'Managing risks and uncertainty in major projects in the new global environment'. In: Cleland, David and Gareis, Roland (eds): *Global Project Management Handbook*, 2nd edition. New York: McGraw-Hill. pp. 9–1 to 9–16.

Milosevic, Dragan Z. (1999) 'Echoes of the silent language of project management'. In: *Project Management Journal*, 30 (1): 27–39.

Moore, J.I. (2001) *Writers on Strategy and Strategic Management: Theory and Practice at Enterprise, Corporate, Business and Functional Levels*, 2nd edition. London: Penguin Books.

Moran, Robert T., Harris, Philip R. and Moran, Sarah V. (2007) *Managing Cultural Differences. Global Leadership Strategies for the 21st Century*, 7th edition. Amsterdam: Elsevier.

Morris, Peter W. G. (2002) 'Research trend in the 1990s: the need now to focus on the business benefits of project management'. In: Slevin, Dennis P., Cleland, David I. and Pinto, Jeffrey K. (eds): *The Frontiers of Project Management Research*. Pennsylvania: Project Management Institute, pp. 31–56.

Morris, Peter W.G. and Pinto, Jeffrey K. (eds) (2004) *The Wiley Guide to Managing Projects*. Hoboken, NJ: John Wiley & Sons.

Muriithi, Ndiritu and Crawford, Lynn (2003) 'Approaches to project management in Africa: implications for international development projects'. In: *International Journal of Project Management*, 21: 309–19.

Murphy, Owen Jay (2005) *International Project Management*. Crawfordsville: Thomson.

Nadler, Lawrence B., Nadler, Marjorie Keeshan and Broome, Benjamin (1985) 'Culture and the management of conflict situations'. In: Gudykunst, William B., Stewart, Lea P. and Ting-Toomey, Stella (eds): *Communication, Culture, and Organizational Processes. International and Intercultural Communication Annual, Volume IX*. Beverly Hills, CA: Sage, pp. 87–113.

National Science Foundation (1999) Regional summary: European Cooperation in Research and Development, www.nsf.gov/statistics/nsf96316/eucoop.htm, accessed 7 April, 2007.

Nonaka, Ikujiro and Nikshiguchi, Toshihiro (eds) (2001) *Knowledge Emergence: Social, Technical, and Evolutionary Dimensions of Knowledge Creation*. Oxford: University Press.

Nooteboom, Bart (2006) 'Forms, sources and processes of trust'. In: Bachmann, Reinhard and Zaheer, Akbar (eds): *Handbook of Trust Research*. Cheltenham/Northampton, MA: Edward Elgar, pp. 247–63.

Nurick, Aaron J. and Thamhain, Hans J. (2005) 'Developing multinational project teams'. In: Cleland, David I. and Gareis, Roland (eds): *Global Project Management Handbook. Planning, Organizing, and Controlling International Projects*, 2nd edition. New York: McGraw-Hill, pp. 1 to 5–19.

OGC (2004) www.ogc.gov.uk/documents/portfolio mgmt.pdf, accessed 6 April, 2007.

OGC (2007) http://www.ogc.gov.uk/introduction_to_programmes_governing_a_programme.asp, accessed 6 April, 2007.

Ohbuchi, Ken-ichi and Takahashi, Yumi (1994) 'Cultural styles of conflict management in Japanese and Americans: passivity, covertness, and effectiveness of strategies'. In: *Journal of Applied Social Psychology*, 24 (15): 1345–66.

OLPC Wiki (2007) The OLPC Wiki, wiki.laptop. org/go/Home, accessed 27 January 2007.

Olsson, Nils O.E. (2006) 'Management of flexibility in projects'. In: *International Journal of Project Management*, 24: 66–74.

Osland, Joyce and Bird, Allan (2000) 'Beyond sophisticated stereotyping: cultural sensemaking in context'. In: *Academy of Management Executive*, 14 (1): 65–79.

Palzer, Michael (2007) Phone interview conducted with Michael Palzer, Head of Communications of Raiffeisen International, 24 August.

Pant, Dinesh P. Allison, Christopher W. and Hayes, John (1996) 'Transferring the western model of project organisation to a bureaucratic culture: the case of Nepal'. In: *International Journal of Project Management*, 14 (1): 53–7.

Parker, Carole G. (2009) 'The emotional connection of distinguishing differences and conflict'. In: Harvey, Carol P. and Allard, M. June (eds): *Understanding and Managing Diversity. Readings, Cases, and Exercises*, 4th edition. Upper Saddle River, NJ: Pearson International Edition, pp. 28–34.

Pearson, Virginia M.S. and Stephan, Walter G. (1998) 'Preferences for styles of negotiation: a comparison of Brazil and the U.S'. In: *International Journal of Intercultural Relations*, 22 (1): 67–83.

Pfleiderer AG (2008) Pfleiderer News, ir2.flife.de/data/pfleiderer/igb_html/index.php? bericht_id=1000001&lang=DEU, accessed 4 December, 2008.

Phillips, Jack J., Bothell, Timothy W. and Snead, Lynne G. (2002): *The Project Management Scorecard. Measuring the Success of Project Management Solutions*. Amsterdam: Butterworth Heinemann.

Pinto, Jeffrey K. and Slevin, Dennis P. (1988) 'Critical success factors across the project life'. In: *Project Management Journal*, 19 (3): 67–75.

Portny, Stanley, Mantel, Samuel J., Meredith, Jack R., Shafer, Scott M. and Sutton, Margaret M. (2008) *Project Management. Planning, Scheduling, and Controlling Projects*. Hoboken, NJ: John Wiley & Sons.

Project Management Institute (PMI) (2004) *A Guide to the Project Management Body of Knowledge*, 3rd edition. CD-Rom.

Putnam, Linda L. (2006) 'Definitions and approaches to conflict and communication'. In: Oetzel, John G. and Ting-Toomey, Stella (eds): *The Sage Handbook of Conflict Communication. Integrating Theory, Research, and Practice*. Thousand Oaks, CA: Sage, pp. 1–32.

Rad, Parviz F. and Levin, Ginger (2003) *Achieving Project Management Success Using Virtual Teams*. Boca Raton: J. Ross.

Raiffeisen International (2007a) Conference Call for the Semi-Annual Report 2007, Raiffeisen International PR document, 9 August.

Raiffeisen International (2007b) Raiffeisen International Pioneer and Powerhouse in CEE. Raiffeisen International Self-introduction, 23 August.

Ramaprasad, Arkalgud and Prakash, A.N. (2003) 'Emergent project management: how foreign managers can leverage local knowledge'. In: *International Journal of Project Management*, 21: 199–205.

Rathje, Stefanie (2004) Unternehmenskultur als Interkultur. Entwicklung und Gestaltung interkultureller Unternehmenskultur am Beispiel deutscher Unternehmen in Thailand. Schriftenreihe Interkulturelle Kommunikation. Band 8, Sternenfels: Verlag Wissenschaft & Praxis.

Rauwerdink, J. (2005) Ein Projekt ist keine Insel. In: VDI (ed.): Projektmanagement Praxis 2005. Sechster praxisorientierter Anwendertag zum Projektmanagement. Expertenforum Hamburg. VDI Berichte 1925, VDI-Verlag: Düsseldorf, pp. 33–37.

Ray, Rebecca and Schmitt, John (2007) *No-Vacation Nation*. Center for Economic and Policy Research. May, Washington.

Rice, Ronald E., D-Ambra, John and More, Elizabeth (1998) 'Cross-cultural comparison of organizational media evaluation and choice'. In: *Journal of Communication*, Summer, pp. 3–26.

Rolls-Royce (2004a) History, www.rolls-royce.com/ deutschland/en/history/default.htm, accessed 14 August, 2007.

Rolls-Royce (2004b) Rolls-Royce Germany – local activities, www.rolls-royce.com/deutschland/en/ activities/default.htm, accessed 14 August, 2007.

Rolls-Royce (2004c) Overview, www.rolls-royce.com/ about/overview/default_flash.jsp, accessed 14 August, 2007.

Rolls-Royce (2004d) Rolls-Royce Germany Products, www.rolls-royce.com/deutschland/en/products/ civil.htm, accessed 14 August, 2007.

RosettaNet (2008) About RosettaNet, www. rosettanet.org/cms/sites/RosettaNet/, accessed 23 December, 2008.

Sahlin-Andersson, Kerstin and Söderholm, Anders (eds) (2002) *Beyond Project Management: New Perspectives on the Temporary–Permanent Dilemma*. Copenhagen: Copenhagen Business School Press.

Sahlin-Andersson, Kerstin and Söderholm, Anders (2002) 'Key features of the Scandinavian School of Project Studies'. In: Sahlin-Andersson, Kerstin and Söderholm Anders (eds): *Beyond project management. New Perspectives on the Temporary–Permanent Dilemma.* Copenhagen: Copenhagen Business School Press, pp. 11–24.

Samsung Corning Precision (2007) www.samsungcorning.com/inc/fla/company_history.swf, accessed 1 April, 2007.

Schein, Edgar H. (1992) *Organizational Culture and Leadership,* 2nd edition. San Francisco, CA: Jossey Bass.

Schindler, Martin and Eppler, Martin J. (2003) 'Harvesting project knowledge: a review of project learning methods and success factors'. In: *International Journal of Project Management,* 21: 219–28.

Schneider, Susan C. and Barsoux, Jean-Louis (2002) *Managing Across Cultures,* 2nd edition. Harlow: Prentice Hall/*Financial Times.*

Schönström, Mikael (2005) 'Creating knowledge networks: lessons from practice'. In: *Journal of Knowledge Management,* 9 (6): 17–29.

Senge, Peter M. (1990) *The Fifth Discipline: The Art & Practice of the Learning* Organization. New York: Currency Doubleday.

Senn, Christoph (2006) 'The executive growth factor: how Siemens invigorated its customer relationship'. In: *Journal of Business Strategy,* 27 (1): 27–34.

Siemens (2007a) Siemens Global Website, www.siemens.com/index.jsp?sdc_p=ft4mls2uo1026935i1327890pcz2&sdc_bcpath=1327890.s_2,&sdc_sid=8920191402&, accessed 4 April, 2007.

Siemens (2007b) Siemens – Global network of innovation, www.siemens.com/Daten/siecom/HQ/CC/Internet/About_Us/WORKAREA/about_ed/templatedata/English/file/binary/Long%20Portrait_1244581.pdf, accessed 5 April, 2007.

SMEDSEP (2003) SMEDSEP components, www.smedsep.ph/components2.html, accessed 7 August, 2007.

SMEDSEP (2006) The SMEDSEP program,http://www.smedsep.ph/the-program2.html, accessed 7 August, 2007.

Spencer, Lyle M. and Spencer, Signe M. (1993) *Competence at Work: Models for Superior Performance.* New York: John Wiley & Sons.

Stahlbauforum (2007) New Bangkok International Airport. http://portal.stahlbauforum.de/projekte/Projekt_AirpBangk.php, accessed 5 April, 2007.

Stanleigh, Michael (2006) 'From crisis to control – a new era in strategic project management'. In: *Project Management Practice,* Issue 6, Summer, pp. 4–6.

Surowiecki, James (2007) 'Die Philanthropie-Maschine'. In: *Technology Review,* January 2007, pp. 28–35.

Takeuchi, Hirotaka and Nonaka, Ikujiro (2004) 'Knowledge creation and dialectics'. In: Takeuchi, Hirotaka and Nonaka, Ikujiro (eds): *Hitotsubashi on Knowledge Management.* Singapore: John Wiley & Sons, pp. 1–27.

Tata Motors (2006) Five years down the line, we see ourselves ahead of market changes. Daily News & analysis, June 7, www.tata.com/tata_motors/media/20060607.htm, accessed 18 December, 2006.

Taylor, Sully and Osland, Joyce S. (2003) 'The impact of intercultural communication on global organizational learning'. In: Easterby-Smith, Mark and Lyles, Marjorie A. (eds): *The Blackwell Handbook on Organizational Learning and Knowledge Management.* Malden, MA: Blackwell Publishing, pp. 253–77.

TED (2006) Talks Nicholas Negroponte: The vision behind One Laptop Per Child, www.ted.com/tedtalks/tedtalksplayer.cfm?key=n_negroponte&gclid=CMSB-vn1gIoCFRiUXgodOGLnMQ, accessed 27 January, 2007.

Thamain, Hans J. (2005) *Management of Technology: Managing Effectively in Technology-Intensive Organizations.* New Jersey: John Wiley & Sons.

The Economist (2006) Carmaking in India: A different route. 13 December, www.economist.com/business/displaystory.cfm?story_id=E1_RQTPTVV, 18 December.

The Economist (2007a) Commercial aviation – barrelling along. 29 September, pp. 67–8.

The Economist (2007b) Coming home to roost? Bird flu flared up again in Asia, reminding the world it is still at risk from a human flu pandemic. 25 January.

The Economist (2007c) DaimlerChrysler Disassembly. 17 February, pp. 61–2.

The Economist (2007d) A new boss for Siemens, http://www.economist.com/research/articlesBySubject/displaystory.cfm?subjectid=1269867&story_id=9214367, accessed 1 September, 2007.

The Economist (2007e) 'Behold, telepresence: Far away yet strangely personal. 25 August, p. 59–60.

The Economist (2008) A new home for the Nano. 11 October, p. 77.

The Inquirer (2006) Four out of five notebooks made in Shanghai. 26 July, www.theinquirer.net/print.aspx?article=33284&print, accessed 25 May, 2007.

The International Project Finance Association (2007a) About us, www.ipfa.org/about.shtml, accessed 31 August, 2007.

The International Project Finance Association (2007b): About project finance, www.ipfa.org/about_pf.shtml, accessed 31 August, 2007.

The World Bank (2005) Program framework document for proposed Loans/Credits/Grants in the amount of US$500 million equivalent for a Global Program for Avian Influenza Control and Human Pandemic Preparedness and Response 5 December, http://sitersources.worldbank.org/PROJECTS/Resources/40940-1136754783560/Avian-Flu-PAD.pdf, accessed 27 January, 2007.

The World Bank (2006a) News and Broadcast: Donors Pledge US $ 475 million at Mali Avian Flu Summit, 8 December, http://web.world bank.org/WBSITE/EXTERNAL/NEWS/0,,conten tMDK:21155963~pagePK:34370~piPK:34424 ~theSitePK:4607,00.html, accessed 27 January, 2007.

The World Bank (2006b): Project Pipeline under The World Bank's Global Program for Avian Influenza (GPAI), http://sitersources.worldbank.org/INTTOPAVIFLU/Resources/AHIProject PipelineMay31-2006.pdf, accessed 27 January, 2007.

The World Bank (2006c) Guidelines: Selection and Employment of Consultants by World Bank Borrowers, Revised October, 2006, http://site resources.worldbank.org/INTPROCUREMEN T/Resources/ConGuid-10-06-ev1.doc, accessed 27 January, 2007.

The World Bank (2006d) Progress Analysis and Recommendations Report for the GPAI, http://sitersources.worldbank.org/INTTOPAVI FLU/Resources/ResponsestoAvianandHumanInf luenzaThreats060630.pdf, accessed 27 January, 2007.

The World Bank (2006e) Guidelines: Selection and Employment of Consultants by World Bank Borrowers, http://sitersources.worldbank.org/INTPROCUREMENT/Resources/ConGuid-10-06-ev1.doc, accessed 23 January, 2007.

The World Bank (2006f) Avian and Human Influenza: Update on Financing Needs and Framework,http://siteresources.worldbank.org/INTTOPAVIFLU/Resources/AHIFinancing12-06.doc, accessed 30 March, 2007.

The World Bank (2007) Projects to Address Avian Influenza Control and Pandemic Preparedness, http://web.worldbank.org/WBSITE/EXTERNAL/T OPICS/EXTHEALTHNUTRITIONANDPOPULA TION/EXTTOPAVIFLU/0,,contentMDK:2086505 8~pagePK:64168445~piPK:64168309~theSiteP K:1793593,00.html, accessed 27 January, 2007.

The World Bank (2006g) Global Program for Avian Influenza Control and Human Pandemic Preparedness and Response, http://sitersources. worldbank.org/INTTOPAVIFLU/Resources/, accessed 27 January, 2007.

Thiry, Michel (2004) 'Program management: a strategic decision management process'. In: Morris, Peter W.G. and Pinto, Jeffrey K. (eds): The Wiley Guide to Managing Projects. Hoboken, NJ: John Wiley & Sons, pp. 257–87.

Thomas, Kenneth (1976) Conflict and Conflict Management. In: Dunette, M. (ed.): Handbook of Industrial and Organizational Psychology, Vol. 2. Chicago: RandMcNally, pp. 889–935.

Ting-Toomey, Stella (1985) 'Toward a theory of conflict and culture'. In: Gudykunst, William B., Stewart, Lea P. and Ting-Toomey, Stella (eds): Communication, Culture, and Organizational Processes: International and Intercultural Communication Annual, Volume IX. Beverly Hills, CA: Sage, pp. 71–86.

Ting-Toomey, Stella and Oetzel, John G. (2001) Managing Intercultural Conflict Effectively. Thousand Oaks, CA: Sage.

Transparency International (2007) What is Transparency International?, www.transparency. org/about_us, accessed 31 August, 2007.

Transparency International (2008) Surveys and indices, www.transparency.org/policy_research/surveys_in dices/cpi/2008, accessed 22 December, 2008.

Trompenaars, Fons and Hampden-Turner, Charles (1998) Riding the Waves of Culture: Under-standing Diversity in Global Business, 2nd edition. NewYork: McGraw-Hill.

Turner, J. Rodney (1993) The Handbook of Project-based Management: Improving the Processes for Achieving Strategic Objectives. London: McGraw-Hill.

Turner, J. Rodney (2003) 'Farsighted project con-tract management'. In: Turner, Rodney J. (ed.): Contracting For Project Management. Aldershot: Gower, pp. 33–57.

Turner, J. Rodney (ed.) (2003) Contracting for Project Management. Aldershot: Gower.

Turner, J. Rodney (2006) 'Towards a theory of project management: the nature of the project'. In: International Journal of Project Management, 24: 1–3.

Tyco International (2008a) Our business overview, www.tyco.com/TycoWeb/pages/Our+Businesses/ Overview.html, accessed 10 November, 2008.

Tyco International (2008b) Tyco at a glance, www. tyco.com/wps/wcm/connect/a8ae3c004b578bb1b

11ef7ac2828438f/Tyco+At+A+Glance_2008.pd f?MOD=AJPERES, accessed 10 November, 2008.

UNCITRAL (2004) Facts about UNCITRAL, www. uncitral.org/pdf/english/uncitral-leaflet-e.pdf, accessed 6 March, 2008.

UNCITRAL (2008) About us, www.uncitral.org/ uncitral/en/uncitral_texts.html, accessed 6 March, 2008.

Uzgalis, William (2007) *John Locke,* edited by Stanford Encyclopedia of Philosophy, http://plato. stanford.edu/entries/locke/#BooI, accessed 6 January, 2009.

Varner, Iris and Beamer, Linda (2005) *Intercultural Communication in the Global Workplace,* 3rd edition. Boston: McGraw-Hill Irwin.

Vonsild, Susan and Becher Jensen, Lene (2006) 'Outsourcing projects between Europe and India – bridging the culture divide'. In: *Project Perspectives,* Annual Publication of IPMA, Vol. XXVIII, pp. 74–8.

Walewski, John A., Gibson, Jr., G. Edward and Vines, Ellworth V. (2006) 'Risk identification and assessment for international construction projects'. In: Cleland, David and Gareis, Roland (eds): *Global Project Management Handbook,* 2nd edition. New York: McGraw-Hill, pp. 6.1 to 6.17.

Weick, Karl E. and Sutcliffe, Kathleen M. (2001) *Managing the Unexpected.* San Francisco, CA: Jossey-Bass.

Weir, David and Hutchings, Kate (2005) 'Cultural embeddedness and contextual constraints: knowledge sharing in Chinese and Arab cultures'. In: *Knowledge and Process Management,* 12 (2): 89–98.

Whitley, Richard (2006) 'Project-based firms: new organizational form of variations of a theme?' In: *Industrial and Corporate Change,* 15 (1): 77–99.

Williams, T.M. (1997) 'Empowerment vs risk management?' In: *International Journal of Project Management,* 15 (4): 219–22.

Willke, Helmut (1998) Systemisches Wissensmanagement. Mit Fallstudien von D. Hnewekow, T. Hermsen, J. Köhler, C. Krück, S. Mingers, K. Piel, T. Strulik und O. Vopel, UTB für Wissenschaft, Stuttgart: Lucius & Lucius.

Winch, Graham M. (2004) 'Managing project stakeholders'. In: Morris, Peter W.G. and Pinto, Jeffrey, K. (eds): *The Wiley Guide to Managing Projects.* Hoboken, NJ: John Wiley & Sons. pp. 321–39.

Wong, Eric (2001) NEC in Hong Kong: an interview with Arthur McInnis, in: *NEC User's Group Newsletter,* No. 18, July, p. 6.

Wong, Zachary (2007) *Human Factors in Project Management: Concepts, Tools, and Techniques for Inspiring Teamwork and Motivation.* San Francisco, CA: Jossey-Bass.

Woodard, Dustin (2004) Costs of hosting the 2004 Olympics, http://mutualfunds.about.com/od/news/ a/2004_olymics.htm, accessed 4 April, 2007.

Yasin, Mahmoud M; Martin, James and Czuchry, Andrew (1999) 'An empirical investigation of international project management practices: the role of international experience'. In: *Project Management Journal,* 31 (2): 20–30.

Yavas, Burhan, F. and Rezayat, Fahimeh (2003) 'The impact of culture on managerial perceptions of quality'. In: *Cross Cultural Management,* 3 (2): 213–34.

Zagarow, Herbert W. (2003) Applying the Balanced Scorecard in Project Management. Published by ALLPM.com, Newletter Article of 17 November, www.allpm.com, accessed 27 May, 2007.

Zigurs, Ilze (2003) 'Leadership in virtual teams: oxymoron or opportunity?' In: *Organizational Dynamics,* 31 (4): 339–51.

INDEX

Page references to non-textual content such as figures or tables will be in *italic* print.

Supporting researchers for more than forty years

Research methods have always been at the core of SAGE's publishing. Sara Miller McCune founded SAGE in 1965 and soon after, she published SAGE's first methods book, Public Policy Evaluation. A few years later, she launched the Quantitative Applications in the Social Sciences series – affectionately known as the "little green books".

Always at the forefront of developing and supporting new approaches in methods, SAGE published early groundbreaking texts and journals in the fields of qualitative methods and evaluation.

Today, more than forty years and two million little green books later, SAGE continues to push the boundaries with a growing list of more than 1,200 research methods books, journals, and reference works across the social, behavioral, and health sciences.

From qualitative, quantitative, mixed methods to evaluation, SAGE is the essential resource for academics and practitioners looking for the latest methods by leading scholars.

www.sagepublications.com

CPSIA information can be obtained
at www.ICGtesting.com
Printed in the USA
LVHW100905030119
602347LV00006B/16/P

9 781412 946209